Performance Approaches
to Teaching Shakespeare

Performance Approaches to Teaching Shakespeare

EDWARD L. ROCKLIN
California State Polytechnic University, Pomona

National Council of Teachers of English
1111 W. Kenyon Road, Urbana, Illinois 61801-1096

Staff Editor: Bonny Graham
Interior Design: Jenny Jensen Greenleaf
Cover Design: Diana C. Coe/ko Design Studio

NCTE Stock Number: 35102

Library of Congress Cataloging-in-Publication Data

Rocklin, Edward L.
    Performance approaches to teaching Shakespeare / Edward L. Rocklin.
        p. cm.
        "NCTE Stock Number: 35102"—T.p. verso.
        Includes bibliographical references and index.
        ISBN 0-8141-3510-2 (pbk)
    1. Shakespeare, William, 1564-1616—Study and teaching—United States. 2. Shakespeare, William, 1564-1616—Study and teaching (Higher). 3. Shakespeare, William, 1564-1616—Study and teaching (Secondary). 4. Shakespeare, William, 1564-1616—Study and teaching—Activity programs. 5. Performing arts—Study and teaching—United States. 6. Drama—Study and teaching—United States. 7. Drama in education—United States. I. National Council of Teachers of English. II. Title.
    PR2987.R63 2005
    822.3'3—dc22
                                                            2005000074

To the memory of

Helene Milich Rocklin (1921–2000)

and

Ralph Joseph Rocklin (1918–2003)

And yet what is said is one of the permanent truths: it is only in degree that any improvement of society could prevent the wastage of human powers; the waste even in a fortunate life, the isolation even of a life rich in intimacy, cannot but be felt deeply, and is the central feeling of tragedy. And anything of value must accept this because it must not prostitute itself; its strength is to be prepared to waste itself, if it does not get the right opportunity.

WILLIAM EMPSON, *Some Versions of Pastoral*

PERMISSION ACKNOWLEDGMENTS

Elements of the prologue are adapted from "How Does One 'Teach' a Play, Anyway?" *California English* 5.1 (Fall 1999): 12–13. Reprinted by permission of Carol Jago for *California English*.

Excerpt titled "A Brief Drama" in Chapter 1 reprinted from *Stan Freberg Presents The United States of America, Volume 1: The Early Years.* © Copyright 1961 by Stan Freberg, Capitol Records.

Chapter 2, "A Pause for Theory: Articulating a Model," reprinted by permission of the Modern Language Association of America from "Performance Is More Than an 'Approach' to Teaching Shakespeare" in *Teaching Shakespeare through Performance* edited by Milla Cozart Riggio, New York: MLA, 1999, pp. 48–62.

Elements of Chapter 5, "*Hamlet*: Opening Playtexts, Closing Performances," reprinted by permission of the Modern Language Association of America from "Exploring *Hamlet*: Opening Playtexts, Closing Performances" in *Approaches to Teaching Shakespeare's* Hamlet edited by Bernice W. Kliman, New York: MLA, 2001: 73–76.

"Defamiliarizing *Hamlet*" exercise in Chapter 5 reprinted by permission of Barbara Hodgdon and the Modern Language Association of America from "Making Changes/Making Sense" in *FOCUS: Teaching Shakespeare II* 12.1 (Fall 1985): 2–11, edited by Ronald E. Salomone, and from *Approaches to Teaching Shakespeare's* Hamlet edited by Bernice W. Kliman, New York: MLA, 2001, p. 222.

The epilogue was previously published as the following: Rocklin, Edward L. "Shakespeare's Script as the Cue for Pedagogic Invention." *Shakespeare Quarterly* 46:2 (1995), 135–144. © Folger Shakespeare Library. Reprinted with permission of The Johns Hopkins University Press.

CONTENTS

Contents

ACKNOWLEDGMENTS

This book has had a long development, and many people have contributed to the volume you hold in your hands. I want to start by thanking Alan Dessen, Charles Frey, Miriam Gilbert, Barbara Hodgdon, Philip McGuire, Paul Nelsen, Randal Robinson, and Audrey Stanley, all of whom have taught me and encouraged me in the project of teaching Shakespeare's plays. To Alan Dessen and Audrey Stanley I owe special thanks for the beautifully designed program titled "Shakespeare Examined through Performance" they conducted at the Folger Humanities Institute during the 1995–1996 academic year. Former Institute director Lena Cowen Orlin and current director Kathleen Lynch provided a supportive environment in which we could perform our intense monthly sessions investigating the dimensions of the texts and the realizations in performance. While all the participants contributed to my ongoing education, I want to thank Dan Colvin, Ed Isser, and Paul Nelsen, who all offered very specific forms of encouragement at different phases of this project. And I must thank the National Endowment for the Humanities for funding such a unique opportunity.

California State Polytechnic University has provided and continues to provide the opportunity to teach the classes on which this book is based. In addition, I have been awarded a number of Research, Scholarship, and Creative Activity grants and several sabbaticals that contributed to the composition of this book. I owe a particular debt of gratitude to Dr. Barbara J. Way, dean of the College of Letters, Arts, and Social Sciences, who has demonstrated her support by finding funds to secure that most precious of all gifts, time, enabling me to concentrate on completing this project during a stressful season.

The anonymous readers for the National Council of Teachers of English made helpful suggestions, and I thank them for the care, clarity, and creativity with which they read and responded to the manuscript.

Lloyd Aquino has performed admirably as my assistant, and his burgeoning research skills have been particularly welcome in the later stages of producing this book. Christian Ramos has not only provided expertise in the use of computers but also demonstrated that hardware and software can actually be shaped to serve the creative purposes of a writer.

At the National Council of Teachers of English, I appreciate the work of Kurt Austin, who has been everything I could want in an editor for this project. And Bonny Graham has made the process of transforming the manuscript into the printed volume a dialogue that I have looked forward to as we worked out choices and corrections.

It is especially important to me to express my deepest appreciation to two people who have supported this book from the moment I conceived of it. Joseph Stodder, for over a decade my senior Shakespeare colleague, encouraged me to experiment in the classroom, and supported every endeavor I have undertaken in the last seventeen years.

I owe most to Kate Massey, my colleague, ally, and wife. Her faith has been, and remains, the steadiest element in my creative life, and anyone who finds nourishment in this book is benefiting from her unwavering belief in what this book could be.

Finally, while I am pleased that this book has had time to mature, I regret that neither my mother nor my father lived to see this fruit of their own belief in education and of the sacrifices they made so that I might pursue that education. Given the asymmetrical nature of our lives as creatures enchained in generations, I can only hope that I offer to others what they managed to secure for me—an opportunity to realize at least some portion of the potential that their care and their love of language helped to create.

Prologue: The Challenge of Teaching Shakespeare's Plays

A Shakespearean playtext is not a series of statements that specify in all respects—or even in all important respects—what must happen during performance. Its statements do specify what cannot *happen, and in doing so they permit whatever possibilities are not prohibited.*

PHILIP C. MCGUIRE, *Speechless Dialect: Shakespeare's Open Silences*

In a call for papers on teaching plays, Carol Jago, editor of *California English*, asked two questions which, taken together, provide an elegant prompt for explaining the logic of the book you have begun to read. She asked, "What does drama do for readers and viewers that different genres cannot?" as well as "And how does one 'teach' a play, anyway?"[1] Briefly put, my response is that if you understand what drama does that is different from prose fiction, then you will also understand the crucial starting point for answering the question "How does one teach a play in an English literature or language arts course?"

It is the premise for the model developed in the chapters that follow—and a crucial feature of this book—that we need to teach drama in two phases. In the first phase, we engage students in a sequence of activities in which they contrast prose fiction and plays and thereby come to grasp the elements that constitute the dramatic medium. In the second phase, we immerse students in an array of medium-specific strategies that enable them to conduct performance-centered explorations of individual plays. In short, we teach drama in general, and individual plays in particular, by teaching students to read and speak in what Harold Clurman has called "a different language" (275). And in that language, students learn to read as experimenters, asking not only "What do these words mean?" but also "What do these words do?" and "What can these words be made to do?" and, in a formulation adapted from J. L. Styan, "What do these words make the actor make the audience do?" (*Elements of Drama* 2).

As the title of this book indicates, I am proposing what is sometimes called, as a shorthand label, a performance approach to teaching drama in literature classes. But in this book the concept of performance is defined more widely than simply "as if one were preparing to perform the play in a theater." The core of a performance approach asks students to analyze, cast, rehearse, sometimes memorize, and perform part of a play, as well as to observe, respond to, and critique these performances. But performance also includes reframing a wide array of concepts and practices traditionally employed in the literary study of drama. And this model also teaches students to work with performance records, film, and video.

Let me offer one simple example of how drama demands that we learn to read in "a different language," and what the consequences of reading in this fashion can be. The example is based on one of the most famous lines in all of Shakespeare, namely, Hamlet's first speech: "A little more than kin, and less than kind."

Given the premises I am advocating, when I teach the play I have to ask students to experiment with the visual introduction that precedes our verbal introduction to Hamlet. So I start by asking questions such as "How is he dressed? When does he enter? Where does he position himself? Or is his position controlled by others, perhaps by nonverbal orders from Claudius or Polonius? Perhaps by other courtiers who either move toward him or away from him?" Next, we proceed to analyze the speech itself, appreciating the way its pattern reveals its speaker as one who deploys precise, elegant, and witty phrasing.

Now we can turn to the question of exploring what the speech *does*; and to enact such an exploration we need to pay attention to how the speech appears on the page of a specific edition. Here is how it appears on the page of *The Riverside Shakespeare* (1192):[2]

> King. But now, my cousin Hamlet, and my son—
> Ham. [*Aside*.] A little more than kin, and less than kind.
> King. How is it that the clouds still hang on you? (I.ii.64–66)

Concentrate, for a moment, not on the spoken words but on that bracketed "*Aside*." The stage direction is in brackets, I explain to students, because it does not appear in either the Second Quarto (1604) or First Folio (1623) texts of the play: rather, it has been added by almost all editors, beginning with Lewis Theobold in 1733. But once you realize that it is not mandated by the original texts of the play, you are free to explore this as a performance choice. This means temporarily setting aside the question "Is it a right or wrong editorial decision?" in order to ask, "What happens if Hamlet performs this line as an aside? What happens if he speaks the line to one or more other members of the court? And what happens if he speaks the line directly to the King?" Furthermore, for each of these questions we must ask not only "What happens within the world of the play?" but also "What happens in terms of the play–audience relationship?"

If Hamlet speaks these words as an aside, as editors direct and as performers have historically chosen to do, then the speech marks him not only as someone who is verbally witty, but also as someone whose wit must be used privately to express his contempt for his uncle-stepfather-king; and the fact that the line is spoken as an aside is itself one enactment of his alienated situation. Furthermore, by opening a gap between himself and all the other dramatis personae, Hamlet also initiates a direct relationship in which we, the spectators, become his confidants, preparing us for the role of tacit co-conspirators we assume during some of his soliloquies—especially the soliloquy in act III, scene iii (although it is not a pure soliloquy) during which Hamlet stands over the praying Claudius and first seems about to murder the King and then decides to murder him at another time.

But what if, as the original texts of the play seem to permit, Hamlet speaks his first words to one or more of the courtiers?

Then, as students soon realize, while the wit of the wordplay remains the same, that wit is now being used to satirize and covertly challenge the new king. In terms of the play's design, furthermore, Hamlet's speech seems intended to split the court, disrupting the harmony sought by the new ruler. For if the courtier or courtiers to whom he delivers or whispers this line seem to respond sympathetically, then Hamlet has established or confirmed (at this point, spectators cannot tell which might be the case) that he has one or more allies in the court—and arouses audience expectations that this may be a play about warring factions. Conversely, if the courtier or courtiers respond by moving away and nonverbally rejecting this invitation to share a satiric, potentially subversive comment, Hamlet's speech serves to emphasize his isolation even as it demonstrates the loyalty of the courtiers to the new regime.

What if, to explore a third option that the original texts of the play also seem to permit, Hamlet speaks his first words directly to the King? Then, while the wit of the wordplay remains the same, that wit is now being used to publicly challenge the new ruler, and to challenge him both as king and as stepfather. In terms of the play's design, this means that the King faces both an external challenge from Fortinbras and an internal challenge from the presumptive heir to the throne during his first public performance of his new office. This also means that the King's next speech represents his apparently deliberate choice to ignore the challenge from Hamlet.

This example, which is by no means exhaustively worked out (the next option clearly is to ask, "What if he directs this remark to his mother, the Queen?," and I leave the pleasure of anatomizing this option to you), demonstrates that one of the simplest but most fundamental skills we must master in learning to read drama is the skill to discover how the same speech can be used to perform different or even radically divergent speech acts, and thus to create surprisingly divergent situations both within the world of the play and in the play–audience relation.

Moreover, small as it is, this example neatly embodies (at least) five of the elements that make reading drama such a challenge for students and that make so many literature teachers ask, "How does one '*teach*' a play, anyway?" First, students need to learn that when a character speaks, he or she is doing something through language: while the words of Hamlet and the King remain the same in any performance, the speech acts they perform can be significantly different. Second, students need to learn how to read not just the speeches but also the whole range of elements in a playtext, including, for example, both explicit and implicit stage directions. Third, students, like actors working through the process of rehearsal, need to learn how to read as experimenters, asking, "What happens if we perform a moment this way? or that way? or this third way?" Fourth, students need to learn how to read Shakespeare texts with an understanding of what editors contribute to these texts, and with a sense of how such editorial choices may at once clarify and foreclose performance options. And fifth, students need to learn to ask, "Will playing this speech in this particular way work with the rest of the scene's or the play's design? Or do other elements of that design further constrain our choices?" When they reach the point of asking this question, students are also ready to return to debating the question I postponed earlier, namely, whether the editorial tradition adding the "Aside" accurately responds to elements in the play's design and thereby correctly specifies "what must happen during performance."

From my own experience, I know that it can be wonderfully liberating for students to discover that different Hamlets can be sharing their contempt as a secret with us as spectators, putting us in the one-up position; or be seeking to create or perpetuate a division within the court, perhaps within the kingdom, using a slyly subversive remark to produce a moment of turbulence in the King's carefully orchestrated scene of harmony; or be directly confronting the new ruler with a challenge to his authority that forces the King to make an instantaneous decision about how he will meet this insulting action from his stepson. I also know that learning to read in this way can be unsettling for some students (as it is unsettling for some readers and critics) who are more comfortable with a more determinate text—and I deal with this issue in the chapters that follow. But in learning to read these elements of the language of drama, and in learning to read as experimenters, students also are learning to experience the power and delight—and, at times, frustration—of becoming co-creators with Shakespeare of the play in performance.

Performance Approaches to Teaching Shakespeare is a book for high school, college, and university English teachers. This prologue is succeeded by two parts and an epilogue. Part I comprises two framing chapters, the first developing the constitutive practices and the second articulating a model for performance approaches in general and mine in particular. Part II offers three chapters, each focused on a single Shakespeare play for which it delineates an array of performance activities and writing assignments. The plays are *The Taming of the Shrew*, *Richard III*, and *Hamlet*. In addition, I offer several major writing assignments for *Hamlet* that demonstrate how to integrate a series of performance activities and writing prompts into a term project. The epilogue suggests how instructors can use the constitutive elements of drama as a cue for their own pedagogic invention. The book concludes with an extensive bibliography of materials that have contributed to the development of the approach proposed in this book.

Let me say a bit more about how this book is organized, in terms of both previewing the individual chapters and laying out the logic of the sequence in which those chapters are arranged.

Although traditional academic presentations almost invariably place theory before practice, it is a premise of the performance model developed here that to understand a playtext your best move is to start by asking, "What do the words *do*?" Fulfilling this logic, the first chapter offers readers a detailed account of how I frame the work my students and I do together and introduce them to the medium of drama, to the elements that constitute the medium, to the challenges of translating a text into a script and a script into a performance, and to the specific challenges of reading Shakespeare's plays in this manner.

In the second chapter, I articulate the model embodied in Chapter 1 and elaborated in subsequent chapters. First, therefore, I articulate how performance can serve as a holistic frame for teaching Shakespeare. Second, I enumerate premises we can use when we ask students to become engaged with the plays through performance. Third, I offer one way of mapping the spectrum of specific performance approaches that exist or can be imagined. And fourth, I suggest, very briefly, how a performance model can be employed for teaching nondramatic literature and composition in English courses—recognizing that developing this suggestion would need another book. Obviously, readers who find the model appealing but have either worked out or feel no need for the theory can proceed to Chapters 3 through 5 to see how they might teach individual plays—and can, of course, return to pick up the theory later when and if they want to.

In Chapters 3 through 5, I offer scenarios for teaching *The Taming of the Shrew*, *Richard III*, and *Hamlet*, including detailed accounts of specific classes so that the reader can see how the process actually unfolds. In addition, I offer several major writing assignments that demonstrate how to integrate a series of performance activities and writing prompts into a term project.

The book concludes with an epilogue in which I articulate some premises about teaching as a form of action that can be understood when seen through the analogy of the dramatic medium itself. That is, I invite teachers who want to try out the performance model proposed in this book to adopt a corresponding stance toward their own activities as teachers. This is a stance that defines the teacher as experimenter, one who, like the dramatist, designs scenarios, if not fully scripted scenes, which are then realized—and, of course, tested—in the performance of the classroom. This chapter opens the door for us to engage in what Donald Schön (*Educating*; *Reflective*) calls *reflective practice*, for it suggests the ways in which asking students to adopt a performance approach not only directly transforms what students do as they read and explore a play but also indirectly transforms what teachers do as they read plays, design their courses, and conduct their classes. For just as Shakespeare's plays invite actors, spectators, and readers to become co-creators in translating script into performance, so a performance approach invites teachers to become co-creators in the unfolding of a pedagogy that can be developed beyond the imagination of any single practitioner—as I know from discussion with those teachers in a number of colleges and high schools who have adopted and adapted the approach in ways I could never have imagined.

What I offer, then, is a book that explains the theoretical basis for this approach; delineates a clear, systematic, and powerful set of basic questions students can be taught to ask of a playtext; presents a wide spectrum of performance activities that are appropriate to the classroom teaching of Shakespeare; integrates these performance activities with developments in the teaching of literature and writing so that students will be working on their critical thinking and writing even as they explore Shakespeare's plays; and offers some carefully refined major writing assignments.

How to Read This Book

> After all, teaching a play should be playful. Recapturing the spirit of play must belong to the formation of teachers, especially English teachers.
>
> GEORGE SLOVER, "Video versus Voice: Teaching Students and Teachers Shakespeare"

This book is put together in a logical sequence insofar as it moves from stating a problem to then offering practice and theory for solving the problem; it also follows a chronological sequence in that Chapters 3–5 deal with three Shakespeare plays in what is probably their order of composition. As I have imagined the range of those who might read and use this book, however, I have also imagined different routes such readers might take, depending on their own intellectual and pedagogical concerns.

Some teachers prefer a model that is as complete and explicit as possible. If you are such a reader, reading straight through the book makes sense. On the other hand, if you have developed your own model, your own frame and style, you may find someone else's model distracting, and you may decide to ignore that frame in order to look for elements and specific activities that appeal to you. In that case, you might turn immediately to a chapter on a play you know and have taught, to discover what you might be able to use. Or you might look at a chapter dealing with a play you have not taught to see how the model meshes with your own imagined classroom designs. If the approach begins to interest you, you might then return to Chapters 1 and 2 and the epilogue. And for those who are teaching teachers, it may make sense to read Chapters 1 and 2 and the epilogue first, since that is where I offer some reflections on the logic of the approach as it applies to changing the teacher herself or himself, and then turn to the prologue and frame before looking at a chapter on a specific play.

Coming at this from another angle, I can imagine readers for whom it is not so much the sequence of the chapters but rather certain features of the chapters that might shape how they read the book.

Some of those who read drafts of this book commented that the framing concepts and activities presented in the first two chapters offer a surprisingly broad lead-in to the study of Shakespeare's plays. "Why is it necessary," they asked, "to spend time studying fundamental elements of drama as a form? Why do you look at this basic material about drama and narrative and the nature of theater? Why can't we just start reading the plays?" I certainly understand and sympathize with these questions, because every teacher realizes how precious and how insufficient—always!— the time is for doing all that students need to do in order to learn what they need to learn. On the other hand, to meet the challenge of teaching these plays, and for a performance approach to realize its potential, *students need to learn to speak in the languages that constitute the medium of drama*. Those languages are, first, the language of stage action inherent in the dialogue and stage directions, and second, the poetic language that Shakespeare, along with his contemporaries, used as the dominant form of dialogue. And anyone using a performance approach is asking students to become fluent in at least *some* of what Patrice Pavis has called *the languages of the stage*. (Only *some* because, for example, I do nothing about lighting or sets, very little about costume, and only a little about properties; although these are areas well worth investigating, I have no training in them and also have little class time to include them.) Thus the activities described in Chapter 1 are designed to immerse students in the medium itself and through that immersion help them become aware of the challenge facing them in reading the words of a play as both text and script. I would add that time spent in having students explore the potentials of different mediums, enabling them to discover how drama works in its own unique way, is rewarded by a deeper, fuller, and more inventive engagement with the plays than I find with students who do not go through this initiation. Furthermore, participation in these opening activities helps nurture the atmosphere of serious play that is essential for the course. Of course, if you work in a system where students come to your class with knowledge about the different mediums thoroughly established, you can move into the plays directly. You can spend more time with the plays presented here, or add another play or plays to your syllabus, and you can also experiment with the approach's potentials, adapting the activities modeled here to others plays or inventing new activities for the plays presented here.

The other feature of some chapters that may shape your way of reading is the relatively high level of detail I have opted for, especially in describing many of the activities. As one supportive but astringent critic asked, "Don't you think your readers may find that they are learning more about a particular class session than they ever wanted to know?" It seems to me that this comment points toward a tension that can be resolved only provisionally in any book on teaching. On the one hand, we can find ourselves frustrated by articles and books on teaching that outline a theory or model but give only the sketchiest detail about how the theory or model works in practice. In these cases, we are given a prescription but no guidance as to what will happen as we start to follow the prescription. On the other hand, we may find ourselves overwhelmed by articles and books that offer great detail and seem to imply, in the very act of such offering, that they are not only offering a prescription but also detailing the one true path we should follow, the only way to teach that subject. I wrestled with this tension as I decided what to include and what to exclude from my records of actual classes. My goal has been not only to supply the scenario but also to offer enough detail so that a teacher can say, "Oh, that's what happens!" Yet while the amount of detail is meant to indicate how a pedagogic script works when translated into a classroom enactment, it is *not* meant to be prescriptive. I am not saying, "This is how it must be done!" but rather, "This is how it is sometimes done" and, in the most detailed presentations, "This is how it once happened." In these detailed accounts, moreover, I have sought to indicate just how inventive, how playful, and, at the same time, how serious students can become in their work with a play—and I hope the detail will also enable the reader to experience the delight that the students themselves expressed in some of these classes.

In terms of how to read this book, therefore, if you think you want the model but not the detail, you can start by looking at the headings that announce each specific activity. You can read the design or script for each activity that usually appears shortly or immediately after the heading introducing that segment and that may be set off from other parts of the text. You can either skim or skip the more detailed accounts, moving quickly through the entire suite of activities for a given play. In that case, you might also want to teach a class using these scripts, record what happens in your own class, and then reread the chapter later to compare your experience with the experience recorded in this book.

Let me conclude this section by noting one other aspect of reading this book. In beginning to illustrate the challenges of reading the text of a Shakespeare play, I chose to initiate our engagement by unpacking a question about address—and this focus on address provides a cue for explaining another feature of this book. In most of the book, I am addressing you, the teacher-reader, but, beginning in Chapter 1 and recurrently in Chapters 3, 4, and 5, when I describe what happens in the classroom I include passages representing my address to students. In order to signal this shift in address without having to state that this is what I am doing, the book shifts fonts, from Sabon to Futura, and drops the quotation marks. Longer student responses also use this font. I hope this convention will make reading this book easier—and that it will provide a cue for reflecting on the tacit knowledge that guides how teachers address their students.

Entering a Conversation: An Invitation

When I first began experimenting with the performance approach over twenty years ago, my work grew out of my dissertation, during the writing of which I taught myself how to imagine performances of plays by Marlowe and Shakespeare; out of experiments in teaching writing; out of reading pieces by Miriam Gilbert,

Morris Eaves, Charles Hallett, and Katherine Burkman; and out of a conviction that students would learn more deeply from such an approach. So I simply plunged ahead, slowly learning how to design activities, seeking to make unsuccessful activities work and successful activities work better. At the Shakespeare Association of America, I met Alan Dessen, Charles Frey, Miriam Gilbert, Barbara Hodgdon, Philip McGuire, Randal Robinson, and Audrey Stanley and found some allies to talk with—and learned that in some cases I was reinventing the wheel. And when I was hired at Cal Poly Pomona, I found myself working with Joe Stodder, who has been not only a fiercely committed proponent of performance approaches but also a colleague whose unswerving support has enabled me to experiment widely in teaching Shakespeare's plays.

Over the last eighteen years, I have also worked with a number of teachers who have plunged into using this approach and generously shared their designs and experiences with me. I have worked particularly closely with four such teachers, Cora Foerstner, Sarah Innerst, Nancy Sassaman, and Wendy Wallin, and I want to acknowledge that their experiments and reports have contributed to my conviction that this approach can be successful in high school and college classrooms. I have also worked with a number of very fine teachers in my capacity as a regional director of the California Reading and Literature Project, and I want to thank those teachers, particularly Donna Heinemann, for their enthusiasm and energy in tackling the activities I asked them to rehearse.

Last but most important have been the students, now numbering well over one thousand, who have taken the eighty Shakespeare and other drama classes I have taught, and many of whom are among the dramatis personae of these chapters. Teaching is always, in the simplest and most mundane sense, an act of faith, and these students have expressed their trust by plunging into the activities I have asked them to perform—and thereby taught me much of what I present in this book.

Anyone who wants to discuss this book, share experiences, suggest extensions, or offer improvements can write to me at the English and Foreign Languages Department, California State Polytechnic University, 3801 West Temple Avenue, Pomona, California, 91768. Or you can e-mail me at elrocklin@csupomona. edu. I am eager to hear about experiments in which you employ the method in innovative ways, since one of the most appealing features of the performance model is its openness to reinterpretation, re-creation, and reinvention by all teachers. In fact, throughout the time I have been developing my concepts and practices, one of the most satisfying experiences has been having a former student return to tell me how she or he has successfully used an activity from my class in a way that I would never have imagined. I hope that those who read this book are able to use it to enter into their own co-creative acts with Shakespeare's plays and their students.

Learning to Read in a Different Language: Framing and Initiating the Study of Drama

Framing What We Do:

Initiating a Performance Approach to Reading Plays

Beckett . . . once wrote to me, saying that "a stage is an area of maximum verbal presence, and maximum corporeal presence."
KEITH JOHNSTONE, *IMPRO: Improvisation and the Theatre*

As I explained in the prologue, it is the premise of the model developed in this book that most students need to study drama in two phases. In the first phase, you engage students in a sequence of activities in which they contrast prose fiction and plays (and, if you have time, poetry) and thereby come to grasp the elements that constitute the dramatic medium. In the second phase, you immerse students in an array of medium-specific strategies that enable them to conduct performance-centered explorations of specific plays. In short, you teach a play by teaching students to read and speak in what the American director Harold Clurman called "a different language."

So this first chapter describes the sequence of activities I use to introduce students to that language of drama by having them contrast the medium of drama, with its double existence as text and performance, with what is, for all but a handful of them, the much more familiar medium of prose fiction. I describe how I set the scene and induct students into their role as active learners. Next I introduce the initiating questions for the course, "What is X? What does X mean? What does X do?" and follow this up by introducing the focus on drama embodied in the questions "What do these words do?"; "What can these words be made to do?";

and, in my reformulation of J. L. Styan's phrasing, "What do these words make the actor make the audience do?" (*Elements* 2).

With this frame established, we move into the next activity, the students' first rehearsal of the process of transforming text into performance, in which they read, cast, rehearse, perform, and write observations about a three-speaker, seven-speech script I call "A Brief Drama." After the performances, we share our notes about how the actors re/created meaning and establish a set of categories for talking about the actor as the medium of performance. We then move from script to narrative as students rewrite "A Brief Drama" in prose. At the conclusion of this suite of activities, students answer the question "What does narrative do?" and wrestle with the even more challenging question "What does dialogue do?"

Our work with "A Brief Drama" also becomes the springboard for the last three activities of this opening phase. Using our experience with this script, we engage in the key task of enumerating some of the constitutive elements of drama. I then move into introducing the challenge of reading differently by identifying some of the performance-centered elements that literary readers find most difficult to envision or perform in the theater of the mind. And I offer a brief preview of reading scripted language to synthesize our work together.

The activities the students and I perform together look different from those enacted in many English classes, even literature classes studying drama, for a number of reasons. These scenes will look different from those experienced by most teachers of Shakespeare in English departments, and indeed from those in their prior experiences as university students, when teachers may have taught drama as literature (although the emphasis on performance has been steadily gaining ground in the last thirty years), and different from how they themselves currently teach drama. They may also look different from the presentations in many other books on teaching drama because I have made these scenes not only quite specific in describing the script for each activity but also quite concrete in describing what students *do* and *have done* in realizing that script. One reason I go into such minute particulars, as Blake called them, is so that you, the reader and teacher, can have a vivid sense of what might happen if you choose to adopt a performance approach to drama. I hope this detailed presentation will help you imagine not simply how the method works but also the way in which it liberates and shapes (and, of course, confines in some directions even as it liberates in others) the energies of students, thereby enabling them to learn more than you or I can teach.

I have also adopted this detailed presentation in part because when I read books on teaching, what I hunger for and often miss is a sense that the approach really has been used in a classroom. So it pleases me when, for example, K–12 teachers taking graduate courses at other universities have read earlier versions of the material in this book and told their instructors that what they have read is written by someone who has obviously spent his life working in the classroom and enjoys it. Finally, just as the text of a play invites all of us to employ our imaginations in its re-creation, so I hope the text of this book invites you to re-create the model in your classroom and stimulates your creativity in imagining, designing, and conducting scenes of learning—and helps you learn from the surprising ways students perform your designs.

Setting the Scene: Initiating Active Learning

Since I think of teaching as a form of action, I use the analogy of teaching being like drama as a heuristic to help me plan the basic scripts for my classes, to guide the improvisation that these scripts produce, to stimulate me as I invent new moves in the course of these improvisations, and to offer me a perspective from which to think about the multiple roles I ask my students to play, as well as the multiple roles I play myself. In this chapter and the chapters that follow, I offer teachers an exploration of some of the options which, although frequently ignored, are available to them as they seek to engage their students and to help them move through the cycles of action, reflection, and re-action that constitute this education in drama. The logic of this analogy thus leads me to think of the classroom itself as the setting in which the action begins, and to carefully choose the ways in which I initially shape that setting and introduce the students, the teacher, and the plays to one another.

I begin by rearranging the room into what is either a circle open at one end or a U-shaped configuration with an open space at the "front"—which means, as the students will soon learn, that we are arranged roughly as an Elizabethan audience at a theater such as the Globe would have been arranged. In the last paragraph of his elegant essay "Original Staging and the Shakespeare Classroom," Ralph Alan Cohen reminds us that we often ignore the simplest of resources for teaching Shakespeare in performance:

> I have argued throughout that a classroom, rightly configured, can show students how the Elizabethan stage unlocks an understanding of Shakespeare's words. One reason is that the Elizabethan stage worked like a classroom in which the audience simultaneously experienced the subject and learned lessons about it. For that reason, teachers who stage their classrooms as Elizabethan theaters will not only find a place from which to view Shakespeare's language more clearly, they will also re-create a venue that teaches as it moves its audience. (99)

And earlier in the essay, Cohen points out that "any classroom with movable seating (chairs or desks) can serve as a model for that stage," remarking that "[w]ith a little effort teachers can virtually put their students into an Elizabethan theatre" (80).

We then move into an activity sometimes called the naming circle: I ask the students to get up and introduce themselves to six people they do not already know. There is usually a momentary hesitation, and I may point out that no one's arms are long enough to do this sitting down. As we begin, I too walk up to students, introduce myself, and shake hands.

After five minutes, we return to our seats, and I call on one of the people I have met to name some of the people she has met. And then I ask one of the people she has named to name still others, although each person is welcome to repeat the names of those already introduced. Eventually—and I am often surprised at how quickly this happens—someone will be able to name the twenty or twenty-five or thirty people present. (For classes of more than thirty-five people, you will probably need several class meetings to begin to master all the names.) And after two or three people have done this as well as they can, I too take a shot at it. There is often much giggling and anxiety and people saying, "Oh, I'm terrible with names!" to which my reply is, "We all have trouble with this—but we can all get this under control in a few days, and we will be doing it at the beginning of class until we do!" No matter how hard I concentrate I often miss a few names and sometimes say, "I know I am going to miss at least three names!" as I start.

Although this is a very simple activity, a number of students, especially first-year students, tell me what a difference it makes to know the names of their classmates and to have twenty or thirty people they know by name as they move through the day; furthermore, this activity, combined with the high level of participation and small-group work, encourages not only friendships but also creation of allies and of informal study groups that sometimes go on meeting after the course has ended. But even without these long-term benefits, the fact that I take time to do this naming at the beginning of class for the first three weeks also lets students draw vital inferences about my priorities.

With the first round of naming complete, I read the course outline. Before I ask for questions about the outline, I stress the point that while students will be asked to do some acting, they are not graded on acting, nor am I teaching acting, nor am I trained as an actor. The point is to use the various performance activities as tools to explore the plays—which means, although students do not know this yet, as tools to unlock their own creativity. Similarly, I stress that we will be using writing as a means of discovery, and that much of this writing, both in class and out of class, will be an opportunity for them to experiment with the new practices. Finally, I note that in the performance activities and in some of these writing activities they will be working in small groups so that they will have the opportunity to create a local community of learners who can function as allies for one another in the risk taking inherent in participating in this sort of course.

Initiating Questions

In this segment, I introduce premises that shape the course, and introduce them in a way that also seeks to embody those premises. Students are always learning from *how* we teach what we teach, and one objective of the version of the approach offered here is to make how I conduct the class as congruent as possible with what I ask the students to learn to do. Thus I initiate our work together by offering some ideas about how we can initiate the study of drama by asking some basic questions.

I think it is possible to argue that, at least in what has been called "the Western intellectual tradition," the questions that initiate a line of inquiry often take three forms: people tend to ask, "What is X?"; "What does X mean?"; and "What does X do?" I would suggest, for example, that if we wanted to generate an oversimplified history of Western philosophy, we could begin by distinguishing members of the thinkers we call philosophers by analyzing whether they prefer to ask "What is X?" or "What does X mean?" or "What does X do?"

Plato, for example, often asks, "What is X?" In his dialogues, especially the early dialogues, he represents Socrates as asking, "What is virtue? What is justice? What is truth? What is the good?" because, Socrates argues, until we have clear, shared definitions of key terms, we may think we are talking about the same thing when we are not. Plato's logic is that if we can find out what things really are, then we will know how to live correctly. If we know what the True and the Good and the Beautiful are, where *know* means knowledge that is certain—and certain because what is known is unchanging, universal, and eternal—then we will be able to choose how to act with as high a degree of certainty as our existence in a truth-clouding world allows. And insofar as Plato is the thinker who established many of the premises of Western philosophy, many philosophers who came after him have attempted to build on his premises and complete the projects that his questions initiated.

Many other thinkers, however, often those working primarily to establish or articulate a religion, have tended to start with the question "What does X mean?" That is, because they believe in a universe created by a deity or deities or transhuman forces, they also tend to imagine that this deity or force not only made things but also made things that carry meaning. They tend to focus on objects and creatures and events not only as the things themselves but also as symbols, assuming that these creatures will convey knowledge of the good and the true to us if only we learn how to employ the appropriate code or symbolism. For such thinkers—and the culture Shakespeare was born into had been powerfully shaped by thinkers of this sort—the universe is filled with objects, creatures, and events with meaning woven into or even constituting their existence. For these philosophers, the questions are not so much "What things really exist?" and "How do we know these things?" but rather "What is the code that will enable us to read the symbolic world we live in?" and "When we do correctly read this world, what do we discover about how we should live?" Many of the ways you have been taught to read literature are adaptations from thinkers who looked at the book called the Bible and looked at what they called "the book of nature" and asked, as English teachers still ask, "What does X mean?"

Yet still other philosophers think we need to start by asking, "What does X do?" This question became much more prominent in twentieth-century philosophy and is exemplified in the work of Ludwig Wittgenstein. In *Philosophical Investigations*, Wittgenstein introduces an image of human beings as (seriously) playing language games that exist within or help constitute what he calls "forms of life."

> When philosophers use a word—"knowledge," "being," "object," "I," "proposition," "name"—and try to grasp the *essence* of the thing, one must always ask oneself: is the word ever actually used in this way in the language game which is its original home.
>
> What *we* do is to bring words back from their metaphysical to their everyday use. (sec. 116, p. 48)

Wittgenstein also critiques philosophers who have made "What is X?" or "What does X mean?" the primary question for those seeking to understand how human beings communicate in words, because in doing so they have detached philosophy from life: "For philosophical problems arise when language *goes on holiday*" (sec. 38, p. 19). Wittgenstein, then, tends to believe that philosophy's primary task is to look at how people act and to consider language as one fundamental medium through which we both take action and create relationships. He thus provides one of the primary instances of a thinker who performs philosophy in a radically different way from both the tradition concerned with discovering real knowledge about real things and the tradition concerned with material things as symbols of a nonmaterial world. He subordinates a concern for what can be known of eternity to what can be known in the public space that comes from shared action through shared language. That Wittgenstein's work itself has been a major force in producing a shift in initiating questions becomes manifest when you discover that the book in which J. L. Austin developed some of Wittgenstein's premises is titled *How to Do Things with Words*.

This is a very abstract presentation, and because it is such an abstract analysis, it might be helpful for the class to apply these questions in a concrete way so that we begin to develop a sense about the differences between these questions. I also use the activity that follows to introduce another element of the course, namely, double-entry writings.

Putting the Questions in Motion: Introducing Writing for Discovery

As many readers will recognize, the writing form I introduce here is a modified form of Ann Berthoff's double-entry journal, which asks the writer to use the right-hand page or side of a page to reflect on an earlier entry on the left-hand page or side of a page. Berthoff has a twofold objective in using this method: first, to encourage student writers to revise their own thinking, and second, to engage students in examination of the very process of thinking and rethinking. Such double-entry writing enables students to become aware of the action of their own shaping imaginations and to draw on the self-renewing stimulus available to writers who return to their own ideas, reflect on their own processes.[1]

In my adaptation of this approach, we do two double entries in the first class meetings, and these entries are also a means by which I introduce the basic sequence of Action-Reflection-Reaction that provides the fundamental rhythm for the classes that follow.

With the page vertically divided, and having announced that students will use only the left-hand side of the page for this first step, I begin the activity by holding up a quarter and asking students to write down five answers to the question "What is X when X equals the object I hold in my hand?" When they have done this, I ask them for three more answers—and then two more, for a total of ten answers. As they work, I suggest that it helps if they can shift their point of view, but I do not explain what this means.

Next, with students still working on the left side of the page, I ask them to answer the question "What does X mean?" for the same object. I note that many people find answering this question more difficult and that we can discuss why later. Again I ask for five answers, then for three more, then two more.

Finally, I ask them to answer the question "What does X do?" I may still ask for five, then three, then two answers, but sometimes I will say, "You *know* I am going to ask for five more, so just do it." Making this move also prepares students for discussing how we perceive pattern in activity, a skill essential to reading playtexts.

Then we go around the room three times, sharing answers to the three questions in turn. As students share each round of answers, I am liable to ask if a given answer fits the question being asked or fits one of the other two questions better, since an answer will sometimes actually belong in another category. In a small class or a class in which the answers seem particularly diverse or innovative, I may go around a second time for each set of questions.

Here is a partial record of the set of answers offered by one class:

What Is X?
A quarter; an American symbol of financial value; a coin; a cylinder with ridged outside edges; imprinted portrait, sculpture, bas relief, profile; dated timepiece, marked with production date—and spatially located with mint mark; a visit from the tooth fairy; a reproduction of national icons; the root of all evil—which someone corrected, saying, "Isn't it the love of money that is the root of all evil?"

What Does X Mean?
Washington was a popular president; that the government controls production of money; freedom to buy necessities; nothing—unless we make it mean something; that we don't trust anybody, because if we did, people would work and barter, and money would not be needed; human beings have developed the skills for mining metals and minting coins; decision making: flip the coin; purchasing power; means one half of a candy bar to a small child.

What Does X Do?
Tightens screws; displays a picture of someone; an ability to play lottery cards and make one rich; causes conflicts; chimes; rolls; reflects light; spins when dropped; exists in space and time; moves goods and services; protects you from a charge of indigence; plays pinball games; allows one to play slot machines; changes in value. [On occasion, a student will respond, "X does not do anything, because it is an inanimate object! People have to do things with X!" This is an answer you can later return to when you discuss the peculiar way in which the playtext *does* things, and the ways in which it makes sense to treat the playtext as if it were an agent.]

What Do These Questions Do?

When we have collected these answers and enjoyed the variety and wit displayed in them, and when people have also begun to achieve a basic sense of how shifting point of view helps us see anew, we are ready to move on. I explain that I want students to move up several levels of abstraction, away from the concrete object, the quarter, in order to look at what happened in answering these questions. This will take several steps.

Step 1: Looking at the patterns within each set of answers. For the first step, I ask students to look at each of the three sets of answers in order to see what patterns they can discover within each set, treated as a separate unit. Here are some answers from the same class: (1) concrete answers, visual, describing the object or giving names to object or aspects of the object—in this sense, objective answers: that is, focused on the physical object; (2) abstractions, more personal and different responses, wider diversity, reflecting the subject's different points of view—more subjective in this sense, bringing in what it *means to the speaker*;

(3) actions: mixture of object with what I do with the object. Next, I suggest we ask the same question but from another point of view: What type of answers, in terms of parts of speech, does each of these three questions tend to elicit? What does the first question elicit? Nouns. Why? Because "What *is* X?" asks for the concrete nature of the item or the abstract essence of the item; it is a question that asks for the names we give X, what we call it. A noun is, as the grammar books tell us, "The name of a person, place, or thing." What does the second question elicit? Adjectives, adverbs, and, most of all, phrases or clauses. Asking "What does X *mean*?" invites us to supply a longer, fuller answer, an answer that is an *interpretation* of X. It offers a different type of explanation, not so much a naming as an unpacking, either of implied significances or inferred qualities—treating the object not so much as a thing but as an expressive entity. What does the third question elicit? Verbs. Why? Because "What does X *do*?" asks for a verb, for an action, for the dynamic possibilities of the subject; it asks us to see the subject in motion.

Step 2: Looking at the entire set of answers as a unit. For the second step, I ask students to reflect on and answer the question "What did the set of questions do?" Answers in this class included the following: (1) each question focuses your attention differently; (2) the set of questions pushes you, forcing you outside your normal thinking; (3) it makes you see your own habitual patterns and provides different perspectives on things you think you know. The main answer, then, is that this set of questions makes you see things from a number of different points of view so that you see the object differently—sometimes so differently that it does not seem to be or sound like the same object. So the set of questions can break the narrowing effect of an individual question.

Step 3: Looking at the question "What do questions do?" Finally, I ask students to respond to the question "What do questions do?" taking the whole set of thirty answers as their data. The questions, they said, take us from the known to the unknown so that we can then ask new questions or form new hypotheses about an object. We discover new ideas because these questions combine an objective view (where the student meant "A focus on the object as a thing in itself") and a subjective view (what the object is, means, or does for the observer). Questions push our thinking beyond our normal realms. They make us think, not just react: that is, after the first question, we cannot give just a reflex response that will let us go on doing or thinking what we already usually do or think. We have to think of something we have not noticed or have not thought of before. "[Questions] create gray areas," said Cathy, "making things you thought or wished were black-and-white more complex, seen from multiple points of view."

I then suggest to students that we recognize two points—namely, that questions are never neutral and that they are always partial. Questions are not neutral because they function as probes that have a direction and a thrust. The question does not predetermine our answer, but it does make certain answers or types of answer more likely, certain answers or types of answer less likely, and certain answers or types of answer nearly impossible.

Let me use three analogies here. First, we can say that questions point us in certain directions, and in doing this they train our eyes on one part of reality and not others: we see or focus on what is in front of us, but we do not see what is behind us. Second, we can say that questions function as though they were flashlights. Like flashlights, questions illuminate; they cast a bright light on some things that will seem to be in the center of a field, but they will cast dim light at the edges of this field, and they will leave other areas in complete darkness. Third, we can say that questions function as if they were lenses. When we employ a lens, we see certain things clearly; we see certain things blurred, so blurred that we may actually distort and misunderstand what we see; and we miss other things entirely. Let me add a specific example. In the fall of 1997, when I was teaching a Shakespeare class, I bought my first pair of glasses with continuous variation. In the material that came with the new glasses, I found the following passage, which I shared with the class: "Allow yourself two weeks or so of continual use with our lenses . . . to attain maximum comfort. This is especially true if you used to wear old bifocal designs. Our lenses are truly superior *but like all lenses, you must learn to use them*" (emphasis added). So, to refocus on my lens analogy, each question focuses and blurs, illuminates and darkens, because it gives us one range of answers and prevents others.

Questions are always partial because they point in one direction but not another and because no single question can prompt all the answers or offer a total understanding of any subject of inquiry. One way of saying this is that there are no 360-degree questions: no single question covers the entire horizon of a life-world, the entire circle of a universe. A question turns our heads toward one part of the landscape and away from another; a question focuses and blurs, illuminates and darkens; and it offers us one range of answers and prevents us from seeing other ranges of answers. A compact summary of what I am arguing here is offered by Kenneth Burke in his famous essay "Terministic Screens," in which he says "Even if any given terminology is a *reflection* of reality, by its very nature as a terminology it must be a *selection* of reality; and to this extent it must function also as a *deflection* of reality" (45). The questions we ask function as reflections, selections, and deflections of the reality we want to probe through the very act of asking those questions. This also means that the person who asks for, is given, seizes, or is presumed to have the authority to set the questions to be answered already has some control over what a group of people will do, think, discover: for whether or not she or he is aware of the fact, the questions (com)posed will fulfill certain purposes or carry out the agenda guiding that individual's actions. And this is what a teacher does. That is, in the classes we take or have taken as students, we are being trained to ask particular sets of questions by all our teachers. Often they do not say this explicitly, but that is what they (and I include myself) are doing: teaching some of the questions that are asked in—that in fact constitute—the discipline in which that teacher functions, *and* teaching what does and does not count as an answer to each discipline-specific question. One outcome of our exploration with questions and a quarter is that students might decide to focus on the questions they are being taught to ask. What I am suggesting is that one part of education can be to think carefully about that education, and in particular to see that education as a form of complex and largely indirect action through which you are reshaping what you do with your mind—including how you use your mind to imagine, recognize or invent, and then choose between courses of action. So in this course, to use Burke's formulation, we will be learning to use a set of questions that enable us to *reflect* the potentials of a playtext; that sharpen our ability to *select* key performance elements of that playtext; but that also *deflect* our attention from other aspects of that playtext, which is why we will also be supplementing these questions with some of the questions and concepts you learned in your more purely literary-focused English classes.

Introducing a Focus on Pragmatics

Using the Three Questions to Explore Speech

As our next step, we turn from things to words and use the three questions from the quarter exercise to examine some aspects of language. On the board I write two groups of words borrowed from literary critic Stanley Fish (*Is There a Text in This Class?*):[2]

He is sincere.

Doubtless, he is sincere.

First, let us ask "What is X?" about each string of words. Each of the two speeches is a group of words and a sentence. The words are made up of sounds, and we can divide the sounds into, for example, number of syllables. Four syllables in the first case, six syllables in the second. And if you shift your point of view? Each also constitutes marks made with chalk on a blackboard or erasable marker on a whiteboard or, ... We can also ask "What does X mean?" about each string. They both mean "This person is sincere." And *sincere* means? Interestingly, students almost invariably start by saying that someone who is sincere is someone who is "honest—someone you can trust." I often ask them to define *insincere* to help them articulate why *sincere* and *honest* are not quite the synonyms they may believe them to be. They generally arrive at a definition of *sincere* as "someone who believes what she or he says and who does not say things she or he does not mean or believe." And what does *doubtless* mean? (You can ask students what the privative suffix "-less" means.) It means that the speaker has no doubt that the person she is speaking about is sincere—that she is absolutely certain of his sincerity.

But when I ask, "What does X do?" the class may divide. Some students say that the second sentence is simply a more emphatic version of the first, equivalent to saying, "You *really* can believe that this person means what he says!" Others, however, will notice that to say "Doubtless" is to raise the idea of doubt even in the act of negating it. As the debate continues, I repeat the sentence, placing a heavy stress on the first word— "*Doubtless* he is sincere"—and ask, "How many people think they know what the next word is?" This question will draw a near-unanimous or unanimous response that the next word is *but*, and I then ask, "How do you know?" It seems obvious that the next word is indeed *but*, yet students sometimes find it difficult to explain how they know this. And this difficulty is a natural cue for talking about some of the more intriguing aspects of what human beings do with language, aspects I amplify with the following example.

The point to notice here, I suggest, is that we can answer "What is X?" in the same way for both sentences: both speeches are strings of words, both strings are sentences, both strings are chalk dust on a writing surface, and so on. And we can answer "What does X mean?" by saying that both sentences seem to *mean* the same thing if we look only at the content of each sentence. But these seemingly identical sentences can actually *do* or *can be made to do* different things. Indeed, as this example reminds us, sentences that seem to mean the same thing can nonetheless be used to create meanings that are directly opposed to one another. One way of understanding how I frame this course, then, is to note that I am interested not only in the fact that what we say or write means something, but also in the fact that what we say and write does something as well. I am interested, that is, in having us recognize and work with the truth that language is a form of action. And, therefore, with learning to ask about the words in a dramatic text, "*What do these words do?*"

Let us explore a slice of language a little closer to home and compose another double-entry writing. Here is a sentence I often encounter in my role as a teacher: *Did I miss anything important?* I ask students to jot down on the left side of this entry all the things they can imagine an instructor might hear in that sentence.

Here is the set of answers from one class:

1. Normally you don't do anything important in class.

2. I didn't think today was (going to be) important.

3. Please spend/waste your time repeating what you said so I can get it.

4. Why should I come to class?

5. I define *important* as "influencing my grade."

6. Your subject is boring, so why should I come to class?

7. I'm more important than your subject, and your job is to make sure you do not make the subject seem more important than the student.

Then I ask the students to move to the right side of the entry and to jot down whatever they have discovered in the course of creating their own list, hearing items from others' lists and from our discussion.

In this move, you open the door for anything the students discover as they reflect on a sentence they may have uttered dozens and heard hundreds of times. I have learned over the last thirty-three-plus years—and this will be true for many of the activities I offer in this book—that while a core of insights emerges in almost every class, student responses will often vary beyond anything I can predict. Thus I have taught myself to listen to and to do my best to make sense of any surprising answers they offer. When a student shares an idea that seems particularly off-the-wall, I often find that a few questions will elicit an exciting connection. Among the ideas students have formulated have been the following:

1. How the same words sound different to speaker and listener: the student may mean the words one way; the instructor may hear them in quite another way.

2. How the different roles people play can change what the words mean.

3. How easy it is to mean more than you intend—and how what the person hears may really be a correct understanding of your motives. Example: the quantifying of the word *important,* when what it means seems to be "what is important for my grade."

4. How students themselves discount other students: that is, only the instructor knows the content and only the instructor knows what part of that content is important; other students don't know or can't tell.

5. Students are not a source of knowledge.

In one class, Mary noted plaintively that all the translations on the first list seemed negative and cynical. Another student, Rosaleen, argued that I had set up the negative response by doing this activity *after* working with "He is sincere / Doubtless he is sincere." Not only did both observations seem correct to me, but they also offered us a fine example of an obvious but often ignored point about the nature of a play in performance—namely, that one of the most fundamental things the dramatist controls is the *sequence* of what the audience hears and sees. For in controlling the sequence, the dramatist controls how a first event becomes the context for a second event and thus shapes the particular meaning or meanings the spectators are likely to create from the second event. (This point about sequence as the dramatist's first element in controlling the experience of the spectators has been made by Thornton Wilder; cited by Robert Hapgood; similar concepts have also been developed by Jean Howard in *Shakespeare's Art of Orchestration.*[3])

A third student, Ellen, a theater major, wrote, "What Rocklin is doing is upside-down in relation to my drama training. We would just go say the line all the possible ways and *then* ask 'What did it mean when you said it that way?' But this class is like being in a glass-bottom boat, underwater!" When she read this entry to the class, Ellen provided an opening that I took advantage of to focus our attention on the aspect of speech we call *stress.*

People with literary training [I pointed out] will focus on the meaning of the words. They will start by imagining possible contexts in which you might mean different things in saying "Doubtless he is sincere" and then try to say the sentence so as to match these imagined meanings. But as Ellen has suggested, we can work from the other direction: we can start by *performing* the line itself in order to *discover* the possible meanings. So let's experiment starting from action rather than intention. What I want you to do is to move systematically through the ways of stressing this line:

Did I miss anything important?

Did I miss anything important?

Did *I* miss anything important?

Did I *miss* anything important?

Did I miss *anything* important?

Did I miss anything *important?*

After each performance, you can ask the class what the sentence would seem to mean—or, conversely, in what context(s), if any, it would make sense to utter the sentence with that particular stress. Here, students will act first and discover or invent the meaning as or after they hear the sound of the words. They will also be replicating the normal way in which we listen to other people, moving from what they say and do to infer the motives that we do not, as a rule, have access to.

As we complete this activity, I note a further point:

What we have done is begin to move into drama, where we will treat words as speech, specifically as *dialogue*, which creates not only the speech but also the context of the speech. I have said that this class seeks to combine literary and theatrical approaches, and this activity, in which we move through two ways of exploring what stress does, offers a very basic example of this process. What becomes evident is that because of the purposes of each discipline, people trained as literary readers or critics and people trained as theatrical readers or performers approach the same text or stretch of dialogue by employing different concepts, categories, and practices. What I hope is also evident is that these moves can complement each other, and that you can learn the set of moves you are less familiar with, add them to your repertory, and be able to explore any play (or novel or poem) in a greater variety of ways.

The activity we have just performed has also taken us through the first two phases of what I describe as the course's basic pattern of action, reflection, and reaction. We have played out the action of a student asking and an instructor hearing the sentence "Did I miss anything important?" and we have reflected on that action in the double entry students have just completed. One purpose of such reflection is simply to see better what the action does. Another purpose is to become aware of other ways one might perform the action, depending on the nature of one's purpose and audience.

What Does X Do? Introducing a Focus on Pragmatics

I conclude this segment by asking students to tell me which of the three questions—"What is X?"; "What does X mean?"; or "What does X do?"—I seem to prefer to start with. That is, one of the things my behavior should enable them to do is to infer which of these questions provides the first step I take in opening a line of inquiry.

Students will cite a number of pieces of evidence, some obvious and some subtle. Some will note, for example, that it was "What does X do?" that I emphasized in both the "Doubtless he is sincere" and the "Did I miss anything important?" activities. Others will note that I was implicitly asking the question "What does stress do?" Or they may note that in exploring "Did I miss anything important?" I compelled the class to look at what their words may do to an instructor. This answer, in turn, is the starting point for me to situate my use of the question "What does X do?" within a network of concepts we will be drawing on as we explore the plays and the plays' language.

As the class discovers, whereas most English teachers start by asking, "What do these words mean?" I start by asking, "What do these words do?" But this does not mean I am not interested in what words mean. I am enormously interested in what they mean, fascinated by the subtle and complex ways that words can invite us to create meaning and, as will become clear soon, eager to trace the ways that the words of Shakespeare's plays compel or invite us to create highly specific meanings. But I think we can get at that meaning more fully if we *start* by asking, "What do these words do?" and by learning to ask, "What can these words by made to do?" and then, "What do these words make the actors make the audience do?" When we are watching a play, I would claim, the meaning of the play emerges from our experience of the action. Thus I am not banishing the question "What do these words mean?" Rather, I am *resequencing* the array of initiating questions: I am asking, "What do these words do?" in order to better answer the question "What do these words mean?" or "What can these words be made to mean?" or "What have these words been made to mean in this specific performance?"

I then introduce another crucial set of concepts we will employ in our work together—the concepts embodied in speaking of the semantics, syntax, and pragmatics of language.

When we looked at the sentence "Doubtless he is sincere" and sought to understand the sentence by defining what the key word *sincere* meant, we were focusing on the aspect of language that is called *semantics*, the study of what words mean. But when we looked at this sentence, we were not just looking at the meaning of the individual words but also at the meaning of the string of words as a unit. So we were also confronting the aspect of language known as *syntax*, which focuses on the ways in which we put words together to create units we call sentences. In the "Doubtless" example, when students said that if I paused rather than put in a period then the next word would be *but*, they were drawing in part on their syntactic knowledge of the patterns we can employ when we speak or write. And when we examined what the string of words *Doubtless he is sincere* could *do*, when we focused on how people use words to get things done, then we were focusing on what is called *pragmatics*. Thus in setting up a frame in which we first ask the question "What do these words do?" I am setting up a context in which we focus on the pragmatics of human communication and, more specifically, the pragmatics of Shakespeare's plays. When I choose to make "What do these words do?" our initiating question, I do so because I believe that to study plays is to recognize that for dramatists the primary functions of the texts they create are pragmatic functions—or, as they would have thought of it in Shakespeare's day, rhetorical functions. But I also stress that in studying plays by Shakespeare we have to work with all three questions and work in all three areas of semantics, syntax, and pragmatics.

From Text to Performance: Exploring What Dramatic Dialogue Does

Although we speak of the play as composed of "dialogue," it is important to be aware that there is a fundamental difference between the dialogue embedded in most narrative fiction and the dialogue that constitutes almost the whole of the play's text, even as it constitutes the verbal component of the performed play, since the stage directions and character descriptions disappear in performance. This segment of the introduction has as its primary function the task of immersing us in the challenge of exploring dramatic dialogue. I introduce this segment by explaining that since I have just claimed that I prefer to start with the question "What does X do?," the only logical thing for me to do now is have the students do some acting. In this next activity, we move directly into the challenges entailed in reading playtexts, and the students move toward answering the question "What are the functions of dramatic dialogue?"

Performing "A Brief Drama"

The class counts off by whatever number is one-third of the total present, rounded up, so that you end up with triads and one dyad. If you have one student left over or if you have a student who absolutely refuses to act, you can ask that student to be a recorder, taking detailed notes on the performances that follow. As I hand out the text of "A Brief Drama," I continue: "Read over this script, discuss it, make sense of it, argue about what it means if necessary, cast it, rehearse it, and settle on how you will perform it. In about fifteen minutes, each of the groups will perform in front of the class."

CHAPTER ONE

A Brief Drama

A: Well all right you could get the men loaded in the other boats, get that out of the way.

B: They are in the other boats sir, they have been for hours. Now if we could just come to some—

A: All right, all right, hold your horses.

B: We—we ate the horses yesterday, sir.

A: Oh yeah, well I'll be with you—

C: Did ya really eat the horses yesterday?

A: I didn't—they did (hm, hm)—enlisted men.

© Copyright 1961 by Stan Freberg, Capitol Records[4]

I include here a record of two sets of performances, the first from a general education course and the second from an inventive group in an upper-division Shakespeare course, to help you envision what follows. First are descriptions of some of the main features in four performances of "A Brief Drama" from a general education class.

Group 1

This group featured a strong, emphatic A. They started with A facing B on a diagonal with C hidden behind A's back (one of the more innovative arrangements). A was pushing to get things done, while B was exasperated with A's hyperactivity and delivered his key line with heavy stresses: "We—we ATE the horses YESTERDAY, sir!" He was implicitly demanding that if A was going to be so peremptory, then he needed to at least know or remember what was going on. C darted out from behind A, who wheeled to face him, and his "hm-hm" came out as a snort of disgust, not, as it frequently does, bemusement. A had not forgotten nor was he surprised at the disgusting baseness of his men.

Group 2

This group did something that happens about every fourth time I have a class perform this activity; namely, they walked in a circle until the very end of the performance, in A, B, C order. The effect was of B and C trying to catch up with A, who was energetic, gestured the most, and became steadily more exasperated. At the end, they moved into an inward-facing triangle as they confronted one another and A gave up.

Group 3

This very lively group produced the strongest A we had—a lion-voiced A, one student later said. A was in control at all times, and he surprised us by shouting, "I'll be with you!" over his shoulder downstage at an invisible other. B was indignant and angry, her rising voice trying to prod A into action, but he remained calm, even stolid. C was writing at the desk, upstage and out of it until his head snapped up and he asked his question. His action left us unclear if he was a civilian performing paperwork or a superior officer, but A did not seem to show the deference we would expect him to show to his superior.

Group 4

Here was a pushy A, playing off against the calmest, most low-key B, almost sleepy-serene, not to be bothered, who said, "We ATE the horses yesterday, sir. . . ." shrugging, arms wide out, as if to say, "What can I say? What else could we do?" and "What's done is done!" C, by contrast, was the brassiest, most inquisitive performance of this role, and in this case it was as if A and C were both trying to get B to respond, to have more emotion than he was showing about the event that they both found out of the ordinary.

And here are descriptions of performances from an upper-division class.

Group 1

This group put more thought into blocking than did most groups and set up a situation built around the desk at the front of the room. A, played by a small, slightly built woman, was seated in front of the teacher's desk in one of the student note-taking chairs, looking nervous. B was upstage right, her back turned, disassociating herself, never once looking at A, never making eye contact, even when she glanced over her shoulder. As the dialogue commenced, C was tapping A's shoulder, frantic to get his attention, circling him, while A avoided meeting his look—and thus C's muteness became a focus of our attention. In the main dialogue, B delivered his lines with great impatience and strong emphasis, looking up and away, disassociating himself, his foot tapping as his exasperation rose, and finally giving a snort of derision in the pause of "We—we ate the horses yesterday, sir!," contemptuous of A's inadequacy, indecisiveness, and fear, and having reached or perhaps gone beyond the limit of what he could endure. Meanwhile, C was getting more frantic until he finally rotated the desk chair 90 degrees so he faced stage left before demanding, "Did ya really eat the horses yesterday?" with a fearful urgency. The startling effect here was that C thus seemed to care about the horses, not to be idly curious, amused, bemused, or amazed, but instead desperate, stunned perhaps that they could have been eaten, almost as if hoping that A would admit that B's words had been a joke.

Group 2
Blocking: A behind the desk, B on the stage-left side of the desk, and C on the same side but down front. Even before he spoke, A was pacing upstage center behind the desk, already angry. As he began to say, "Well all right you could get the men loaded in the other boats," he smashed his knee (as it seemed) into the desk, so that he interrupted himself to yell, "Get *that* out of the way!," turning beet-red as he did so. As the scene continued, A grew steadily angrier, and there was not a trace of joking in his final line. Unlike most As, then, he was always the dominant figure, and B's quietness seemed to most of us to be a response combining fear with an attempt to pacify A. C spoke his line in the common "hick" interpretation, but he added "sir?" at the end, which of course made him part of the hierarchy—and also someone we had to see as either especially dumb for risking A's wrath, or impervious to attack, insouciant, perhaps somehow having a license to ask questions, almost like a Fool. In fact, when we asked afterward, Margaret did not realize she had added the "sir?" and it may well have been an improvisation that responded to how dominating and threatening A appeared to be—a placatory gesture.

Group 3

This group surprised us with an adroitly improvised setting and props. As they moved into position, C drew the skull-and-crossbones flag on the board, immediately creating a specific setting that was enacted by A, who stood on the desk-top, manning the ship's wheel. He had also turned a bracelet into a huge silver ornament in his left ear. He shouted his first line to his right, which provoked B into climbing to the upper deck. A's shouting, unlike that of A in the first group, was the voice of a man in command and enjoying himself, heavily stressing words as if shouting over a storm. When B climbed up, he was clearly subordinate, even fearful, and he showed exasperation only when he turned away and muttered, "Oh brother!" under his breath before saying, "We— we ate the horses yesterday, sir." At this, C, who had been seated below in front of the desk/deck, rose up and delivered his line, trembling so much that we had to wonder if he was shivering from fear, seasickness, or illness. Obviously, hearing about eating the horses added to his shocked and fearful state. Like group 1, this group had invented a production option for C that was out of the ordinary and yet strikingly effective. It also, of course, illustrated how much the more open nonverbal element could supply a context that transformed the meaning of the seemingly more closed verbal element.

Group 4

This group also had a prop, in this case a chair-desk, which C carried around as the scene began, hunched over, officially respectful but in fact insubordinately scowling. As A completed the first order to load the boats, C slammed down the desk, almost on A's feet, so that A drew himself up with contained anger and snapped "Get that out of the way!" Again, the truth about the horses was a secret, so B whispered, "We— we ate the horses yesterday, sir," but C overheard and was provoked into a Cockney snarl: "Did ya really eat the horses yesterday?," anger, disgust, and contempt mixed together. C thus provoked A beyond endurance, so that A addressed the last line to the audience, flung his notebook on the floor, and stalked off. In this group too, then, the main tension was between A and C, not A and B.

In the discussion that follows, my goal is twofold: first, to collect responses, noting what was striking about each performance and what the actors did that created the particular meanings projected, and second, to initiate one ongoing process involved in teaching Shakespeare, namely, the retraining involved in learning that in reading, rehearsing, performing, or watching drama, we are concerned with both *reading differently* and *seeing differently*. Besides the specifics we share, this segment takes another step in helping students learn to sharpen both their sight and their vision.

Establishing Categories to Describe What Actors Do

Before the class period ends, we quickly jot down a list of everything the actors did that "added"—and I'll later (or at the next class) explain why I put "added" in quotes—to the text in creating their performances. This move often needs to be negotiated so that the students shift down to the appropriately concrete level: that is, students will often say that actors "added emotion," and I must push them to produce detailed descriptions of the behavior that creates and conveys emotion. Once we get started, the board fills rapidly, until we have twenty or thirty items. Then I say:

> Please categorize the list in some way that allows you to have three to six categories that cover all the things we have said the actors added. Remember that an ideal category system is both exclusive and exhaustive: that is, the boundaries between the categories can be sharply defined, and the set of categories as a whole comprehends the entire range of the phenomenon you are studying. This is an ideal that, in fact, many category systems do not and in some cases cannot achieve, but even if you cannot achieve this ideal, keep it in mind as a guideline. The categories you create can become a heuristic: a good set of categories becomes a set of questions that helps you cover the major variables as you try to imagine how a scene might be staged. And a good set of categories *also* provides us with a common vocabulary that can enable us to communicate

either what we perceive or what we imagine with greater precision and mutual comprehension.

If the class seems to be having trouble, I point out the obvious distinction between verbal and nonverbal items. This simplifies the problem, allowing them to concentrate on categorizing the diverse range of things actors do nonverbally. This is another activity students usually do in small groups, since debate about possible categories can provoke useful collaborative analysis, with students compelling one another to refine their ideas.

I then collect several of the categorizations by having one reporter from each team of students put that team's categorization on the board. Then we discuss them, discover where they overlap and where they diverge, and in this way further refine our perceptions of what actors do to create meaning.

At this point, I also offer the class the set of categories presented by Daniel Seltzer in several essays on Shakespearean drama. As Seltzer himself puts it in "The Actors and the Staging," he wants to present "four aspects of acting style which, taken together, cover everything an actor can do (physically) on stage":

> (1) *Stage business*, ranging from small details of action relating to the character's own person to facial expressions and movement carried out on lines; (2) *Voice*, primarily in terms of pitch and volume, but including special uses such as parody, and extending as well to such matters as the pacing of speeches, special pauses, tonal quality, and the like; (3) *Stage movement*, in terms of "blocking," but also considerations such as which areas of the stage were apparently considered "strongest" and which were utilized for different kinds of action; (4) *Address*, that is, literally the direction of the actor's speech—when he is alone on stage (as when, in a meditative speech, he may as it were address "himself" only; or, in an explanatory vein, or comic routine, address the audience; or, in a speech of apostrophe, usually in strong emotions, address an imaginary hearer) or with other actors (when he may speak to one or more at a time, or speak without actually addressing any, or in asides to the audience, or alternate among actors, or between them and the audience; also when his speech covers the exit or anticipates the entrance of another actor). (38)

I resequence the list, making voice the first category. Voice, stage business, stage movement, and address, I suggest, are concepts we can employ as we discuss the complex things we can imagine actors doing and the complex things we see actors doing, whether the actors are the members of the class, live actors at a performance, or actors in a film version of a play.

You also may want to use Seltzer's categories as you start working on the first play. Ask students to read, say, a short opening scene or the opening fifty lines four times, using a different category each time to help them imagine a performance or performances; or create four groups, each group exploring the scene through the lens of one category. This exercise can also help students begin to discover how Shakespeare packs his lines with implicit stage directions. Again, you can use this activity as an assignment for small groups or in asking a student to direct a performance. Or it can be assigned as double-entry writing homework.

If, as frequently happens, we have reached the end of the period, I assign some or all of the following tasks:

1. List the steps in the process your group went through to move from asking "What's going on here?" to its performance of "A Brief Drama."

2. List features of the text (features you might ignore when reading fiction) that you had to pay attention to in carrying out this task.

3. Write a full description of how your group performed the scene, using the categories of voice, stage business, stage movement, and address to help you re-create what you did.

4. Write a narrative version of this drama: that is, embed the dialogue in the sort of narrative you would create if you wrote this as a short story. I will collect your narrative, but not the first three items.

A Note on the Rest of the Chapter

What follows from the action of performing "A Brief Drama" is a series of interlocking cycles of reflection and reaction in which students explore what they have done in order to discover some fundamental features about dramatic texts, about performances, about the relation of performances to texts, and about the constitutive elements of drama. The series is complex but also allows for extensive adjustment and improvisation. Indeed, this book may be thought of as being like an accordion: I present this accordion with the bellows expanded, but you are free to collapse some segments, shorten others, and invent new segments, depending on your purposes, your students, and the time available. In fact, I rarely have time to do the entire sequence of activities in any single course, but, as noted earlier, I aim to offer more material than you can use in one term, trusting readers to design sequences that work for their own needs.

From Script to Narrative

So far, the class has focused on a script, moved from text to performance, and then stepped back to analyze some of the elements the performance offers the spectator that the text does not offer the reader. What I aim for in this sequence is to have students gain insight into the nature of the dramatic medium through a series of engagements that use contrast to lead students to answer the question "What is drama?" by answering two other questions, "What is the nature of the dramatic medium?" and "What does drama do and how does drama do what it does?"

Two principles are at work in this sequence of activities: (1) such a definition is best arrived at through direct experience of the different potentials of the medium to be defined; and (2) such a definition must also work through contrast with an alternative medium. The definition students need, after all, is not some verbal formula transmitted by the teacher, but rather a definition-through-action that enables them to experience the medium and to contrast it with a related yet different medium.

Thus the next step is to have the students translate "A Brief Drama" into a narrative text. I simply say, "Please transform this miniature play into a short story: that is, write it as a prose narrative. You need to keep the same seven speeches in the same order, but I want you to do more than just write a paragraph that describes the setting and then put the dialogue in as is at the end. You need to invent a context for the dialogue and then write a full-scale narrative that includes the dialogue."

If we have time, students write their narratives on the spot, but this rarely happens, and I find their narratives are more illuminating pedagogically if they are written for the next class. In that class, I ask for volunteers and, when necessary, for versions that are quite different from those we have already heard. Eventually we hear a set of variations that exploits the main alternatives of the narrative medium, and once again I ask for a list: "Please list the different things that the narrators you created did."

Described the scene.

Described the history of the people involved: took us back in time.

Took us forward in time, past the end of the script.

Told us what one or more of the characters was really thinking.

Wrote the story from one character's point of view.

Wrote the story from an outsider's point of view.

Made fun of one or more of the characters.

Took sides, supporting (say) B against A.

Described their gestures.

Told us what to think of different characters.

You are now ready to ask the class the more general question "What does a narrator do?"—a question that may spontaneously emerge in the course of the discussion, depending mostly on how sophisticated your group already is about such concepts. Compiling this more abstract list will naturally move the class toward discovering or recalling the fundamental concept of point of view and the distinctions in knowledge and person, as well as distance in time and space, that represent fundamental choices facing a writer as she or he exploits the potentials of the narrative medium. Depending on how thorough you want to be, you can simply list the main categories or ask the class to create a more complex enumeration of the narrative medium's potential points of view.[5]

For the next step, I propose another question. Even when

they work in the narrative medium, most writers create dialogue for their characters, and we need to ask why they take the trouble to do this. That is, what is it about dialogue that makes it worth creating even though many novelists say that writing good dialogue is terribly hard? In short, we need to ask, "What does dialogue do that narrative cannot do?"

The students often have difficulty formulating what it is that dialogue does, and does in a way that narrative cannot seem to do. They may start by saying things such as, "The dialogue is more real than the description!," thereby substituting the creation of an evaluative hierarchy for the analysis of different functions. I use such comments to suggest that for analytic purposes, sometimes describing what things do works better if we suspend the impulse to say that different equals "better or worse."

When pressed to say *how* dialogue is more real, someone may say, "It gives you the character's personality," an answer that can be followed up in interesting ways. What students will perceive is that dialogue gives us "more" in the sense that it gives us not just the content of what a character says but also *how* she or he says it: and in giving us the specific words a character is supposed to utter, dialogue performs several functions. First, it offers us the word choice, syntax, and pragmatic style of the speaker, as well as cues for rhythm, tone, and implicit action. Second, it invites us to use our imagination to animate the written text, just as we did in actual performance, exploring alternative performances of the dialogue. Third, when the author provides a scene in which several characters speak, she or he offers implicit information about the *interplay* between speakers, the way they modulate or do not modulate what they say, in both substance and style, in response to the particular spoken language of the other(s).

Eventually we can clarify some other crucial points about dialogue and in particular the dialogue that constitutes the text of a play. Put simply, the most fundamental things that dialogue does are to put us *in the present and in the presence of the speakers* and to make us *witnesses* to their words in action, inviting us to read the scene with at least as much precision and subtlety as we bring to reading other human beings in our own lives.

The simplest way that dialogue is "more real" is that dramatic dialogue is always in the present tense, which is to say in the present, and because in live theater this dialogue is spoken by actors, we are not only in the present but also in the presence of the virtual human beings created by those actual human beings, the actors. Furthermore, the manner in which actors can incarnate the roles from the page in real bodies creates the experience of risk that, in supreme moments of live theater, can leave a spectator as shaken as Samuel Johnson claimed to be merely by reading the death of Cordelia at the climax of *King Lear*. This is the power that English Renaissance playwrights such as Ben Jonson in *Volpone* claimed might bring spectators to recognize their follies, and that playwrights from William Shakespeare in *Hamlet* to Philip Massinger in *The Roman Actor*—when they created characters who articulate exalted defenses of the actor's art— claimed might make a murderer watching a play confess his or her crime. Dramatic dialogue makes us witnesses, and may even make us feel as if we were participants, in a way that neither prose fiction nor film does, and it thereby invites us to undergo a particular form of powerful artistic experience.

We can also come at this contrast from the reverse direction if we return to "A Brief Drama." In this case, I ask the students to enumerate all the activities they had to carry out in order to translate "A Brief Drama" into performance. Here is the list created by one class, interwoven with my commentary:

1. *Context*. The student actors had to discover or invent a context in which these speeches make sense, which meant looking for cues to context in the dialogue. The use of *sir*, for example, suggests a military or other hierarchic context, such as master-servant: B "sirs" A, but A does not "sir" B, so it seems clear that A is superior to B. At the same time, tracing the use of *sir* does not solve all the problems since C does not address anyone as sir nor is she or he addressed as sir. Furthermore, C's "Did ya?" suggests to some of us that C is less educated than A and B. And putting these two cues together, most groups performed C as not being part of a hierarchy and as less sophisticated than A and B. But, as happens in some classes, C can be played not only as outside but also as at the top of the hierarchy.

2. *Address.* Even if they never consciously asked the question of address, students were in fact deciding issues of address. Their performances showed them deciding the question "Who is C asking his or her question of?" Surely she or he asks B, since it is "We ate" and "Did ya" —but A answers. But then they confront the question "Who does A address?" And there is another question: "Does A point to anyone when she or he says 'enlisted men'?"

3. *Self-revelation.* Furthermore, whether they noticed this or not, all performances decided the question "Did B eat horse?" That is, "We ate the horses yesterday, sir" seems to mandate that B partook of horse, but she or he can make it clear that "we" refers to the group membership she or he shares with others and yet that she or he did not eat horse.

4. *Pronouns.* Students discovered that pronouns are always potentially problematic since their referents must often be inferred from among two or more possibilities. Take, for example, the line "Get that out of the way": while most people take the pronoun as referring simply to the topic of conversation, getting the men loaded in the boats, other performances make it evident that *that* refers to a physical object, perhaps a prop that A has stumbled over, or even to character C. In these performances, the line is actually spoken as "Get *that* out of the way!" Similarly, "I didn't—they did—enlisted men" can be played to include B or not, and may also include us, the audience.

5. *Sounds.* All groups tend to struggle with the sounds indicated by "hm, hm," not merely as to what sound to make but also what that sound expresses.

6. *Punctuation.* Some students are nonplussed by the lack of commas in the first phrase "Well all right you could get the men loaded" since they felt that it should be "Well, all right, you could get the men loaded in the other boats," but they acknowledged that it makes sense without commas.

7. *Pauses.* We can examine the variety of pauses they created.

8. *Stresses.* We have already touched on the ways students must read in order to make choices about what to stress, as in the case of the pronoun *that* noted previously. As another example, a number of groups delivered the pivotal line as "We ate the HORSES yesterday," which seems to imply a three-step narrative: The day before we ate (say) the rabbits; yesterday we ate the horses; and tomorrow we will eat the cattle—a demonstration of how complex their reading experiments can become as students become more sophisticated performance readers.

9. *Props and bodies as props.* In one group that had only two students for the three parts, the performers turned this apparent deficit to advantage. A spoke to B while holding a cell phone to his ear. His prop, which at first looked merely cute, paid off in laughter as we realized that C was listening to A's conversation with B, and as A projected C's line as a high-pitched voice coming over the phone. Furthermore, if the students do not make this point, I draw attention to the ways in which they use their bodies as props. One of the more striking examples was a group that created a shipboard scene not by drawing emblems such as a sail or a pirate flag on the board but simply by having all three actors stand and sway in unison throughout the performance.

Reading Differently: Exploring Semantic, Syntactic, and Pragmatic Elements

Another way to explore the subtleties of what scripted language does is to turn again to the categories of semantics, syntax, and pragmatics and ask the class, as students work in their performance groups, to enumerate all the things they did in translating the text from page to stage using these three concepts. This activity has the added benefit of demonstrating how subtly dramatic dialogue can operate in something as seemingly minute as the dash that marks an interruption. When asked to examine the challenges of reading differently using the categories of semantics, syntax, and pragmatics as their lenses, students produce this analysis:

Semantic Elements and Sounds. Here students always consider the "hm, hm" sound. As readers we have to ask first what sound this is. How is A going to say it? But of course this depends on what the team imagines A wants the sound to mean (and to do—the categories cannot be kept absolutely separate). The single most important semantic element, students realize, is the unexpected shift from figurative to literal language as the phrase "hold your horses" elicits the unexpected reply "We—we ate the horses yesterday, sir." Students may also note, depending on the performances, the possible pun, which this time seems to move from literal to figurative, in the phrase "get the men *loaded* in the other boats."

Syntactic Elements. I often start this segment by pointing out that every performance supplies what students seem to think of as "missing" commas, because they have A say, "Well, all right, you could get the men loaded in the other boats." I say the line without the commas, to show it can be done, and ask, "Why do you add the commas?" Their answer usually starts with "Because that's how we usually say it!" and it takes some effort for them to realize that they want the commas as a means for the actor playing A to suggest some hesitation in speech—that is, to make it seem as though the character is fishing around for something to order B to do to get rid of him. (Again, what starts as a syntactic element spills over into pragmatic considerations.) Students also note that the dashes signal both interruption and self-interruption, *and* present some intriguing cues for actors to solve. There is B's speech: "We—we ate the horses yesterday, sir." As readers they had to ask, "What makes B interrupt himself?" Either he does not want to admit what A does not know, or he does not want to remind A of something that might upset A or that is shameful to the men. We can now ask if the next line helps us make a choice about the reason B interrupts himself. I sometimes model the experimental reading approach I want them to adopt by asking, "Or does the interruption occur because for a moment B himself forgets what they did?" and then I perform the speech this way. Students find this option unconvincing, and we move on, turning to the self-interruptions of A's final speech: "I didn't—they did (hm, hm)—enlisted men." Why the two pauses or shifts? Is it because A is doing one thing? Or is he doing three things? If A is doing three things, the scene might look like this:

First, he says "I didn't" to indicate "I am innocent" of the implicit charge in C's question; and his tone can range, for example, from indignant to smug. He can say "—they did—(hm, hm)" while pointing, so as to create a sharp contrast, a signal of his distance, which might also be a statement, whether conscious or not, about rank, class, morality, culinary taste, or something else. Finally, he may say "—enlisted men" as an assertion of hierarchic difference, perhaps class difference, implicitly asking, "What can you expect of *them*?" Pragmatic considerations will again come into play as you look at the options for address. It might be the case, for example, that A addresses three different individuals or groups: imagine that A first speaks to C, announcing "I didn't"; then either speaks to B or about B and the enlisted men when he says "—they did (hm, hm)," perhaps pointing to draw a sharp contrast, as well as making whatever sound he makes; and last of all, turning to the audience, says "enlisted men" in a tone which, as we saw from the performances, can be contemptuous, bemused, affectionate, or hostile.

Pragmatic Elements. The pragmatic focus is inherent in trying to make sense of any playtext and also foreshadows the heuristic titled "Performing an Action" that I introduce when we explore *The Taming of the Shrew*. Students answer the questions "Who are these people? What are their relations? And what is the situation?" The details of "A Brief Drama" indicate that the characters are situated on land but near water, whether ocean, lake, or river; that they are part of an institution, probably a military force with a hierarchic structure, probably all male, indicated by the use of "sir"; and that this moment comes after or at the end of a sequence covering the last several hours or days. One question students confront is "Who is C?" They argue about whether C is "uneducated" because he says, "Did ya really—?," or whether this is an expression of surprise. C seems obviously out of the hierarchy since he does not use "sir"—but in some performances C is clearly part of the hierarchy, above A, hence does not use "sir" in addressing A, while A *forgets* to use "sir" when addressing C because he is so incensed about what the men did. On the other hand, some argue that C is an enlisted man who did not eat the horses—perhaps even loves horses (I am waiting for C to be depicted as an animal rights advocate)—and who is so stunned and appalled that he forgets the protocols of rank.

Synthesizing the Categories to Explore an Open Moment

Finally, I focus on an example that shows how we can—and how actors must—draw on all three elements of semantics, syntax, and pragmatics to solve a subtle aspect of the dialogue as written (or, to be more precise, as I have chosen to transcribe it from the recording). I ask the class to return to the first interruption, "Now if we could just come to some—," pointing out that actors must always be prepared to complete any interrupted sentence in case their partner does not perform the interruption precisely on cue. I ask students to write out words that might complete this sentence, and then we collect their choices: *understanding, compromise, decision, conclusion, agreement, consensus, choice,* and so on.

"Now, if you are performing B, are there any considerations in the semantics, the syntax, or the pragmatics that might make one word more probable than another?" After giving students a few minutes to respond, I either run through each proposed word systematically or ask for a volunteer to argue for one word, with support from whoever else chose it, followed by challenges and counterpropositions. We may or may not reach a consensus, but in the course of the argument students themselves demonstrate the wide and subtle array of considerations that can come into play in doing something as apparently simple as inferring a word to "complete" a speech. Among the key factors they work out is that B probably cannot use *agreement, compromise, consensus,* or *understanding,* since in the hierarchic situation he is subordinate to A. Furthermore, given A's function, *conclusion* and *choice* are not likely candidates because what A needs to do, and what B wants him to do, is not merely to come to a conclusion but to take action—in fact, to issue an order. At the same time, students recognize that B is trying to prompt A to issue an order yet trying not to be or appear to be insubordinate, and this helps them discover that the crucial variable is B's use of *we*. For if we substitute *you* and make the sentence "Now if you could just come to some—," the subtlety of B's choice comes sharply into focus. Students now can see how B is using the first-person plural to evade the appearance of blaming his superior, speaking as if they are a team (in other words, almost making it appear that they are equals) yet also preparing to use the key word *decision*. Eventually, many but not all students come to agree that *decision* is the most probable selection, as B balances the need to prompt A to make a choice and issue an order against the need to avoid appearing insubordinate. In moving through this activity, students get a preview of the complex and subtle details that may be packed into scripted language and of the disciplined process an actor may move through in anatomizing those details in order to make performance choices.[6]

Some students either infer that "A Brief Drama" is a parody of Washington crossing the Delaware or are familiar with the Stan Freberg album (originally issued as an LP in 1961, when I first heard it, and recently reissued as a CD) from which this excerpt comes, and are not surprised when I play the full segment for the class.

At this point, we pause so that students can do some reflection, using two consecutive prompts: "One thing that is becoming clear to me about what dramatic dialogue *does* is—" followed by "One thing that is becoming clear to me about what I need to do when I *read* dramatic dialogue is—". Neatly summarizing much of what we had done, Liz wrote, "One thing that is becoming clear to me about what I need to do when I *read* dramatic dialogue is that I need to learn to articulate inferences about characters and action, and to question my assumptions about characters and about the relationships between characters."

Reading Differently: Two Examples from Romeo and Juliet

Formulations such as the one offered by Liz are my cue to follow Barbara Hodgdon ("Making") in applying this model of reading differently to a speech from Shakespeare. First, the students and I look at a single line from *Romeo and Juliet*, applying the sharpened sense of reading actors must use when they read, and then move on to performing the first segment of the opening scene of that play to experience how the energy and sweep of the language work to carry spectators along even though they have no time for such close analysis.

We start by working with a speech that I write on the board: "Nurse, where's my daughter? Call her forth to me." (I do not tell the students who is speaking, although some of them will recognize this as Lady Capulet's first speech in act I, scene iii.) As Barbara Hodgdon reminds us, the actor exploring this line needs to ask, "What do these words reveal (1) about the speaker? (2) about the speaker's state of mind? and (3) about the speaker's relationship to the daughter and the nurse?"[7]

What often becomes clear with the first few comments is that some students encounter a semantic issue as they assume this is a medical nurse and proceed to draw quite plausible inferences about the context of the scene and answer the three questions. Other students will either know or infer that "nurse" is short for "nursemaid," but discussion reveals that the single speech does not provide evidence to help readers decide with certainty between these two readings. Students quickly realize that the speech implies a number of things. The speaker assumes that the nurse knows or should know where the daughter is, and this implies that the nurse is closer to the daughter than the speaker is. The speaker also expects instant obedience from both nurse and daughter. The fact that both these people are referred to by function or kinship, not name, indicates the speaker's formal (some students, going a bit further than the speech actually warrants, say distant or cold) relationship with both, as well as a certain focus on other people only in relation to the self. Often a student will observe that the speaker sounds harsh or angry with the daughter. When challenged on the source of this reading, the student points to the use of the imperative: this reminds us that syntax is an important resource provided by dramatic dialogue and also provides an opening to note how the social structure of Shakespeare's world makes it natural for some speakers to issue such a command—an action that some students say they would find uncomfortable. (If you want to pursue this issue of master/mistress-servant relations, the interaction of Lady Capulet and the Nurse certainly provides a rewarding scene to study.) At the end of this activity, we locate the speech in the text so that students see that it is Lady Capulet's first line in act I, scene iii. This also allows us to begin discussing how important a character's first line can be in establishing an initial impression. Discussion also demonstrates how rich dramatic dialogue can be, and how even a single line of dialogue can constitute an entire context in itself, providing cues for readers to unpack if they choose to read the line in slow motion as we just have. And students have yet another concrete example of how considering semantics, syntax, and pragmatics allows them to use the individual words, the sentence structure, and the implicit information about relationships as cues for their interpretation of the line.

We then shift to the second example, in which students read the opening sixty-four lines of *Romeo and Juliet*—that is, up to the moment when the servants actually begin to fight. Although I tell students that they need not do any acting, many of them start to act, and indeed to insist on doing some acting, as they get into the reading. Usually, after they finish the first reading they want to try again, and we have a second run-through in which they become more actively engaged.

The students will supply their own immediate responses, some unique to the specific performance in your class. But as the discussion proceeds, you will want to stress certain ideas. In particular, as Hodgdon suggests, you will want to (1) note how quickly the action, whether comic or serious, develops, and how strong a response, either laughter or intense curiosity, the performance evokes from the spectators; (2) note how easily language translates into speech, how some meanings emerge from *hearing sounds*—that is, *from listening to the words and the interplay of words*; and (3) note "how, even though words disappear fast in performance, they *are* comprehensible." ("Making" 4)

At the end of this discussion, you can also pause for students to add another "One thing that is becoming clear to me about Shakespeare's language is—" entry.

Enumerating Some Constitutive Elements of Drama

Next, I ask the class to use the rich work we have done so far to help them answer the question "What are some of the constitutive elements of drama?" This is a difficult question, and I start by explaining the concept of constitutive elements.

The concept of "constitutive elements" is a way to look at some of those activities that human beings carry out in a systematic fashion. Such activities can be said to be constituted by the presence or participation of certain elements or the existence of certain rules that make the activity uniquely itself. The clearest instances are probably rule-governed activities such as games, in which the concept can be stated with particular clarity because we can distinguish constitutive from regulative rules. This distinction was originally presented by John Rawls and has been elaborated by John R. Searle, who formulates the distinction in this way:

> As a start, we might say that regulative rules regulate antecedently or independently existing forms of behavior; for example, many rules of etiquette regulate inter-personal relationships which exist independently of the rules. But constitutive rules do not merely regulate, they create or define new forms of behavior. The rules of football or chess, for example, do not merely regulate playing football or chess, but as it were they create the very possibility of playing such games. (33)[8]

An obvious analogy is the United State Constitution, which is the document that constitutes our country's government and the country.

As a constituted activity, drama can be understood as a system, but a system composed not so much of the sort of rules that create games but rather by the participation of certain groups of people in particular spaces and operating within certain tacit conventions. Or, following Wittgenstein's (*Philosophical*) idea of looking at language games, we can think of drama as a particularly complex game that some societies invent. What I am asking students to do is to articulate the elements that constitute the game of drama as it has been played in the tradition that came into existence shortly before Shakespeare began his career as a dramatist. And I am pointing out that the work we have done, particularly in performing "A Brief Drama" and transforming drama into a narrative, is evidence from which they can discover those elements that constitute the activity we call drama.

In the discussion that follows this explanation, the students usually manage to articulate three or four of the constitutive elements of drama. Their formulations become the starting point for my own more detailed presentation, in which I remind them that my own list is not exhaustive and that someone in this class may help us add to the list.

The first element is the intangible *network of conventions*, the tacit knowledge that allows the public representation to take place. In *Drama from Ibsen to Brecht*, Raymond Williams has provided an essential formulation:[9]

> In the actual practice of drama, the convention, in any particular case, is simply the terms upon which author, performers and audience agree to meet, so that the performance may be carried on. *Agree to meet*, of course, is by no means always a formal or definite process; much more usually, in any art, the consent is largely customary, and often indeed it is virtually unconscious. (13)

That such conventions exist, and that they embody complexly interlocking social, political, cultural, and aesthetic agreements, is testified to by the riots caused by some plays and by the variety of reasons for which audiences have rioted.

The second and more tangible element is the *performance space itself*, that feature Peter Brook has called, in the title of his famous essay, "the empty space." The nature of this space offers different potentials to the dramatists who write for and the actors who work in that space. Indeed, the director Max Stafford-Clark has reminded us that "[a]ll acting is a response to architecture." In particular, the literal distance between actors and spectators makes possible different types of player–spectator relations. So each playing space tends to make possible some types of playing and to foreclose others, and thus helps to shape the particular realizations of play–audience relations that develop during the course of the single play and of a period of drama.

The third element is the *presence of the actors*. As has been noted by many writers, the actor is the medium of drama, which means that, as Bert O. States puts it in *Great Reckonings in Little Rooms*, "Composing for the actor, whether for the actor within oneself or the actor in one's theater company, means simply composing for the human instrument with all its stops and ventages. Thus everything that takes place on the stage, apart from scenic and sound effects, must be impersonated" (131). The presence of the actor, then, means that the text is incarnated in action, and that the characters of the play seem to be physically present to one another. The rise of computers, with their attendant vocabulary, has provided one way to make a key distinction between the way in which the actors and the characters are present: the actors are actually present whereas the characters are virtually present. The virtual presence of the characters to one another is, of course, the source of drama's power within its fictive world. At the same time, the actual presence of the actors is the source of the play's existence as a living event, changing from performance to performance both because each individual actor will vary his or her performance and because the ensemble of actors will respond to how the spectators respond to a given performance.

The fourth element, which is the direct correlate of the third (so that a student might plausibly argue that these are two halves of a single constitutive element), is the *presence of the spectators*. This presence also operates in several ways simultaneously. Most obviously, the presence of the spectators allows them to experience the presence of the characters, to experience the corporeal reality that readers of a play cannot experience. At the same time, as Michael Goldman reminds us, the spectators can also experience the presence of the actors and how the actors not only play a part but also play with/in a part (*Actor's Freedom* 29–35). And it is crucial to how theater operates that the members of the audience are present to one another. As Emrys Jones argues, when the play begins the spectators become a united group as shared responses lead to the emergence of what he calls an "audience mind" (4–8). This is not a mystical phenomenon, but follows from the way the response of one spectator can be magnified by the resonance it generates in other spectators. The obvious examples are the way laughter and tears can ripple through the audience, but subtler effects also occur, including those that follow from divisions within the response of the audience. (This point is developed in studying *The Taming of the Shrew* when we ask the question "What does the title do?") The magnifying effect of mutual presence creates a significantly different experience from that of a solitary reader.

The fifth element can be defined as the *presence of linear time*. As part of its mimetic dimension, the performed play moves through time, takes place *in time*, and seems to unfold (within and through various enabling conventions) as life unfolds. This unfolding of the play in a temporal dimension performs several different functions, perhaps the most important of which is the way this imitation of the time flow of human existence tends, in Western drama, to emphasize two fundamental conditions of human existence: our mortality and our subjection to unforeseen, unintended, and unwanted consequences of our choices and acts. Drama tends to emphasize how we must make choices, and make choices based on inadequate information and in contingent circumstances, even though those choices are irrevocable and even though we must live with all the consequences of our choices, as we live with the knowledge of our eventual death. Thus the plot of a play often emphasizes the way in which the choices made by a character lead not only to consequences the character foresaw and intended to achieve, but also to consequences the character tried to forestall and to consequences the character neither foresaw nor sought to forestall—even to consequences that are a reversal of those intended. Along with its focus on moments of choice, drama emphasizes how the characters must endure, confront, or seek to alter unforeseen and unwanted consequences.

The other major effect of the play's temporal dimension is that as members of an audience we cannot stop the action as we can when reading a poem or a novel. Nor can we turn back to reread an earlier part of the play. The play thus has the potential to make us feel the inexorable movement of time so that the performance controls our temporal experience as a printed text cannot. In exchange for this powerful temporal control, the dramatist has to rely much more heavily on the audience's ability to make connections in the midst of the action, which means that the performed play is shaped by its dependence on human memory. (This is explored when we study *Richard III* and answer the question "What does repetition do?")

The sixth element is the *objective form of presentation*, which can also be phrased as the *absence of a narrator*. In drama, as Thomas Van Laan (*Idiom*) notes, speech follows speech, and all characters are, or seem to be, on an equal plane within their reality, hence no one seems to possess greater authority or to enjoy the privileged position that the narrator in prose fiction can enjoy. This constitutive element thus raises a fundamental question, crisply articulated by Van Laan, namely, "How can the dramatist, working in such an apparently objective medium, manage to control his spectators' responses so that they ultimately see his play as he sees it himself?" (5; Van Laan's entire first chapter, "The Limitations of Dramatic Speech," is well worth reading in terms of understanding the constitutive elements of drama.)

Occasionally, a student will remember that some plays do have narrators, although few if any students will know that Shakespeare also created narrative figures, most notably the chorus in *Henry V* and Gower in *Pericles*, as well as such narratorlike figures as Rumor in *Henry IV, Part II* and Time in *The Winter's Tale*. When examples are introduced, they can lead to interesting discussions of how such figures nonetheless function differently than the narrators of prose fiction. In a play such as *The Glass Menagerie*, for example, we can see how Tennessee Williams attempts to compensate for this constitutive element by creating a narrator. But we can also see how Tom Wingfield, because he is personated by an actor, is a limited figure in a way that a narrator in prose fiction need not be. Even if no student knows or recalls such an onstage narrator, you can ask them to look for answers to the question "What do dramatists sometimes do to compensate for the absence of a narrator in their seemingly objective medium?"

The seventh and eighth elements both entail making somewhat problematic distinctions but are nonetheless worth enumerating as part of the effort to enable students to accurately perceive the unique aspects of the medium of drama. The seventh element, the *verbal medium of dialogue*, might be thought of as simply an aspect of the actor's presence, since that presence includes both body (action) and voice (speech). But it is worth distinguishing as a separate element because in Shakespeare's plays that medium is not a simple imitation of everyday speech. The verbal medium is more specifically the blank verse or unrhymed iambic pentameter that is the basic form of speech in Shakespeare's plays. Shakespeare also employs other verse forms, such as iambic pentameter couplets, octosyllabic verse, and songs. The blank verse plays off against the variable use of prose, which functions in particular ways in different plays, creating different contrasts (prose/verse for a single character, prose speakers versus verse speakers, and so on) in different contexts. The iambic pentameter verse has its own set of constitutive elements, some of which we explore when we study specific plays in Chapters 3 through 5. (For readers who want to explore the nature of the verse in depth, there is no substitute for George Wright's *Shakespeare's Metrical Art*.) Furthermore, that verbal medium includes the specific functions of the language seen not only as the dialogue between characters but also as instructions to the actors to transform the words into characters.

The eighth element is the *script*, which functions as the performance's blueprint, shaping the experience the spectators will undergo. The script in drama is a peculiar constitutive element. First, there is a spectrum of types of drama that ranges from scriptless drama (pure improvisation), through the scenarios of commedia dell'arte, to the fully scripted drama. Second, even in forms of drama that are based on written scripts such as those of Shakespeare's plays, the script disappears when the play is performed. (For readers who know it well, however, the script can function as a mental template to which the performance is compared; this is almost surely *not* an effect intended by Shakespeare for his original audience, but it is a potential created once the plays are printed and intensified when they are taught in formal education.) Third, it is particularly important for students to learn to read the script not only for the more obvious purposes of discovering plot and character, but also so that they learn to perceive how the script functions as a score for creating a performance—a score that mandates some actions, delimits others, and leaves some areas open to the performers' decisions (Brook).[10]

This list, while not exhaustive, does give us a useful outline of the complex constitutive elements that create drama in performance, and they give us terms for further exploring the nature of Shakespeare's plays. As the academic term progresses, we return to these elements, using our knowledge of them to help us explore the text and imagine performances—and in turn use the performances we imagine, read about, and witness to help us refine our sense of the constitutive elements of Shakespeare's text.

When combined with our exploration of the functions a narrator can perform in transforming "A Brief Drama," the act of enumerating the constitutive elements helps us recognize why reading the text of a play can be so challenging. What becomes clear is that as a solitary reader you are without the presence of actors; you are without the responses of other spectators; you are without the insistent pressure of time; you are without the physical reality of the virtual world created on the stage; and you are without the guidance, especially in composing a point of view, that the narrator in prose fiction so often supplies. But it is also true that as we learn to use our imaginations and to read in different ways, the text of a play can be especially rewarding to read.

Reframing the Challenge of Reading Differently

When I say that in studying plays we must engage in learning to read differently, I am focusing our attention on a truth the students have experienced firsthand: in order to perform "A Brief Drama," they had to read differently than if I had handed them a narrative version to read and interpret. As discussion demonstrates, to make sense of the simple three-person playtext they had to be(come) alert to context, address, self-revelation, pronouns, punctuation, sounds, pauses, stress, and props.

At this point, I seek both to summarize key points from our experience and to preview some of the elements of the language of drama that students will become familiar with. In effect, I outline a range of elements in the language of the stage that literary readers will usually ignore but that, by the end of our work together, I hope students will have incorporated as elements they are habitually alert to when they read dramatic texts. In particular, I emphasize learning to read for the visual and auditory dimensions the text will produce when the play is performed. That is, as students learn to read differently, they will be teaching themselves how to imagine the incarnational and temporal dimensions of the experience that is latent in the words on the page. They will, in the words of director Harold Clurman, be learning to read "in a different language":

> The art of the theater does not consist in adding actors, scenery, movement and music to a dramatist's text, as one inserts a set of illustrations into a published book. What we call a play in the theater is something radically different from a play on the page. The dramatist expresses himself mainly through words, the director through *action* which involves people amid the paraphernalia of the stage. . . .
> Theatrical action is virtually a new medium, a different language from that which the playwright uses, although the playwright hopes that his words will suggest the kind of action that ought to be employed. The director must be a master of theatrical action, as the dramatist is master of the written concept of his play. . . .
> In a sense the playwright's text disappears the moment it reaches the stage, because on the stage it becomes part of an action, every element of which is as pertinent to its meaning as the text itself. A change in gesture, inflection, movement, rhythm or in the physical background of a speech may give it a new significance. . . .
> The written play is not the goal of the theater—only the beginning. If the play at the end is not something beyond what it was at the beginning, there is very little point in the process of transposing it from the book to the stage; very little point, that is, to the whole art of the theater. (273, 275, 276, 278)

Clurman's words also explain why, when I ask students to list all the things the actors "added" to the script of "A Brief Drama," I put the word *added* in quotes: if the actors truly are the medium of drama, then when they perform they do not "add" the physical reality to the words as we "add" decoration to our clothes; rather, they fully incarnate what is only potentially present in the words of the play. This is another way of phrasing the idea that learning to read a play's text is learning to translate from one language to another.

What readers often ignore is what happens when the words on the page are performed by the actors, which is to say that readers ignore the vocal aspect of the verbal dimension as well as most aspects of the nonverbal dimension. What actors can do with their voices, including what they can do by *not* speaking, for example, is one aspect consistently ignored by readers. Let me enumerate some of the key elements we want to train ourselves to be alert for and to imagine.

Pauses. I start with an example that also reminds us how moving from page to stage is an act of translation. This example is based on Hal Holbrook's performance of the opening lines of *Huckleberry Finn*:

> You don't know about me, without you have read a book by the name of "The Adventures of Tom Sawyer," but that ain't no matter. That book was made by Mr. Mark Twain, and he told the truth, [long pause] mainly. There was things which he stretched, but mainly he told the truth. (17)

Despite the fact that I manage nothing like Holbrook's skilled performance, the first "mainly" draws a laugh from students. This laughter is interesting because it is created by an effect that is unlikely to happen for a reader of Twain's text. When Holbrook's Huck pauses, he creates an effect, at least for hearers who have not read or do not remember the text, that is dependent on not knowing what comes next and on the surprise that comes when the qualifying "mainly" is delivered in such a manner that it undercuts what the sentence has said up to that moment—namely, that "Mr. Twain, he told the truth." This effect is one that readers are unlikely to experience because as they read their eyes take in the comma and the following word. Thus for the reader the comma works quite differently than the pause does for an audience. Readers trained to read texts as literature are unlikely to pause the way an actor may pause, and in this case readers will lose some of the pleasure the line can create—and lose the potential for a certain type of wit in Huck himself, who in Holbrook's version becomes a more knowing figure than he is usually taken to be, especially by first-time readers of the novel.

When I ask, "What does a pause do?" the class can discover that pauses are one of the simplest devices for creating suspense and surprise, and that pauses are also capable of changing the meaning of a line and even, in some cases, of reversing either what the line means or what the line does, or both.

What I say about pauses may seem so obvious as to be hardly worth mentioning. Yet one of the more vivid moments in a class session occurred when one student blurted out: "I've always thought you have to keep reading straight on—and now I realize that you can stop, you can pause at *any* moment in *any* line! You can pause *anywhere* to see what happens!" While some readers may murmur "'Tis new to thee!," that is precisely one of the reasons for employing a performance focus, so that students can make discoveries whose resonances will liberate their imaginations.

Silences. I start the next item as follows: "Differentiating a *silence* from a *pause* may be easy for a reader but works differently for a spectator. For one thing, when a pause or silence begins on stage, we do not know—." There will be silence in the room for a few seconds, then people shifting in their chairs, and then they will start to fill in answers, watching me, and catching on at different moments to what is happening as I keep nodding yes or looking puzzled or gesturing for a speaker to say more. I may also write their answers on the board, turn back, and wait for more ideas to emerge. I have never yet let my silence last the rest of the period, although in one very strong class I was able to remain silent for about fifteen minutes while students supplied completion after completion, answer after answer, and even, in some cases, began to talk to one another with no (other) prompting on my part—but the point gets made. What they begin to discover is the range of things silence can do: it can be an answer or a refusal to answer; it can be a negation of something a character has said or done; it can be the silence of death; and, of course, it can represent extreme conditions. If, as I sometimes do, you have the class read a chapter from Philip McGuire's *Speechless Dialect: Shakespeare's Open Silences*, students will also learn to distinguish between open and closed silences.

Interruptions. Interruptions relate to silences insofar as they are sometimes the means by which one speaker silences another, or silences herself or himself, much as Bottom interrupts himself when he awakes from his dream in *A Midsummer Night's Dream* (IV.i.200–219). Like pauses and silences, interruptions tend to have a much greater impact when you witness a play, because the act of interrupting another speaker is usually a pointed one. The class can quickly see some obvious things that interruptions do. Like pauses and silences, interruptions create a form of suspense, as we wonder how the interrupted speaker might have completed a thought. We may also begin to supply possible completions, so that the dramatist has again impelled us to participate in the play. Interruptions are also symptoms of the condition of the inter-rupter and can, for example, signal the inability of the interrupter to restrain herself or himself from speaking or, conversely, signal how effective a speaker has been in touching a raw nerve of the interlocutor. Interruption may be a refusal to cooperate or a form of protest, and it can be a fruitful assignment to ask students to note patterns of interruption in a given play's text. You can also ask students to reexamine how the two mandated interruptions in "A Brief Drama" were performed by different groups, and hence how they functioned to create different meanings in those performances.

Asides. Asides function in a number of ways, but they are most important in transforming the play–audience relation. When a character utters an aside, he or she creates a powerful and di-rect relation with the spectators, giving us privileged access to otherwise secret thoughts. (I sometimes use the example of Hamlet's "A little more than kin and less than kind" on the first day of class, but you can also use that example here.) In "Quince's Questions and the Mystery of the Play Experience," J. L. Styan provides a concise summary of what asides do; speaking of the Elizabethan period, he says,

> This period and the eighteenth century were the great age of the aside, that electrifying device that can set a whole theatre by the ears. Insignificant in reading and thus often ignored in literary criticism as a frivolous appendage, it is always of major effect in performance and central to the mechanism of a scene. And it has the power to grant that ironic double vision which persuades the spectator that he is not only watching the play, but also *having a hand in creating it.* (13)

The class itself frequently provides an opening for an example of the power of asides. In many of my classes there are students who have taken one or more previous classes with me, and as I go through these opening activities, I may say, "And, as Mary knows, the next question is—." When we come to discussing asides, I ask the students who have not taken a class with me before, "What did that aside to Mary twenty minutes ago do to you?" Usually, the answer is that for a moment the student felt excluded, an outsider listening to insiders. Thus we also establish that an aside, to extend Styan's point, can function both to include and to exclude groups of people.

Bodies—and entrances and exits. One of the most elementary facts about drama as an incarnational medium is that the people on stage can create both local effects and larger rhythmic effects as the number of bodies on stage fluctuates, moving from a full to an empty stage. These effects are especially important in Elizabethan drama with its relatively bare stage. Developing the ideas presented by Barbara Hodgdon in "Making Changes/Making Sense," I sometimes have students look at the opening scene of *Romeo and Juliet* simply to trace the flow of bodies and thereby begin to understand the basic experience of life in Verona this scene establishes. Schematically, the scene builds as follows:

Sampson and Gregory	=	2 bodies
+ Abram and Balthasar	=	4 bodies
+ Benvolio	=	5 bodies
+ Tybalt	=	6 bodies
+ 4 Citizens	=	10 bodies
+ Capulet and Lady C	=	12 bodies
+ Montague and Lady M	=	14 bodies
+ Prince and Train	=	20 bodies
Exeunt, leaving		
Montague, Lady M, Ben	=	3 bodies
+ Romeo	=	4 bodies
Exeunt, leaving		
Benvolio and Romeo	=	2 bodies

In short, the scene starts with two characters, increases to four and then six as it bursts into violence, escalates with fearsome rapidity to twenty people—more, if the theater can afford more extras, and quite a few more in some films—before that violence is quelled and the scene rapidly depopulates, until only two people are left. What a purely literary reader is likely to miss is a central element of the theatrical experience—namely, an introduction to Verona as a place where tensions run so high that a person walking through the streets on an errand or on no errand at all may suddenly find himself or herself caught in a potentially lethal brawl. We also discover that to wear a sword and to use it in an attempt to keep the peace may actually have the opposite effect, for the scene's design mandates that Benvolio's act of drawing his sword could easily become a fatal mistake with the entrance of Tybalt. Most critically, we discover that whether this violence seems comic or tragic is a performance decision. That is, in some performances the brawl may be staged so that, Tybalt aside, the participants seem engaged in a ritual with no real intent to harm one another—something on the order of a food fight between rival fraternities. On the other hand, the brawl may escalate to real violence, with some of the participants seriously injured or, in some cases, mortally wounded. Since, as Susan Snyder (*"Romeo"*; *Comic Matrix*) has demonstrated, *Romeo and Juliet* is a tragedy built from a comic matrix, either choice makes sense. The comic brawl helps emphasize that the tragic encounters of Act III and after are a shocking divergence from what should be a comic outcome, wherein the young lovers outwit the blocking elders; whereas a brawl that inflicts serious injuries emphasizes that Verona is a powder keg that, because of the prince's failure to exert sufficient authority, erupts into an orgy of violence that wipes out an entire generation of young people. (This analysis also suggests that casting the prince is itself a crucial choice: his failure to control the violence, which is of course mandated by the text, can be made to seem the inexperience of a young ruler, the weakness of a middle-aged ruler, or the declining power of an aging ruler; and each of these choices will add another element to a complex mixture the audience must interpret.) This opening choice will in turn shape how spectators interpret the ending, where the final stage directions do not mandate the return of Benvolio. Thus what we see in the final scene are the corpses of Paris, Juliet, and Romeo (since Romeo says, "Tybalt, liest thou there in thy bloody sheet?" [V.iii.97], it might seem that the text mandates the presence of another corpse, but it is by no means certain that in the original performances the corpse was not created simply by Romeo's address, as is true in many modern productions), and the remnant of the older generation, namely, old Capulet, Lady Capulet, and old Montague, who informs us that his wife has also just died. (In the First Quarto, Montague adds, "And yong *Benuolio* is deceased too").

Similar patterns occur in many of Shakespeare's plays, and it is rewarding to learn to read for the flow of bodies not only within but also across scenes. The opening two scenes of *Hamlet*, for example, move through a sequence that includes a small group, fluctuating from two to four to three to four (with the ghost) to three; then the stage is flooded as the first court scene begins, only to have the flood wash away, leaving Hamlet alone—the first of many moments in the play when the stage is commanded by a solitary figure. The filling and emptying of the stage is particularly crucial for how a play ends, yet the complex possibilities will be ignored by readers for whom "Exeunt" makes all the characters vanish instantly and simultaneously. Such readers will miss the richness in something as simple as the sequence in which characters exit, miss the different potentials available, for example, if Isabella, or the Duke, or even Barnardine is the last character to exit at the end of *Measure for Measure*.

Dead bodies. Dead bodies (which offer another form of silence) are also easily ignored since, when reading prose fiction, we simply forget about them unless the narrator recalls their existence. But on Shakespeare's stage, a dead body remains until it is taken off, and it may well be the case, as is true of Caesar's corpse, that while other characters continue to speak, the dead body will be the center of attention, its very stillness and silence intensifying our focus on it. Furthermore, on an Elizabethan stage, what to do with a dead body can be an important decision, since when it is removed and who does the removing can also create meaning.

Costume. While those who know something about semiotics will be aware of clothing as a form of communication, most readers ignore costume, as they do so many other visual elements. Yet costume can be used in a wide variety of ways. Consider, for example, the good and evil angels in *Doctor Faustus*. The reader, who has the speech headings, knows more than the spectator, who must infer which angel is which. The director could decide, for instance, to dress the good angel in black and the evil angel in white, either to make Faustus's perplexity, if he sees the angels, greater, or to forestall a too-easy reading of the moral bearings in the play's universe.

Disguises. Costumes can also function as disguises, especially in intrigue plots, and again, like asides, they open a gap between characters, creating either a bond between the audience and the disguised character, if we are aware of the disguise (as we usually are in Shakespeare), or a powerful surprise if we are not aware. Both costume and disguise are issues that come to the fore in *The Taming of the Shrew*, when these points become more vivid for students.

The responses of listeners. Although the list of the critical elements of performed drama can be extended, I end by stressing that as readers we tend not to imagine how characters who are listening respond. When we read fiction, unless the narrator or writer calls attention to it, we simply do not think about nor (usually) do we have access to nonverbal responses by characters in a scene. But in performance, much of the acting is done by those who are not speaking, and in observing how nonspeaking characters respond we learn much of what we need to know.

Although this is a point that opens out into much larger considerations that I usually introduce only later in a course, they can be introduced here. In particular, the meaning in many scenes depends on the nature of a listener's unspoken response. Again, this is a point students have already illustrated in performances of "A Brief Drama," in which some of the humor and perhaps some of the more memorable images derived from the nonverbal responses of A, B, and C in the second half of the playlet. One issue I do raise is that in drama there is always a question about the fit or lack of fit between what a speaker says in describing a nonspeaking character's stage business and what we actually see on stage. If, to give a melodramatic example, a character shouts, "Put down that knife!," we assume that in performance the person he shouts at will indeed be holding a knife; but if she is not holding a knife, the impact of the speech is reversed, and instead of focusing our attention on the supposed knife wielder, it focuses attention on a speaker who is either hallucinating or carrying out some other objective. I also point out that the words of one character can sometimes *create* the reality of another character. Since, for example, even the most physically accomplished actors usually cannot blush or turn pale at will, a dramatist who wants to mandate a blush or a sudden paleness will have another character note the change, creating it as a reality even if it is not physically manifest—as happens when, after the ghost of King Hamlet has exited after his first appearance, Barnardo observes, "How now, Horatio, you tremble and look pale" (I.i.53). The actor playing Horatio presumably will have no trouble performing "trembling," but he may not be able to turn pale at will; the speech should ensure that spectators "see" him doing both.

Finally, this discussion also prepares for a point we will explore when we turn to the first play of the term, namely, that there is an enormous difference between scenes with two and scenes with three characters, and that one of the most significant choices Shakespeare faced was precisely whether to have two or three characters in a scene.

At this point, I usually ask the class to stop and shift from note taking to another written reflection, suggesting they begin with "One thing that is becoming clear to me about the dramatic medium is—" or "One thing that is (still) confusing to me is—." After students have written for five minutes, I ask them to share insights, confusions, and questions so that I can clarify things, but also so that they can hear what their peers are discovering and thus push the discussion further. This discussion almost invariably provides a natural cue for the next subsegment of these framing activities.

Performance as More and Less Than Text and Vice Versa

Some students ask if I am saying that I think the performance is superior to the text, that the theatrical is superior to the literary approach. But I am *not* arguing that seeing a performance is better than reading in every way. There is a complex relation between text and performance that needs to be clarified and that I start to clarify by saying that the text is both less and more than the performance even as the performance is both more and less than the text. The text obviously gives us *less*: we get words, not full action, not the full incarnation of the play. And logically it follows that the performance gives us *more* than the text precisely by giving us all the physical, visual, kinetic, and vocal elements we have been exploring—it gives us a full embodiment. But it is also true that performance gives us *less* than the text, for every performance is an interpretation of the text, and in offering one possible interpretation it suppresses others. In fact, the stronger the performance, the more fully it liberates our imagination in one way, the more fully it also ensures that we do not think of other interpretations. Neither a single production nor all the productions ever mounted to date can exhaust the potential performances latent in the text of the play. Susanne Langer rightly calls the text of the play "the commanding form" (385) from which we create all the productions. But Langer's key point needs to be combined with Philip McGuire's counterpoint: "For me a play is not identical with the words that make up its text (or texts), even if those words are Shakespeare's. A play by Shakespeare consists of—is—both its words and its performances" (*Speechless* xxv). The relation of text and performance is complex and asymmetrical, and the really interesting challenge—and the challenge I hope this book helps teachers master—is to enable students to immerse themselves deeply in the words and the performances (imagined and actual), and to learn more about a play through such double engagement.

Drama as Process(es)

Finally, I ask the students to turn their attention back to what happened when they performed "A Brief Drama" and to list the different activities they had to engage in, and therefore the number and variety of roles they had to play, in moving through their performances. The list of roles the class produces will include at least the following: dramatist, director, actor, spectator, reviewer, literary analyst. As we return to these roles throughout the term, students discover how people make choices in each role, how they can perform each of these activities. When I say that we are learning to read differently, I am also saying that I will ask them to perform a number of different roles that will broaden the ways in which they can become engaged with a dramatic text and its performances; they will reflect on what happens when they play these different roles and on how playing the different roles will lead to different, and sometimes conflicting, forms of knowledge about the play.

Reading Dramatic Language

I summarize what we have just done as follows: We have just spent time practicing two basic ways of reading, as actor and as spectator, that are core activities of this course, from which the more complicated activities I am going to ask the students to perform will follow. One way of reading is the way of an actor: it is an intense close reading, looking for clues packed into the language; it is also an experimental form of reading in which the actor tests possible inferences through alternative possible performances. The actor's way of reading has to do with inferring what the words instruct the actor to do as she or he is constructing a performance—it is reading from the inside. Another way of reading is the way of the spectator: this is a form of intense attention to all that happens, in both verbal and visual dimensions, aimed at grasping as much as you can of the unfolding and vanishing event—making sense of what we hear and see.

I put the verbs in this order because I want to make another point about the nature of drama in Shakespeare's day: at a crucial moment, Hamlet asks, "Will the King hear this piece of work?" (III.ii.46–47), whereas we would say, "Will the King see the play?" One difference, then, between Shakespeare's conception of a play and our own seems to be that we assume, without noticing that we assume, that drama is a predominantly visual form, while Shakespeare and his audience seem to have assumed—and perhaps did not notice that they were assuming—that drama was a predominantly oral and aural form, in which language had primacy and in which rhetorical shape, musical cadence, and figured poetry were among the primary delights offered by their medium. In that sense, there has been a substantial transformation in the conception of performance from Shakespeare's day to ours, a transformation in which the visual dimension has in many ways displaced the verbal dimension, reversing our concept of which is the dominant sense in the theater. If we are to read Shakespeare well, we need to keep in mind that in his dramaturgy the verbal is the equal of the visual dimension.

The point is not to set up a ranking of different types of reading. Actors, at least actors of Shakespeare, need to know as much as they can about the literary features of the playtext. And literary readers are better readers if they can use an actorlike process to hear more in the words of the dialogue than readers usually do. Throughout the course, we will move between the two ways of working with and responding to a playtext. One objective of the course is to learn to ask questions of a play script from these different points of view and with these different actions in mind.

In an even briefer summary, what this chapter suggests is that drama is—and there is no religious meaning here—an incarnational art and that learning to read drama means learning to read as an experimenter. In studying the plays, then, we will be shifting between reading the text and exploring how the text is incarnated in performance; and we will be developing our ability to experiment as both readers and actors.

A Pause for Theory:
Articulating a Model

Having presented the scripted activities that initiate students into exploring Shakespeare's plays, as well as detailed accounts of what students do in performing those activities, I turn to articulating the model shaping this practice. The objective here is not simply to make that model explicit but to make it available so that you can use it to design effective courses and classes. To begin, I offer a vignette that echoes but also amplifies the image of the challenge of reading drama presented in the prologue of this book.

At workshops on teaching Shakespeare, actor Patrick Stewart often demonstrates how a small role ignored by most readers and even by some actors and directors offers opportunities for performance as surprising in their diversity as they are striking in their potential for creating meaning. Examining the opening of *King Lear*'s act V, scene iii, Stewart asks, "Do we know that the Captain whom Edmund sends with secret instructions to murder Cordelia is a captain when the scene begins?" Imagine, he continues, that Edmund says, "Come hither," to a soldier who steps forward, then visibly starts with surprise as Edmund continues, "captain," and is still recovering his composure when he hears, "One step I have advanced thee." In this staging, what seems a purely functional summons becomes a promotion—a promotion that serves as a bribe to ensure that the Captain will carry out the command contained in the note Edmund offers him. Stewart also points out that the text does not mandate when Edmund actually gives this note to the Captain, nor whether the Captain reads the note on stage. As Stewart prompts them, workshop participants invent performances that, in a full production, would contribute a small but telling episode to the emerging design. If, for example, the Captain reads the note, looks appalled, and starts to refuse the commission, spectators, recalling the rebellion of Cornwall's servant at the climax of act III and the earlier revolt of Kent in the opening scene of act I, may hope for a third revolt here in act V.[1] Such a staging may strike some readers as a radical departure from what the text of the play mandates, but it can also be seen as another way in which the actors could realize the play's design of repeatedly raising but then shattering audience expectations that good will finally defeat evil. Confronting such a performance, spectators would repeat Edgar's discovery that "the worst is not / So long as we can say 'This is the worst'" (IV.i.27–28).[2]

In *Speechless Dialect*, the examination of Shakespeare's "open silences" I quoted earlier, McGuire devotes a chapter to surveying how open silences have been staged in productions of *King Lear* and also explores how else they might be performed. Turning to the ending of *King Lear*, McGuire shows how its open silences have been performed to support opposed readings. Yet he suggests that the range of recorded performances has not taken advantage of just how open this ending is, and he supports this claim by delineating an array of stagings for Lear's "Pray you, undo this button" (V.iii.310). McGuire's analysis can be reformulated by saying that, from a director's point of view, three crucial questions must be answered to shape the staging of this request. First, is Lear referring to a button on his own gown, to a button on Cordelia's gown, or to no button at all, and to whom does Lear address his request? Second, how do those around Lear respond to his request and, whoever responds, how does that person perform that action? Third, what meaning is created if there is no direct response to Lear's request? Theatrical tradition has it that Lear is referring to the top button of his own gown and that Kent responds, but this is not mandated by any of the early texts of the play. McGuire explores six possible stagings to show how each will complete and modify the meaning created by the pattern of the play's previous action, providing different balances of hope and despair for this notoriously disturbing ending (97–106).

These examples, the work of a literarily attentive actor and a theatrically engaged literary critic, represent the rich potential of

performance approaches to Shakespeare, approaches that combine the most attentive reading of the text as a design with reading the text through the body—using our bodies as the tool we
experiment with. And in recent decades, these approaches have
won a central role in the teaching of Shakespeare in many secondary school and college literature classes. At the same time,
these examples also remind us of just how fundamental the challenges are when we sit down to read a play or ask students to do
so. For instance, when we ask students to read *King Lear*, what
usually happens can be thought of as a narrow use of the senses:
it is possible for literarily trained students to use their eyes only
for reading and their ears not at all. One reason students have
trouble reading Shakespeare is that they are not trained to transform the words on the page into imagined voices and imagined
actions, nor to imagine how radically the meaning of the words
uttered by such voices can be transformed through a performer's
choice of action.

Therefore, one way to reformulate the challenge of teaching
Shakespeare's plays in literature classes is to ask, "How do we
teach students to read in the ways enacted by talented interpreters such as Stewart and McGuire?" And, taking a step back, "How
do we compose pedagogic designs that will enable students to
rehearse and master the art of reading drama in this way, so that
they can continue to develop and mature as inventive readers
long after they leave our classrooms?"

What Stewart and McGuire demonstrate is that the challenge
is a problem of translation, since a Shakespeare play is written in
two languages that look like, but are not identical with, the language of a purely literary text: first, the language of the script, a
special form of writing in which the words on the page serve
both as speeches by characters and as instructions to actors; and
second, the language of the stage, in which the medium is the
actor, not the text nor even solely the spoken word. In this sense,
both the dramatic medium of the theater and the dialogue are
"second languages" to our students, and teaching Shakespeare
therefore means teaching them to read Shakespeare through performance—that is, to help them develop ways of using their minds
and bodies not taught in most literature classrooms. Furthermore,
for teachers the pedagogic challenge also includes designing classes

that do not merely teach the results of the performance approach but that teach the approach itself: for surely one objective of any serious effort to teach Shakespeare through performance must be that students learn to enact the approach on their own.

The objective of this chapter is to articulate the core of a performance model. In restating my objective in this way, I am distinguishing a performance approach from a performance model. For while there is an enormous variety of successful performance approaches, what I want to offer is a model that can be used as the basis for many such approaches. First, therefore, I discuss how performance can serve as a holistic frame for teaching Shakespeare. Second, I enumerate premises we can use when we ask students to become engaged with the plays through performance. Third, I offer one way of mapping the spectrum of specific performance approaches that exist or can be imagined. And fourth, and very briefly, I suggest how a performance model can be employed for teaching nondramatic literature and composition in English courses, recognizing that an adequate presentation of this idea would itself demand another book.

But before beginning to articulate this performance model, I need to make explicit a key issue implicit in what I have said so far.

Drama's Double Nature: Clarifying a Complexity

The argument for employing at least some elements of performance in teaching Shakespeare seems unassailable since, as the examples from Stewart and McGuire remind us, much of the potential of playtexts becomes fully intelligible only when we read them as scripts, designed to enable actors not only to re-create what must be spoken and done but also to discover and invent those elements necessary for a full production.[3] In fact, the point may seem so self-evident that some readers may find themselves asking, "What's the problem? Why is there even a need to argue for employing a performance approach to teaching Shakespeare's plays?" At the same time, as some readers may have noted, my use of Patrick Stewart and Philip McGuire as exemplary figures has already hinted at the nature of the problem, which is sometimes given shorthand expression when we speak of "the double nature of drama." This, therefore, seems a logical moment to unpack another aspect of the challenge of teaching Shakespeare's plays.

Drama's double nature is clear from the fact that when we speak of "the play," we can be referring either to a written (and enduring) text or to a live (and, until the twentieth century, mostly transient) performance. Problems for teachers and students of drama in general and of Shakespeare's plays in particular arise not only from the doubleness itself but also from how that doubleness has been and still is embodied in educational practice, especially as that practice is shaped in colleges and universities, where drama is taught in both English and theater departments. Institutionally, theater practitioners present drama as one of the performing arts and the play as performance, whereas literary critics tend to perceive drama as one of the humanities and therefore analyze the play as a literary text. Furthermore, each discipline has an inherent imperative to privilege its own version, one group arguing that the play is "really theater," the other arguing that it is "really literature." The division has been reflected in the way some scholars have decried how performers distort plays instead of doing them "straight," even as some performers have decried the way scholars show no respect for the always contestable yet inescapably necessary interpretive and inventive contributions that theater practitioners make to productions—contributions that, as Harold Clurman reminds us, make producing and performing a play a project worth doing in the first place: "The written play is not the goal of the theater—only the beginning. If the play at the end is not something beyond what it was at the beginning, there is very little point in the process of transposing it from the book to the stage; very little point, that is, to the whole art of the theater" (278)

Indeed, we can see one manifestation of this doubleness when we recognize that for those trained and working within the theater it would ordinarily seem either utterly redundant or mystifying to speak of a performance approach to drama, since those whom we call the players—actors, directors, designers, stage crew, and others—and those who teach the players in schools, colleges, academies of drama, and universities would ask, often with some incredulity, "What other approach is there or could there be?"

But, of course, as those in theater know, there has been and is another approach, the literary approach employed by teachers of English at all levels. In fact, *performance approach* is a shorthand term used to denote the approach developed by those teaching English literature who, having become dissatisfied with reading plays only as literature, did two things: they widened the focus of inquiry from the play's text to include the performed play as the subject of study, and they gradually developed ways of reading the text that were in part very much like, although not identical with, the ways of reading and exploring a script developed by actors, directors, and others who work in the theater. Thus, when the phrase "performance approach" is used to describe a way of teaching, it is really shorthand for "a performance approach to drama used in language arts, literature, and English classes."

The temptation to treat plays as if they were literary texts has been, is, and perhaps always will be particularly strong in the case of Shakespeare because his plays are so exceptionally rich and so extraordinarily successful as texts to be read—that is, in purely verbal or poetic terms. And certainly, until the advent of film in the twentieth century, most and perhaps all of the plays had been more read than witnessed. *Love's Labour's Lost*, as Miriam Gilbert (*Shakespeare*) reminds us, was "not performed between 1700 and 1800" (21), and other Shakespeare plays, while they did not suffer such an extreme eclipse, were also performed infrequently. In addition, from the reopening of the theaters in 1660 until the end of the nineteenth century (and in some cases into the early twentieth century), the play on the stage was often not the play on the page, since what was performed was often an adapted version. To take an extreme but well-known example, from 1681 until 1838, if you went to the theater to see *King Lear* what you heard and saw was Nahum Tate's version of the play, with a "happy" ending in which Lear is restored to the throne by Cordelia (which in fact was a return to the pre-Shakespearean version of the Lear story that Shakespeare himself had radically altered) and Edgar marries Cordelia. If you wanted to encounter Shakespeare's *King Lear*, you could do so only by reading the text.

Perhaps in part because of this divergence between the text and the performance and in part because of the rise of prose fiction, the dominant forms of criticism in the late nineteenth century treated the plays as if they were novels, while the dominant forms of criticism in the first half of the twentieth century treated the plays as if they were extended poems. Yet starting about 1950, literary critics became increasingly conscious of the disabling effects of treating these plays as if they were novels or poems and (re)turned to looking at the plays as plays. These developments have been usefully summarized by T. J. B. Spencer:

> A stage play is usually an ephemeral thing, and we may be prepared to forgive the quiet assumption by many critics of the late nineteenth century that, as works of literature, the writings of Shakespeare belong to much the same literary kind as *Middlemarch*; and the equally tranquil assumption by many critics of the twentieth century that his writings belong to much the same literary kind as *The Waste Land*.
>
> Other works of art offer difficulties to criticism. . . . But Shakespeare has, perhaps by accident, made it peculiarly difficult to ascertain the basis of our criticism. There is a fundamental uncertainty about what we are dealing with, what kind of work of art we must talk about. (3)
>
> . . . But if the plays are "literature" they are literature of a very odd kind. . . . We do not *know* that Shakespeare intended his plays to be "dramatic poems" which have had a book-existence. Equally we do not *know* that he intended them to have no literary existence, to be merely theatre scripts. There is some evidence to the contrary. . . .
>
> But in trying to assess the kind of work of art that Shakespeare wrote, we can at least feel certain about one thing: he was taking part in a collaborative and composite artistic activity; he was creating a show, with the help of actors, musicians, and other artists, in a particular playhouse or special kind of playhouse. As an artist Shakespeare thought in terms of the stage, whatever other kinds of "publication" he may also have envisaged. We may, perhaps, without having any evidence to produce, consider it incredible that he should not have expected his plays to be read as well as performed. But we are on safe ground in working on the assumption that his dramatic art was primarily a theatrical art. (5–6)

Thus literary critics and teachers began to confront the ways in which the intellectual and institutional split between literary and theatrical approaches, while necessary for the development of these disciplines, tended to become an obstacle to teaching Shakespeare's plays. And it is a perception of the disabling effects of this split that has prompted a number of people to propose that it makes more sense to approach plays in general and Shakespeare's plays in particular as being both literary and theatrical in nature. Rather than an either/or situation, it seems that only a both/and approach can do justice to the full potentials of a Shakespeare play. At least some critics and teachers, myself included, argue that it is better to see plays as existing in both disciplines and to think of Shakespeare's plays as *performing texts*—a term intended to suggest the intersection of performing arts and literary texts.

Using the term *performing texts* also emphasizes that the double existence of drama is irreducible. For at the same time that we have turned away from reading Shakespeare's plays as if they were identical with novels or poems, and turned toward recognizing them as being written by someone who conceived of them as "primarily a theatrical art," we have nonetheless also recognized that it can be reductive to treat plays only as theater. As Bert States puts it in *Great Reckonings in Little Rooms*:

> Shakespeare, theater people are pleased to note, was an actor; he wrote for the stage and went to his peace little caring about the survival of his texts, even for future actors' use. His plays—and by extension all plays—are essentially scripts, or scores, that exist only in a literary limbo until actors, the musicians of the tribe, arrive and give them sound and sensible motion. This is an innocent enough fiction, notwithstanding the fact that there are as many things about *Hamlet* one cannot possibly appreciate in a performance as there are things in a performance that elude the most sensitive reader. But this has less to do with art than with biopsychology—that is, with the range of responses awakened by different senses and stimuli. (130)

What has emerged, it seems to me, is a pedagogy that employs many of the concepts and practices that have been forged by those studying the plays as literature *and* many of the concepts and practices deployed by those examining or producing the plays as theater. What has been created, furthermore, is best seen as an interlocking array of approaches, no one of which is exhaustive, but which, taken together, enable us to arrive at a more comprehensive knowledge of the play as text and performance. In these approaches, we see drama as a complex entity that exists both as the potentials of the text and the realizations of performance. Certainly what we have created so far is a spectrum, and what we have are performance approaches, plural, with different people each proposing *a* performance approach, just as I offer one approach here in this book, even as I seek to offer a more encompassing model or framework in this chapter. The image of a spectrum also helps us recognize differences and even incompatibilities between performance approaches. At one end of the spectrum, someone who proposes a model based primarily on the literary aspects of the text will find people in theater arguing that this model ignores too many aspects of performance. Conversely, someone who focuses primarily on the theatrical nature of the play will find literary colleagues complaining that in focusing attention on actual or imagined performances this approach renders essential literary features invisible. But across the middle of the spectrum, many proponents of performance approaches believe that the best option is to combine these varied but equally disciplined ways of knowing. Although (based on evidence beyond the scope of this book to discuss) it may not be possible to produce a comprehensive synthesis of literary and theatrical disciplines, it is possible to articulate premises for a performance model that undergird many of the more specific approaches.

Articulating a Performance Model

While the arguments for adopting a performance approach in the most literal sense have been accepted for several decades, the logic of performance is wider than many proponents realize. I would argue that performance is not simply "another approach" to Shakespeare: rather, performance provides an encompassing frame for teaching Shakespeare's plays.

This frame can be articulated as a series of three interlocking assumptions. First, this model assumes that it is pedagogically enabling to define "English" as the study and practice of rhetoric, if rhetoric is conceived of in Kenneth Burke's terms as includ-

ing the noncoercive means by which human beings seek to persuade one another to adopt an attitude or take an action.[4] Second, this model assumes that students can be introduced to
rhetoric through the medium of drama precisely because drama
directly represents human beings engaged in action. Third, this
model assumes that drama functions persuasively not only in the
direct action represented on stage but also in the indirect action
on spectators—what Burke defines as "persuasion to attitude"
(*Rhetoric* 50)—as it does when Hamlet's first speech, if performed
as an aside, functions to make us his confidants, and thereby also
places us in a position of superiority to the king, queen, and the
court.

Within this frame, we can discern the core components inherent in the medium of drama and in the occasion that is the
dramatic event—the performance of a play—namely, the playwright and playtext, the players, and the playgoers.

One component is the text of the play, which serves as what
Susanne Langer has called a *commanding form*: it mandates what
must happen, what must be said, and in what order, but conversely, what it mandates also defines what it leaves open (385).
That is, when a text is treated as a script, it functions as a set of
instructions that specify much but not all of what must happen
during a performance, while also leaving some of what happens
delimited and other aspects of what can happen open to invention by the performers. As McGuire points out, "A Shakespearean
playtext is not a series of statements that specify in all respects—
or even in all important respects—what must happen during performance. Its statements do specify what *cannot* happen, and in
doing so they permit whatever possibilities are not prohibited"
(*Speechless* 139). The second core component is the disciplined
activity of actors and directors who use their imaginations, bodies, and voices experimentally, inventing and rehearsing ways of
acting and speaking the lines that are not specified by the text
and that, with further refinement, may prove to be both valid
and producible. So an actor playing the Captain might discover
the option to protest, and such a performance would invite spectators to connect his action with the earlier actions of Cornwall's
nameless servant and of Kent. And the third core component is,
of course, the audience, whose primary activities are to enjoy

and to make sense of the performance. So spectators watching the performance in which the Captain reads and protests the command in Edmund's letter might find their hopes rising as they connect his action with the earlier actions of Cornwall's nameless servant at the climax of act III, scene vii and Kent's protest against Lear's folly at the beginning of act I, scene i.

The text as commanding form and the actor as experimenter intersect to generate the various forms of the initiating question I introduced in Chapter 1. John Barton phrases the question as "How does Shakespeare's text actually *work?*" (3). Alan Dessen (Editorial Note) phrases it as "What do these words do?" And, transforming Styan's (*Elements*) statement into a question, "What do these words make the actor make the audience do?" (2). Put in a more abstract form, we can initiate exploration of a play from the two core disciplines by teaching students to ask "What does X do?" where X is any element of a Shakespeare play, ranging from something as specific as the title to something as encompassing as the play's action; from something as minute as a single pause or aside to a pattern of language that pervades a play; from the contributions of a role constituted by a single speech to the design embodied in a title character; and from the function of the smallest scene to the multiple dimensions of a 500-line concluding act.[5]

Articulating Premises for Teaching Shakespeare's Performing Texts

I now offer a coherent set of six premises that are shared by many such approaches. In articulating these six premises, I am building on the work of numerous predecessors, but I am most directly indebted to Robert Hapgood in *Shakespeare the The-atre-Poet*, both for a general definition of the performance ensemble and for the map offered in the second premise.[6]

1. A performance-framed model enables students to explore the nature of the dramatic medium and the *theater event*. The word *theater* calls attention to the complex ensemble of playwright, whose ideas are embodied in the playtext; players; and playgo-

ers; and to the ways in which the players and playgoers must function as co-creators of the performance—and thus focuses on the collaborative nature of the medium. The word *event* focuses attention on the temporal nature of the play in performance: the event is temporal not only in that a sequence of activities leads up to and includes the performance and subsequent discussion and reflection by spectators, but also insofar as the audience experiences the play as an act that unfolds in time. This focus on the event also reminds us that readers of the playtext must attend to the temporal nature of the imagined event, and also may attend to the temporal nature of their own experience of reading the play. (An expectation log—an activity introduced in the next chapter—is the primary tool that enables students to both record and reflect on their experience of reading the play as a temporal event.) Furthermore, when we teach drama using a performance model, we need to offer students an opportunity to contrast drama with prose fiction in order to discover the constitutive elements of the medium. This understanding of the nature of the different mediums becomes the foundation on which students construct their engagement with both the theater event and the reading event, both as processes and as subjects of inquiry.

2. A performance model enables students to explore the playtext in the roles of playwright, players, and playgoers, which means, to employ another phrasing from Hapgood, that students are taught to move through phases of conception, enactment, and reception. (This point is amplified in the next section of this chapter.) Moving from one of these roles to another also affords students opportunities to develop a variety of engagements with the play as well as to use the very diversity of these engagements as a tool to gain perspective on both the text and their initial responses to the text.

3. A performance model initiates students into reading the playtext as script, reading the words on the page as a design for eliciting their own explorations as potential actors and directors. In particular, such a model teaches students to ask, "What do these words do?"; "What can these words be made to do?"; and "What do the words make the actors make the audience do?" Asking

these initiating questions means that a given word may not have a determinate meaning until we have discerned its function in a speech or explored and chosen from among alternate functions that speech might perform. As Patrick Stewart's workshop demonstrates, the word *captain* can change its function as the actors reimagine the context and the action emerging in that context. Through such work, students will learn how a script mandates some elements, offers a controlled range of options for others, and leaves still other elements open to the inventiveness of players and readers.

4. A performance model builds on students' skill in exploring literary elements of the script and on the option to read the text as literature as well as to perform it. The model will thus also focus attention on the *reading event* for considering the play as a text: *reading*, because we focus on the active, co-creative participation of the reader, and *event,* because we focus on the temporal dimension of reading as well as on the options for recursive action that distinguish readers from spectators. Students will not only become better able to consider literary features but also learn to analyze which features can be realized in performance and which can be realized only by readers. This means that students will also have an opportunity to explore difficult questions raised by the relation of producibility and validity in interpreting plays.

5. A performance model assumes that the words of a playtext are both open and closed. As a text, the words of the play are open to multiple interpretations. But when the play is performed, the performers must to some extent make choices that close this range of interpretive possibility in order to present a coherent production to the spectators. The point has been usefully explained by Stephen Orgel in the introduction to his edition of *The Tempest*:

> Shakespearian texts are by nature open, offering the director or critic only a range of possibilities. It is performances and interpretations that are closed, in the sense that they select from and limit the possibilities the text offers in the interests of producing a coherent reading. [To examine the text as script in this fashion] is to indicate the range of the play's possibilities; but it is also to acknowledge that many of them (as is the nature of possibilities)

are mutually contradictory. There is nothing anomalous in this. The text that has come down to us is poetry and drama of the highest order, but it is also, paradoxically, both less and more than literature. It is, in its inception, a play script written to be realized in performance, with broad areas of ambiguity allowing, and indeed, necessitating, a large degree of interpretation. In its own time its only life was in performance, and one way to think of it is as an anthology of performances before Ralph Crane transcribed it for the printer in 1619 or 1620. As a printed text, it is designed to provide in addition the basis for an infinitude of future performances, real and imagined. . . . For Shakespeare and his company, the text was only the beginning, not the end, of the play. (12)

As students move toward creating a specific interpretation through closing some (but not all) of the open elements in a playtext, they continue to explore the co-creative roles the dramatist offers to the other members of the performance ensemble.

6. A performance model teaches students to compose multiple, conflicting, or even contradictory performances and to learn more about the potentials of the text from that range of performances. At the same time, it teaches students to recognize the constraints that the design of a play as a whole places on the moment-to-moment potentials. In short, it introduces the difficult but vital questions about whether an interpretation seems valid and whether a valid interpretation is always producible.

Another way of grasping the imperatives embodied in these premises, as well as of understanding the centrality of the question "What does X do?" in generating the model's practice, comes into focus if we return to the analogy of learning to speak in a different language. For within that analogy it makes sense to say that this is a model that asks students *to learn to speak drama.* This phrase emphasizes that we are not primarily asking students to acquire information, nor asking them to learn about something—say, "about Shakespeare" the man—but rather asking them to learn to do something. This helps us recognize that in a performance model we seek to balance training in the arts with training in the humanities. Thus, although the model I propose is not simply an arts model, it draws on the logic of education entailed in training people who are apprentices in disciplines in which the goal is primarily to become a performer. This logic, which can be conceived of as "an arts approach to English," has been developed by Peter Abbs ("Meaning") and colleagues in the Association for the Verbal Arts:

> An arts approach to literature [is] committed to establishing and making current those kinds of knowing most appropriate to what is being studied. . . . Thus the aim [is] to bring the student's feelings, sense-perceptions, imagination—and the intelligence active in all of these—inside the text in order to comprehend it. What is being asked for is a refining of the mimetic imagination, an anchoring of thinking in the aesthetic response. . . . What we are out to establish is a thinking *within* the actual medium rather than an immediate thinking *about* the explicit content. (170)

Furthermore, in developing this arts model of English in *A Is for Aesthetic*, Abbs articulates another key premise of the performance model: namely, that while we can distinguish between performance, the usual goal of the arts model, and interpretation, the usual goal of the humanities model of English, performance can unite these two approaches because "*Performance is critical interpretation kept within the medium of the art-work*" (72).

As the idea that we should be teaching students to think "within the medium of the art-work" implies, this version of English is centrally committed to and achieves part of its value by teaching us to read *through* the text—and indeed this book aims to enable its readers to teach Shakespeare *through* performance.

In a performance model, then, students become immersed in the playtext so that they can respond to its cues as fully as possible, thereby exploring its designs, including its designs on its spectators and/or readers. Through lending the text their energies so that it can exert its power, however, students are in turn also empowered, since they become free to re-create the playtext using their own creativity to invent new possibilities. If, in one sense, the playtext as script shapes what we do, in another sense we also reshape the playtext. Reanimated by our energy, it rewards our partial submission to its designs with a chance to explore, stretch, and refine our own inventive and expressive pow-ers, even as we seek to develop an interpretation through the medium of the performed artwork itself. And these acts of en-gagement can also prompt us to detach ourselves from the power of the play, shifting our ground so that we can reflect on and critique our immersion in the codes embodied in the play. For teachers whose objectives include ensuring that their students do not let themselves be shaped by the codes or ideologies that seem inherent in the texts of Shakespeare's plays, I suggest that perfor-mance activities sometimes provide the quickest means for foregrounding, detecting, and stepping back from codes or ide-ologies—for example, the patriarchal assumptions inherent in the very title of *The Taming of the Shrew*—that teachers fear students will unwittingly adopt in part because of the canonical status of Shakespeare.

Mapping a Performance Model

I spoke earlier of a spectrum of approaches, but I think the model developed so far offers another way of mapping the array, with the map itself (see Figure 2.1) also prompting us to develop fur-ther aspects of performance-centered teaching. In its simplest form, the map helps us see how a performance model emerges from the constitutive roles or functions and the constituting processes of drama by correlating the three roles for the participants in the performance ensemble with conception, enactment, and recep-tion.

First of all, the performance ensemble comprises people in the roles or positions of playwright, players, and playgoers. These are not exclusive but rather interlocking roles or positions, so that in each position one of the agents is foregrounded, but foregrounded in relation to actions of the other two ensemble members. This model can also be thought of as a three-phase model of how the theater event comes to be. When we speak of roles (or functions, or positions), we emphasize the choices we can make to adopt the stance or perform the role of playwright and dramaturg, actor and director, or spectator and reader in defining a given activity. When we speak of phases, we empha-

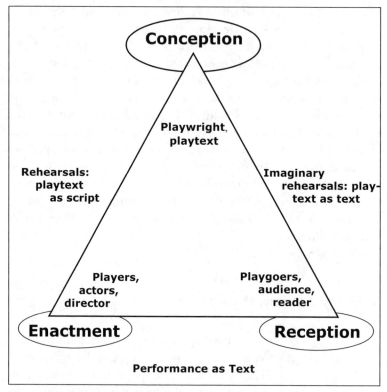

Figure 2.1. *Mapping options for a performance model: Roles, activities, and relations performed by members of the theater ensemble.*

size the sequential nature of these positions or roles and the constituting relationships. Not only are these relationships multiple but they also form complex and reciprocally modifying processes, so that what at first appears to be the "receptive" partner in a relation may nonetheless impel the "active" partner to significantly reshape what he or she does. This map, then, lays out the three primary participants in the performance ensemble, and it points toward the roles, relations, and processes we ask students to assume and carry out in many of the activities designated as performance approaches to drama.

In the following paragraphs, I suggest ways in which the map can help to organize an array of performance concepts and practices for literature classes. In adapting Hapgood's model, I divide enactment into two subphases, rehearsal and performance.

Conception: Composing the play, anatomizing the composed design. The map starts by focusing on the playtext itself as the commanding form, in which Shakespeare created a design that, while not identical with any performance, nonetheless is the source for all performances and can be read as both process and product. Initially, that is, we can read the text as registering some of the compositional choices the dramatist made or can be conceived of as making. In the case of many of Shakespeare's plays, for example, we can ask students to look at how the dramatist transformed his sources, and how those transformations—such as the decision to have Cordelia murdered in *King Lear* or the decision to have Isabella refuse Angelo's corrupt bargain in *Measure for Measure* (in both cases, Shakespeare radically altered the narrative presented in his sources)—illuminate the intentions embodied in the design. Or we can focus attention on a play such as *King Lear*, for which there are significantly different early texts, namely, the First Quarto (1608), the Second Quarto (1619), and the First Folio (1623). Even without accepting the strong claim that the Folio *King Lear* represents a systematic revision of the First Quarto, we can ask students to step into the playwright's role to explore what revised elements of the design emerge in the Folio version and what changes in performance. We also can ask students to treat the text as not yet completed by offering their own revisions, or ask them to examine the revised *King Lear* by Nahum Tate (1681) for what that comparison reveals not only about the original design but also about contrasting cultural presuppositions about drama and about the representation of human action operating in two periods. (It is worth focusing, for example, on the contrasting conceptions of the relation of human justice to the natural order, a topic that received explicit formulation in Samuel Johnson's famous comments on the superiority of Tate's ending to Shakespeare's.) Or students can investigate the design in terms of elements such as the plot; the sequence of scenes; the scenic form, with its subordinate segments; the roles from which actors create characters; and, moving on to the smaller elements, word choices or questions about punctuation. Or, starting from a temporal focus, they can ask such questions as "What does the beginning do?" and proceed to analyze what the opening encounter of Kent, Gloucester, and Edmund does to initiate the action of *King Lear*, establish an initial relation between the play and the spectators, and elicit spectator expectations about and commitments to the events that follow. In exploring Gloucester's speeches and Kent's responses, for example, what options can students discover for establishing the audience's initial relation with and expectations about Edmund? And how does that initial relation shape what an actor might do in addressing Edmund's subsequent soliloquies to that audience?

Enactment: Rehearsal, discovery, and performance. As we move down the triangle of Figure 2.1, we see that the two legs represent the routes of actors and directors and of readers as analogous yet different engagements with the text. Directors engage in close reading but for purposes different from those animating literary readers; and directors and actors enter into a rehearsal period in which they play with the text, using themselves as the medium of exploration. If we ask students to put themselves in the player's role, we can draw on a wealth of activities, theater games, and improvisatory techniques to help them grow into and become productive in that role. The map also emphasizes that actors are pivotal agents in two phases: rehearsal and performance. In the first phase, director and actors explore and re-create the text. The emphasis here is on two things: (1) how the actors transform the role—the words on the page—into the character, the fully performed virtual being; and (2) how the director and, depending on the director's style, the actors, working with others such as the dramaturg and designers, transform the playtext's potential into a completed experience that is at once more and less than the script. In the second phase, the text disappears as it is transformed into the language of the stage, and here we look at the interplay between the range of possibilities explored in rehearsal and the actual choices made in performance. Readers with literary training can simply employ their strategies to read the playtext as they would a novel or poem, and when they do so the map collapses into a single straight line between text and reader. But readers learning to use a performance model can engage in practices analogous to, although usually not identical with, those engaged in by actors and directors, including what Hapgood defines as *imaginary rehearsals*. Along this route, the model emphasizes a process of discovering alternative performances and then selecting those performances that students wish to convince others to accept.

Reception: The spectator's dance with the performance. Through enactment activities, we ask students to become spectators and critics. In the role of playgoer, students respond to their experience of an unfolding event and reflect on the completed event. They respond to patterns enacted, imagined, and projected in their work in class or in performances in the theater or on film or video. And as they reflect on the completed event, students become critics as well, drawing on selected models for responding to the play in performance. The types of criticism include traditional forms of literary criticism of the text and reviews of performance; theater history; and emerging forms, such as the study of film-as-text and performance-as-text. In addition, students can engage in forms of criticism that compare different incarnations of a play, as does Marvin Rosenberg in his "Masks of" series exploring *Othello, King Lear, Macbeth,* and *Hamlet.* As you will see, the essay assignments presented later in this book are designed so that students must move through several roles, operating from different positions on the triangle and thereby developing suites of partial analysis that can be combined into more complex critical wholes.

Finally, note that this map makes no effort to chart other dimensions, such as the wide variations in our courses, classrooms, programs, and students, especially variations in our purposes and the purposes of our students.

CHAPTER TWO

Making Drama a Frame for English: Extending the Model

At the beginning of this chapter, I suggest that not only can we employ performance as a frame for teaching Shakespeare but also that we might choose to move drama to the center of the literature class or even the center of a more broadly conceived English curriculum. Obviously this maneuver entails articulating a more encompassing version of the frame. And although completing such a project is work for another book, I can briefly sketch an outline for how such a project might be developed.

One way to begin this recasting is to say that if the current paradigms in English often define themselves as teaching students to read either *with* or *against* the grain of the text, a performance-centered paradigm widens the curriculum by teaching students to read *through* the grain of the text. That is, this model for reading drama engages students in ways that ask them to immerse themselves in the power of the text yet also invite them to develop their own power through rehearsing and shaping that text in performance (Rocklin, "'Incarnational'"). One pivotal maneuver is to ask students to extend the model from playtexts to other texts, since many other texts can be seen as scripts that offer cues for re-creating a reading. Thus—and this may seem paradoxical—the model proposes that we start by asking students to learn how drama is *different* from prose fiction, and therefore how to read drama differently; yet eventually the model, in a recursive maneuver, invites students to apply these new drama-shaped practices to poetry, prose fiction, and expository prose (Rocklin, "Converging"). One obvious extension is to poems, such as those by Donne, Herbert, Marvell, and Browning, which feature a dramatized speaker; another extension is to those works, such as Thomas More's *Utopia*, which are written as dialogues. Students who have mastered the model in some of my classes have proceeded to use the model to explore dialogues such as More's *Utopia* and Castiglione's *The Courtier*, as well as to analyze aspects of novels such as D. H. Lawrence's *Women in Love*.[7]

Furthermore, because the performance approach also focuses on the design of a text and the choices embodied in that design, the very acts by which we invite students to learn to read differently also serve as an indirect cue for them to think about themselves as writers. Thus, if we teach students to ask, "What does the title of this play *do*?" (an activity detailed in the chapter on *The Taming of the Shrew*, where we can see that this particular title arouses expectations and creates divisions between members of an audience and within the consciousness of an individual spectator), it is a short step to learning to ask, "What does the title of my essay do?" And when the model works, this is a step some students take on their own.

Moreover, the formulation "What does X do?" naturally prompts the reflective move of self-examination that teachers interested in critical pedagogy especially value. Students for whom asking "What does X do?" becomes second nature will, either on their own or with the lightest prompt from the teacher, turn the question back on itself, asking, "What does using this initiating question and the whole model embodied in this question do?"

Since this model of performance can be widened reflexively to our own work as teachers, implicit in my presentation is another maneuver. If we recognize that the classroom is itself a scene of action, then we also recognize that teachers can use the dramatic model to invent, refine, and critique their own teaching. Working with a performance model of drama enables us to discern cues for our own creativity as inventors of pedagogic designs latent in the playtexts we teach. In addition, an understanding of drama and the concept of performance becomes a tool for our work as teachers in two phases. One phase is our work as pedagogic designers of whole courses and individual classes; the other phase is our work as stage managers who partially direct scenes of learning as they unfold (see Rocklin, "Shakespeare's"; "Mapping"). I delineate in the epilogue to this book an understanding of how the constitutive elements of drama can become a heuristic for examining the way we design and conduct our classes—that is, to employ a formulation from Theodore Sizer, the way we design scenes that will provoke people to learn (2).

This argument can be summarized in a sequence of points that suggest all composition, including literary composition, can be seen as a performance by the writer; that all texts, including literary texts, function in ways analogous to the ways that playtexts function as scripts; that all reading is a form of virtual performance; that all teaching and learning is also a form of performance, so that we are, among our other roles, analogues of the dramatist; that what we compose are scenarios in which students become participants in designed experiences; and that our primary choices as creators of designed experiences concern the potentials of the design we offer our classes, the roles we invite students to play, the richness of the experience that emerges as the pedagogic script is played out, and the ways in which we remain open to seize on the improvisations of our students as cues for further invention and learning. By this argument, the practices we develop are as decisive as the theories we espouse, since our pedagogic choices become premises that simultaneously liberate and inhibit the creativity of our students.

Epilogue

I have suggested that one way to formulate the challenge of teaching Shakespeare's plays in literature classes is to ask ourselves, "How do we teach students to read in the ways enacted by talented interpreters such as Patrick Stewart and Philip McGuire?" You will have noted that the model proposed here suggests that at times we ask students to step into the role of the playwright, in this case the role (so to speak) or position of Shakespeare. You may wonder whether I have an idealized view of our students, perceiving them not only as developing readers and apprentice writers but even as artists. My reply is that to make a performance model work, you only have to believe that students can be asked to act as if they are artists for the purposes of eliciting and exercising their own creativity. Thus I would suggest that another point of adopting a performance model is that it will help elicit the students' own creativity as a complement to the creativity of the artists we ask them to read. In this sense, what we should be aiming for is a model of "English" in which the creative and the interpretive functions are much more fully integrated.

II

IMAGINARY REHEARSALS
AND ACTUAL ENGAGEMENTS

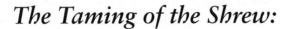

The Taming of the Shrew:
Action and Scene, Role and Character

Prologue: Why Start with a Comedy?

> Precisely because Shakespeare's central concern in this particular play is with action, characters, and ideas, rather than with poetry and atmosphere, and because the play relies for its effect on broad and obvious contrasts between characters and attitudes instead of subtle discriminations between them, it loses much less in the process of translation than do such comedies *A Midsummer Night's Dream*, *As You Like It*, or *Twelfth Night*. Essentially of the theatre and for the theatre, *The Taming of the Shrew* goes on living because it has, in the first place . . . a delight in vigorous events subjected to the discipline of a coherent, well-organized, and significant plot. (*Taming*, Hibbard 11)

Although there are a variety of ways to organize any course or set of courses on Shakespeare's plays, if you choose to follow a basically chronological sequence, and if you believe that Shakespeare mastered comedy and history before tragedy and tragicomedy, then it makes sense to begin with a history or a comedy. My own experience suggests that it is easier to start with a comedy because, in addition to the major translation problems, the histories add another obstacle, namely, the sheer unfamiliarity of the events on which they are based. If, for example, you make the otherwise plausible choice to begin with *Richard III*, you encounter the problem that the play demands knowledge of the entire pattern of the War of the Roses as developed in the *Henry VI* trilogy for its retrospective design to achieve its full impact. Indeed, when I have begun with *Richard III*, students have had great difficulty with these issues. Furthermore, even if students are familiar with the history, the history plays have the largest casts of any Shakespeare plays; *Richard III* has thirty-seven roles and clusters of functional parts. This means that as readers expend energy just keeping track of possibly forty-plus participants, they will have less energy to translate the play into an imagined performance.

The comedies, furthermore, tend to seem much more accessible than the histories, even if this apparent accessibility hides major cultural differences. Most of the comedies initially look less time-bound because the characters seem self-explanatory, because the plots are self-contained, and because the plays seem to be about immediately recognizable, "universal" themes. Any of the three early comedies, *The Comedy of Errors*, *The Taming of the Shrew*, and *The Two Gentlemen of Verona* might be chosen. Each has received support as Shakespeare's first comedy, and each, as critics note, represents a different major comic tradition—Plautine comedy, commedia dell'arte, and romance. One could argue for each of these, but my own choice has been *The Taming of the Shrew*.

Few critics claim this is a great play. Michael Goldman seems to be nearly alone when he says that "[t]he *Taming of the Shrew* . . . [is] a masterpiece so easy and robust that we seldom give it a second thought" (*Actor's Freedom* 131), and even Goldman, I suspect, would agree that while it may be a theatrical triumph it is certainly not a literary masterpiece. But if we formulate the task of teaching Shakespeare as the task of learning to translate the different languages of the dramatic and poetic mediums, then beginning with this play offers a number of pedagogically useful features.

First, the induction makes the "Taming" a play-within-a-play and therefore is useful for introducing the challenges facing a dramatist designing the beginning of a play. Second, the use of disguise in the Bianca-Lucentio plot exemplifies some of the most important resources available in drama, as well as some of the primary difficulties involved in reading a play. Third, the use of intertwined plots, each with a contrasting style, introduces the key issue of learning to read multiplot drama. Fourth, the relatively prosaic language of the play offers students an opportunity to learn to read and perform blank verse without having to attend to more complex potentials of the medium, and to focus on rhetorical elements so crucial to Shakespeare's early style. Fifth, the explicit and apparently unironic endorsement of patriarchal order that concludes the play offers an opportunity to confront the ways in which students' assumptions diverge from (or converge with) those of Shakespeare's day—as well as an excellent cue for exploring how performance can subvert explicit doctrine. Sixth, the tensions in the play itself and the resistance it has aroused mean that, as Ann Thompson puts it, "throughout its stage history *The Taming of the Shrew* has probably received fewer completely straight performances than any other Shakespearean play of comparable popularity on the stage" (*Taming*, Thompson 24). Starting with this play, then, enables teachers to focus on performance history, as well as on issues of gender, and to draw on the rich array of feminist criticism this play has elicited. Indeed, our exploration of the play, including Michael Billington's 1978 review (republished in *One Night Stands* 123–24) will drive home a point first made in the course outline, namely, that Shakespeare's plays have been reviled as well as revered.[1]

The ten activities that constitute our work with this play focus on these opportunities. And these activities introduce four key elements that constitute the language of drama: the paired concepts of action and scene and the paired concepts of role and character. Students rehearse the practices by which they can use these concepts to enter the play's design and conduct explorations of and experiments with the text as a blueprint for performance. Subsequent chapters offer opportunities for further rehearsal with these key elements of the language of drama, even as they introduce other primary elements of that language.

Using the materials in *The Riverside Shakespeare*'s general introduction and the illustrations—material you can supplement with books such as those by Gurr (*Shakespearean Stage*) and Kinney—as our starting point, we spend some time delineating the construction of the English Renaissance theater, and thus beginning to learn the elements of that particular theatrical language. Next, students share the responses recorded in their expectation logs, and this small-group sharing becomes the springboard for us to collect their initial responses to the play as a whole. We then turn our attention to the induction and the way the induction frames the "Taming" play; this two-scene prologue offers an excellent, tightly focused example of the challenges facing a dramatist who is designing the beginning of a play. At the same time, exploring the induction offers an ideal opportunity to distinguish different concepts of action essential to the dramatic medium and to understanding the functions of a scene within that medium. This look at action and scene leads to asking the question "What does the title do?" We complete our initial work with these two concepts by defining the terms *scene* and *scenic form* (as developed by Emrys Jones), with particular focus on act II, which provides an especially rich illustration of scenic form, and then mapping the play as a whole in terms of both its acts and its actions.

We next turn to working the second pair of concepts and practices, introducing a simplified form of Stanislavski's model for reading as an actor (using only the concepts of objective, unit, and subtext) to transform a role into a character. These concepts are immediately put into practice as students work with the roles of Petruchio and Katherine in act II, scene i, beginning to learn how a role or part in the text becomes a character in performance. We then examine the pivotal act IV, scene v in terms of Katherine's choices when she confronts Petruchio's "sun/moon" dilemma.

Our work with these four basic concepts comes together in examining act V, where students begin asking, in effect, the questions "What does the ending do?" and "What can the ending be made to do?" So in examining the intriguing ending of *Taming*, they explore Petruchio's last playlet primarily through rehearsing Katherine's last act, the choices she makes before, during, and after delivering what might be called her "homily on obedience." After a close segment-by-segment analysis of the speech, students develop alternate performances in which Katherine may not only submit but also qualify or subvert that overt submission as part of a process of negotiating her relation with Petruchio.

Finally, individually and as a class we return to the focus on learning to read differently by reflecting on new concepts and new practices—and setting goals for *how* students will read the next play.

The Shakespearean Stage: Elements of a Different Language

> To take full advantage of reading Shakespeare, we must cultivate both the mind's ear and the mind's eye; we must learn to hear the verse spoken aloud as we read it, and also to see the drama enacted in an imaginary theatre. (Harry Levin, General Introduction, *The Riverside Shakespeare* 14–15)

When I assign the class their first reading of *The Taming of the Shrew*, I also ask them to read the general introduction in *The Riverside Shakespeare*, concentrating on "The Theatrical Setting." Since all the major one-volume editions of Shakespeare's plays and most of the single-play paperback editions have a section on the Elizabethan-Jacobean theater, you can make the appropriate reading assignment in your class. Many editions have a reproduction of Johannes de Witt's sketch of the interior of the Swan Theatre, made about 1596, as copied by Aernout van Buchel. I supplement this with the reproduction and mini-essay published in *Illustrations of the English Stage, 1580–1642* (Foakes 52–55), which not only explains the elements of the drawing in detail but also describes problems in interpreting the drawing not evident to a novice reader. Examining these materials enables us to take the vital step from recognizing the general problem of translating a playtext into the language of the stage to tackling the specific problem of translating *this* text in terms of the potentials of *this* particular type of stage. In taking this step, I am making explicit the challenge of learning the theatrical language that was the language "spoken" by the dramatists, actors, and spectators of the period. It is important for students to realize that, as is true of most conventions, this language was rarely made explicit in the scripts of plays, and hence must be recovered by the sort of detective work they are beginning to learn to perform.

Since I want students not simply to memorize but also to use this information, beginning to integrate it with the challenges of reading the first play in terms of the specific physical and conventional properties of the stage the play was written for, I may also give them a short writing assignment:

> As you read the assigned material, would you please note the distinctive features of what is often called the Elizabethan stage, and describe how it is similar to or different from the parallel feature of the modern realistic stage.

> When you have finished, please write a second entry in which you begin to describe how actors on the Shakespearean stage would perform differently from the actors working on a modern proscenium stage. It may help if you pick a specific moment in *The Taming of the Shrew* and sketch out how this moment would be performed on each stage, and how these different performances might elicit different responses from the spectators. To start, you might ask yourself where Sly and his deceivers sit when they begin to watch the "Taming" play presented by the traveling players.

What I offer here is a set of categories with key pieces of information in each category. This material is drawn from Andrew Gurr's *The Shakespearean Stage, 1574–1642*; from Gurr and Ichikawa's *Staging in Shakespeare's Theatres*; from Arthur Kinney's *Shakespeare by Stages: An Historical Introduction*; and from Alan Dessen's "Shakespeare and the Theatrical Conventions of His Time." I have reorganized this material using categories employed by Bernard Beckerman in *Shakespeare at the Globe, 1599–1609*. And, as noted earlier, I also have the students read R. A. Foakes's short essay on the drawing of the Swan Theatre.

As we begin, I return to the words of Harry Levin quoted at the beginning of this section, suggesting that our goal is to learn as much as we can about the real theater in order to help us more accurately "see the drama enacted in an imaginary theatre."

The Theater: The Globe

Located in Southwark, Bankside: out of City's jurisdiction, in sporting district, which included arenas for bearbaiting and houses of prostitution.

The first Globe was probably a 20-sided polygon; the Fortune was a square.

Dimensions: perhaps 100 feet in diameter outside; 70 feet inside.

Stage occupies nearly half the yard space, so the spectators are never more than 30–40 feet away from the actors.

The yard, where people stood. Three levels of galleries, which were the more expensive seats. Audience: 2,000–3,000: say 800–1,000 spectators in yard, entering for a penny; some 1,500 in the galleries, paying one or two pennies more for better seats.

The Stage

Stage occupies nearly half the yard space: approximately 44 feet broad, 23 feet deep. About 5 feet above the ground.

The Swan drawing shows:

> Three galleries, two entries from yard.
>
> Stage, three players. Tiring house facade: two doors.
>
> Partitioned gallery/arras, with players, musicians, or spectators.
>
> Two carved stage posts support the cover/heavens, which is tiled.
>
> Hut, trumpeter, flag above. There are bulks or trestles beneath stage.
>
> Below stage trapdoor/Hell. A throne or other descending device from heavens. Possible third door or discovery area.
>
> Tiring (attiring) house (dressing rooms): two/three doors, possible curtain/arras area. Did the curtain color signal genre?
>
> Above: possible upper windows (false Vincentio, Juliet).
>
> Aloft: third level, musicians, sound effects. Hut: flag, trumpeter.
>
> Roof: "shadow" or "heavens" covered most of stage: zodiac underside.
>
> Actors could be lowered from heavens in some theaters.
>
> Posts, which might have been used for hiding, eavesdropping.
>
> Trap: to pit below stage. Could be a grave, as for Ophelia; but metaphysically Hell.

The Acting: "Will your majesty hear the play?" (Hamlet)

Basic style: this was a more verbal and less visual theater, with emphasis on words creating reality. The words were the core of the experience.

Actors: emergence of companies with patrons, of permanent theaters.

The development of acting style was probably explosive, and Shakespeare may have written with specific actors in mind: Burbage, Kemp, Armin.

Boy actors: boys played all women's parts. This convention has aroused intense controversy about what effects were created by boys playing women, especially when they played women who disguised themselves as boys or men.

The Staging: Physical features and metaphysical dimensions

Open stage: little scenery, few props, so not realistic in modern sense.

No curtain, no scene changes as we think of them.

Continuity, not division, is the principal feature of the curtainless stage: bodies are dragged off, as Hamlet drags off Polonius, and the practical and the fictional merge on this stage.

Place was created mainly by dialogue, perhaps by signs, say for towns.

Three types of place (Beckerman): unlocalized, generally localized, particular.

Indoors/outdoors not visually as important.

Little scenery, then; some spectacular props.

Major expenditure on costumes, which might cost more than the script.

Lighting: during daylight, lighting is not illusionistic but signals location or time of day. Light does not actually illuminate.

Symbolic or metaphysical vertical dimensions: the globe, world, universe.

Day: lighting was daylight, hence torches and candles did not illuminate (more light to create dark) but signaled night or indoors or both.

Costume: flamboyant, expensive (more than the play), perhaps discarded clothing from nobles.

Spectacle: no scenery, but much spectacle: hangings, costume, pageantry.

Sound, and some properties, such as thrones, beds.

Duels: staged to display skill, appreciated by knowing spectators.

Battles: staged with a few actors entering, clashing, exiting, reentering.

Action: continuous, nonlocalized, verbal scene-painting if needed.

Space: movement is fluid, scene shifts at will and at word (*Antony and Cleopatra*: 42 scenes).

Time: also shifts freely (although *Comedy of Errors* and *Tempest* have unity of time).

Acts: perhaps music between acts; act intervals necessary at indoor theaters such as Blackfriars while candles were trimmed. Music between these breaks was added.

Scenes: no divisions. Option to explain the "Law of Reentry."

Address: soliloquy, aside. Use of couplets to signal conclusion.

I ask students to spend a few minutes on the theater's physical structure first, as well as on the distribution of the spectators (which opens up class and economic issues you may want to pursue). Frequently our classroom is about the dimensions of the stage; I point this out and have one student simply cross the room so that we can grasp the time an entry probably took on the original stage.

Working from these basic facts about the theater, I ask how the actors must have performed on such a stage, and we begin to work out the detailed comparison of the Elizabethan stage and the modern proscenium stage. The comparison between an outdoor theater with performances in daylight and an indoor theater using modern lighting provides a simple but vivid example of how differently the older stage functioned—and of how unobvious the conventions we take for granted actually are. Students find it striking, for example, that on the Elizabethan stage darkness was often indicated by adding more light to the scene in the form of torches or candles—and that these lights not only indicated time of day but also could be used to distinguish between outdoor and indoor scenes. Similarly, on the open stage there were only a few props, and these props carried a much greater signifying potential than most props carry in a modern realistic setting. (We do activities with props for the second and last scenes of *Richard III*.)

In discussing the question of setting, I point to the crucial difference between the realistic stage, which almost invariably gives us a specific, detailed visual representation of each scene, and the open stage, where location is indicated only when that is necessary for the action to be intelligible. The emergence of more representational drama, even as early as 1700, led editors to insert specific locations for almost every scene in these plays. We also look at how this type of drama handled time, with its much greater freedom or its much slighter interest in specific time and timing—although when Shakespeare wants us to be aware of time, as he does in *Romeo and Juliet*, for example, he ensures that we are, and in these plays we need to attend to the pattern of time and timing.

In this first discussion of stage and staging, I do not go into great detail, but I do stress one point, which is the sharp contrast in how divisions are made in the action. The classic modern stage, with discrete scenes signaled by the fall and rise of the curtain and its announcement of time intervals in a program, stresses discontinuity; the Elizabethan theater, with no curtain, continuous action, and free shifting of place and time, stresses continuity. Thus part of learning to translate this theatrical language is learning to recognize how the dramatist asks us to connect the different scenes of the play rather than to think of them as separate and self-contained units. This becomes more evident as we discuss the way in which entrances and exits function to make connections visually, so that we may see one group of characters exit as another enters, thereby connecting groups of people who never meet on stage.

One way to summarize much of this material is to introduce two interlocking distinctions we can make between Elizabethan and modern drama, the distinctions between presentational and representational production styles and between symbolic and naturalistic staging. When students grasp these distinctions, they will have a convenient way of keeping in mind the array of more specific differences that are a key to learning to read differently.

Presentational and Representational Theater

The fundamental difference here is between those methods of production that acknowledge the reality of the play situation and those that attempt to create a full illusion of representing reality. That is, presentational styles acknowledge the reality of the theater; they acknowledge that the play is a play; and they acknowledge the presence of the spectators. Indeed, presentational styles may permit or even encourage direct address by characters to the audience, securing our participation in a way that also reminds us of our role as spectators. Representational styles, in contrast, ignore (that is, pretend to ignore and invite spectators to ignore) the reality of the theater; they seek to replicate an extra-theatrical world as completely as possible, tacitly denying that the play is a play, and they are performed as if the audience were not present. Representational styles suppress anything that would break the illusion, especially any form of direct address to the spectators.

Symbolic Dramaturgy versus Naturalistic Dramaturgy

The distinction between the two types of theatrical language correlates closely with the two methods of production. The naturalistic style aims to reproduce reality, conceived in the modern sense of the material world: the aim is to imitate as fully as possible the actions of people in an extra-theatrical world. The symbolic style, in contrast, follows from the logic of a nonillusionistic theater: since this theater does not aim at illusion, the performers are free to stress symbolic dimensions of their action and to ignore at least some of the imperatives that would drive their characters if those characters were projected as fully individualized people operating under the pressures created by our environment outside the theater.

These two fundamentally different stage logics are embodied in different acting conventions, where a *convention*, as Raymond Williams defines it, consists of "the terms upon which author, performers and audience agree to meet, so that a performance may be carried on" (*Drama from Ibsen to Brecht* 13). Alan Dessen

(*Elizabethan*) offers an excellent example of a modern production in which the two conventions were in collision:

> To see such interpretive logic in conflict on stage, consider a moment from the Oregon Shakespearean Festival production of *King Lear* in 1976. Here, in a rendition of III.iv, Denis Arndt as Lear took upon himself the role of a lecturer with Poor Tom as his visual aid ("consider him well") in order to raise an essential question ("is man no more than this?") by placing particular emphasis upon nakedness ("uncovered body," "the thing itself," "unaccommodated man," "a poor, bare, forked animal"). At the same time, Ron Woods as Tom was building his characterization upon his iterated line "Tom's acold" and was therefore shivering, "playing cold," grasping at anything that would provide warmth. As a result, at one performance the two actors engaged in a strenuous struggle for Tom's blanket (his only possession other than a loin-cloth), with Lear trying to pull it off in order to display a naked or nearly naked figure (to establish his thesis) while Tom, with equal vigor, sought to pull the blanket around him (to gain warmth). Tom won—perhaps at the expense of the larger implications of Lear's speech.
>
> Note that the two actors were responding to two different sets of signals that then led them in two different directions. Woods, as a modern actor conditioned by the logic of naturalism, was reaching out for appropriate stage business to resolve the question: how would a nearly naked man obviously suffering from the cold "behave" in a storm? In contrast, Arndt was drawing upon previous speeches about naked wretches in the pitiless storm and was therefore treating Tom as a theatrical expression of images crucial to this part of the play ("is man no more than this?" can "man" be reduced to this?). The two different kinds of interpretive logic (physiological-naturalistic versus imagistic-symbolic) are not necessarily incompatible but were at odds in this wrestling match where Poor Tom as stage image linked to the particular coordinates of this scene did not mesh comfortably with Poor Tom as a "man" or "character" responding to blasts of cold. (2–3)

The easy transition here is simply to begin working with the induction since the induction leads immediately to a number of problems in staging the scene, and will lead to the crucial question of where Sly and his practicers sit when "The Taming of the Shrew" begins.

Introducing the Expectation Log

As I explain in the course outline, students produce an expectation log for each of the plays they read (see Figure 3.1). (For *Hamlet* they perform an analogous activity in which they read the play twice, first without and then with the soliloquies, and answer some questions about this double reading.) In the log, they will record, and therefore be able to reflect on and share, their experiences in reading the assigned play. These expectation logs are not graded, but turning in a completed log for each play is necessary in order to pass the course. Thus, before they read *The Taming of the Shrew*, I hand out the expectation log—informing students that they can download the log from my home page—and review the basic procedure. They fill in the first box after they finish reading the first act of the play. In the top middle box, they record what they expect to happen in the next act. After reading act II, they fill in the lower left-hand box. Then they return to the upper right-hand box to compare their predictions with what happened in act II. I comment that the point here is not to "keep score" but rather to reflect on their guesses. Students repeat this process for the remaining acts, except that they do not have to write a summary for act V (although some of them will do so).

Expectation logs are a way of catching our minds in motion, thereby enabling us to respond to the play in several ways. When we watch a play, one of the things we do is formulate expectations as the action unfolds. Some of these expectations will be fulfilled, while others, although quite logical or plausible, will not be fulfilled because the dramatist has designed the play to arouse but not fulfill some guesses. (Some well-known examples include the beginning of several of Shakespeare's tragedies. The opening of *Hamlet* invites spectators to expect a war between Denmark and Norway that never occurs, although the leader of the Norwegian forces becomes king without firing a textually mandated shot. The opening of *Othello* obviously prompts spectators to project that a war between the Venetian Republic and the Ottoman Empire will be at the heart of the play, but at the

Expectation Log: _____

Briefly summarize what happened and who surfaced as main characters.	Predict what may happen next and who will be involved.	After reading the following act, briefly evaluate how closely your expectations were met and what, if any, surprising events occurred.
Act I	Act II	Act II
Act II	Act III	Act III
Act III	Act IV	Act IV
Act IV	Act V	Act V

FIGURE 3.1. *Expectation log.*

beginning of act II they learn that the Turkish fleet has been destroyed in a storm. And the opening of *King Lear* hints that a civil war between the Dukes of Albany and Cornwall may be at the center of the action, whereas the climactic battle is fought by British forces against an invading French army led by a British princess.) Recording expectations helps us perform at least three functions in immersing ourselves in and discussing each play.

First, keeping the log enables each of us to record some of our transient responses and guesses, material we ordinarily forget, both because later actions overwhelm early experiences and because we prefer to forget our mistaken projections. But these mistaken guesses are well worth recalling because they can illuminate crucial elements of the play's design and our own mental processes. In recording and comparing their predictions with the action, students reflect on both their on- and off-target surmises, and thereby learn something about how the dramatist shaped the event so as to direct or misdirect the spectator's feelings and thoughts.

Second, because everyone does a log, each student can work with other members of the class to compare responses and expectations and thereby learn something about where the dramatist impels people to formulate the same idea, where the options seem more open, and, perhaps most important and illuminating, how differently people can respond to the same text.

Third, for some of our later assignments and particularly for writing essays, the log becomes a tool to help writers demarcate how their interpretations of a play have changed over time.

When we begin our study of each play, students work in pairs comparing where they had the same and where they had divergent expectations. They analyze what elements of the play and what in the experiences they bring to the play prompted them to formulate these expectations; and each pair articulates what they have discovered through this discussion.

Of course, *The Taming of the Shrew* adds an extra wrinkle since those students who are first-time readers do not know that the opening two scenes form an induction, and that this induction will provide a frame for the "Taming" play that follows. Nor do they know that in Shakespeare's text this frame is never completed. Thus students' first expectations often have to do with what they take to be an ongoing plot focused on Christopher Sly. One student wrote, "In Act I, I think Sly will find out he is the butt of the jokes, become angry, but be powerless to do anything about it. I'm sure we will meet more characters. Who is the Lord?" And in the evaluation box, this student wrote, "Sort of a false start there. I take it that the inner play is the important one? Since Sly is the focus of the Intro, will Tranio be more important than Lucentio? My guess is Tranio will 'Tame the Shrew' since Lucentio and Bianca have so much in common as to be made for one another." Having recorded her responses in this manner, the student could engage in a very specific discussion of how the double beginning of the play shaped her responses, and of how the design of the induction led her to make her intriguing guesses about the plot of the "Taming" play. While her specific guesses turned out to be off-target, her basic move in seeking analogies between the characters and the internal play is precisely the move spectators need to make if they are to answer the implicit question "Is there any connection or connections between induction and 'Taming'?"

I sometimes assign a play in two segments, frequently breaking the reading between acts I through III and acts IV and V. This works quite well for *The Taming of the Shrew* and *Richard III*, which are examples of what Emrys Jones convincingly argues are Shakespeare's two-part designs. This is not, however, the way I shape the reading of *Hamlet*, for example, nor does it work for *Measure for Measure*, for which I ask students to read acts I and II and then acts III through V. (In the case of *Measure for Measure*, you might experiment by asking students to stop at act III, scene I, line 150, at the moment the Duke intervenes and begins to resolve the tragic impasse.) Furthermore, I may ask students to do other small activities while completing their logs, such as composing three alternate titles or composing a title for each act.

If you use the expectation log, you will be rewarded with increased specificity of student response, effective cues for small-group and whole-class discussion, and insights into how your students are reading the plays.

What Does the Induction Do?

As I do with each play, I make a simple request: "Tell us about your responses to *The Taming of the Shrew*." The goal is to initiate a discussion in which students share what excites, repels, enthralls, or puzzles them and ask the questions that seem most urgent to them—as well as take the risk of asking the "foolish" questions they are embarrassed to ask. It is important to accept their responses, especially the responses students themselves fear are too naive or negative, for only by understanding what is blocking them can you clear up problems or devise moves that lead to fuller engagement. In this opening dialogue, we also begin to formulate some of the primary questions and central issues that will guide our work. While many responses will be unique, here are some major issues that usually come up.

First, they are often puzzled about the framing story of Christopher Sly: "Why an induction? Isn't this confusing? What is the relation of the story about Sly to the 'Taming' story? What happens to Sly? Why does he seem to disappear? Has he really fallen asleep? Is he still on stage even if he isn't speaking? Why doesn't Sly reappear at the end? If Shakespeare wasn't going to bother with Sly at the end, why introduce him at the beginning?"

Second, many find the Bianca-Tranio plot confusing. Most of all, they note that the play is *hard to read*. "There are all these people in disguise, using other names, and you have to remember both names when you read their speeches. It makes your head spin, and you have to keep referring back to the list of characters!"

Third, the multiplot drama often does not make sense to them. "What is the relation between the different plots? Where does the Widow come from? Is there any relation between the two main plots and the framing Sly plot? And if the Sly plot is never completed, how can we work out such a relation?"

Fourth, students will have sharply divergent responses to and interpretations of the ending. The issue frequently emerges in a response like that of Kathryn, who asked, "Did they really believe all that stuff about men being superior? And that speech at the end—what happened to Katherine? Why did she give up?" Such questions take us back to the beginning of the play as people argue about whether we are supposed to believe that Petruchio really loves Katherine or only wants her money.

Student responses open the door for spirited debate, a debate that often runs its course with minimal intervention on my part. In fact, I prefer to wait until the debate is at its most heated and then ask for another short writing that formulates the issues. These pieces can be collected, reproduced, and distributed: such a collection provides an excellent starting point for further discussion and allows you to ask students to do a focused short writing when you finish the play that compares the writer's first and later responses in order to say (1) how they have (or have not) changed; (2) something about the process of change or strengthened conviction; and (3) how understanding the process may suggest strategies to use in reading the next play.

Introducing a Concept of Action

At this point, I shift our focus, moving to connect questions about the Sly plot to our discussion of the physical theater. The objective in this activity is not only to enter the play but also to begin employing students' new but general knowledge of the Elizabethan stage, and to learn about how Shakespeare wrote the cues for playing in the scripted language of the text. At the same time, the induction provides a moment to introduce the concept of action, the first of four performance-centered concepts that constitute the core of our work with this play.

"Some of you who asked 'What is an induction?' may have guessed that I will reformulate that question as 'What does this induction do?' We can begin to answer the question 'What does the induction do?' by doing the induction. Could we have two volunteers, please, who will start by simply reading the short segment between the hostess and Sly?"

In one class, the two volunteers were Toni as the hostess and Erik as Sly, and when they had reread the opening segment, I asked the class as a whole to begin analyzing the words of the scene for the cues about context and action they offer actors, and then ask themselves how the actors would project that context to first-time spectators.

What is the context? "Sly is drinking, has broken glasses, owes the hostess for drink and glasses, and the hostess is running him out to save her remaining glasses, while also asking for payment." So we are outside a tavern and, using Beckerman's (*Shakespeare*) categories, in a generally localized but not specific place. How would the spectators come to know this? "There might be a tavern sign over one of the stage doors, but probably costumes and behavior would be the primary signals: the hostess would be dressed in clothes signifying her occupation, and Sly would be dressed poorly; his actions and his speech would indicate his drunkenness." (You might ask, "What happens if we hear the sound of breaking glass just before this pair comes on stage?" Not only does this hint at the scene and action but it also foreshadows the role of noise in this play.)

What about the action? The hostess seems to be her own bouncer, and this raises the question of how physical the scene is. Is she a strong woman? Or is she successful mainly because Sly is drunk? In particular, how much physical contact or violence might there be? What else do we discover about the hostess? "She is unafraid, and probably righteous because she believes she has the law on her side." What else do we discover about Sly? "That he is drunk and that he is ignorant but trying to sound educated, and that he comes from a poor class." (Given Sly's speech in the induction, scene ii, lines 17–21, in which he says he has been a card-maker and bear-herd and is now a tinker, some students wonder if his drinking might explain the change of occupations.)

After a few minutes of discussion, Toni and Erik played the scene again. This time they invented more action, so that the potential of performing this segment as farce began to emerge. Indeed, the hostess ended by shoving Sly hard enough to knock him down, and Sly's final defiance, shouted from the ground, drew laughter for his surprising tumble, as did his imitation of a drunk trying to stay awake. Both actors received nice applause.

"If we stop the play here, as if using a freeze-frame in a movie, then we can ask, 'What has the play done so far?' That is, if we imagine ourselves as first-time spectators, who have only the title and the experience of these first few minutes of action, what are we thinking?"

We will be trying to locate ourselves in relation to this action, which seems to have come to an odd pause as the man who calls himself Sly sinks into drunken sleep. Our obvious move is to attempt to use the title to make sense of what we have seen. As one student remarked, "We will be asking ourselves if the hostess is the shrew. If the hostess is the shrew, it certainly does not look as if Sly will tame her!" And of course we have no idea that we are watching an induction: Shakespeare has designed the induction so that it not only grabs our attention but also leaves us slightly off balance.

As we come to the end of the first scene—either through completing a performance or through a quick discussion—we have reached a perfect moment to introduce the fundamental idea of action, and prepare for introducing the concepts of the scene as a unit of action and of scenic form.

> We need to distinguish two senses of the term *action* and to see how a scene can function as a unit of action in the second sense. The first, more obvious meaning of *action*, which we can call Action$_1$, is simply all the physical things the characters are doing: here, fighting, falling down, rushing off, falling into a drunken sleep. The second, less obvious meaning of *action*, which we can call Action$_2$, is the central event being performed through the physical and verbal action of the characters. This concept of action is also connected with a concept of expectation. What the dramatist does is shape the action of one scene so as to invite us to formulate a guess about what the action of the next scene (or of a later scene, in the case of multiplot drama) will be. What I want to emphasize is the way in which the Action$_2$ of one scene functions to impel us to define the Action$_2$ of the next scene. So would you please formulate as fully and precisely as you can what this scene suggests will be the Action$_2$ of the next scene. Remember that when you are looking to define the Action$_2$ of a scene, you want to choose the verb that most precisely captures the core of this event.

ERIK: The scene sets us up to watch whether the Lord succeeds or not.

INSTRUCTOR: Good! Can anyone include Sly in their definition of the action?

CATHY: The scene sets us up to watch carefully, to see how successful the Lord is in his attempt to transform Sly's preexisting character or personality or identity.

INGA: Here is another definition of the action. We will see the scene as a struggle between the Lord's attempt to fool Sly and Sly's attempt to fool the Lord into thinking that Sly is fooled!

INSTRUCTOR (joining the murmurs of appreciation provoked by Inga's comment as we recognize a twist many people had not imagined): If the action of the first scene sets us up to ask, "Will the Lord succeed in transforming Sly's identity?," then the next step is to look at how Shakespeare writes in signals that enable actors to re-create that action. Would you please find all the cues in the scripted language that tell us how the contest should be played out?

This activity can be done individually or in small groups, and I usually give students about ten minutes before we begin to share ideas. If students seem to be having difficulty grasping the concept of Action$_2$ or knowing how to look for cues, I add, "If you find it difficult to begin this analysis, you can ask yourself some more specific questions: When does Sly stop resisting the new identity? What seems to be the statement or action that convinces him to adopt a new identity? What is the sequence of moves made by the Lord and his followers that brings Sly to this decisive point?"

ERIK: Sly resists until he says, "Am I a Lord?," when he must realize, "Hey, this can be to my advantage! Why not? What have I got to lose?" So even if he's not convinced, he is rationalizing accepting that he is a lord.

LADONNA: Maybe Sly doesn't really believe but just stops resisting because he realizes he has nothing to lose. The signal is that he shifts from arguing to asking questions, which shows him accepting this identity and trying to learn the details, which he could not "remember." So I agree with Erik; he shifts when he asks, "Am I a Lord?"

STEPHANIE: Up to line 20, Sly resists. Then there is the long stretch where he is silent while the Lord talks: he is listening hard, and something must happen in there while he listens. Maybe we can see what happens from his expression, maybe not.

LINDA: We will see the wheels turning in this section. And I think that Sly would know the Lord was a lord because the

servants, no matter how good their acting, would uncon-
sciously still defer to him—and because the Lord has the
longest speeches.

CATHY: I want to go back to Erik's point: when he says, "Am I a
Lord?" *Sly shifts from prose to verse*, which means he shifts
into the language that everyone around him is speaking. Is
Sly conscious of this? Probably not, but it is a signal to the
actor that the character is picking up the sound of how they
speak.

INSTRUCTOR: Cathy's point emphasizes something crucial about
scripted language, namely, the two levels on which the
dramatist must write. Shakespeare is composing a complex
moment in which the *social action* by this group seeks to
reconstruct Sly's reality, so he builds in signals that show this
change happening. And he is composing for his fellow actors,
so he needs to write cues for the *dramatic action* using
language that offers them clear directions about how to
perform the change. So we can extend Cathy's point by
asking, "What are some of the other indicators of social
action we can discover here?"

The two key elements that will elicit detailed exploration are
the business with the drink and the sexuality that is introduced
with the appearance of the page as Sly's "wife." As students discover, there will be a number of questions about the drink and
about the comedy that emerges from the choices made in performance. Does Sly get a drink when he first calls for it, or only
when he repeats his request? Does he even notice when the servant corrects his behavior, offering him sack instead of ale and
offering the drink in an aristocratic cup instead of a plebeian
pot? The point is to notice that Sly is speaking in verse like a lord
but still drinking like a poor man. And what happens when he
tastes sack, which he has never tasted before?

The entrance of the "Lady" adds other rich possibilities. On
the one hand, here is the moment when Sly can be played as
becoming completely convinced of his new identity, so that his
startlingly direct line, "Madam, undress you, and come now to
bed," can be Sly shedding the last vestiges of doubt as he starts to
shed his clothes. On the other hand, it can also be the moment
when Sly lets us know that he knows he is being gulled, with a
look and a wink conveying his knowledge and in effect saying,

"Oh, is that your game?! Well let's see how far you will go!" This can be a moment when he almost turns the tables on his deceivers by taking them more seriously than their pretense can sustain. And there is, as Inga added, a third possibility: "He can be trying to fool them into thinking he has accepted when he doesn't believe it, but then he is fooled himself about the lady." As you discuss this scene, you can also introduce students to the pervasive sexuality in these plays, particularly in "Ay, it stands so that I may hardly tarry so long."

It is worth pointing out that Sly changes how he speaks, starts to acquire new tastes in liquor, attempts to master new forms of address, and attempts to make love to his "wife." Language, food, distinctions of class, and sexual relations: only when you enumerate the list in this fashion is it evident how neatly the transformation of Sly introduces some of the basic dimensions in which Petruchio and Katherine will play out a parallel "taming." If you want to explore larger issues of culture, this is a fine moment to introduce the idea of cultural codes and the analysis of how such codes shape behavior even as they operate in ways beyond the intentions and control of the individual.

Reflecting on Our Practice: Reading Differently

"Write a short record of the specific moves we have just rehearsed. Remember that you want to move from the specific to the general, formulating concepts you can use to guide future reading." Here is a list developed by one class.

1. *Prose-verse shifts.* These can signal a variety of shifts, transits, or changes: in this case, an ascent in class and a solitary figure joining a group.

2. *The functions of a character's questions.* Asking questions can signal doubt or a change of mind in a character who is confronting choices. We can ask ourselves, "What does the asking of this question at this moment allow us to infer about the character?"

3. *Nonverbal response.* One type of silence occurs when one character is listening to long speeches aimed at him: a key choice here is whether the character offers nonverbal cues as to what he or she is thinking.

4. *Forms of address.* The forms of address such as "Lord" can convey complex relations depending on what term is used and how it is spoken, and can create powerful effects when a character changes a form of address.

5. *Eating and drinking.* Simple but fundamental actions such as eating and drinking can create bonds between characters, and on the stage they usually have a much more direct effect than on the page.

6. *Clothing.* The clothes a character wears are crucial, especially in a society where the types of clothing indicated rank and occupation and where sumptuary laws regulated or attempted to regulate who could wear what. Having a character change clothes is one of the fundamental resources of the theater.

7. On an open stage such as this, there are relatively few props: those that do appear often are highly charged with symbolic meaning.

As the final step, I ask students to list specific aspects they will work on as they reread the play for the next class. You can also collect writings in which students show how they use their new ability to focus on their chosen aspect to offer a more detailed reading and exploration of the possibilities in a small segment of the playtext.

What Does a Title Do?

What follows is a five-step activity designed to prompt students to think not only about the title of this play but also about the title of any text they read, and perhaps about the titles they give their own compositions.

I have suggested that we can best begin exploring any given element of a play by asking, "What does this element do?" Having begun to answer this question about the induction, let us look at an element that, at least for readers and those attending modern performances, comes earlier and ask, "What does the title do?" As a first step, would you please invent five titles for the play . . . and three more . . . and two more. . . . You want to go past the obvious and into more imaginative possibilities so that you can capture unexpected patterns and make surprising connections.

We collect one title from each class member, writing them on the board and copying them down as well. Here is one set:

The Last Laugh	Sly's Revenge
Katherine & Petruchio	Christopher Sly's Dream
O Cursed Kate	Disguise Within
The Wedding Account	What You See Is What You Get
Beyond Desire	Opportunities of a Shrew

And here is a set with a different range:

Love & Marriage: A Matter of Control	Katherine the Untouchable (or So We Believe)
Subservient Kate	Once a Shrew Always a Shrew
Petruchio Beaten	
To Woo a Recalcitrant Wife	Man's Taming
Far Cry from Freedom	All's Fair in Love and Padua
Unethical Approach to Love	Let's Make a Deal
The Liberation of Kate	Once a Shrew, Now a Wife
Failure of Feminism in Renaissance Drama	An Onion Will Do as Well
	Surrender in Padua
The Wrath of Kate	The Sly Way In
She *Will* Love Me	Beauty and the Beast
Lessons [Lessens?] in Love	Selling of a Daughter
Spare the Rod & Spoil the Wife	Handy Man Throw No Petals on the Ground

As a second step, would you please classify the set, arranging them in no less than three and no more than five or six categories.

This can be done in groups, where debate forces discussion of the categories and hence draws attention to the functions that titles perform. With the second set of titles given above, for example, students created groups that were based on the focus of the titles: (1) Outcome, (2) Conflict, (3) Subject, (4) Genre, (5) Point of View, (6) Protagonist, (7) Allusions, (8) Abstractions.

> For the third step, please pick out the three titles that most appeal to you, note why they appeal to you, and then analyze what each title does. To put this question another way, ask yourself, "What effect would Shakespeare have been seeking to create if he had chosen this title?"

In the first set, for example, "Christopher Sly's Dream" drew a strong response because it explained the relation of the framing and the taming, and implied what might happen at the end. Another favorite was "The Last Laugh" because it told us how to take the ending yet left open who had the last laugh. Finally, some appreciated "Opportunities of a Shrew," which reversed the negative interpretation of the word *shrew*, thereby inviting us to think about the possibility that, whether or not she had consciously chosen this role, Katherine might have found some advantage in being seen as a shrew.

> As a fourth step, look back at the titles you invented, the categories you created, and our discussion, and answer the question "What can a title do?"

For this activity, students often return to their categories and supply verbs for them. They discover that a title can announce a subject, preview an outcome, create suspense, misdirect attention, set up a surprise, suggest a point of view, challenge some cultural expectation, raise a controversy, stir debate, offer a theme, inform us about the genre of the play, allude to other contexts, and so on. Or a title can tease us by making us wonder how it "fits" the play, so that we must explore different ways to apply it to the action.

> As a fifth step, now answer the question "What does the title of this play do?"

Students' initial answers will be that the title arouses interest by suggesting an exciting but disturbing conflict; that it focuses on the process of taming; that it seems to announce an outcome;

and that it directs spectators to a particular attitude toward the shrew. Even in these answers, students are still mainly focusing on the question "What does the title mean?" so that they need to be pushed to ask, "What does the title do to the audience?"

The key point here is that insofar as it announces that the play will be about what the Elizabethans would recognize as the struggle for mastery between women and men—what has come to be called "the battle of the sexes"— it will divide the audience into (at least) two groups. Thus the question must be restated: "What will the title do to women? What will the title do to men?" The short answer is that the title seems to reflect a culture that sees shrewish women as a source of disruption in the community, a culture whose imperatives include the idea that men are the "governors" of their households and must therefore rule "their" women—which means control their wives and raise their daughters to be obedient. The title seems based on an expectation that most men will be in favor of a shrew being tamed, and therefore they can expect to see a performance they will enjoy.

But what about the women? We know, from the evidence of Shakespeare's other plays, as in the epilogue to *As You Like It*, and from other testimony, that women constituted a substantial portion of the original audience, and that the players were well aware they needed to please women as well as men. But while some of these women might have endorsed this patriarchal order, many women in the audience would not have simply accepted the patriarchal norm. At least some of these women would have had a sense of how this norm oppressed them. All the participants would have been aware that there was a strong, unmarried woman on the throne of England, which meant that even the highest-ranking peers found themselves the subjects of a woman.

In fact, the prevalence of shrewish women as a topic for public reprehension and literary production, however much it may have been in part a literary convention, also testifies to the widespread existence of women who did *not* accept these normative beliefs. After all, you do not spend time attacking as subversive those visions, values, and practices that nobody is currently professing or performing. So for at least a portion, and perhaps a sizable portion, of Elizabethan women, the title would impel them to ask if they would be watching a play whose action they might find hard to stomach. The title, in short, also serves to arouse resistance. And for both women and men, the title may also make them wonder if they will applaud or deplore the outcome. This act of dividing and subdividing the audience is one of the most interesting actions performed by any of Shakespeare's titles.

In the class that produced the second list of titles, Jackie, an English major who also worked extensively with horses, pointed out that we had missed another crucial aspect of the title: "The title says 'tamed,' not broken: when you tame something you want to win its love; when you break it, you only win its obedience, but you lose its spirit. And if you break it, not tame it, you can never trust it, because it will always want to rebel." Such an observation shows us that the simple either/or divisions the title seems to elicit may become more complex in the action that follows. It also models the vital process of exploring a metaphor for its range of functions, for the ways the analogy may play out.

> There are two assignments for next class. First, reread act I and, in addition to employing the practice you chose for yourself, concentrate on the concept of action. Specifically, please begin to examine how a play's actions operate in two dimensions: for each action you define, briefly state what that action does within the play's own world and in the play–audience dimension.
>
> Second, read the excerpt from *Scenic Form in Shakespeare* by Emrys Jones, which is the first twenty-two pages of the first chapter, titled "The Scenic Poet." Please do the following: (1) State the concept of scenic form in your own way but using Jones's key terms. (2) Look at his model scenic form analysis of *Titus Andronicus* act III, scene i—a scene you may want to read since you have the play—and formulate the most important moves the critic makes in performing this analysis. (3) Drawing on your own understanding of the concept of scenic form and the insights gained from looking at his model analysis, proceed to analyze the scenic form of act II of *The Taming of the Shrew*.

Learning to Explore Scenic Form

In exploring the induction, students are introduced to the concept of dramatic action. In exploring act I, scene i and act II, we shift our focus to the primary unit in which action is embodied, namely, the scene. Here students are introduced to the concept of scenic form as they read the excerpt from *Scenic Form in Shakespeare* (Jones), work with the concept in performance activities, and collaborate on their own scenic form analyses.

The concept of scenic form is important for at least two reasons. First, the ability to discern the form of a scene is one of the most effective tools for investigating the design of a play and what that design does when it is put in motion. Second, as students wrestle with the practice of analyzing for scenic form, they also become engaged in a process that helps them learn to do criticism in a new way, wherein they not only read for content but also to grasp how the critic performs a particular type of inquiry. Acquiring this ability to analyze and then rehearse a critic's practice is a talent they will be able to use in future courses in literature and drama; it also aims to empower them by offering a model of learning to learn that can last a lifetime.

Since "The Scenic Poet" is a difficult reading, I assign a double-entry journal.

In the opening chapter, Jones establishes his critical tools, which are the concepts he uses throughout his book to produce analyses of individual plays. In the left column of your double-entry journal, list the key terms of his critical vocabulary. When you have finished your first list, please put an asterisk next to the core terms necessary to discuss scenic form, especially as you can see these terms embodied in Jones's own analysis of act III, scene i of *Titus Andronicus*.

Introducing the Concept of Scenic Form

The first discussion of scenic form will almost certainly be more energetic than clear, both because the concept itself is complex and because it runs counter to the emphasis on words that will have dominated most of the training students have received in reading, interpreting, and writing about literature. Therefore I encourage students to be as explicit as possible about what they understand and what they feel uncertain about, and listen carefully so that I can help them move toward a better grasp of the concept.

I start by simply asking for responses to the excerpt from "The Scenic Poet." Part of what makes the task difficult is that Jones is introducing his more encompassing concept of drama and defining some of drama's unique formal properties, some of which we have already discovered in our earlier activities and analyses, particularly our delineation of the constitutive elements of drama. Part of what we do in this first discussion is sort out the core concepts of scenic form from other related concepts of drama. Thus, as the students share their reformulations, I listen for the moment when it becomes useful to sharpen the discussion by asking, "What are the key terms that Emrys Jones introduces and employs?"

As we collect these terms, it becomes clear that students are fascinated by two later sections from the excerpt. In one section, Jones shows how to analyze the pattern of speakers (A/B/C/A/B/A/B, etc.), and in the other section he shows how Shakespeare reemployed forms he had learned from the work of other dramatists or developed in his own earlier work. These ideas, however, are peripheral, and the preliminary list will be too inclusive. So we return to the opening paragraphs of the excerpt:

> It can be an illuminating experience to see Shakespeare acted in a completely unfamiliar language [*Macbeth* in a Japanese version]. . . . But the extraordinary vitality of some of the great scenes of the play survived with surprisingly little loss. One of them, the banquet scene, came across as a dramatic invention of the highest power; even without Shakespeare's words, the scene made a strong effect. . . . When the scene is acted in English or read in its full poetic context in the play as Shakespeare wrote it, so much significance of a verbal and poetic nature claims attention that it is possible, perhaps even natural, to overlook or not to notice its basic structural shaping: that formal idea which gives the scene its dramatic unity and which was made to stand out in the film and opera. What Shakespeare has invented is something—a structure, an *occasion*—which may be said to be (however dangerous the phrase) independent of the words which are usually thought to give the scene its realization. This "something" we may call a "scenic form."
>
> Plays are made of scenes before they are made of words (although a play of Shakespeare's . . . may be as great a poem as it is a play). The dramatist's first and proper task is to dramatize;

and the scene is the primary dramatic unit, the unit in terms of which he will work out his play. If we look for a reason why Shakespeare's plays hold the stage as well as they do . . . at least a partial answer will be found in his mastery of scenic construction. A play can hold an audience even though written without much verbal distinction; what it cannot overcome is defective scenic organization. (3)

I ask students to (re)write a brief definition of scenic form in their own words. In one class, some of the definitions offered were:

The structure of a play that not only complements the dialogue but can also stand apart from it. —Richard

A structure that sequences the events that make the actors and audience feel emotion. —Lisa

Scenic form is the structure of a piece and its pattern and the relationship between its parts. It's why and how units are put together. —Debbie

Scenic form: Structure of an occasion or event and the resulting patterns exhibited in dramatic form in relation to the "audience mind," expectations and emotions. —Sue

Scenic form is the structure and sequence of events that produce the ultimate effect of the scene. It is the medium by which the information contained in the scene is most effectively communicated to serve the playwright's purpose. —Cathy

Scenic form is the element of the play in which the author reaches the audience's emotion. It is the part of the play that doesn't depend on words. It is separate from the text, and it is even present before the text ever was. It is visual, the action. —Angela

Scenic form deals with the structure of a performance—beyond the text—and deals with the relation between actor and audience—where the audience is more than just spectators. A good dramatist makes them a part of the action in a "co-partnership" where the drama develops the tension to a point for emotion, then gives the audience a moment to step back. —Robert

Scenic form: That "something" in a play which is separate from the words of the play, that gives the play life and emotion. Jones calls the "something" an occasion or structure. It seems to me that it is all the patterns and structure in the action of the play which are separate from the dialogue, and which involve the audience in the play. —Linda

Scenic form is the structure of visual properties that gradually carry an audience to a specific reaction, whether deliberate or not on the author's part. —Inga

After we heard this set of definitions, we listed what they seemed to have in common:

1. The idea that the dramatist invents an *occasion*, an event that is the seed for an effective scene. What the dramatist invents is "independent" of the words because it can be thought about as an idea or, better yet, a *design* that is in a sense logically, if not chronologically or psychologically, prior to the words.

2. The idea that the dramatist shapes the invented occasion and that the finished dramatic unit can be seen statically as a structure: a whole with subordinate parts that can be distinguished in various ways.

3. The idea that we can shift from looking at the static structure in the scene on the page to looking at the dynamics of the scene as a live event in which the actors animate this structure by moving through the parts.

4. The idea that this embodied design or enacted pattern in turn moves the spectators, offering them a shaped experience to respond to and digest; alert spectators can, in fact, rearticulate the design or $Action_2$ incarnated in the $Action_1$.

Thus students keep offering, challenging, and refining definitions, returning to the text to see if we have grasped all the constitutive elements. In another class, a key moment occurred when I asked them to revise their definition by answering the question "What is the central aspect of scenes that Jones is trying to analyze?" Leslie offered her refined definition, saying, "The core of scenic form is the phases of action that create and release tension in both the characters and the spectators."

What Does Act I, Scene i Do?

Eventually we reach a point where further refinement of the definition in a vacuum ceases to be productive. At that moment, we move from defining scenic form to doing scenic form analyses of acts I and II, analyses that become more complex as the students begin to grasp both concept and practice. We start by analyzing the form of act I, scene i while integrating the concept of action, and in doing so we are also dealing with what this second beginning of the play (or beginning of the second play) does. This first analysis is also very controlled, providing more explicit modeling of some basic steps in scenic form analysis, rehearsing students before the more demanding task of analyzing act II.

> As a first rehearsal in doing a scenic form analysis, we are going to look at act I, scene i. Remember that when I asked you to reread the first act, I also asked you to concentrate on analyzing the Action$_2$ of each scene, as well as to begin differentiating the action in terms of the play's two dimensions. Those dimensions of action are what the play does within its own world and what the play does in terms of the play–audience relation. What we are doing, then, is analyzing the functions the scene performs.

In this preliminary activity, I do some of the analysis. Specifically I show students that you can always start a scenic form analysis by marking phases based simply on the entrances of different characters or groups of characters (which is what we were tacitly starting to do in looking at the induction). In this case, the result is that the scene divides into four phases, plus the final few lines the "Presenters" speak. If you omit that last segment, you can divide the class into groups, with each group working on one phase:

1. Lucentio and Tranio	(1–47)	47 lines of verse
2. Baptista, daughters, suitors	(48–104)	57 lines of verse
3. Hortensio and Gremio	(105–145)	41 lines of prose
4. Lucentio, Tranio / Biondello	(146–248)	103 lines of verse

Working in their groups, students quickly analyze each segment, and we then collect each group's enumeration of these functions. In this first round, I tend to be more directive, modeling the formulation of the action, in both dimensions, that is necessary for doing a scenic form analysis—and for doing many other types of critical performance as well. What we end up with is a list that looks like the following (I have put these in full sentence form, but you may use a much shorter form that focuses on the verb for each segment):

First segment: We are introduced to Lucentio and Tranio
1. Their opening speeches introduce Lucentio and Tranio, who answer questions about who, what, where, when, how, and why they have come to Padua.
2. Their speeches establish the audience's relation to these two.
3. Their speeches also establish our sense that these are conventional figures: the young lover and the tricky servant.

Second segment: Setting the plots, opening the gaps
1. Baptista's first words set both plots in motion, establishing the situation in which Katherine must be married for Bianca to be wooed.
2. The first words spoken by each sister also introduce us to the apparently radical contrast between defiant Kate and obedient Bianca.
3. In inviting Bianca's wooers to send tutors for her further education, Baptista opens the door for the disguises and intrigues that follow.
4. Lucentio's and Tranio's asides and dialogue open a gap between the two groups, and in opening this gap they place us, the audience, in a superior position.

Third segment: Plotters and eavesdroppers
1. The dialogue between Hortensio and Gremio establishes their temporary truce to cooperate in finding a husband for Katherine.
2. Their dialogue also establishes our sense of the conven-

tional nature of each character, for instance, that Gremio is "a pantaloon."

3. Because Lucentio and Tranio hear what Hortensio and Gremio are up to, this segment puts the Pisan team one up on the home team.

Fourth segment: The eavesdroppers construct their own intrigue

1. Lucentio reveals that he has fallen in love with Bianca.

2. Depending on how Tranio speaks the line "Nay then, 'tis time to stir him from his trance" (I.i.177–78), this segment establishes a direct relation between Tranio and the audience, or Tranio and Lucentio and the audience.

3. The scene also introduces the plot that Lucentio and Tranio create so that Lucentio can woo Bianca.

4. Lucentio and Tranio begin to put their plot into action and switch costumes in front of us, helping us keep track of the disguises.

Obviously, students will have questions about both the process and the formulations, but in this activity I usually ask them to formulate the questions while holding off on attempts to answer them until we have done the second round of analysis, when further experience and more extensive discussion will enable them to arrive at their own answers.

Applying the Model of Scenic Form Analysis to Act II

If you do not do the preliminary activity, you will simply organize small groups that use the concept of scenic form to analyze act II. Part of the reason I introduce the concept of scenic form here is that the example from *Titus Andronicus* that Jones analyzes is a 300-line scene that, as most editors believe, was also the entire act III of the original play. It thus provides an excellent model since act II of *The Taming of the Shrew* comprises a massive 411-line scene.

After the groups are formed, I add: "As you move through this process, as you look for the designed occasion or occasions

Shakespeare created here, you are also looking for Action$_2$, which is the core of the scene. In fact, in a long scene such as this there are often several actions, and you might look for a pattern of repeated action that constitutes the form of the scene or that is its designed occasion." These are the breakdowns the students in one class came up with.

Group 1

1–36	The fight
37–113	Hired as tutors
114–141	Petruchio asks Baptista for Kate's hand
142–168	Kate demonstrates she is a shrew
169–324	Do they marry? Kate and Petruchio
325–411	Who gets Bianca (bidding for Bianca)?

Group 2

1–36	Enter Baptista
23–30	Bianca's exit
31–37	Kate's exit
38–53	Entrance of Petruchio et al.
54–61	Petruchio presents "Litio"
62–71	Introduction of Petruchio
72–110	Tutor and suitor
111–141	Petruchio and Baptista
142–159	"Litio"'s entrance
160–168	Exit all but Petruchio
169–181	Petruchio's soliloquy
182–278	Petruchio and Kate
279–324	Enter Baptista et al. Exit Petruchio & Kate
325–399	Vying for Bianca
399–403	Exit Gremio
404–411	Tranio's soliloquy

Group 3

1–22	Fight

23–36   Enter Baptista

37–40   Introductions

41–55   Intro of Petruchio

56–60   Intro of Hortensio as "Litio"

61–70   Discussing Kate

71–79   Intro of Lucentio as "Cambio"

80–85   Intro of Tranio as "Lucentio"

86–110   Exit tutors

111–141   Discussion between Petruchio & Baptista

142–168   Exit all but Petruchio

169–181   Kate enters

182–242   Verbal sparring

243–278   Petruchio's long speeches

279–324   Discussing marriage

325–385   Tranio & Gremio compete

386–404   Exit all but Tranio

405–411   Exit Tranio

Group 4

1–36   Fight between sisters

37–181   Lull, preparing for Kate

182–278   Fight between Petruchio and Kate

279–324   Lull

325–411   Exchange between Tranio and Gremio

As often happens with segmenting activities (see the section on segmenting the first scene of *Hamlet* in Chapter 5), whereas some groups (1 and 4) see lines 1–36 as a single unit, other groups (2 and 3) delineate three units. But three of the four groups agree that line 36 is the end of a segment. Similarly, all four groups agree that a unit begins at line 325, although two groups see this as beginning the last unit of the scene and two groups discern three segments in the last 87 lines of the scene. If you ask, "Why do all the groups start a phase here?," the answer is that they see the exit of Petruchio and Kate as signaling a major shift: the central figures of the play are gone—or to put it another way, the star characters exit. As we discuss each group's work, we will engage in a debate during which the diverging analyses enable everyone to keep refining and sharpening their understanding of the scene's form, even as the discussion also enables me to guide students to further insights about the nature of scenic form and scenic form analysis. At this point, while I continue to ask guiding questions, I also do my best to let the students make discoveries themselves. In these sessions, students become very excited as they realize that they can indeed do a new form of analysis and thus have added a new critical practice to their repertory.

An Analysis of Scenic Form in Act II: Four Contests

Another reason I introduce the investigation of scenic form here is that act II is one of the most elegant examples of a clear yet complex design in Shakespeare's early plays, a point made by Brian Morris in his introduction to the Arden edition of this play (104–6). So as the class discussion reaches the limit of what students can articulate, I either present Morris's analysis as a handout or present my own amplified version of Morris's analysis. I do this because this analysis will help them gain a firmer grasp of scenic form and of the relation of action to scenic form.

What Morris demonstrates is that act II consists of four segments in which the action of each segment is a contest. Here is my own charting of act II, scene i to show the underlying pattern of action:

1st contest, Katherine versus Bianca: physical. 1–37 = 37 lines.

Katherine & Bianca (1–22)	Bianca's hands tied; Katherine strikes her.
+ Baptista (23–37)	Exit Bianca, exit Katherine.

2nd contest, Petruchio versus Baptista: verbal. 38–141 = 104 lines.
Bargaining over Katherine's dowry. Petruchio talks of money, Baptista of love.

+ Gremio, Luc (Cambio), Hort (Lit)

Pet, Tran (Luc), Bion (38–110)	Exit Luc (Cam) and Hort (Lit), Bion.
Petruchio & Baptista (111–141)	Bargaining for Kate.

3rd contest, Petruchio versus Katherine: verbal/physical/verbal.
142–324 = 183 lines.
Set up by offstage contest of Katherine versus Litio: physical.
Delayed yet intensified by Petruchio's first soliloquy.

Hort (Lit) (142–69)	Lute breaking, exit Bap, Grem, Tran (Luc), Hort (Lit).
Petruchio (170–181)	Petruchio's 1st soliloquy.
+ Katherine (182–280)	Wooing Katherine: she strikes Petruchio, Petruchio threatens her.
+ Bap, Grem, Tran (Luc) (281–324)	Pet announces wedding, P & K exit.

4th contest, Tranio-as-Lucentio versus Gremio: verbal. 325–411 = 87 lines.
Bidding for Bianca's hand.

Bap, Grem, Tran (Luc) (325–398)	Grem & Tran (Luc) bid for Bianca; exit Baptista.
Grem & Tran (Luc) (399–403)	Gremio: warning speech and exit.
Tranio (as himself) (404–411)	Soliloquy: plan to get a "father" for Lucentio.

Here is a prose expansion of what this chart represents:

Contest 1, Kate versus Bianca: A Physical Contest (1–37 = 37 lines). The short first contest that opens the scene shows Katherine apparently dominating her younger sister. Coming after her verbal sparring with her nonsuitors and her father, this action shows Katherine escalating to physical violence. The performance variables are how painfully Bianca is tied, how forcefully Katherine "strikes" her, and whether Bianca in any way seems to provoke this response. Katherine's acts not only indicate that she is capable of violence but also set a threshold for her violence—just as his beating of Gremio in act I, scene ii sets an initial level to the violence we can expect from Petruchio. Therefore, how Katherine treats Bianca will shape our sympathy with or distaste for Katherine and will help shape the degree to which we become interested in or committed to her "taming." While the initial impulse of most women and some men will be to take Katherine's side, and while the scene can be played to support that impulse, it can also be played to make Katherine's violence seem unprovoked and outrageous.

Contest 2, Petruchio versus Baptista: A Verbal Contest (38–141 = 104 lines). The bargaining over Katherine's dowry is the second contest. On the one hand, since it is a verbal contest, it seems less intense than the physical opening. On the other hand, since it will shape Katherine's entire future, it seems more fundamental. And the context created by the earlier segment may highlight the tension between Baptista's talk of winning Katherine's love and Petruchio's talk of gaining her dowry. Certainly this segment establishes an economic focus that will reemerge in the wager that closes the play. This segment also raises a problem about Baptista, a father who speaks of the need for a suitor to win his daughter's love but seems to contradict this concern by agreeing to the match before Petruchio has even seen Katherine. Simultaneously we also face a problem about Petruchio, namely, is he as mercenary as he seems to be? If not, what else motivates him? That is, we wonder if Petruchio has been putting on an act from the beginning or has begun putting on an act here.

Contest 3, Petruchio versus Kate: Verbal/Physical/Verbal Contest (142–324 = 183 lines). Overtly, this seems to be a contest about whether Petruchio and Katherine will be married at all, but of course Petruchio has already ensured that Baptista will go along if he can win Katherine's "love." As Morris points out, Shakespeare does two things that shape the context in which we watch this contest. First, he provides the offstage contest of

Katherine versus her tutor, the disguised Hortensio. What is crucial is that Katherine uses violence with a man. She thinks that this man is an inferior, but her action impels us to wonder how far she will go with Petruchio, her equal. This escalation of Katherine's "shrewish" behavior makes Petruchio's task look more formidable. Second, Shakespeare provides Petruchio's soliloquy. As he speaks to us (or to Sly, as students sometimes suggest), Petruchio forces us to revise our sense of his objectives, and may make our allegiances more complex. We also note how confident or dubious he is about his success: that is, we will be watching to see if the violence to "Litio" has in any way unnerved him, provoked second thoughts, or piqued his interest. Morris is correct when he says of the play:

> It is a special example of the theme of "the battle of the sexes"
> ... and every live performance of *The Shrew* sets up a tension
> between one half of the audience and the other, a tension which
> can be resolved in many subtly different ways, depending on the
> actors, the theatre, the aims of the production, and, above all,
> the text. (104)

But I would add that the scene is designed to elicit complex responses. The play invites us to sympathize with Katherine if we see her as ignored in favor of her sister, but it also makes us see her mistreating that sister. And because we hear Petruchio's soliloquy, we know, as Katherine does not, the strategy he proposes to employ in wooing her. Thus the design impels us to internalize the conflict and, perhaps, to become less one-sided in our allegiances.

Contest 4, Tranio-as-Lucentio versus Gremio: Verbal Contest (325–411 = 87 lines). As Jones notes, Shakespeare often ends a scene with a quieter segment that allows us to reflect on the more intense events we have witnessed. This scene ends with a relatively low-key phase in which the contest for Bianca is played out between Tranio, disguised as his master Lucentio, and Gremio. This phase can be seen as a single unit focused on the bidding for Bianca, or else as a two-part unit, first staging the bidding in which Tranio scores an apparent victory and then leading toward the signing of the marriage contract itself, which, as Gremio points out, is not yet accomplished.

Finally, because the last phase is also the fourth contest we have witnessed, it functions to complete a definition of the world of Padua. The whole pattern shows that at the core of this world, and particularly in how it arranges the marriages it needs to sustain itself, this is a society that constitutes itself through competition and contest. Moreover, this Action$_2$ also links the world of Padua to the world of Sly, where the Lord has undertaken his own (one-sided) contest to change the identity of Sly—who can be played, as students note, to show that he consciously decides to "lose" that contest in order to "gain" material advantage.

To conclude this activity, I ask students to map the last three acts of the play in terms of scenic form. As part of the assignment, I suggest that in this mapping the two key elements to come up with are a title for each act and a verb that sharply focuses the underlying action. Asking the students to map the play as a whole is also the expedient moment when I introduce a reference to one of the play's sources, and in particular to the title of that source. In the *Riverside* edition, Ann Barton offers this convenient introduction:

> The Bianca plot is derived from a play by George Gascoigne, *Supposes* (1566), in itself an adaptation of Ariosto's comedy *I Suppositi* (1509). Both plays declare their Plautine ancestry. They are concerned almost entirely with plot "mistaking," false "supposes" about the identity of characters and the nature of situations. (139)

Alternatively, you can use a summary offered by Stanley Wells in *Shakespeare: The Writer and his Work*:

> "Supposes" is as much a key-word in *The Taming of the Shrew* as is "errors" in *The Comedy of Errors*. The Induction displays the trick by which Sly is made to suppose that he is not a tinker but "a mighty lord." In the play performed for Sly's amusement, Lucentio, wooing Bianca, employs various "counterfeit supposes," but they are superficial.... And the most vital part of the play demonstrates the "suppose" by which he [Petruchio] transforms the shrew into the ideal wife. (27)

Thinking of this as a play about poses and supposes, I suggest, may help students formulate the pattern of action and the labels as they map the last three acts of the play.

Mapping the Play by Acts as Actions

The assignment to map the play in terms of its major actions, as we have just mapped act II's four contests, is a move that allows students to gain perspective on the design of the play as a whole after they have been immersed in a specific unit of the play. When I make the assignment, I point out that many of Shakespeare's plays have such 300-line or 400-line act-length scenes. To learn how to do the sort of analysis modeled here, therefore, is to learn a move they can apply to almost any Shakespeare play they will ever read or study—and indeed can apply to plays written by many other authors as well. When we discuss their maps in the following class, I point out that while the maps have much in common, the differences demonstrate some of the multiple ways an act can be perceived and some of the interconnections between the acts. (A further discussion of mapping is offered in a parallel assignment on *Hamlet*.)

Toward the end of this discussion, I offer students my own map so that they can see how I see the play, so that they can challenge my analysis, and so that they can ask questions about how I do such mapping. For *The Taming of the Shrew*, my map looks like this:

Induction:	Framing the Action and the Audience
Act I:	Exposition through Disguise and Intrigue: Opposing Wooings
	Setting up contests, alternate outcomes.
Act II:	Four Contests: The Competitive World of Padua
	Inducing the audience to choose sides, dividing our loyalties.
Act III:	Petruchio Weds Katherine / Suitors Woo Bianca
	Getting married, but not yet being married.
Act IV:	Taming the Shrew / Winning the Maid

From getting married to being married: Petruchio & Katherine (re)negotiate or Petruchio imposes their relation.

Act V: Three Marriages Celebrated and Contrasted

The outcomes of the supposes reviewed in a final contest, in two phases:

Scene 1: The intrigues completed, disguises unmasked.

Scene 2: The wager: the different choices compared, the different methods evaluated, and a winner declared.

Reading as an Actor: Transforming Role into Character

If, as I do, you think of a course on drama as a single action whose objective is to have students acquire and employ new concepts for translating the dramatic design of a text into the medium of the play in performance, then so far students have acquired two of the core concepts needed to speak the language of drama: they have acquired a concept of action and they have acquired a concept of scenic form as the tool for analyzing what is obviously the primary temporal unit in which Shakespeare embodies that action. Now we turn to the other obvious unit of Shakespearean drama, the dramatis personae.

As is true with most readers of fiction and most literary critics, students initially think of the dramatis personae as characters. But as the study of performance has emphasized, and as people in theater know, it is extremely useful to distinguish character from role. Put most simply, the role is what the dramatist creates in composing the text of the play, while the character is what the actor creates when she or he transforms a role into a performance.

The point of introducing this distinction is to separate these two elements, as we earlier separated the two senses of the play (as text and as performance) in order to create a more precise and productive understanding of the play. The role consists of all the speeches that constitute a particular part; any description of the part (Gremio is "a pantaloon"); any delineation of costume (Petruchio must dress fantastically for his wedding); any necessary action, whether mandated implicitly in dialogue or explicitly in stage directions (Katherine must strike Petruchio in act II, scene i); and, not to be overlooked, the way the words and actions of other dramatis personae help create the role. In contrast, the character is the incarnation of the role crafted by the actor in a production. As is true for the playtext and the performance, here also we have a nonsymmetrical relation: the character created by an actor is always more than the role because it is a full realization, and it is always less than the role because it is only one possible realization.

Act II provides excellent opportunities to make this distinction between role and character and to begin rehearsing some of the practices by which many actors are trained to transform a role into a character. These practices come from the system developed by Constantin Stanislavski, and while later thinkers have critiqued the psychological premises Stanislavski took for granted, and while theatrical innovators have offered us different systems, the core of Stanislavski's model still provides an effective starting point for learning another approach for transforming the words on the page into performance. What we will be doing as we work on Petruchio's soliloquy in act II, scene i, then, is to introduce some of the basic processes by which an actor can transform the multiple potentials latent in the role into a specific character design he will seek to project in performance.

After I have introduced the distinction between role and character, I hand out the following summary of the concepts of unit, objective, and subtext taken from the work of Stanislavski.

Playing an Action: Moving from Role to Character
Using the Concepts of Objective/Action, Unit/Beat, and Subtext

It seems obvious that in the plays we are studying the basic unit is the scene. Certainly the scene is the unit that is most obvious to us when we are in the position of spectators at a play. But while thinking about a scene as a whole yields rich insights, it also can prevent us from getting a more detailed perception of the internal movement of the scene—and we want to capture that movement as a means for deepening our engagement with a play, for improving the imaginary performance in our mental theater, and for sharpening our perception of any productions we may see. In particular, we also want to learn something about how the role on the page becomes the performed character on the stage.

Another way into a play is to study the scene as an actor might explore it. At first sight, it seems that the actor's task is to ask, "What are the words I have to say?" and "What are the actions I have to perform?" But that is too general to be much help. The challenge is, more specifically, to make sense of the role in order to be able to create the character, so that when the actor speaks the lines and performs the actions the audience perceives them not as memorized speeches and re-hearsed gestures but as springing from a unified life which is virtually present as it is re-presented before them.

Thus many actors—that is, many actors trained in the late nineteenth and throughout the twentieth century—have been and are taught, as part of their discipline, to ask certain fundamental questions as they begin to learn and rehearse a part:

Who am I?
Where am I?
Who else is here?
Why are we here? or Why am I here?
What are we doing? or What am I doing?
                              and, most important,
What do I want?

These questions offer actors a powerful heuristic for moving from the outside, the words on the page, to the inside, the virtual life of their roles, so that, as Ellen O'Brien puts it, the actor can inhabit "the mental universe of his character" ("Inside Shakespeare: Using Performance Techniques to Achieve Traditional Goals," *Shakespeare Quarterly* 35 [1984]: 625.) This heuristic is, as some of you may have recognized, based on the network of practices and concepts developed by the Russian director Constantin Stanislavski (1863–1938). For our purposes, we need only three of his basic concepts: the objective, which is also called the action; the unit or beat; and the subtext. What I am presenting here is a very stripped-down introduction to these concepts. The concepts will become useful for you only if you repeatedly rehearse them, for it is only in the slippery business of employing abstractly defined terms that one takes control of them and discovers their power—that is, what they can help you do.

Objective

The objective or action is what the character is trying to accomplish at any given moment, as distinct from the physical actions she may be performing, which may have nothing to do with the objective she hopes to achieve. These actions may be overt and explicit, but they may also be covert and implicit.

> Action (or Intention) means what is really happening on the stage, regardless of what you are saying. It is, in a sense, your reason for being on the scene. We know that in a play, especially a good play, as in life, one does not always mean exactly what one says. Of course it is perfectly possible that you *can* mean exactly what you say: one character may say to another, "I love you," and that may be exactly what is meant and all that is meant: that *I*, this man, *love you*, this girl. . . . But it is also possible that something quite different is intended by those words. You might hear one character *sneer* the words, "I love you." It's perfectly clear that he is trying to let the other one know he *despises* her, yet he's using the very same words. His intention, therefore is quite different this time. . . . The reading of the words, "I love you," is only part of acting: it is *what you wish to convey* with those words that is important. Now this process of intention goes on not only when you are speaking; it is present all the time, whether you are speaking, listening, or standing alone on the stage, thinking.
>
> —Robert Lewis, *Madness—or Method*
> (New York: Samuel French, 1958): 30.

The objective or action is the character's intended outcome, and *it must be stated as a desire or wish*, with an active verb in the infinitive form: "I want to escape from this madhouse," "I want to persuade my friend to go with me to the grave," "I want to persuade my friend to help me assassinate Caesar," "I want to get an A in English," "I want to make it through the night." Once you have found the objective for a character, furthermore, it is useful to look for the *obstacles* which that character must try to overcome in order to achieve her intentions. These obstacles, of course, are frequently the objectives of one or more of the other characters—so another benefit of analyzing the objectives of all the characters in a given scene is that it helps you discover how the scene itself emerges from the tensions between their actions. And articulating these actions will lead you to think about both the units and the subtext.

Unit / Beat

When trying to learn a part, the actor needs a manageable unit: act and scene are too large to be useful at first, while the line (for example, a line of verse or a sentence in prose) is (usually) too small. What the actor needs is a manageable unit within the scene upon which to focus attention. In conjunction with the objective or action, this is what the concept of the unit or beat provides.

> A [unit or] beat is simply the distance from the beginning to the end of an action. A beat may be as short as a pause, a look, a gesture, or it can remain unchanged through pages of dialogue. A new beat begins when something occurs to change the direction of a scene. Most commonly, a change in beat occurs when one character's action [objective] is confronted with the conflicting action [objective] of another character, and an adjustment must be made.
>
> —MARY DEVINE AND CONSTANCE CLARK,
> "The Stanislavski System as a Tool for
> Teaching Dramatic Literature,"
> *College English* 38 (1976): 17.

Breaking a scene into units allows you to chart it, both for the individual characters and for the ensemble. And it is another tool to help you enumerate and clarify the actions or objectives of the characters (as well as the adjustments and key activities they perform). Using these two concepts, you can arrive at a much more detailed grasp of three questions that we can ask about any of the characters: "What does she do?" "Why does she do it?" and "How does she do it?" You will also begin to develop a much clearer grasp of the interplay *between* the characters, and hence a much richer grasp of the *dynamics* of the scene as a whole.

Subtext

The simplest definition of the subtext is that it is the unspoken but inferable thoughts of a character. The concept of the subtext follows directly from the nature of the objective as defined above. People in life and characters in drama do not explicitly state all their objectives, nor do they articulate all the thinking that occurs as they choose their objectives and the means by which they will achieve them. The subtext, then, is "a psychological interlinear translation of the play" as Devine and Clark put it (16), the ongoing stream of thought by which the character makes the choices which issue in the speech and action the audience actually witnesses. The subtext is the moment-by-moment inner dialogue out of which the overt dialogue and action grow.

One way of articulating the founding premise of this model is to say, as Cary Mazer writes, "that an actor plays not a mood or an effect but an action or objective" ("Playing the Action" in *Teaching Shakespeare through Performance* [1999]: 158). Obviously, working with these concepts to transform a role into a character takes intense effort, but as Miriam Gilbert has pointed out, that intense work has a logic of its own and offers some exciting rewards:

> Actors *must* discover what they are saying, and for a number of highly practical reasons: it is much easier to remember lines if you know what they mean; it is much

easier to speak the lines convincingly if you have found connections between them; it is much easier to play a scene with other actors if your lines are genuine responses to what has been said (even an evasion or a silence is a response) rather than merely memorized words. Thus the rehearsal process becomes a time of first finding and then refining the connections among words—one's own words, and those of the other characters on stage. . . . Whatever the motivation, the actor needs to find it so that the lines become character, not just words.

—MIRIAM GILBERT, "Teaching Shakespeare
through Performance," *Shakespeare
Quarterly* 35 (1984): 603.

And this kind of in-depth study of small sections of a playtext will also help us, as students, to possess and be possessed by the play in ways that neither reading nor seeing the play can achieve—and give us extraordinary rewards as well.[2]
ELR 11/03

To help students begin their work of transforming the role of Petruchio, I point out that to articulate an objective usually entails looking at the immediate context the dramatis persona finds himself or herself in. What is Petruchio's situation as he begins this speech? At this point, Baptista and Petruchio have completed bargaining over Katherine's dowry, and suddenly the supposed music tutor enters, reeling, to explain how Katherine has broken the lute over his head. This event is timed so that at the very moment Petruchio is insisting, "I am rough, and woo not like a babe" (II.i.137), Katherine is demonstrating that she does not respond like a babe. In effect, Katherine's act functions as an implicit challenge to his claims and elicits an important performance choice in Petruchio's response to this violence: "Now by the world, it is a lusty wench! / I love her ten times more than e'er I did" (160–161). One question to ask is *how* he speaks the lines, and I suggest two primary decisions the actor playing Petruchio must make: first, how does he respond to the fact of what Katherine has done, and second, is that response modified in any way by his need to maintain a particular image of himself in front of the others? While he can mean that this evidence of Katherine's tempestuous nature makes her an exciting challenge, he can also be startled to discover that he must confront a woman whose defiant energy is much more than he bargained for, so that he may even show a moment's doubt as to whether he can succeed.

After ten minutes, we begin discussion. What is Petruchio's objective? "He needs to think about Katherine!" I remind students that they need to state objectives in the first person: "I need to think about Katherine." Does this meet the definition of an objective? Not yet, because the speaker has not decided to do anything. But we soon get sharper objectives: "I need to think about what I know about Katherine in order to decide how I will meet her!" We experiment with refined phrasings: "To plan the encounter, to set up my moves, to prepare myself for a battle." And finally they offer on-target formulations such as "To prepare a plan of action for dealing with the moves that I anticipate Katherine may make." Next, we share ways of dividing the speech into units and of inferring the subtext connecting those units. Some students mark a unit with every "Say" and "If" clause, while others see clusters and offer divisions such as this:

> *Pet.* I pray you do. I'll attend her here,
> And woo her with some spirit when she comes.
>
> Say that she rail, why then I'll tell her plain
> She sings as sweetly as a nightingale;
> Say that she frown, I'll say she looks as clear
> As morning roses newly wash'd with dew;
> Say she be mute, and will not speak a word,
> Then I'll commend her volubility,
> And say she uttereth piercing eloquence;
>
> If she do bid me pack, I'll give her thanks,
> As though she bid me stay by her a week;
> If she deny to wed, I'll crave the day
> When I shall ask the banes, and when be married.
>
> But here she comes, and now, Petruchio, speak. (II.i.168–181)

In the first two lines Petruchio not only bids farewell to those exiting from the scene but also states his objective, and we can ask what is the subtext that gets him from "And woo her with some spirit when she comes" to "Say that she rail, why then I'll tell her plain." The answer seems to be that he must move from announcing his intention to asking himself, "But given what I already know about her, and especially this last bit of evidence from smashing the lute, it may not be an easy task! Simply being a courtly gentleman won't work, so *how* am I going to woo her?"

In the second unit he moves from asking "How?" to devising specific tactics. In fact, his three examples are all instances of the same principle: "If she does some negative action, X–, I will say it reveals the contrary positive attribute, X+." We can ask what plan seems to lie behind the tactics he chooses. "He decides to confuse her because he realizes she is too strong for him to directly overpower her—he has to throw her off balance!" In fact, we can trace a more precise pattern in this second unit: as he goes from "rail" to "frown" to "mute," Petruchio moves from imagining a Katherine who at least responds verbally to one whose response is nonverbal rejection and then to one whose response is complete silence—each of which offers less and less chance for him to engage in any wooing at all. Thus we can discern the transition that at once separates and connects the second and third units: "What if these first three moves fail? What if she attempts to put an end to all wooing? What if she just laughs and tells me to get lost?" Petruchio's answer, in the "supposes" of the third unit, is to extend the principle of deliberate reversal, shifting from (mis)describing Katherine's attributes to (mis)understanding her rejections of his whole enterprise.

Finally, as he sees Katherine, he shifts from planning to action. What is he doing in the last line? "He speaks to himself in the third person because he is getting himself psyched up for the encounter." Even more specifically, he is commanding himself to seize the initiative so he can preempt whatever move Katherine may have prepared for their encounter.

If you hold performances, students will begin to see how the design of the role offers an array of potential Petruchios, as well as how this type of detailed exploration enables the actor to project a very specific Petruchio. Performances also allow you to introduce the crucial issue of choosing between the two basic forms of address, to himself and to the audience, which confront an actor delivering a soliloquy.

After the analysis and any performances, we move into the question "What does this soliloquy do?" Within the world of the play, the soliloquy functions representationally as a moment in which the character reveals something of himself. It is a moment when the performer makes a crucial choice about whether his particular Petruchio is simply proceeding as he has begun or else taking off or putting on a mask. In one class, while some students suggested, "He takes off his face, the face he is using with others," some students asked, "Or does he put on a face at the end of the speech?"

Discussing this issue moves us to consider what the soliloquy does in the presentational dimension. Most obviously, it opens a gap between Petruchio and the other characters, putting us one up on the other characters in general and Katherine in particular. Insofar as Petruchio is sharing a secret with us, the implied intimacy invites us to reciprocate by sharing his point of view. By having Petruchio tell us *what* he is going to do, furthermore, Shakespeare frees us to concentrate our attention on two other aspects of the wooing, namely, *how* Katherine responds as she tries to figure out what this man is up to, and *how successful* Petruchio is in carrying out his original plan.

Yet this soliloquy will make our response more complex, especially in the gender-specific terms established by the play's title. For any of the women and men who do not endorse the normative premises the title seems to invoke, this speech will force them to share the consciousness of the would-be tamer at the very moment they are likely to be resisting his point of view. At the same time, they will be watching Katherine with whatever qualifications her earlier treatment of Bianca may have created in their initial sympathy with the "shrew."

At this point, I ask for another short piece of writing, beginning "One thing that is becoming clear to me about how to do an actor-based analysis of a role is —." This is followed by a second entry, beginning "One result of doing this type of analysis will be —." In discussion I focus on what students are learning about the concepts and practices, and on difficulties they have experienced in using these concepts. As we talk, they also begin to identify what cues in the speech itself most helped them perform the analysis so that they can see how the speeches that constitute a role are written not only by Shakespeare the dramatist but also by the figure Ann Pasternak Slater suggests we recognize as "Shakespeare the director." (See especially Slater's first chapter, "Action and Expression.")

Petruchio and Katherine: Working with Two Roles

To help students master this process of transforming a role into a character, we repeat the activity, this time working with two roles. While the concepts and basic practices remain the same, the addition of a second role changes the process, just as the entrance of a second person into a scene changes that reality.

Once more, the first task is to analyze the design of this segment of text by analyzing the speeches of the two roles, but now students must deal with the design of the scene created by the interplay between the roles. First, with the entrance of a second person, we encounter the fundamental reality of conflicting objectives and the way a clash can force each of the dramatis personae to modify his or her objective. Second, the functions of the subtext become more diverse as each speaker makes choices under the pressure of the other's presence. Third, marking the units will also be more difficult since the units now are defined by the interaction between the characters, and that interaction is in part a contest to see who will control the action. Therefore students will confront three ways of dividing the scene: from Katherine's point of view; from Petruchio's point of view; or from the point of view of the scenic form, in which the units may not coincide with the units as seen from the point of view of a specific role.

If you have the time, it is worthwhile to have each partner rehearse both roles. Students will grasp how the scene looks from the two points of view and more easily perceive how the scene looks in terms of its form. This move also raises issues of gender and may prompt some dyads to perform with a man playing Katherine and a woman playing Petruchio.

Since we have studied Petruchio's trajectory and his state of mind at the moment this phase begins, we now do the same for Katherine. Again, discussion helps students start to formulate an objective for Katherine, a task made more difficult by the absence of a soliloquy. We move from the moments of Katherine's existence we have seen to the life implied in those moments as I ask, "What have we witnessed in the previous scenes that lets us infer her point of view and the pressures she is responding to?"

First, Katherine has heard her father's plan. On the one hand, Baptista is using his power to ensure that Katherine will be married. On the other hand, Katherine recognizes that because of her dowry she will be sought as a wife in spite of her reputation as a shrew. Katherine is thus placed in a situation in which being seen as an undesirable shrew gives her a certain power: she can thwart her father's plan and deny her sister and her sister's suitors the satisfaction they seek. But exercising that power has its price.

During this scene, Katherine has moved through a sequence of striking encounters: she has attacked Bianca to find out which suitor her sister favors; she has been caught and chided by her father; and she has vented her fury by breaking a lute over the head of a tutor. We can imagine that when she enters, Katherine is enraged about her father's plan and her sister's surplus of suitors; that she is frustrated by Baptista's favoritism, Bianca's popularity, and the mockery of those wooing her sister; and that while she may have found satisfaction in the lute smashing, it may also have left her seeking further outlets for that rage. Overall, she has been through a sequence of events in which her apparent preference for confrontation has been thwarted in a number of ways. Now she finds herself sent out to meet a man whom she has either explicitly been told or must implicitly expect will present himself as a suitor.

This last point raises a crucial question—which students may realize they missed in reading the scene—namely, "What has Baptista told Katherine?" Has he told her of the marriage he has arranged with Petruchio? Or has he told her that she has a suitor? Or has he simply told her that she is to meet a man named Petruchio, so that she has assumed this man must be a suitor?

Interestingly, the text does not answer this question. Of course, if Katherine does know of the tentative bargain, she may be curious and excited, but she also may be infuriated at being consulted after the fact. To formulate an objective, we must make a decision about how much Katherine knows and, even more important, how she feels about what she knows.

As we watch students' performances, some of which are summarized in the following section, we begin to see how the scene actually moves and to focus once again on how the actors, unlike readers, confront inescapable physical decisions. This scene is a particularly vivid instance because it mandates that Katherine strike Petruchio and that Petruchio prevent her exit ("Let me go," II.i.241). The most vivid demonstration of this point comes in those performances in which, despite the fact that the *Riverside* text includes the Folio's direction "She strikes him," the actors do not realize, or realize only when they are onstage, that Katherine must at least swing at Petruchio. But even if every performance includes Katherine's lashing out, the problem is still demonstrated because some pairs simply are not willing to lash out in any realistic, forceful manner. They are hesitant for good reason, of course, since they do not know how to stage a slap with apparent violence but actual safety; if you know such maneuvers, you may want to teach them. Indeed, the first performance in which Katherine does make solid contact usually produces a gasp. One of the simplest but most essential points this scene demonstrates is that the theater entails physical danger in a way that reading does not.

The scene is incarnational in another sense, of course, for it is highly carnal, and as students both rehearse and perform, you will hear the nervous, suppressed laughter that usually arises when dealing with sexuality in the classroom. So we must begin to look at the larger issue of sexuality in this play, as well as the specific issue, already present in Sly's encounter with his "lady," of Shakespeare's prominent use of bawdy language.

Six Performances

1. Katherine = Rosaleen, Petruchio = Brenda
In this performance, the sexual banter was emphasized, espe-

cially in tone and expression, until Katherine became really of-
fended, her face and posture clearly expressing shock and outrage as she tried to leave. When Petruchio blocked her path, this
further outrage frightened Katherine enough to cause her to strike
him. The class felt that in this staging Petruchio was in control,
that Katherine spoke with him only because her father had ordered her to (a point inferred from her initially submissive manner), that Petruchio's jokes went too far, and that he knew he was
going too far and did so as a means of increasing his control.

2. Katherine = Marian, Petruchio = Dennis

This Katherine was more an equal, and Petruchio's initial attack
sparked her retaliation; the escalation was mutual rather than
one-sided. This was a pair like Beatrice and Benedick, two wit-
loving people looking for a worthy partner to play the game.
This Katherine turned her back on Petruchio, who grabbed her
shoulder and thereby provoked the slap, which was delivered
with an energy to match his own. Petruchio, not Katherine, made
the first physical contact. This time the question we were impelled to ask was "Is their sexual banter an expression of sexual
attraction?" It was hard to tell who started the bawdiness and
most spectators felt it was "in the air." It seemed that this
Katherine slapped Petruchio because for once a man was standing up to her; slapping him was not so much a move to escape as
the result of her surprise that she could be challenged or perhaps
beaten at her own game. This meant that while the slap was a
way of topping him, it was also a tacit confession of failure, since
she had run out of verbal comebacks. This second performance
thus raised the question "If this is a competition between two
game players, how do they assess the outcome of their first encounter? And how do we like the outcome?"

3. Katherine = Jana, Petruchio = Ann

This performance emphasized the bawdiness, relished by both
participants and played with high energy. Katherine was played
by the much larger of the two women, and this size difference
either made Petruchio seem bolder or emphasized Katherine's
restraint. There was no physical violence.

4. Katherine = Nancy, Petruchio = Greg

This was a much tenser, more reserved Katherine, warier, angrier, and very physical, who slugged Petruchio so hard on the shoulder that she drew a mixture of gasps and laughter. This Katherine would continue to fight back, so Petruchio was in for a long, difficult contest in which his success was not assured.

5. Katherine = Stephanie, Petruchio = Linda

This was a lively performance by two ebullient people. Katherine in particular seemed intensely engaged, thinking through her responses, dueling seriously with this man. The stakes felt high, and the language seemed alive with nuances. The slap was awkward, and Petruchio held Kate, but a bit late. The full engagement of Katherine and the underplayed violence made the shift in power seem less emphatic: these two seemed more equal, the scene more comic.

6. Katherine = Ken, Petruchio = Samara

This performance surprised us by the gender reversal, emphasized by the fact that Ken is very solid and well muscled, while Samara is slender and slightly built. This Petruchio stressed the repeated "Kate"s and provoked real sneers from Katherine, who had a deprecating tone. Although they projected a sense that they could really offend each other and might easily come to hate each other, a peculiar sense of intimacy was created by the fact that they sat side by side on the desk, Petruchio sliding toward Katherine and Katherine sliding away but not jumping off or fleeing. Thus there seemed a discrepancy between the verbal and the physical dimensions of the action, a discrepancy that suggested how very complex the negotiation of their marriage would be.

Exploring the Alternate Productions and Basic Design

While there are a number of ways to begin unpacking these performances, I find the most direct way is to ask, "Why does Katherine strike Petruchio?" This action, after all, is a turning point, and the question opens up discussion of everything leading up to this moment as well as of how the moment shapes what follows. Asking this question about each performance impels us to examine how the language operates to direct the complex dance that begins here. During the discussion, I keep asking students to articulate the key choices the script offers for each role. Some key choices can be framed in the following questions:

1. What is Katherine's immediate response to Petruchio?

2. How does the battle over her name function?

3. How do they negotiate the physical distance between them?

4. In the duel leading up to the slap, what are the phases through which the pair moves? And how does each use puns as a weapon?

5. How does Katherine strike Petruchio, and how does he respond?

6. What is Petruchio doing when he says, "I swear I'll cuff you, if you strike again"?

7. Why is Katherine silent during Petruchio's two long speeches? Is it because she is left speechless? Or is Petruchio somehow stopping her?

8. How does Katherine respond to Petruchio's announcement that her father has agreed to a marriage between them?

The first three questions focus on the beginning, the next three on the middle, and the last two on the end of this part of the scene. Each cluster helps open up the complex ways in which the language functions not only as speech but also as a cue to invent the nonverbal action that constitutes part of this wooing. They also help us explore the interplay between dialogue and action.

The first cluster focuses on some of the specifics through which the collision of Katherine and Petruchio is played out in performance. You are asking students, "How do Katherine's and Petrucio's use of interpersonal distance and the battle over Katherine's name establish the initial conditions of a relationship?" The point is that Shakespeare's design focuses on fundamental aspects of a relation that people must negotiate when they meet: "How will we name each other?" and "What physical distance will we establish to reflect our understanding of the relation between us?" These questions are particularly urgent when one person sets out to woo another, because naming and controlling distance are the means of establishing or forestalling intimacy.

You might ask one pair to reenact their performance in slow motion while you and the class ask further questions. What happens as Petruchio refuses to accept Katherine's preferred version of her own name, even though the right to decide the form of our name others will use is one of the most basic forms of self-definition between equals? How does Katherine respond to Petruchio's use of a form that implies an intimacy she has not granted? What happens when he says, "You lie, in faith, for you are call'd plain Kate?" Certainly as readers and even as performers, students tend to ignore what a truly extraordinary act it is to say, "*You lie*," to someone less than a minute after meeting him or her. Furthermore, in terms of the play's focus on gender and gender roles, it is worth pointing out that in the original context, if Petruchio called a man of equal rank a liar, this insult—"the lie direct"— would create a situation in which the other man would have no choice but to challenge Petruchio to a duel. Once you recognize this fact, Katherine's act of slapping Petruchio looks less startling, since being called a liar may have intensified Katherine's already aroused combativeness.

The middle cluster focuses on the battle leading up to the slap, and here you are probing two issues: (1) how does the language, especially the use of sexual puns, delineate the shifts in control between Katherine and Petruchio? and (2) how do the two protagonists shift between the verbal and the physical dimensions of their contest? In fact, these questions continue the work of the first cluster insofar as the issue of naming becomes the issue of naming each other sexually, and insofar as the issue of physical proximity becomes the issue of physical contact.

In slow-motion replay, you can begin to delineate more explicitly and precisely these complex and rapid shifts, asking students to become more aware of the ways in which, despite Petruchio's framing of the scene, Katherine seems to gain control in the verbal duel. Does Petruchio shift from verbal to physical attack with "come sit on me" because he recognizes he is getting nowhere with (im)pure wit? Again, you can focus on a single phrase to raise the magnification of your questions: "What happens when she says 'and so farewell,' leaving Petruchio to face the moment he imagined in 'If she do bid me pack'? How do they get from this to the stage direction *She strikes him*? and to 'I swear I'll cuff you, if you strike again'?" You can also ask, "Does Katherine surprise herself, or did she know what she would do? How long a pause is there after the slap? What registers for each of them and for us in that pause?"

The third cluster focuses on the puzzle—a puzzle that will recur in all but the last scene in which she appears—of why Katherine remains silent during Petruchio's two long speeches. Is he, as in some stagings, covering her mouth? How does she deliver the line "Where did you study all this goodly speech?" (262)? How does she respond to his announcement that "your father hath consented / That you shall be my wife"? (269–270). Why does she not rebel more when her father reappears? How do the others respond? In particular, how forceful is her "I'll see thee hang'd on Sunday first" (298)? Certainly, Gremio and Tranio take her remark seriously, the latter's "Nay then good night our part" (301) indicating that he fears he will never be able to woo Bianca.

I ask students to begin recording the discoveries they have made about the process of moving from role to character and the range of possible performances of this scene. This is a rewarding moment as they seek to capture the excitement generated by the different performances, the surprising nature of some of the inventions, and the further development of their ability to enact this way of reading a script. Part of the power of performance, it seems to me, is precisely that the act of embodying the script naturally leads back to writing that attempts to record and extend the acts of discovery students have made as performers, and the way that recording these acts, in turn, helps students become positively addicted to further exploration of the text.

Katherine's Choices in Act IV, Scene v

The idea of "coverage," as Miriam Gilbert ("Teaching Shakespeare 602–3) has convincingly argued, has always been an illusion when teaching a Shakespeare play; even teachers using a purely literary approach to plays have always had to slight scenes, characters, themes, and images, and of course they have largely or wholly ignored the reality of performance. On the other hand, as Gilbert admits, performance approaches are time intensive: you create detailed exploration at the cost of even less coverage. From my own experience of teaching a ten-week course on the Quarto and Folio texts of *King Lear*, I would add that even when you spend an entire term on a single play, this deep immersion still tends to leave students vividly aware of what you have not managed to cover. Perhaps we had better recognize not only that coverage is an illusion but also that part of the greatness of these plays, as has often been suggested, is that they cannot be exhausted by any reading, even as their potential cannot be realized by any single performance. Given the inescapable need to select how and where you become immersed, I do not present here detailed activities for exploration of acts III and IV. But from my perspective, there is one scene the class must deal with, and that is act IV, scene v—what is sometimes called "the sun/moon" scene—in which Katherine finally yields, in some fashion, to Petruchio's demands. This scene is another of the powerful conversion scenes that Jones describes as a prominent aspect of Shakespeare's dramaturgy.

To deal with this scene, the class must have at least a basic grasp of what happens in act IV, scene iii, the previous scene between Katherine and Petruchio. At a minimum, I ask students to do some writing on act IV, scene iii that allows them to continue working with the questions used by actors.

> (1) In this writing, please articulate Katherine's situation as the scene begins. Again, do this as an actor might in working with the role. (2) Analyze Katherine's speech at the beginning of act IV, scene iii in order to learn how Katherine herself understands her situation and how she construes the action that Petruchio defines as "taming" her. (3) Next, please reread act IV, scene iii as a whole and imagine possible stagings, focusing on the different ways Katherine's role might be transformed into the character on stage: what range of performances does the role make possible? (4) Where is Katherine at the end of the scene? How does she understand what happened to the clothes ordered for her? How does she understand Petruchio's apparently irrational attempt to control what time it is?

The key point is to enable students to recognize the dilemma Katherine faces. She wants her first visit as a new bride to her family and her city to be a triumphant return in order to show them how they have misapprehended her all along. And she wants to defeat Petruchio. But defeating Petruchio apparently means either not returning home or returning home in disharmony, hence proving accurate her family's vision of her and of her marriage, thereby allowing them to validate their mocking definition of her as a shrew. Alternatively, she can return in triumph, but only, apparently, by giving in to Petruchio and appearing "tamed"— an act of submission that, as she says in this scene, reduces her to a "puppet." Formulating Katherine's dilemma is a necessary step for working with act IV, scene v.

In exploring this scene, we use all four of the primary concepts: action, scene and scenic form, role, and character. First of all, what Petruchio and Katherine *do* in this scene demands a careful analysis in order to articulate fully the complex Action$_2$ they perform, especially since so much of that action is not only unspoken but also obviously depends on complex inferences. Second, this complex, subtextual, and nonverbal action means that the *form of the scene*, in terms of the unfolding of the different phases, also must be worked out with some care. And third, the roles at this point demand acute attention to the potentials in the scripted language, even as they also offer particularly rich alternative possible performances for creating quite different (even incompatible) versions of Petruchio and Katherine.

Here is the assignment, which may be given at the end of the previous class, that provides the starting point for our work on this complex scene:

> In preparation for the next class, please read over act IV, scene v and do the following: (1) Analyze the form of the scene, delineating the phases and the tensions between the objectives of Katherine and Petruchio. (2) Focus especially on the first phase(s), the "sun/ moon" phase between Katherine and Petruchio, and the "mistaking" of Vincentio. How do you understand what is going on here? (3) List what you think are the critical points in this segment, and define some of the key alternate choices that the roles offer to the actors playing Katherine, Petruchio, and Hortensio. (4) Imagine several contrasting performances—or if you can work with other members of the class, try rehearsing different performances.

If you do not make this assignment or if you want to initiate this activity in class, you can simply ask for four volunteers to read the scene through. In that case, you might want to stop just before the entrance of Vincentio, when the design (re)connects the two plots. Reading will let the class begin to hear the language and discover the challenges. After that, students can move into groups of four to begin preparing performances.

As always, the initiating question is the one Miriam Gilbert (Hodgdon, "Making Changes") has taught us to ask, namely, "What is going on here?" The central challenge to answering the question is that we must make explicit what is left implicit, because the core of whatever happens in this scene occurs in the tacit communication, or failure of communication, between Petruchio and Katherine. Indeed, this is one scene that absolutely requires readers to stretch their ability to invent performances, since so much of the action is played out through the medium of the actor's body through gesture, business, and blocking (to return to Seltzer's ["Actors"] categories). In Kenneth Burke's great phrase, this negotiation takes place as the dancing of attitudes (*Philosophy* 9), even if one of these attitudes may seem to be a refusal to join the dance.

Here is the first phase in the complex action by which Petruchio and Katherine (re)negotiate some element(s) of their marriage—and I remind students to consider how the words *sun* and *son* will function when they are heard rather than read:

> *Pet.* Come on a' God's name, once more toward our father's.
> Good Lord, how bright and goodly shines the moon!
> *Kath.* The moon! the sun—it is not moonlight now.
> *Pet.* I say it is the moon that shines so bright.
> *Kath.* I know it is the sun that shines so bright.
> *Pet.* Now by my mother's son, and that's myself,
> It shall be moon, or star, or what I list,
> Or ere I journey to your father's house.—
> Go on, and fetch the horses back again.—
> Evermore cross'd and cross'd, nothing but cross'd!
> *Hor.* Say as he says, or we shall never go.
> *Kath.* Forward, I pray, since we have come so far,
> And be it moon, or sun, or what you please;
> And if you please to call it a rush-candle,
> Henceforth I vow it shall be so for me.

> *Pet.* I say it is the moon.
> *Kath.*   I know it is the moon.
> *Pet.* Nay then you lie; it is the blessed sun.
> *Kath.* Then God be blest, it [is] the blessed sun,
> But sun it is not, when you say it is not;
> And the moon changes even as your mind.
> What you will have it nam'd, even that it is,
> And so it shall be so for Katherine.
> *Hor.* Petruchio, go thy ways, the field is won.
> *Pet.* Well, forward, forward, thus the bowl should run,
> And not unluckily against the bias.
> But soft, company is coming here. (IV.v.1–26)

As the groups work on their scenes, or as the class works through the design and performance possibilities, you can have them list the more specific formulations of the question "What is going on here?" that the scene elicits. Among these questions, I find that three best initiate exploration of the scene. One is to ask why Petruchio repeats his line "I say it is the moon." Another is to ask a question Katherine herself must confront, namely, why doesn't her first submission work? A third is to start with Hortensio's plea to Katherine, for the fact that he intervenes as well as how he intervenes makes it clear that Hortensio believes the couple has reached a complete impasse:

> *Hor.* Say as he says, or we shall never go.
> *Kath.* Forward, I pray, since we have come so far,
> And be it moon, or sun, or what you please;
> And if you please to call it a rush-candle,
> Henceforth I vow it shall be so for me.
> *Pet.* I say it is the moon.
> *Kath.*   I know it is the moon.

Even though Katherine apparently listens to Hortensio's exhortation, even though she does indeed seem to "say as he says," and even though Katherine, Hortensio, perhaps the servants, and even some spectators expect him to proceed, Petruchio does *not* move forward. Instead, he repeats the phrase with which he initiated this confrontation; so why does he not move? Once launched into answering these questions, students will grapple with the rich potentials of this scene.

Petruchio's Last Play and Katherine's Last Act (V.ii)

Just as I want students to explore what the beginning of a play does, so also I want them to explore what the ending does. In terms of the model offered here, we can begin to investigate *what* the ending does by looking at *how* the ending does what it does. If you look at how *The Taming of the Shrew* ends, you will see that it offers two endings and points toward a third. The first ending occurs in act V, scene i with the completion of the intrigue plot. The second ending occurs in act V, scene ii with the wager on the obedience of the wives, and it functions as a thematic ending, prompting us to articulate a new perspective on the action as a whole. The third ending is the one that would occur if the Sly plot were completed—as it is completed in the non-Shakespearean text of *The Taming of a Shrew* (Bullough 108). (This analysis of the separate plot and theme endings also offers a prototype for analyzing the design of other plays such as *A Midsummer Night's Dream*, in which the entire fifth act is a thematic ending that comes after all the plots have been completed in the fourth act, and in which there are also three consecutive, distinct endings.) Another way to make this point is to say that the final scene is not strictly necessary to complete the plot. But a wager scene is an integral part of the folk motif on which the taming plot is based, and in shaping this scene the dramatist reaps the reward for having taken the risk of bringing together the two quite different stories centering on Baptista's two daughters. For through the direct interaction initiated by the wager, the playwright prompts the spectators to articulate a vision encompassing the action as a whole, including the action in the plot to transform Christopher Sly. Indeed, the completion of his design actually seems to have stimulated Shakespeare to go past the wager itself, inventing the new actions that culminate in what we might call Katherine's Homily on Obedience, that performance that constitutes nearly one-quarter of the final scene and contains over one-fifth of Katherine's lines in the entire play.

That is, while the wager comes from the basic folktale that is the origin of the shrew plot, Shakespeare does not close the play with the triumph of Katherine's return. In fact, in terms of scenic form, what is striking here is the nature of the structured occasion Shakespeare creates. He shapes a design in which, after the reversal that completes the wager, there are three more phases as Petruchio issues three further commands to Katherine, instructing her to (1) "fetch" the other wives; (2) throw down and step on her cap; and (3) deliver a homily on obedience to the two other wives. We see the final instance in which Petruchio frames a scene, but this time the scene is one in which Katherine may well be the star performer, not the unwitting object—although much depends on the specific performance. The scene thus becomes both *Petruchio's last play* and *Katherine's last act*. While you can develop activities for each segment, I present only an activity for the last segment here.

Katherine's Last Act: A Homily on Obedience

When we come to the third of these challenging commands, students offer strong initial responses. In one class, when I asked, "How should Katherine's speech be played?," Mary answered, "Not at all!" For Mary the speech revealed the inescapable power struggle in an all-or-nothing situation that Katherine confronted and was defeated by—defeated by the disturbing use of torturelike conditions: loss of sleep, starvation, and the threat of physical violence. Against this position, other students offered other arguments. Judy, for example, answered by saying, "Katherine started the violence; she was violent to everyone else—her sister, her father, the tutor, Petruchio—and all that happened was that she met someone willing to be violent in return. She meets an image of herself, a man who says, 'Hit me again and I'll hit you back!'" Mary replied by pointing out that there can be a contrast in how the violence is staged: Katherine's can be gentle, Petruchio's extreme; he can seem genuinely dangerous, while she is violent only from weakness.

A response as vehement as Mary's, which demonstrates that Shakespeare's plays can be reviled as well as revered, can serve as a cue to share Michael Billington's review of the Royal Shakespeare Company's production of the play as directed by Michael Bogdanov, which opened in May 1978. Bogdanov's production became instantly famous for having Jonathan Pryce's Christopher Sly emerge from the audience and seem to cause an onstage riot in which the set apparently collapsed; for having Pryce's Sly become Petruchio; and for having Petruchio use a level of violence so extreme that when Katherine gave her speech on obedience even Petruchio himself seemed repulsed by what he had wrought. Billington concluded his review by asserting:

> There is, however, a larger question at stake than the merits or otherwise of this particular production. It is whether there is any reason to revive a play that seems totally offensive to our age and our society. My own feeling is that it should be put back firmly and squarely on the shelf. (124)

Interestingly enough, in his foreword (dated January 1993) to the volume in which he reprinted this review, Billington conducted an internal debate "about the merits of the overnight versus the morning-after review" in which he also added a second thought about his response to *The Taming of the Shrew* and several other plays:

> More seriously, the overnight reaction of critics to plays such as *Waiting for Godot, The Birthday Party, Saved,* and *Serjeant Musgrave's Dance* doesn't exactly encourage one's faith in the wisdom of instant judgement. Looking through my own work, I pause to reflect on my call to banish *The Taming of the Shrew* from the British stage or my brutal put-down of Pinter's *Betrayal* on its first appearance. I include these pieces because they are an honest record of how I felt at the time; but the problem with one night stands is that things often look different by the sober light of dawn. (xii–xiii)

Especially when sharpened by reading Billington's review and reflection, discussion will produce a spectrum of images of how students are imagining the speech being staged. At one end, just short of "Not at all," students will suggest a Katherine who displays resistance and even hatred in submission; or a mixture of love and hate; or what might be called submission-with-spirit. Others will imagine a couple that projects the sense of sharing a secret, playing a game with the world, as they did with Vincentio earlier. Toward the other end of the spectrum there will be suggestions that Katherine can be played to indicate the covert dominance of a woman fooling Petruchio with the appearance of obedience. It is worth pointing out that such performances will suggest a surprising shared identity between Katherine and Bianca: Bianca, after all, may be seen and played as someone who hides her "shrewish" spirit before marriage, reveals it after marriage, hence disappoints her husband, and thus establishes conflict; Katherine is openly shrewish before marriage, lets Petruchio think he has tamed her, and hence has him thinking that she is now obedient—as obedient as Bianca appeared to Lucentio when he first set eyes on her. This last connection reminds us that we will evaluate the marriage of Katherine and Petruchio in part based on how their marriage looks compared to other marriages presented.

Exploring Katherine's Objectives

At this point, we return to the steps by which we can explore a role in order to create a character. We start with analysis of the speech using the objective, the unit, and the subtext. To stimulate thinking about what objective(s) Katherine might propose for herself, we need to think about both the immediate and the wider contexts. The immediate context is Petruchio's command:

> *Pet.* Katherine, I charge thee tell these headstrong women
> What duty they do owe their lords and husbands.
> *Wid.* Come, come, you're mocking; we will have no telling.
> *Pet.* Come on, I say, and first begin with her.
> *Wid.* She shall not.
> *Pet.* I say she shall, and first begin with her. (V.ii.130–135)

How might Katherine respond to this context? Presuming she is not so tamed as to be "broken"—which is, as productions from 1970 onward have demonstrated, a producible interpretation, although one with severe consequences for not only the play but also the spectators—how might she formulate her own purpose even as she sets out to obey and, in some cases, qualify Petruchio's command? Given the dilemma Katherine faced as she set out for Padua, how has her experience on the journey and at the feast led her to resolve or dissolve or intensify that dilemma? Has what has happened at the feast reshaped the dilemma itself?

Katherine must be asking herself what she wants to do not only in terms of Petruchio but also in terms of the other people present. These are people who a few minutes earlier were teasing Petruchio about marrying a shrew, teasing Katherine herself, and attacking her marriage. At the same time, she has just triumphed over these two women, their husbands, and her father. She may well catch the irony that her own obedience has revealed the disobedient, "shrewish" side of the two "good" wives. Furthermore, there is a choice that readers can easily ignore but that tends to be much more obvious in performance, namely, that depending on the timing of her reentry Katherine may have heard that she has helped Petruchio win a very large wager.

When students have formulated an objective for Katherine, divided the speech into units, and articulated subtext, we begin performances. I often start with the speech performed by an isolated Katherine. But either in the course of the first performance or during the second performance, it becomes clear that we need to add the other people to the scene, so six students assume places on stage, and we resume Katherine's speech—and what comes into focus is the question of address. At this point, you have the option of asking students to amplify their analyses of the speech by deciding whom their Katherine is addressing in each unit and where and how she shifts address. Some students, especially those most actively teaching themselves to read dramatically, will already have considered this dimension, but some will not.

Introducing this question here is also a way of modeling the long-term objective of having students become fluent in the different practices. The true challenge, after all, is not in learning the different concepts and practices, but in learning when and how and in what combinations to employ them. As Donald Schön (*Reflective*; *Educating*) has argued at length, there are no rules for acquiring and using this type of tacit knowledge, although it is precisely this type of knowledge that makes someone a skilled performer. Only when students can coordinate such conceptual tools can they produce richer, more integrated explorations of a play. If you want to be more explicit, you can suggest that for each unit students may want to answer four questions: (1) Who is Katherine addressing? (2) What is she saying? (3) What is she doing? (4) Whoever she is directly addressing, how is she also indirectly addressing Petruchio?

One possible division of the speech into units follows, with some key points that emerge in the performance and discussion of each unit. In my comments, I answer the questions just listed, although not necessarily in order.

> *First unit: Probably addressed to the Widow*
> Fie, fie, unknit that threat'ning unkind brow,
> And dart not scornful glances from those eyes,
> To wound thy lord, thy king, thy governor.
> It blots thy beauty, as frosts do bite the meads,
> Confounds thy fame, as whirlwinds shake fair buds,
> And in no sense is meet or amiable. (V.ii.136–141)

Katherine presumably does begin with the Widow, whose expression she seems to be describing in the first two lines. In this rebuke, Katherine establishes the basic premise of patriarchy in Renaissance England, the metaphor that equated the king as head of the nation with the husband/father as head of the family. It was an equation that made the man the king of the household and all other members his subjects. This metaphor also performs the crucial task of naturalizing a culturally created reality, implying that a woman's function is to bloom as a plant, not storm as a tempest. At the same time, the last three lines also afford Katherine a chance for a remarkably personal attack, and the actor has the option of playing them to emphasize the resemblances to some of the attacks Katherine has earlier endured herself. It is also worth pointing out that even if the speech is addressed primarily to the Widow, when Katherine speaks of "thy lord, thy king, thy governor" she has the option of turning to Hortensio and then back to the Widow.

> *Second unit: to Widow, to Widow and Bianca, or to some or all of the men*
> A woman mov'd is like a fountain troubled,
> Muddy, ill-seeming, thick, bereft of beauty,
> And while it is so, none so dry or thirsty
> Will deign to sip, or touch one drop of it. (142–145)

Katherine generalizes as she shifts from "thy" to "A woman," and this shift seems to be a cue for a shift in address: having attacked the Widow with startling directness, she now widens her focus to include Bianca as well. What she adds here is a threat, suggesting that if Bianca behaves as the Widow has been behaving, she too will cause her husband to withdraw from and neglect her. Katherine may be drawing on, if not consciously recalling, recent experience when her own "muddy" and rebellious behavior caused Petruchio to withhold the sustenance she needed. At the same time, it is possible to imagine this segment as addressed to Petruchio; to all three husbands; or, interestingly, to Hortensio and Gremio, who in the first scene so vividly rejected even the idea of wooing Katherine precisely because she was "troubled" or turbulent. If she plays this last option, Katherine would be acknowledging the logic of their complaints, although whether that acknowledgment was straightforward or ironic would still be a question for the performer(s) to decide.

> *Third unit: to both women, perhaps moving between them—or to the husbands?*
> Thy husband is thy lord, thy life, thy keeper,
> Thy head, thy sovereign; one that cares for thee,
> And for thy maintenance; commits his body
> To painful labor, both by sea and land;
> To watch the night in storms, the day in cold,
> Whilst thou li'st warm at home, secure and safe;
> And craves no other tribute at thy hands
> But love, fair looks, and true obedience—
> Too little payment for so great a debt. (146–154)

The primary point here is to make a contrast, stating explicitly the manifold benefits that the lord-husband offers to the wife-subject who is obedient and loving, while seemingly demanding nothing like an equal "labor" from the woman who reaps all the benefits while taking none of the risks. Of course, this formulation ignores the extensive work the wife would do to carry out the enterprise of running a complex household. Katherine thus makes explicit how apparently unequal is the division of obligations and responsibilities, so that the husband as lord is seen as apparently risking all and yet asking little.

The word *debt* provides a cue for an interesting option, namely, that Katherine stresses this word with a significant glance at Petruchio. If she has heard enough to know that her obedience has won at least "a hundred crowns," then she may seize the opportunity to remind Petruchio that it was her act that enriched him. If this seems implausible, here is Ralph Berry's description of the 1981 Stratford Festival of Canada production:

> The suburban bickering of Act V was convincing enough, and the great final speech came over with entire conviction, as why should it not? Naturally, it can be delivered with the irony it asks for. . . . On the other hand, there's no reason why Katherina shouldn't mean every word, in context. The key is that Petruchio has won a bet, and Katherina knows it. . . . The glance that Sharry Flett shot at her groom registered the point fully. (*"Did you? Good for you! And now you can buy me another gown."*) I see no reason why Katherina, alone in Padua, should be untouched by the economic drives sustaining that community. (Bulman 285–86)

The point is not only to become aware of the variety of ways in which Katherine can communicate indirectly with Petruchio but also to recognize that she may wield more power precisely because she is communicating indirectly and thus cannot be directly rebuked.

> *Fourth unit: explicit address to the women, implicit address to the men*
> Such duty as the subject owes the prince,
> Even such a woman oweth to her husband;
> And when she is froward, peevish, sullen, sour,
> And not obedient to his honest will,
> What is she but a foul contending rebel,
> And graceless traitor to her loving lord? (155–160)

Katherine makes the analogy explicit but, more important, works it out in enough detail to also imply the limits on the husband's authority in this patriarchal order. Overtly, she is continuing her attack on the two women as "traitors," but covertly she can be warning Petruchio and the other husbands. In the previous section, she had insisted on "true obedience": here, in a neat correspondence, she insists that what a subject is obedient to is the man's "honest will." In both cases, Katherine can achieve her immediate objective by the stress she places on the crucial adjectives. This qualification can be hinted at first in the opening line of the unit, for "Such duty as the subject owes the prince" can be spoken so as to imply "Such duty and no more": this prepares alert auditors to grasp the implicit equation of the key phrase "his honest will." Some students will suggest, as Mary did, that in fact this argument frees Katherine from obedience since Petruchio has been exercising a *dis*honest will: he has been in disguise the whole time, and in subjecting her to various forms of deprivation he has tyrannically abused his rights. This issue can be a cue for further debate, inviting students to investigate the political theories and realities of gender and gender politics in Elizabethan England as well as contesting views of those theories and realities in modern study. (Christina Luckyj's essay "Historicizing Gender" offers a powerful activity for initiating such an exploration.)

> *Fifth unit: including herself in her address*
> I am asham'd that women are so simple
> To offer war where they should kneel for peace,
> Or seek for rule, supremacy, and sway,
> When they are bound to serve, love, and obey.
> Why are our bodies soft, and weak, and smooth,
> Unapt to toil and trouble in the world,
> But that our soft conditions, and our hearts,
> Should well agree with our external parts? (161–168)

One of the most striking features in this part of the speech is that after addressing her sister and the Widow and speaking of "thy lord" and "thy husband," Katherine now includes herself as one of these shame-causing rebels whose haughty behavior denied the natural order. At the same time, it seems important that she includes herself in this fashion only *after* she has also implied that the man is the woman's "lord" only when his will is "honest," leaving her listeners—and of course those listeners, both on- and offstage, may make quite different inferences—the option to infer that both subjects and women are free to meet a dishonest will with passive resistance. Again, she can be speak-

ing indirectly to Petruchio, confessing her own simplicity in seeking to "rule."

> *Sixth unit: to both women—moving from rebuke to exhortation*
> Come, come, you froward and unable worms!
> My mind hath been as big as one of yours,
> My heart as great, my reason haply more,
> To bandy word for word and frown for frown;
> But now I see our lances are but straws,
> Our strength as weak, our weakness past compare,
> That seeming to be most which we indeed least are. (169–175)

"Come, come" signals a transition not only because it is an exhortation but also because it initiates a move toward the act of at
least verbal submission that will climax the speech. The plural
indicates that this section is addressed to both women, and as
she includes herself Katherine eventually shifts to the inclusive
"our." The mention of "external parts" in unit five is also a cue
for the reintroduction of a sexual dimension. The sexual imagery
becomes more pronounced, and it will be up to actors and directors to decide what Katherine may be using the imagery to do.

Again some of the richness of the speech lies in its qualifications and forms of indirect address. When Katherine says, "My
mind hath been as big as one of yours," we too can recall the
evidence of pride. But when she adds, "My heart as great, my
reason haply more," she adds an interesting distinction. As far as
our experience extends, she can accurately compare her reasons
only with Bianca's, suggesting that her reasons for being so rebellious were in fact "stronger" (*Taming,* Oliver 231) because
Bianca was treated as a favorite child; this was an option realized
by Blaire Chandler's Katherine, who, in the Shakespeare Santa
Cruz production in August 2004, turned and, with some asper-
ity, delivered this half-line to Baptista. Thus, even as she continues the act of submission that stuns and delights her father,
Katherine may find a way to rebuke him, recalling her accusation that not only did he favor Bianca but also that his favoritism
led him to neglect his duty to find a suitable match for Katherine.
And although Baptista may, as was the case with Dominic
Hoffman's performance in the Santa Cruz production, seem
unfazed by his daughter's implicit criticism, the actor can use

expression and gesture to show that Katherine's remark hits home. In fact, through the wager Katherine has been offered and seems to be seizing the opportunity to upstage that favored sister, so that Bianca's experience of being displaced parallels Katherine's experience of being upstaged at her own wedding.

> *Seventh unit: to the women and to Petruchio*
> Then vail your stomachs, for it is no boot,
> And place your hands below your husband's foot;
> In token of which duty, if he please,
> My hand is ready, may it do him ease. (176–179)

As she moves into the conclusion signaled in part by the couplets, Katherine seems prepared to perform a startlingly literal act submission. The first couplet is a direct command to her immediate audience, the other two women, and it seems likely to draw a strong nonverbal response from them (ranging from stunned submission to some form of protest; in the Santa Cruz production, both Bianca and the Widow exited at this point, departing in different directions), even as it is likely to draw strong nonverbal responses from the men. And this gender-divided response will once again bear some complex relation to the gender-divided responses in the audience as well. Thus Katherine's last action is open to a variety of performances, ranging from simple and apparently complete submission to simple and apparently unequivocal warning (for example, she trips up Petruchio), with more complex mixtures possible. And whereas the stage direction in the non-Shakespearean text of *A Shrew* mandates that "*She laies her hand under her husbands feete*" (Bullough 107), there is no such stage direction here, which means that while Katherine must offer to make the gesture, it may not be completed because of a choice either she makes or Petruchio makes.

As we move through cycles of performance and analysis, we refine our sense of the variety of things Katherine can make this speech do and of the variety of things the play does through what Katherine does. That is, this activity encourages students to become aware in very fine detail of the way in which performing the text may also transform the nature of what is said, so that the speech may become something much more than the mere articulation of the official doctrine of patriarchal ideology. While

Katherine delivers this speech on demand from Petruchio and, in a sense, on his authority, it is also the case that she has center stage, with all attention on her. And with the stage hers, she delivers a speech that is not only eloquent but also the longest in the play. Thus, in creating tensions between doctrine and performance so central to the final "taming" action, the play also implicitly raises questions about how the patriarchal order actually operates: as a complex performance can suggest, embodying that theory in individual human lives can produce discrepancies between what the theory says should be and what happens in the carnal world.

Given the complexity of what Katherine may be doing, we also need to be aware of the range of responses open to Petruchio. At one extreme can be the lack of response embodied in the 1978 production directed by Bogdanov, starring Paola Dionisotti as Katherine and Jonathan Pryce as Petruchio:

> Kate's famous speech . . . is delivered in a spiritless, unreal voice and received without much appreciation by the men, and with a smouldering resentment by the women. The main feeling is of shame—and that the systematic deformation of Kate's character (the deformity of submission on top of spite) is being revenged in the weariness and boredom of the men. When Petruchio says "we'll to bed" it sounds as if they have been married for years. It is an interesting and courageous (not to say feminist) way to interpret the play. (Lorna Sage, qtd. in *Taming*, Thompson 22–23)

At the other extreme is the performance imagined by Brian Morris in his Arden edition:

> Petruchio responds to this unsolicited act of love and generosity with one of the most moving and perfect lines in the play, almost as if he is lost for words, taking refuge in action: "Why, there's a wench! Come on, and kiss me, Kate." I believe that any actor striving to represent Petruchio's feelings at this moment in the play should show him as perilously close to tears, tears of pride, and gratitude, and love. (149)

But while you can offer examples of such extreme responses (in the Santa Cruz production, Robertson Dean's Petruchio was indeed moved nearly to tears), either after students' own exploration or before they begin, as a stimulus for invention, the focus usually will be on a middle range of possibilities.

Certainly in Petruchio's first speech there is room for a range of emotion. "Why, there's a wench!" can be delivered to indicate Petruchio's sense of "I knew it all along! I knew I had you all fooled!" if he is thinking of his own certainty as a gambler. Or it can be played to indicate "What a relief! This risky gamble has paid off!" Or he can deliver the line quietly, with greater wonder, to indicate his admiration of Katherine's performance, in which she surpasses anything he had imagined. The key difference, as we work this through, becomes our sense of whether he is saying, "I really can trust my judgment! and trust that I have made her submissive!" or "I really can trust Katherine!" or "I really can trust us as a couple!" or, as in Bogdanov's production, "I am ashamed at how brutally I have coerced this person into self-abasement!" For positive interpretations, he can project a sense that he can stop testing her because he has reached a point where he realizes, "I really can trust that we are a team!"

With the second phrase, "Come on, and kiss me, Kate," we have room for a variety of performances not only of the speech but also of the action that follows; as at the end of the previous scene, much of the impact will depend on how the kiss is performed and on our sense of what sort of passion and affection (if any) that kiss embodies and recalls.

One more issue seems important here, because Petruchio's "Come Kate, we'll to bed" raises an interesting question. Although the point is easily missed, it seems to be the case that the couple has not yet consummated their marriage. The point is made by Ann Thompson in annotating the servant Curtis's statement that Petruchio preaches "continency" (IV.i.182–183) and Petruchio's concluding "Come, Kate, we'll to bed" (V.ii.184):

> The specifically sexual reference here neatly counters the commonplace innuendo of "in her chamber." It is important that the marriage is not actually consummated until after the last scene of the play. (*Taming* 125)

> Given the reference to Petruchio's "sermon on continency" on his wedding night (4.1.154) and his policy of depriving Katherina

of food, sleep and other physical gratifications, we must assume that the marriage is now about to be consummated. (161)

If the characters suggest they are going to make love for the first time, and also convey delight in the prospect, they powerfully reinforce a sense of triumph. However, students for whom any positive ending of the play seems unacceptable, or who want to argue that whatever Shakespeare's original intentions the text of the play is open to subversive performances, can also imagine stagings that convey other responses and create other experiences. This is Petruchio's third request for a kiss and, as with the previous two requests, Katherine can respond in ways that negate as well as fulfill the presumption that such a kiss will signal a harmony between husband and wife. Katherine can refuse to kiss Petruchio (or refuse to kiss him until he performs some further action—say, giving her the money from the wager), or, as is more probable, can kiss him in a manner or location that negates the request, raising real doubts about just how tamed she is. Just as Baptista's initial conditions made Bianca's marriage hostage to Katherine's marriage at the beginning of the play, so here at the end of the play Petruchio's insistence on repeatedly proving his control of his marriage renders him hostage to Katherine's decision about whether and to what degree she will cooperate with his commands.

Reflecting on Newly Rehearsed Practices

Introducing the last activity, which follows our work with each play as a whole, I ask the students to reflect on the concepts and practices we have added to their repertory of ways for reading differently.

A simple in-class move is to begin writing in response to the prompt "One thing that is becoming clear to me about how we read this play is —" or "One new practice that really struck me and that seemed rewarding to me was when we—." As students share their entries, you can keep a running list on the board and prompt others to read their entries by asking, "Who found themselves thinking about another new move or practice?" Obviously the list of new concepts and practices is a review of the work you have done together. This activity works for both the spatial dimension of the play's design and the temporal dimension of the play's performance as an event. The goal is to gain perspective on the new concepts and practices for reading a play's text.

As we complete this review, I sometimes suggest that students think of themselves as creating their own handbooks for reading drama.

> First, please write up one new concept in your own words; provide at least one example from our work together, and add one new example of your own. Second, set an objective for yourself as you begin to work with the next play. You might write, "As I read *Richard III*, I want to concentrate on reading differently by using this particular practice." Or you might think about the fact that you will read the play several times, and say, "When I read this play the first time, I want to concentrate on using concept A, and when I read this play the second time, I want to concentrate on using concept B."

Again, we share these commitments as a means of helping students review the work to date and so that we will be prepared to ask one another how using concept A or B worked in practice.

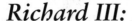

Richard III:

Framing and Reframing Actions

Prologue: New Concepts, Recursive Practices

I have noted that starting with one of the history plays presents problems that are avoided by starting with a comedy, but a history play makes an excellent choice as the second play for the course. *The Tragedy of King Richard the Third*, Shakespeare's early theatrical masterpiece, offers ample opportunities for students to employ the previously introduced concepts and practices in reading a dramatic text as a script, even as it offers rich opportunities to introduce new concepts and practices that will help students read the two languages of a Shakespeare play. It also, of course, compels you to find an effective way to introduce the historical context necessary to help students make sense of the play's retrospective design.

In particular, the play offers a protagonist who acts as an onstage dramatist, numerous soliloquies, a striking use of rhetorical language, and a clear two-part structure that highlights the nature of design in drama even as it amplifies the concept of scenic form. In addition, Richard's performance as a comedian of evil forces students to confront their tendency to oversimplify their responses to dramatic characters, as well as to ignore the way in which moral judgments can be made more complex by dramatic frames.

The activities offered in this chapter introduce these additional concepts while building on the concepts of action, scene, role, and character introduced earlier. After collecting the students' initial responses, we move directly to the challenge of a play that opens with a soliloquy by a villain who woos us as he later woos almost everyone else in his world. By asking "What does the opening soliloquy do?" and by performing the opening scene, students confront the complex relationship that Richard-as-dramatist establishes between himself and the audience even as they confront the complex challenge that Shakespeare sets for that audience as it finds itself invited to enjoy the comic talents of a self-announced villain. In this way, we build directly on our exploration of the beginning of *The Taming of the Shrew*, just as Shakespeare almost certainly learned to create the opening of *Richard III* in part by reflecting on his earlier use of the induction.

In working with the play's famous second scene, we further our study of Shakespeare's language: students first stage the so-called wooing scene between Richard and Anne as a sound-and-movement exercise, without any language, and then answer the question "What does the language do?" This exercise helps them recognize and exploit the complex rhetorical patterns that were a prominent feature in Shakespeare's day but are largely ignored in present-day education.

Looking at the play's opening scenes in detail also provides a perfect cue for introducing the concept of discrepant awareness as a central element in the grammar of theater, and for exploring how the dramatist uses discrepant awareness to create complex ironies that we share with the villain even as we sooner or later reject his moral code. As they perform Richard's encounters with Clarence and Hastings, students begin to rediscover the excitement that must have gripped Shakespeare as he realized the enormous dramaturgic potentials embodied in an actorlike character who showed how histrionic skill could shape history. In the course of our work, students will trace the consistent use of discrepant awareness in acts II and III.

Next, I introduce the terms *framing* and *alignment* to explore how in act IV, scene iv Queen Margaret begins to prompt spectators to reframe the action and realign themselves in relation to the competing frames proposed by the play. Focusing on this scene helps us work with act IV, scene ii, learning about the specific dramaturgic methods through which the play transforms our relation to Richard, closing the original gap and opening a new gap between Richard and the spectators. That is, the class explores how Shakespeare employs a number of subtle but powerful devices to transform our previously established point of view.

I introduce another element of Shakespeare's dramatic language by asking, "What does repetition do?," and students proceed to explore how repetition functions on every level from the largest units of dramatic structure to single words. By looking at how they might stage the scene in which the ghosts appear to Richard and Richmond, they observe how a dramatist weaves a large dramatic design using a specific scenic form, discrepant awareness, and rhetorical patterns of language to compose a powerful whole.

This focus on repetition in turn leads naturally to asking a question that mirrors the question "What does the beginning do?" namely, "What does the ending do?" We approach this question by returning to our exploration of the difference between the naturalistic, representational drama of the proscenium stage and the symbolic, presentational drama of Elizabethan stage, as students imagine and orchestrate various ways to stage the final duel between Richard and Richmond. As they perform this activity, which builds on our work with the ending of *The Taming of the Shrew*, they can learn more about how alternate performances embody alternate stage logics, and how these different endings can complete different potential designs inherent in the play's text. They thus encounter another crucial difference between text and performance, namely, that the text remains open while the performance seeks closure.

Finally, we turn to the issue of genre, examining why the play might be called both a tragedy, as it is in the title, and a history, as it is by its placement in the Folio. The aim here is not to settle this debate but to see what we can learn from it and to lead us to ask the question "What does a genre do?"

A Word about the Recursive Design of the Course

As the class begins a second play, you set in motion a recursive process and also open the door for other types of assignments that I will sketch out here. The process is recursive in the simplest sense—it makes students use the same questions they employed to explore the first play; it does this not only to prompt analysis of the second play but also to help them realize that these questions do work for Shakespeare's plays in general. Students need to rehearse the concepts and practices as soon as possible after beginning to acquire them so that these concepts and practices become second nature. At the same time, you want students to see that if these questions are to yield rich results, students must learn to use them flexibly, adjusting them to the contours of the specific play.

Furthermore, by asking the same questions of several plays you have an opportunity to develop further assignments focused on the parallels in the action of two plays and on the development of Shakespeare's dramaturgy. You might, for example, design an assignment to compare Petruchio's wooing of Katherine with Richard's wooing of Anne. Not only are both scenes moments of conversion, as Jones would call them, but both also involve a man apparently pushing a woman to or beyond her limits, as Kate slaps and Anne spits at the man wooing her. Looking at Richard's action might lead some students to a clearer sense of the violence in Petruchio's action, even as looking at Petruchio's action might lead them to a clearer sense of the strategies employed by Richard. Such exploration might lead some students to object to calling one or both of these scenes a wooing: the parallels in the ways Katherine and Anne find themselves driven to extremes may suggest, as some feminist readers would argue, that, from the woman's perspective, another term might more accurately name this event. Shifting from content to craft, students might begin to trace the unfolding of Shakespeare's dramaturgy; you might, for example, ask them to compare the induction of *The Taming of the Shrew* with the first scene of *Richard III*, which functions as Richard's induction to the play he believes he is staging.

As we begin *Richard III*, then, and depending on how thoroughly the students have already grasped the model, I may make the recursive nature of the process explicit.

I hope it is clear that in asking you to repeat these questions my purpose is to have you incorporate them in your nervous systems, so that they become, in that revealing phrase, *second nature* for you. If they become second nature, you will have taken over the model, and you will pass beyond the need of a teacher for this type of inquiry. When you read or see a play, you will be able to continue employing what you have learned in this course throughout your life. If this happens, you will have learned more than I can teach—and that is one of the greatest satisfactions I or any teacher can have.

Opening *Richard III:* First Responses and Framing Issues

"What are your responses to the play?" As with the first play, some student responses recur almost every time I teach this play, because of fundamental challenges in reading the history plays in general, because this history play in particular comes at the end of a four-play sequence, and because this play challenges some expectations that present-day spectators and readers bring to the encounter. Recurring responses include the following questions:

Who are all these people?

Who is Queen Margaret? Where does she come from and go to?

Why does Anne yield to Richard? Is it credible that Anne would yield?

If it is not credible, then why does Shakespeare offer us such a scene?

How is Clarence killed?

Who is Richmond?

Why does Queen Elizabeth let herself be fooled by Richard when he woos her to woo her daughter?

Why are so many of these people fooled by Richard?

About Richard himself a number of questions emerge:

How is he deformed?

How can he manipulate people so well?

Why does he enjoy playing with words and punning?

Why does Richard have an attack of conscience at the end when he has never seemed to have a conscience before?

Most of these issues will be dealt with as we move through the activities, but some we need to deal with before we begin work on the first scene.

I usually respond first to the question that spotlights the most obvious reason students find this play difficult to read: "Who are all these people?" *Richard III*, Schoenbaum notes, is one the most crowded plays in the canon:

> *Richard III* offers thirty-seven roles, besides guards, halberdiers, gentlemen, lords, citizens, attendants, soldiers, two murderers, the Keeper of the Tower, the Lord Mayor of London, messengers, a priest, a scrivener, two bishops, a page, the sheriff of Wiltshire, the ghosts of Henry VI, Edward, Prince of Wales, and Richard's other victims. (54)

Since the *Riverside* edition offers a genealogy, we turn to these pages. (If the edition you use does not have such a family tree, you will want to reproduce one for your students.) We may go over the complex relations among the Plantagenets, or I may ask that students use the genealogy, coupled with the brief segment "The War of the Roses" presented in the introduction to the three parts of *Henry VI*. If I want to offer cues for this assignment, I say this:

> Before you reread the play, master the basic information this chart offers you. The problems it visually emphasizes are that Edward III had seven sons; that he outlived his eldest son and heir; that as a result his grandson became king at an age when he was too young to rule; and that during the minority of this king, Richard II, rivalries were formed that eventually led to civil war within the royal house. You also need to realize that, in the official beliefs of the Tudors and in the minds of some of Shakespeare's contemporaries, the events of Richard III's reign form the last act of an immensely long drama that encompasses the fall and redemption of the kingdom. As you reread the play, you want to correlate both the people you meet and the people referred to—for example, the corpse of King Henry VI in act I, scene ii—with the chart in order to understand these patterns.

Second, we spend some time discussing the nature of Richard's deformity. "How is he deformed? How much does the deformity show? How much is it emphasized in this opening scene? How accurate is the play's account of the deformity?" I find it useful to distinguish four types of answer: (1) There is the modern answer formulated by present-day historians. They stress how speculative all answers must be, but the current consensus is that while Richard may have been deformed, it seems not to have been in the massive way described in the sources. Certainly the story that he was two years in the womb, born with teeth, and so on, is hyperbole invented by those who served the dynasty that killed Richard and usurped the throne. (2) There is the Tudor answer given in Shakespeare's sources, specifically, the history written by Thomas More who, many think, got his information from the Bishop Morton who appears in act III, scene iv—a man who was Richard's enemy, as the play makes plain. In the play, Shakespeare seems to accept the version presented in the histories by Holinshed, Hall, and Grafton, all of whom essentially repeat, and in our terms, plagiarize, More. This is a version that makes Richard a monster at birth and a hunchbacked, crippled tyrant in his life. (3) There is the theatrical answer, which involves the performance history of the play. The answer here is that Richard has been played with an amazing variety of deformities, from slight to overwhelming, including a famous production in 1984 in which Anthony Sher played Richard on crutches. (4) There is another part of the dramatic answer, which reflects both the biased and the more objective histories, almost all of which agree that whatever his physical deformity, Richard was a good general and a courageous fighter. Shakespeare's play seems to accept this assessment. We deal with this issue when students imagine alternate ways of staging the duel.

There is also a historical consideration of another sort, namely, the different cultural contexts of the 1590s and our own time. Each context makes disability or physical deformity a condition with a very different significance, and at some point you need to shift attention from the nature of Richard's deformity to the significance of his condition in the cultural frame. This is also a moment to bring in any reading you may have assigned on the culture of the 1590s.

What students need to grasp is the fundamentally different view of nature that was still dominant, although being seriously contested, when the play was written and performed. This was a view that used "Nature" to denote a single creation designed as a whole by God; that believed God had structured this whole into a complex hierarchy, the "great chain of being," in which every creature and element had its precisely defined place in the graduated series that formed the universe; and that also believed the hierarchy repeated itself, with correspondences between levels (as we saw in *The Taming of the Shrew*) and between different dimensions. In a culture that took analogy to be a primary means of understanding the world and a source of authoritative insight, these correspondences were signs that could be read in both directions: a spiritually deformed creature was assumed to be physically deformed, and a creature who was physically deformed was assumed to be spiritually deformed. Thus, in its original context, Richard's physical deformity warns of his moral deformity and foreshadows his spiritual destination. For us, however, such a physical condition or disability is usually seen as the result of some genetic or environmental cause, with absolutely no relation to the true nature of the person afflicted: a person who suffers from a disability bears no moral responsibility for that condition; nor does that condition shape her or his moral character; nor is she or he to be judged or prejudged on the basis of that condition. If anything, people born with a disability who go on to reach the level of achievement Richard reaches as a warrior, for example, are judged as heroic precisely for overcoming such an obstacle. In fact, in contrast to Elizabethans, people holding this widely accepted view today would look at the disjunction between physical condition and achievement as adding to the stature of the person so regarded. Furthermore, the current emphasis is on how people who have disabilities can be integrated into our society.

With our radically different view of nature, we find the Elizabethan view extremely cruel, and many students will feel an initial pity for Richard and some indignation at how other characters treat him. This is not to say that Shakespeare himself might not have been capable of responses closer to our own, but simply that his culture provided a very different frame for perceiving physical defects. On the other hand, it does not seem likely that all Elizabethans—so divided in their beliefs that we recognize it does not make sense to speak, as Tillyard and others have, of "*the* Elizabethan mind"—would have been incapable of feeling pity for Richard, nor that it would have been impossible for some of them to imagine or know what being treated as Richard is treated might do to him or her. Therefore it seems to me that while we should not ignore all such responses because they are "modern," we may nonetheless want to temporarily dampen these responses in order to see Richard through the lens of this earlier construction.

Third, the students are puzzled, intrigued, and frequently shocked by the wooing of Anne. For many of them, it seems incredible that Richard should succeed in wooing her when he is so obviously her enemy, although some of them will also connect their response to this scene with their responses to similar elements in *The Taming of the Shrew*. Fourth, and following directly from the shock of Anne's response, they also wonder why all the other people whom Richard seeks to manipulate allow themselves to be fooled. I note that we will be able to answer these questions better as we explore the first three acts of the play. These questions are also important in that they set up the later discovery that Richard can be seen as wooing—at least in his own terms—almost everyone he encounters, including us, the spectators. Fifth, the ghosts interest the students, and they ask about how the ghosts are staged. In addition, some students wonder why Richard suddenly has a conscience at the end when he seemed so conscienceless up to that point. Again, this issue is one we will become (re)engaged with when we do the last two activities.

What Does Richard's Opening Soliloquy Do?

In the case of a villain-hero in tragedy like Richard III or Macbeth, it is a matter of the greatest importance that the actor get into immediate touch with his audience lest its thought and feeling be allowed to drift and escape. Whether Gloucester declares the winter of his discontent in the shape of a catlike Emlyn Williams (Old Vic, 1937), a smooth-tongued tyrant like Donald Wolfit (Strand Theatre, 1942), a chillingly ironic intellectual like Laurence Olivier (New Theatre, 1944), a leering Alec Guiness [sic] jogging his legs as he sits on the balcony (Ontario, 1953), a giant crab like Douglass Watson (Connecticut, 1964), a wounded spider

like Donald Madden (New York, 1970), or the beetle of Anthony Sher on his crutches (Royal Shakespeare Theatre, 1985),
the first perverse objective of that remarkable opening soliloquy
is to accommodate the monstrous "received idea" that legend
has imposed upon the audience to this play. *Richard III* opens
with its actor alone on the empty stage for a lengthy period of
time to ensure that his audience learns to collaborate with villainy: the playwright and not the historian is to take possession
of the action, and against all reason we willingly participate in
the outrageous events of the play. (Styan, "Stage Space" 198–99)

To focus discussion on the opening scene, I ask three encompassing questions: "What does beginning with Richard do? What
does Richard himself do with this opportunity to introduce himself to the spectators? And what does Shakespeare achieve through
what Richard does in this self-introduction?"

Students may begin by recalling our discussion of Richard's
appearance. In one class that had been especially intrigued by the
question of his deformity, students immediately focused on the
visual dimension, demonstrating that they were learning to translate a text into an imagined performance. They suggested that
because we first meet Richard by himself, we must confront and
deal with whatever type of deformity he presents and establish a
level of (dis)comfort with that deformity. One student returned
to the discussion of Lavinia in Jones's example from *Titus
Andronicus*. "We see Lavinia after she is mutilated, we experience the shock, but then we have time to recover so that we are
free to watch how others react to her. Here we have time to ad-
just to Richard and can observe how other characters react to his
deformity." It is also crucial that Richard reveals how he feels
about his deformity before we see how others respond.

Then I ask for volunteers to perform the opening speech. We
often start at one end of the spectrum with a self-pitying performance, which leads me to ask, "What does a self-pitying performance do?" Students realize that self-pity largely tends to turn us
off, so in the theater it can be counterproductive. A second performance is likely to present a Richard who projects anger through
sneering contempt, a harsh tone, and a driving delivery. An angry Richard may elicit more empathy, yet he too may keep us at
bay because such anger blinds him to a more precise understand-

ing of his own situation and the ironies of his enterprise. A third possibility is a more gleeful performance, mixing contempt with flippant mockery. Here the effect may seem more appealing insofar as we can share the hope of revenge, the sense of control experienced by anyone who has a plan to obtain a goal, and the glee that comes from imagining being one up on other people.

If students stop here, I reopen the door: "We said earlier that on an Elizabethan stage the actor can address other characters or the audience. So let me ask, 'Who is Richard talking to?' You have played this soliloquy as overheard speech, but what happens if he directly addresses us, the spectators?" Sometimes I ask half the students to rehearse how they would deliver the speech as if we are overhearing Richard and the remaining half to rehearse the speech as if Richard is openly addressing us. Here is a description of key elements from two performances in a general education Shakespeare class. The first was by Solveig, who kept her eyes down throughout her speech and dropped her voice to a whisper on "Plots have I laid." In contrast, Glen started with his back to us, whipped around in a sharp turn, and spat out, "Now —". Where Solveig kept still, Glen circled the room, cutting awkward, self-mocking "capers" (I.i.12) even as he spoke of his inability to do so, and he stressed *dogs* and *I* in ways that made us hear the words differently.

"What did Solveig's eyes and whisper do?" I asked. "No eye contact made him separate," someone said. Another added, "Not making any eye contact tells us that the character is using the convention that a soliloquy equals overheard speech: if the character does not see us, it signals that we are not there for the character." "And the whisper?" "It makes us listen harder." So it turns out you can signal "This part is important!" both by having a character raise his voice and by having him lower it: the contrast is what directs how we listen. "A whisper also signals 'This is a secret!,' which does what to us?" "If Richard is confiding a secret to us, it is as if we are his friends, his allies, his accomplices. Even though he ignores us, which would seem to push us away, the whispering pulls us in; we become more engaged—and perhaps compromised."

"What did Glen's initial move, his circling and capering and his stress of *dogs* and *I* do?" Turning his back created suspense and made us want to know who the person is, what he looks like. The whirling around made us jump and foreshadowed his desire to surprise people. The stress on *Now* sharpened the sense that *now* something will change. As he circled us, he took us in; he could move around us, so that we were caught in his world while he was freer than we were. And the stress on *dogs* and *I* made it seem as if everyone, human and animal, had contempt for him. But then stressing *I* was a response in which he threw contempt back: "They may think nothing of me, just as you may be thinking nothing of me, but you had better watch me carefully!"

After the performances, we take a closer look at the design of the speech. As with *The Taming of the Shrew*, I start with the movement of the speech's larger units, and this means a focus on the *rhetorical patterns*. The rhetorical patterns of the speech are so prominent because the speech is clearly composed by someone thinking specifically in rhetorical terms, so starting this line of inquiry enables you to sharpen students' awareness of the strong rhetorical patterning in most early Shakespeare plays. Furthermore, it is important for students to see that Shakespeare creates rhetorical patterns that, even before they shape the audience's experience, direct the actor as to how to transform the role into the performed character, prompting him to imagine how that character delivers the speech, defines the world, and attempts to situate the spectators.

Whether to introduce a concept of rhetoric at all will be a significant decision for anyone teaching Shakespeare's plays. But if you decide to introduce the concept, you confront a challenge of scale: how full a presentation do you need to offer in order to provide students with a usable concept of rhetoric? Part of the challenge concerns the scope of the definition you employ, since current definitions move in concentric circles from the broadest, Burkean definition, in which rhetoric as all forms of persuasion can seem to include all speech and written acts, to the narrowest definition of the "ornament" that speakers and writers add to their content, the most common definition in public discourse. Your decision, of course, depends on your context. In high school, even if rhetoric is taught in some form in English classes, the curriculum may not introduce the concept. In college, with the emergence of composition as a discipline, the resurgence of the study of rhetoric, and the rethinking of the relation of writing and reading in English departments, students may come with some knowledge of rhetoric. Whatever the level of your students' background, your introduction can be kept to a minimum.

For a definition of rhetoric, I find Richard Lanham's mini-essay in the second edition of *A Handlist of Rhetorical Terms* very useful. Or you may start with something as simple as C. S. Lewis's famous passage in *English Literature in the Sixteenth Century* in which he calls attention to how alien any concern with rhetoric as Shakespeare and his contemporaries knew it had become in mid-twentieth-century England and America:

> While Tudor education differed by its humanism from that of the Middle Ages, it differed far more widely from ours. Law and rhetoric were the chief sources of the difference. . . . Rhetoric is the greatest barrier between us and our ancestors. If the Middle Ages had erred in their devotion to that art, the *renascentia*, far from curing, confirmed the error. In rhetoric, more than in anything else, the continuity of the old European tradition was embodied. Older than the Church, older than Roman Law, older than all Latin literature, it descends from the age of the Greek Sophists. Like the Church and the law it survives the fall of the empire, rides the *renascentia* and the Reformation like waves, and penetrates far into the eighteenth century; through all these ages not the tyrant, but the darling of humanity, *soavissima*, as Dante says, "the sweetest of all the other sciences." Nearly all our older poetry was written and read by men to whom the distinction between poetry and rhetoric, in its modern form, would have been meaningless. The "beauties" which they chiefly regarded in every composition were those which we either dislike or simply do not notice. This change of taste makes an invisible wall between us and them. (60–61)

And there is Francis Bacon's famous assertion: "The duty and office of rhetoric is to apply reason to imagination for the better moving of the will" (qtd. in Lanham 131). As the second part of this introduction, you can simply refer to the contents of a book such as Thomas Wilson's *The Art of Rhetorique*. The first answer Wilson offers is that rhetoric means "Eloquence," and that the study of rhetoric is the study of how to create eloquent compositions in speaking and writing, prose and verse. Wilson also rehearses a version of the classical model at the core of education in Tudor England:

(1) The matter whereupon an Oratour must speake.

(2) Of questions.

(3) The ende of Rhetorique. To teach. To delight. And to perswade.

(4) By what means Eloquence is attained.

(5) To what purpose this arte is set forthe.

(6) Fiue things to be considered in an Oratour.

    i. Inuention of matter.

    ii. Disposition of the same.

    iii. Elocution.

    iv. Memorie.

    v. Utterance.

(7) There are seuen parts in every Oration.

    i. The Enterance or beginning.

    ii. The Narration.

    iii. The Proposition.

    iv. The Deuision or seuerall parting of things.

    v. The confirmation.

    vi. The confutation.

    vii. The Conclusion.

(8) There are three kindes of causes or Orations, which serue for euery matter.

The kind Demonstratiue, wherein chiefly it standeth.

An Oration deliberatiue

Of an Oration iudiciall.

As we work with the plays, we will find ourselves amplifying our understanding of rhetoric as well as coming to appreciate some of the "beauties" that at first may seem alien to our own deployment of language.

There are five main features of Richard's speech that I want students to discern:

1. The rhetorical pattern of the speech as a whole, especially the basic syllogistic structure of the first three parts, which is indicated clearly by the shifting pronouns that move from *we* to *I*.

2. The contrast between this three-part syllogism and the fourth part, which shifts from "Prove a villain" to the very different formulation of "Plots . . . inductions."

3. The function of the last line both as self-direction and as complex instruction or invitation to the spectators.

4. The complex act of self-definition performed here, in which Richard both fulfills yet subverts expectations that the play, by its title and the history known to much of the original audience, would arouse.

5. The complex way in which we are framed and invited to align ourselves with Richard, adopting his stance as the stance from which to watch and appreciate the rest of the scene.

"What does the rhetoric do? That is, what does the patterning of the language indicate that Shakespeare wanted his actor to re-create as he transformed the role of Richard into the character? What can these words be made to do? What can the actor make these words do, and therefore mean?" Students should understand that performances should be inventive yet responsive to the intention mandated in the playtext's design:

> [Glou.] **Now** is the winter of **our** discontent
> Made glorious summer by this **son** of York;
> And all the clouds that low'r'd upon our house
> In the deep bosom of the ocean buried.
> **Now** are **our** brows bound with victorious wreaths, 5
> **Our** bruised arms hung up for monuments,
> **Our** stern alarums chang'd to merry meetings,
> **Our** dreadful marches to delightful measures.
> Grim-visaged War hath smooth'd his wrinkled front
> And **now**, in stead of **mounting** barbed steeds 10
> To fright the souls of fearful adversaries,
> He **capers** nimbly in a lady's chamber
> To the lascivious pleasing of a lute.
> But **I**, that am not **shap'd** for sportive tricks,
> Nor made to **court** an amorous looking-glass; 15

I, that am rudely stamp'd, and want love's majesty
To **strut** before a wanton ambling nymph;
I, that am curtail'd of this fair proportion,
Cheated of feature by dissembling nature,
Deform'd, unfinish'd, sent before my time   20
Into this breathing world, scarce half made up,
And that so lamely and unfashionable
That dogs bark at me as I **halt** by them—
Why I, in this weak piping time of peace,
Have no delight to pass away the time,   25
Unless to **see** my shadow in the sun
And **descant** on mine own deformity.
And **therefore**, since I cannot **prove a lover**
To **entertain** these fair well-spoken days,
I am **determined** to **prove a villain**   30
And **hate** the idle pleasures of these days.

As I delineate here how a class analyzes this speech, I follow the five points listed above, but remember that in most classes the answers will usually emerge in a scattered fashion. If you want to direct work more precisely, you can also ask, "How do you divide this speech into its major units? What patterns enable us to project the shape of the speech embodied in those units?"

Even on the page, students can see, as some will have heard in the performances, the repetition of "now" and "our" that marks the first thirteen-line unit, and this perception will prompt them to identify the shift that occurs at "But I" and the shift that occurs at "And therefore." Eventually they will see how the speech moves through a progression that corresponds to a syllogism. The remaining part of the speech will seem a single unit to some, while others will see the last line as a separate unit. Thus the most common analyses perceive four or five units, although some students subdivide the units to end up with a higher total.

With the primary pattern for the first thirty-one lines laid out, we concentrate on patterns within the first three units. Looking at the first unit, I ask, "How do *now* and *our* operate? What is the name for the rhetorical figure here?" Usually at least one student will know this is an *antithesis*, but if no one knows the term, I supply it. I also introduce the idea of a rhetorical figure using Lanham's definition:

> The term *figure* in its most general meaning refers to any device or pattern of language in which meaning is enhanced or changed. The term has two subcategories:
> 1. Figure of words
>   a. **Trope:** use of a word to mean something other than its ordinary meaning—a **Metaphor**, for example.
>   b. **Scheme:** a figure in which words preserve their literal meaning, but are placed in a significant arrangement of some kind.
> 2. Figure of thought: a large-scale trope or scheme, or a combination of both—**Allegory**, for example. (178)

It is a pleasure to let students explore the figures from which the first two units are woven, working out how *now* and *our* set up multiple antitheses, and to make explicit the full antithesis when Richard gives only half. The stress on *now* is an implicit contrast to *then*: *then* there was winter, *now* there is summer; *then* we wore helmets, *now* we wear the wreaths of victors; *then* we rode horses to battle with other men, *now* we dance with ladies. The stress on *our* functions as an implicit contrast to *their*: our discontent is over, theirs has begun; our brows are bound with victory wreaths, theirs are bloody and unbound, and so on.

Answers to the question "What does Richard use these antitheses to do?" may be slower to emerge. Behind the public antithesis between York and Lancaster as respectively successful and defeated parties is a private antithesis between the other Yorkists and Richard, in which Richard sees himself as a man defeated by the success of his party. Thus Richard sets up a contrast between a public *now* and his own private *now*: for the "now" which is positive for "our" side is negative for the dissonant "I." Furthermore, students discover that Richard uses these antitheses to create satire. For even as Richard reenacts the way this world mocks how his "deformity" renders him unfit for the world in peace, so he enacts a mockery of that world as one where undeformed men embrace deforming occupations.

Students should also see the other major rhetorical shift that appears on the page as a matter of punctuation: whereas the first unit is three more or less equal sentences (4 lines, 4 lines, 5 lines), the second unit is a series of clauses punctuated by the stabbing emphasis of "But I, that am not shap'd . . . / I, that am rudely stamp'd . . . / I, that am curtail'd / . . . Why I . . ." followed by unequal units of shorter duration and greater intensity. This creates a difference in rhythm and tone: the first unit is relatively calm, but the second unit intensifies, with the contrast interrupted by the repeated "I"s that return attention to the speaker before the next wave of self-description. The second unit reaches a crescendo at the dash, with the following "Why I" a diminution as Richard seems to subside into contemplation of his condition. In the third, shorter unit, the parallel clauses bring together the previous antitheses as the larger movement brings together major and minor premises to conclude this syllogism:

> And **therefore**, since **I** cannot **prove a lover**
> To **entertain** these fair well-spoken days,
> **I** am **determined** to **prove a villain**
> And **hate** the idle pleasures of these days. (28–31)

One reason we find the speech intriguing is that we find ourselves listening to a man who seems to be reasoning his way to doing evil through a clear-eyed analysis of his world.

We focus next on what happens as Richard moves from "prove a villain" to "Plots have I laid." The question is "What are the two ways Richard defines himself here? And what does this double self-definition do to define how we understand him?" Although Richard has completed a logical argument for being "a villain," we do not know what this choice will mean in practice.

> **Plots** have I laid, **inductions** dangerous,
> By drunken prophecies, libels, and dreams,
> To set my brother Clarence and the King
> In deadly hate the one against the other;
> And if King Edward be as true and just
> As **I** am subtle, false, and treacherous,
> This day should Clarence closely be mew'd up
> About a prophecy, which says that G
> Of Edward's heirs the murderer shall be.
> Dive, thoughts, down to my soul, here Clarence comes! (32–41)

When we hear "plots" we think of a conspiracy. But a second meaning is the theatrical one of plot as a play's design, and "inductions" emphasizes this second meaning: for if we ask, "What is an induction?," the answer is that it is the start of a play in which, as in *The Taming of the Shrew*, one action frames another. Richard speaks the language of the figure the Elizabethans called "Machiavel," based on their (mis)reading of Machiavelli, but he also speaks the language of the Elizabethan dramatist, saying that his story is going to frame the play, that his villainy will be performed in theatrical terms.

In defining himself as a villain, Richard seems to place himself in an objective moral context in which we should respond by condemning his vision, his values, and his actions. In defining himself as a dramatic agent, however, Richard seems to place himself in a context in which we are unsure of what to make of his vision, values, and proposed actions, since we assume that the dramatist's aim, given Elizabethan rhetorical theory, is to move, to delight, and to instruct us. The challenge for us as spectators is to work out the relation between Richard's explicit self-definition as a villain and his implicit self-definition as a dramatist. The rest of the scene, by showing us *how* Richard enacts his plot, enables us to discern how the design of the play prompts us to understand Richard's self-definition.

Then I ask what the last line does. The line functions as a direction the speaker issues to himself, in which Richard is not only hiding his thoughts but also disguising himself, as Petruchio does in a parallel situation. But this also signals a shift in roles from playwright-spectator to actor-participant. Furthermore, the line functions as a direction to the spectators, for in the very act of redefining himself Richard seeks to redefine us, encouraging us, as Styan ("Stage Space") notes, to shift how we align ourselves with the play.

We are now ready to perform the rest of the scene so that students can grasp in detail how the play veers from our expectations. You might simply let three students rehearse and perform the next segment, or you might divide the class into triads so that everyone gets to explore the scene. Here are some useful questions: (1) What role does Richard play? (2) Do Clarence and Brackenbury believe his performance? (3) What does his performance show us about Richard? (4) How does Richard take advantage of the gap between his persona and the self he has shared with us so as to produce a double performance?

The first three questions can be quickly answered: (1) Richard plays the role of a grieving, loyal brother and presents himself as a man too simple to deal with the scheming people who surround him. (2) Obviously, they both believe his performance completely. (3) His performance shows us that Richard is a brilliant actor, able to take in even someone whose presumed intimacy should make him proof against such dissimulation.

The fourth question directs us toward a more complex answer. Richard's self-professed villainy is actually carried out by performing as a comedian in the little play he stages, and he packs his performance with humor, more specifically with irony. That humor consists of jokes that only he and we understand—jokes that usually take a few minutes to discover, since they involve unfamiliar forms such as the royal "we" in "We are not safe, Clarence, we are not safe" (70), which continues the pronoun play begun in shifting from *our* to *I* in the soliloquy.

Once the nature of this ironic comedy begins to emerge, the next question is "How does Richard's irony function to further shape our responses?" That irony invites us to acknowledge and even admire Richard's cleverness. This also means we are invited to see the others as gullible and to feel superior to those whom Richard dupes. This can be made plain when a student performs Richard's soliloquy after the departure of Clarence and Brackenbury, and when you discuss how repetition of the same game with Hastings adds to our relation to Richard.

> *Glou.* Go tread the path that thou shalt ne'er return:
> Simple plain Clarence, I do love thee so
> That I will shortly send thy soul to heaven,
> If heaven will take the present at our hands.
> But who comes here? the new-delivered Hastings? (117–121)

Performance makes explicit the fact that Richard sees himself as a comedian. The jokes about Clarence, coupled with the repeated use of the royal "we," express a glee at his plot. The ironic humor in his execution of that plot is in surprising contrast to, even contradicts, the moral frame invoked when Richard calls himself a "villain." And the performance with Hastings adds to our sense of Richard as comedian, so that we become better prepared for his irony, listen more closely, and catch it more easily.

> *Glou.* He cannot live, I hope, and must not die
> Till George be pack'd with post-horse up to heaven.
> I'll in, to urge his hatred more to Clarence
> With lies well-steel'd with weighty arguments,
> And if I fail not in my deep intent,
> Clarence hath not another day to live:
> Which done, God take King Edward to his mercy,
> And leave the world for me to bustle in!
> For then I'll marry Warwick's youngest daughter.
> What though I kill'd her husband and her father?
> The readiest way to make the wench amends
> Is to become her husband and her father:
> The which will I, not all so much for love
> As for another secret close intent
> By marrying her which I must reach unto.
> But yet I run before my horse to market:
> Clarence still breathes, Edward still lives and reigns;
> When they are gone, then must I count my gains. (145–162)

Still surprised at the sudden shift from self-proclaimed villain to actor-comedian, first-time spectators will doubt that Richard can succeed in deceiving Anne as he has deceived Clarence and Hastings. After all, he will be confronting an enemy, not a brother or long-time ally, and confronting her while she is still in mourning for the king, her father-in-law, and that king's son, her husband, both murdered by Richard himself.

I ask students to do some writing in which they articulate answers to the question "What sort of relation between Richard and the audience does this scene establish? That is, what is the Action$_2$ of this scene?" I suggest they concentrate on finding the verb or verbs that most precisely describe what Richard was doing or attempting to do through speaking to us in just the way he spoke to us.

A crucial discovery, it seems to me, comes when we look again at what Richard says he cannot do, focusing on how he describes himself in his opening speech: "But I, that am not shap'd for sportive tricks, / Nor made to court an amorous looking glass" (14-15). Yet he ends the scene by telling us that a wooer is the challenging role he will take up in his next scene. "And now, looking back, what else can you say about the first scene?" If Richard is about to woo or court Anne, then it also seems true that he has spent the first scene wooing or courting us. You may have students share what they write, or you may collect the entries and reproduce some of them for the next class as a means of helping students see how clearly this process of inquiry can produce written critical insight.

Finally, I make an assignment for the next class. "As you read the rest of act I and acts II and III, please analyze as best you can the pattern of Richard wooing Anne. Imagine how you want it staged. Why does Anne yield? How do you think Richard makes this happen? What does his (apparent) success here do to us?"

What Does Shakespeare's Language Do?

In this activity, we continue to pursue the objective of improving fluency in reading the two languages in which Shakespeare composed. By removing the words of the play, I ask students to focus on the dramatic language of stage action. Then when we return to the words, I ask students to take another step in learning how Shakespeare's language guides actors and readers in transforming roles into characters. We also continue our work of learning to understand the functions of the playtext's rhetoric. Students who learn some elements of the sort of rhetoric that was the core of education in Elizabethan England improve the precision with which they can read the play's language since familiarity with and sensitivity to such patterning was one of the dramatist's primary instruments for instructing actors how to perform and spectators how to hear and experience his plays. Although few people now possess the rhetorical knowledge that Elizabethan dramatists could expect from some spectators, students can learn to recognize and exploit rhetorical elements if they encounter these elements not as inert categories but as moves that adept speakers could, did, and still do employ in their efforts to persuade others.

It may seem peculiar to start an activity focused on prompting a deeper engagement with Shakespeare's language by taking that language away, but Gilbert has argued cogently for employing this process:

> Performance-oriented activities seem . . . most useful when they
> are designed to get students involved directly with the language.

Of course, having to speak the lines seems the natural tack to take, but let me suggest some related possibilities. To move to the other extreme, *not* speaking the language—finding out what happens when you remove the language—is one way of discovering how the language really works. The principle is to deprive the student of language and then restore it. In a sound-and-movement exercise students work in pairs, or threes, preparing a short scene for which they will present the central emotional story with movement, gesture, and sound, but not with language. . . . But what is the point of all this? One part of the work that you're really trying to get students to do consists in their collaboration, as they try to figure out what to present. Discussion should produce argument about the scene itself, plus close attention to the text to see what images can be used for the exercise. The second part of the work comes in the full class discussion after the presentations. . . . Usually it's helpful to have several versions of the same scene, so that students can try to account for the variations. . . . What in the text, I ask, did each group stress—and what did they leave out? Were there sections of the scene which didn't translate easily into movement? What can we learn from that? Not only does it help to have multiple "readings" of the same scene, but an overview of a character or group of characters develops when one watches a series of exercises based on the same characters at different moments in the play. . . . By moving away from the text and then back to it, students discover its strength. ("Teaching Shakespeare" 604–5)

As with many activities in this book, the process works through contrasting constitutive elements to clarify the functions those elements perform.

In the first of the two classes described here, I initiated the sound-and-movement exercise when some students noted that we had not done any performances in several classes—a moment I savored as a sign that at least some of them were becoming positively addicted to performance as exploration. Other students pretended to be appalled but proceeded to offer a rich array of performances and ended the period by noting how pleased they were to have done this activity.

Sound-and-Movement Activity

I pair the students, although you can experiment by having some pairs and some groups of four so that some actors can perform as guards, pallbearers, Berkeley and Tressel, or the corpse of Henry VI.[1] As they begin, I add another point: "When you do this type of sound-and-movement activity, you are looking again at scenic form as Emrys Jones defines it: you are exploring this scene as if it were the occasion without the words—doing it as what Shakespeare himself might have called a dumb show." Here is a brief description of the performances in one class, focused on the striking features in each version.

1. Anne = Marian, Richard = Dennis

Anne looked up to heaven to indicate her grief; when Richard approached, her look was a form of "unhand me, sir!" Richard made a gesture that was clearly moustache twirling and that, as well as labeling the character, was the visual equivalent of a verbal aside; it also set up the same use of the gesture to initiate the soliloquy at the end of the scene. At one point, Anne crossed herself, as if dealing with a vampire, a striking effect.

2. Anne = Leslie, Richard = Kathryn

This Richard was meek, pleading with and fawning on Anne. In contrast, Anne was extremely forceful in remonstrating with Richard, waving her arms, shaking a finger, driving Richard away, so that for a while it seemed unlikely he would get anywhere near wooing her. Part of the striking quality of this reversal came from the fact that this Anne was a good six inches taller than Richard.

3. Anne = Mary, Richard = Ellen

Suggesting doglike devotion, Richard was on the floor as Anne attacked him, lying in fetal position, supplicating. Anne was haughty, looking up to heaven, making scornful gestures. These students used the *Riverside* Shakespeare, heaviest of one-volume editions, as the weapon, with Anne holding it above her head, poised and still for a long time before she tossed it away; the noise it made when it landed caused a number of people to flinch. Richard then handed it back to her. As Richard knelt, he put his head against Anne's (visibly pregnant) stomach.

4. Anne = Joanna, Richard = Mary

This Richard energetically pursued Anne, and Anne surprised us by polishing the ring while laughing at Richard, as if he were a fool. Yet her sense of having the upper hand was negated by Richard's own asides of gloating laughter.

5. Anne = Ellen, Richard = Nancy

This was a very moving Anne, repressed yet explosive as she backed away from Richard, frightened, trapped, and cornered. When she held the sword (a pen) and paused, the intensity of her expression made it seem possible that she would indeed stab Richard. The same repressed violence emerged as Anne twice knocked the sword away when Richard reoffered it to her. Anne was puzzled by the ring, looking very troubled. She let Richard put his arm around her to walk her off.

6. Anne = Cathy, Richard = Mike

Both Anne and Richard were energetic. Richard swung his sword at the guards, and Anne responded with equal vehemence. When Anne lifted the sword, a brief evil look suggested she could not only stab him but enjoy it as well. Richard took off his jacket and started to take off his tie. He gave Anne the ring and when she accepted, the scene ended with a silently chortling Richard.

7. Anne = Joyce, Richard = Jack

Another energetic pair, in which Anne wept and Richard several times did a shoveling-it-on gesture to indicate to us his assessment of his flattery. After he gave her his sword and knelt, Richard had to writhe around the floor to follow Anne as she turned away. This Richard also did pelvic thrusts to indicate his real intentions, and he repeated these after Anne's exit.

8. Anne = Rosaleen, Richard = Brenda

This Anne was flustered and frightened, fighting Richard off, constantly batting him away with her hands. She also covered her ears, although we couldn't tell whether this was from disgust or fear of being tempted. She seemed to find Richard awful, and remained a wild creature, starting away from physical proximity, let alone touch. This Anne also made one of the more realistic spitting sounds. Richard escorted her off, his arm around her, but she looked dubious to the end.

9. Anne = Ani, Richard = Nancy

This was a calculating Anne, looking at Richard and the ring and clearly asking, "What's in it for me?" Richard knelt, passionately mouthing lines, and strong expressions crossed his face as he waited for the stroke of the sword.

Because the scenes move quickly, because most of us are not trained to remember visually, and because it is so hard to record, we pause to write a minute-long note after each performance. After the note for the last performance, I ask students to write from the prompt "One thing that strikes me about these performances is—." Then I throw open the floor for what is usually a vibrant discussion.

In the first part of the discussion, we focus on enumerating the physical elements in each scene and on the challenges that the imperatives of a wordless performance spotlight. Indeed, almost the first aspect students comment on is how pervasively physical the scene is, especially with the shocking act of one human being spitting on another—and how incompletely many of them had realized this physical dimension in first reading the scene even though, following their developing model of reading differently, they sought to imagine its staging. What the performances had demonstrated was what an array of complex alternative choreographies the mandated physical action invites us to invent.

These performances also illuminate an essential issue for reading not only this but many other scenes, namely, "Who is in control?" What becomes clear here is that however much this seems to be Richard's scene to a reader, in the theater there is a genuine question about who is in control of the scene. Since Richard not only dominates his own play but so easily dominates critical discussion of the play as a whole, it is important to sustain this focus on Anne as a way of beginning to grasp how Shakespeare uses the group of women who, as a number of critics have noted, function as a chorus to articulate the vision that eventually displaces Richard's vision in the second half of the play. It is vital that we explore the range of possible Annes and the range of motives these Annes manage to project. The students' performances gave us Annes like those most of the students had imagined, passive and easily manipulated by Richard. But there were Annes who were much stronger, who looked as if they might kill Richard, and who seemed to yield not primarily or only out of fascination with Richard but out of their own motives. How actors project motives for Anne is critical in opening up the text in exciting ways. On the one hand, students discover another difference between playtext and prose fiction, in which the narrator can supply motives, give characters an opportunity to discuss motives, or explain motives that characters are not or cannot (afford to) be aware of. This also helps students begin to see the complex analogy between what narrators can do or invite readers to do and the concept of subtext in drama. On the other hand, they also see yet another way that the script in effect invites our creative co-participation: the actors must probe and articulate motives if they are to project a coherent version of Anne, and a version for whom spectators can at least tentatively answer the question "Why does she give in?" Thus, when we read the play with an actorlike engagement, we too are free to accept the invitation to imagine performances that contrast with, conflict with, or even contradict one another.

I maintain this focus by asking, "What happens to Anne?" Spitting obviously indicates that she is pushed past her boundaries. I ask, "If this happened to you, what would happen to your sense of balance, of knowing where you are in the world?" Joanna said, "I'd be terribly confused and enraged." Joyce noted that she simply cannot accept that Anne gives in; what she wanted to project in her performance was a belief that Anne must be secretly planning revenge. Mary supported Joyce in simply not believing Anne would succumb.

The second moment students focus on is when Anne does not kill Richard: as we saw, some Annes started to, whereas some Annes seemed incapable of killing Richard. The question they wrestle with is "Why can't she kill him?" One answer is, "She finds it impossible; she does not want to be left alone, powerless." Another student commented, "If she thinks it through, she must either decide he is faking, which makes her a fool, or that he is for real. She wants his love to be genuine so she is not a dupe taken for the worst ride of all."

The spitting is also important because it forces the students to confront the physical nature of performance. "When you started rehearsing, almost immediately I heard nervous laughter about the spitting. What did that indicate, and how did that nervousness influence the performance you actually gave?" This discussion will, sooner or later, focus on the way that spitting on another human being is a forbidden act, so that to think of doing it arouses intense discomfort, and even pretending to do it in a dramatic fiction seems repellant. (And with awareness of AIDS, this sense of crossing a limit is radically intensified.)

We also explore the sword. Some Annes, students note, were ladylike, barely holding it, or holding it at arm's length, so there was clearly no real possibility she would use it. If Anne clearly could never kill Richard, and if we and the guards know this, the result is that Richard looks overtly manipulative and also appears to be not as much of a risk taker as he pretends. In other performances, such as those by Ellen or Mary, we felt a real possibility that Anne would stab Richard; such performances made us acknowledge that, whatever else was true about him, Richard may be willing to gamble with his life.

Students also realize that these Annes made the scene stronger. First, even if only for a moment, the level of risk increases sharply; second, if it seems that she accepts Richard's proposal only after calculating how it might advance her, we can speculate that she might prove to be dangerous to Richard, even perhaps become the agent of revenge she herself has so insistently prayed for. Of course, a strong Anne also makes Richard appear more daring because he is taking a greater risk. And when he succeeds, he tends to win more of our respect, however grudging, and from some even more hatred because he succeeds when he might have been killed. As noted, several people were startled to think that sexual desire—his, hers, or both—could be at work here: "It *humanizes* him," said Mary, to which Joyce responded, "No, it *dehumanizes* him, because it makes him an animal!"

I turn to a second class to add two vivid performances that highlighted elements of drama in the scene that do not always emerge.

10. Anne = Josette, Richard = Sara

Anne stopped the corpse (which was a student desk placed center stage). She touched the imagined face and loud sobs rose from her chest. When Richard entered, Anne let out a yell compounded of pain, anger, and outrage at the violation she felt at Richard's appearance at Henry's funeral. At first she hid her face, weeping, and then she looked scornfully at Richard. When he offered the sword, she grabbed it and instantly started a downward thrust, checked this motion with great effort, and then violently threw the sword away, turning away herself. She collapsed on her knees, weeping. Richard knelt to place the ring on her finger. Her resistance was weakened by grief. Anne looked at the ring, and we wondered if she was puzzled or interested. The actors rose and exited to loud applause.

11. Anne = Judy, Richard = Rosemary

This pair also moved a student desk center stage and then placed the small lectern from the front desk on it. Judy put her sweatshirt over the coffin so that Henry was covered with a shroud. This Anne gave a tremendous performance, really mourning the corpse, stroking it, pointing at it. When Richard appeared, Anne shouted "NO!" Her face was enraged as she lifted the cloth; she used a tissue as if it were part of the corpse's clothing now issuing blood. Anger drove her to confront Richard so that when she spit at him their faces were only inches apart; the spitting was truly venomous and done with enough realism to make us flinch even as it drove Richard back, his hand rising (as if) to wipe it off. Anne took the sword, looked up to heaven, and dropped it. She pulled back as Richard offered the ring, so they were at arms length, tensed, as Richard held her hand and slid on the ring. Anne held it up to the light—it was almost as if she were giving Richard the finger. This Richard also did a fuller soliloquy, looking down at his shadow and preening in a mimed mirror, before turning to us and then, smiling, exiting.

Josette and Sara made us aware that no one else had used the sound part of sound-and-movement so fully: as one student noted, "First of all, it stunned us. Second, it seemed to break the rules: we didn't feel secure because we didn't know what might come next." There were equally strong responses to Judy's Anne, who projected a sense that Richard's behavior was so monstrous that if the heavens did not strike him down, her faith in an ordered universe would crumble. It also made everyone see the significance a bleeding corpse could have for those who accepted it as a sign.

Working through Scripted Language

Eventually we come back to the language, and I initiate the next phase of this activity by asking, "What is missing when we take away the language? Or to return to our framing question, 'What does Shakespeare's language do?'"

> At the risk of being simplistic, let me suggest that what we want our students to look at is the language—the central problem in understanding (or performing) Shakespeare, and so basic as to be overlooked or taken for granted. What students, actors, audiences, and even critics do not understand is the language—by which I mean not only the literal language, but its implications about characters' feelings and their relationships, the signals given by the choice of prose or blank verse or rhymed couplets, the resonance for the character (not just the theme) of images, and even the silences. If we do not slow down to look at such implications, whole sections of the play float by us, as they sometimes do in the theatre, full of sound and beauty, but without power or meaning. John Barton's recent nine-part series for British television, and the book which serves as both record and expansion of that series, is an attempt to fill the remarkable vacuum which exists in print/media on the subject of actually speaking the words. Or, as Barton puts it, "How does Shakespeare's text actually work?" (Gilbert, "Teaching Shakespeare" 604)

Again, one way of opening up the question of what the language does is to focus on a rhetorical figure. Just as antithesis dominates the opening soliloquy, so stichomythia is the prominent figure here. Students will already know this pattern if you studied it in the first scene between Petruchio and Katherine:

> *Glou.* Vouchsafe, divine perfection of a woman,
> Of these supposed crimes, to give me leave
> By circumstance but to acquit myself.

Anne. Vouchsafe, defus'd infection of [a] man,
Of these known evils, but to give me leave
By circumstances [t'accuse] thy cursed self. (75–80)

Or I may ask students to infer the rules that Anne and Richard seem to employ to play this linguistic game. The basic rules seem to be: take the phrase, clause, or sentence used by your opponent; keep the same syntactic and syllabic pattern; change one or two words, or parts of words; and do all this to make your sentence come out sounding nearly identical with and yet meaning the opposite of the sentence spoken by your antagonist, thereby producing a sentence that in some way "tops" your opponent— as in the two "Vouchsafe" speeches above.

Articulating the rhetorical pattern is a cue to introduce the concepts of pressure and direction. *Pressure* is a term for the force one character exerts as she or he seeks to get another character to do something. *Direction* describes the trajectory that results from the interplay of pressures exerted by different characters. The point is to integrate the rhetorical and theatrical considerations so that students see how the rhetorical patterns help constitute the pressures exerted by Anne and Richard, and how the direction the scene takes is a result of these pressures. Again, they will learn a rhetorical figure in a context in which rhetoric is seen as a form of action. "When does the stichomythic exchange begin? Who begins it? When does it stop? Why does it stop? What functions does it perform in the scene? What does the stichomythia do in terms of directing the actors in how to play the scene? in helping us understand what is happening between the characters? in understanding how Richard woos Anne?" I have the class explore these questions while looking at the scene in phases.

First Phase. "What is Richard's problem as he enters the scene?" Students often begin with answers that are too subtle: "He has to bring up the subject of love" or "He has to convince her that he really did this for her" and so on. So we imagine ourselves as Richard, and they soon see that the first problem is a simple physical challenge, namely, "How do I get these people to stop this funeral procession?" This is no mean challenge since the sanctity of the funeral rite exerts its own pressure and direction. From Richard's speeches, it seems that part of the strategy he uses is indirect: to stop the rite, he concentrates on overawing the guards, perhaps hoping to indirectly overawe Anne. We also look at the key decision each performance will have to make, namely, does Richard use a weapon or only words when he threatens the guards? Each choice establishes a different sense of Richard's authority and has an effect on whether he later draws his sword for the first or the second time.

Second Phase. Having stopped the procession, Richard's new problem is "How do I stop Anne's curses?" He tries to stop her when she pauses after attempting to exorcise him ("Avaunt . . . Therefore be gone"), but far from succeeding, he gets another, longer tirade. Then he lets her rage on. What is the logic of his choice here? "When someone is in the grip of a powerful experience," I comment, "they have to talk about it, no matter what— and they will get enraged if anyone tries to stop them. In fact, such people often cannot even *hear* any other topic, and remain unable to hear anything else until they are done. And that's what I imagine Richard recognizes: that until he lets her vent her grief and rage, Anne will not hear any other topic. Furthermore, Richard must see that if he cannot stop her use of the corpse to condemn him, he will never be able to begin his wooing." Theatrically attuned students realize that the script strongly implies that Richard must get Anne away from the casket, as in Judy's performance, where the bleeding corpse renewed her rage and grief and could easily continue to do so.

"And when he senses she has finally begun to exhaust her rage, why does Richard introduce the idea of charity?" As Linda realized, Anne herself first uses the phrase "charitable deeds," and Richard uses it when he responds, "Sweet saint, for charity be not so curst." He is trying to find a way to turn her religious convictions from revenge to forgiveness. *Charity* is also an ambiguous term, and Richard will soon try to confuse Anne by sliding from agape to eros, just as he will seek to have her confuse "turning the other cheek" with "falling in love." Also, we can see that Richard is listening intently: he not only decides to let her spend her anger but also seems to realize that the more she talks, the more she offers him cues to shape his specific attack.

Third Phase. But when Richard tries again to shift focus, Anne initiates the stichomythic duel. "Anne answers Richard; she is always topping his lines. He keeps looking for an opening, and she keeps out-dueling him." But we need to ask, "How does the duel work for Anne?" Even though she continues to curse Richard, she too must listen carefully to his words in order to shape her reply. Thus, even though the pressure and direction initially seem to be controlled by Anne, Richard gains purchase by impelling Anne to listen to him. You can also get at these issues by asking, "What motive can we imagine that keeps Anne attacking rather than walking away?" One answer is that, in a world where women cannot take physical revenge, Anne seeks verbal revenge. That is, impelled by a sense of absolute righteousness, Anne believes she is presented with an opportunity to force Richard to confront the evidence that can shame him into admitting his guilt—an opportunity she cannot possibly suspect also puts her at risk of becoming the object of the curse she has uttered minutes before.

Fourth Phase. The first phase of their duel shows Richard that Anne's fury is not spent, and through the next two phases the pressure is still apparently hers, so that it seems as though she is driving him across the stage. He then retreats a third step and concedes that she is correct in her charge that he killed King Henry. This seems to mark a moment of defeat, and yet it is also a moment when, surprisingly, Anne's pressure slackens a bit. Anne gets the admission she must have thought she would never get, yet apparently she does not experience the triumph she might have anticipated. Although Richard's concession that Anne's charges are true does not stop her thirst for revenge, his yielding seems to exhaust her forward drive. And now Richard begins to exert pressure as he shifts to overt sexuality, proposing himself as lover. He makes his obscene suggestion and at that moment tops her line. That is, one of Shakespeare's cues is the reversal in the pattern of stichomythia.

> *Glou.* For he was fitter for that place than earth.
> *Anne.* And thou unfit for any place but hell.
> *Glou.* Yes, one place else, if you will hear me name it.
> *Anne.* Some dungeon.
> *Glou.*   Your bedchamber.
> *Anne.* Ill rest betide the chamber where thou liest!
> *Glou.* So will it, madam, till I lie with you.
> *Anne.* I hope so.
> *Glou.*   I know so. But, gentle Lady Anne,
> To leave this keen encounter of our wits
> And fall into a something slower method. (108–115)

What is the turning point? "She slows down, loses ground, and he asks that they 'leave this keen encounter . . . / And fall . . . slower method.' He gets them out of the verbal duel and out of having her accuse him of all his crimes." Anne has been cursing the man she hates, yet Richard not only declares himself a would-be husband but also reframes the duel not so much as combat but as play, in which they are partners. And he is right that they have been performing an action in which, in a limited way, she has had to be a partner, even if she has hoped it would prove to be a dance of self-condemnation for her enemy. Furthermore, when Anne utters the line "If I thought that—," she not only conveys her shocked incredulity about his love but also admits her sudden horrified doubt: she simply cannot believe this, but she cannot absolutely reject it either.

Thus we return to asking what drives Anne to spit, and to exploring what she thinks and feels in the seconds after she spits. The aim is for students to see how the action works dramatically for both the characters and the audience. "The problem here is that when you cross a line such as this one—for Anne, Richard's proposal; for Richard, Anne's spitting—you cannot pick up a book of etiquette that answers the question 'What do you do when someone spits in your face?!' You are in no man's or no woman's land."

"Which is perfect," said one student, "because now she is in Richard's country."

Anne shows that she has no words left but also that she still sees Richard as less than human. At the same time, spitting signifies her inability to stop him. It is her tacit admission that in fact she has no hope of converting him to seeing himself as the hellish being she believes he is. It is also, as a feminist reading would point out, the moment when Anne's violation of decorum clearly expresses her sense that she has been violated by his horrific use of "love" as the classic excuse for violence. She must also therefore be realizing how terribly she has lost control, how badly Richard has shaken her.

Conversely, what happens to Richard in being spit on? Being spat on, after all, makes it evident that someone thinks you are beneath contempt; it says more vividly than words, "*I despise you!*" So on the one hand this is a moment of extreme public humiliation. On the other hand, he can see that she has also been *reduced* to spitting on him, that she is shocked into speechlessness and has run out of other responses. And he may recognize that she has humiliated herself as well—or probably can be made to think and act as if she has humiliated herself. In that sense, he has succeeded.

"And how can Richard respond to her spitting?" You want to explore the range and, even more important, the responses that can project the enormous tensions Richard may experience and that we may be trying to imagine or grasp as we watch him in the silence that, in most performances, follows her spitting. We know of his murderous heart, so we imagine his instinctive, almost reflexive impulse to strike back, which may show up as anything from the slightest suppressed movement to an overt, barely restrained reflex action. At the same time, this is a moment that, because it severely tests his self-control, teaches us about the ratio of impulse to discipline in each particular Richard. So what is this moment like from Richard's point of view? As Inga blurted out, "When she spits, Richard has the opportunity to really turn the other cheek!"

It is in this context of turning the other cheek that Richard offers to let Anne kill him. Given the cue from Inga, we can revise the question as follows: "How does Richard use the fundamental roles, which the Elizabethans often called offices—namely, Anne's roles as Christian, as woman, as object of love in the courtly code—as weapons against her?" The point is for students to articulate the imperatives that constituted these offices. Thus students can work out that a woman's office as Christian means she should be charitable, not vengeful. Her gender, going back to the pattern of courtly love that Richard's wooing language seems designed to invoke, means that although a woman may be married, she must hope to be wooed by a lover who is not her husband and by a man who will do anything for her love—the more a man does for her, the more he proves he loves her, even if he kills her husband for love of her. And as a woman, she is supposed to be protected by the man and, because of such protection and her own frail nature, is utterly forbidden to commit any violent act herself.

Together with your students, you can work out some analyses of the rest of this scene. I note in passing one of the most striking discoveries, again made by Inga, who asked, "Suppose Anne actually begins to kill Richard? Suppose she actually cuts him, sees blood, then stops?" This was a possibility none of the students had imagined, and I include it here as emblematic of the fact that no matter how often you do this activity there is always the potential for new inventions and new insights, and thus for students to teach one another previously unnoticed and unimagined potentials of the playtext. Indeed, one of the premises of the performance approach is that the openness of the playtext means that it is impossible in principle to exhaust the potential performances, hence it is impossible in principle to produce a complete enumeration of producible and valid performances, no matter how brilliant someone is at performance or production analysis. This is a blessing not only for actors and directors but also for students and teachers—and a blessing that has sustained my efforts in teaching my classes and in composing this book.

Creating and Exploiting Discrepant Awareness

Work with the first two scenes of *Richard III* brings us to an ideal moment at which to introduce the concept of relative awareness as a central element in drama. One of the great resources of the medium, the maneuver of opening gaps in awareness between characters and between characters and spectators can, as the example of *Oedipus Rex* famously demonstrates, produce some of the richest and most heart-stopping effects achieved through per-formance. In the activities that make up this segment, we begin to explore how the interaction of the constitutive elements creates this feature of the dramatic medium—a feature which, to borrow a concept from the sciences, can be recognized as an emergent property of the medium. One benefit of beginning with *The Taming of the Shrew* and *Richard III* is that both plays employ an intrigue plot, and such plots are ideal for introducing the exploration of relative awareness since it is precisely this property of the medium that the playwright exploits when he creates the intrigues. Equally important, students are now equipped to conduct a substantial analysis of how the dramatist uses the discrepancies produced through the use of relative awareness to create complex ironies that we share, for example, with the villainous Richard, even as most of us, as spectators or readers, continue to oppose his moral code.

What *The Taming of the Shrew* and *Richard III* also show us is that in an intrigue plot characters can disguise themselves in at least two different ways. As the Bianca-Lucentio plot demonstrates, characters can disguise themselves literally by changing costumes, taking on a new name and a new identity. But as the Katherine-Petruchio plot shows, characters may also disguise themselves not by changing costume but rather by hiding or distorting their nature and identity. In writing *Richard III*, Shakespeare was obviously fascinated by this second type of disguise and seized on the enormous potential for complex plotting open to a character capable of disguising himself simply through acting. In *The Taming of the Shrew*, Shakespeare exploits this potential intermittently, but in *Richard III* he exploits it systematically, producing one of the most fundamental and powerful elements of his dramatic design.

When embodied in an intrigue plot, however, relative awareness is also the source of some of the more difficult translation challenges that confront us when we read plays. The difference between reading an intrigue plot, with its exasperating demands on readers to keep track of disguised characters moving through intricate levels of awareness, and seeing an intrigue plot unfold in performance, where it offers us effortless and explosive delight, is one of the most striking instances of the gap that can exist between page and stage. The problem is one that students will have already raised, and they are pleased to know that critics have recognized this problem. Here, for example, is G. R. Hibbard who, in his introduction to *The Taming of the Shrew*, notes that it can be difficult

> for the reader who, deprived of the bustle and animation of the stage, may well find it hard to develop any very lively interest in the elaborate intrigues of Tranio, Lucentio, Gremio, and Hortensio, particularly as their names, disguises, and disguise-names make it far from easy to keep one distinct from another. (9–10)

As readers, we find ourselves repeatedly making an effort to recall who is disguised as whom, and the effort we expend remembering that, say, Cambio is really Hortensio in disguise tends to leave us less likely to re-create the effects that are the dramatic point of the disguise. The mental gymnastics entailed in reading this way is nicely captured in a stage direction in the *Riverside* edition: "Enter Gremio, Lucentio in the habit of a mean man, Petruchio with [Hortensio as a musician and] Tranio [as Lucentio] with his boy [Biondello] bearing a lute and books" (12). The repeated formula of "A as B" is a shorthand for the act of attention through which we remember a series of equations without which much of the meaning and the comedy does not exist. Introducing students to the concepts of relative awareness, discrepant awareness, and dramatic irony refines their ability to analyze how an intrigue plot works and develops their skill in translating such plots into imagined performances, in which they can appreciate the complex effects achieved by these intrigue plots.

In class I hand out material from *Shakespeare's Comedies* by Bertrand Evans because it remains the best introduction to the concept of relative awareness in drama:

> The world's dramatists—indeed, the world's storytellers—might be classified in a rather fundamental way according to their preferences in the handling of the relative awareness of audience and participants. Three possibilities are available to a dramatist: he can keep the audience less informed than the participants, equally aware with them, or more aware than they. The first way, of

course, has always been a favourite of mystery writers. . . . The second, if one were to make a statistical survey, would doubtless be found the most prevalent way for both dramatic and narrative story-tellers past and present. . . .

But the third way is Shakespeare's. It is the way of other great dramatists also . . . but it is not so consistently *the* way of any other dramatist.

The degree of Shakespeare's devotion to a dramatic method that gives the audience an advantage in awareness, and thus opens exploitable gaps both between audience and participants and between participant and participant, can be partially suggested through some simple but extraordinary statistics. The seventeen comedies and romances include 297 scenes, in 170 of which an arrangement of discrepant awareness is the indispensable condition of dramatic effect; that is to say, we hold significant advantage over participants during these scenes. Further, the comedies include 277 named persons (and unnamed ones whose roles have some importance), of whom 151 stand occasionally, frequently, or steadily in a condition of exploitable ignorance; that is to say, we hold significant advantage at some time over these persons.

Or to put these general facts in another way: more than half the persons in the comedies and romances are shown as speaking and acting "not knowing what they do" in about two-thirds of the scenes in which they appear. When only principle persons and scenes (omitting, for example, the many mainly expository scenes) are counted, the proportion is far higher: then roughly four of five persons are shown acting ignorantly in four of five scenes. Or to put the matter in yet another way: if a comedy requires two hours and a half to perform, attention is centered for nearly two hours on persons whose vision is less complete than ours, whose sense of the facts of situations most pertinent to themselves is either quite mistaken or quite lacking, and whose words and actions would be very different if the truth known to us were known to them.

Though these figures barely hint the story, they do suggest that Shakespeare's dramatic method relied heavily on arrangements of discrepant awarenesses, and that examination of his management of these can shed light on some fundamental principles of his dramaturgy. (vii–ix)

I also delineate the key terms. In drama, *relative awareness* denotes the fact that there is always a potential for differences in awareness both between dramatis personae and between most dramatis personae and the audience. We see a scene between characters A and B that character C does not, so that we, along with

A and B, simply know more about events than character C does. This is the simplest sort of *gap in awareness*, but it is not the sort of gap that interests us. The critical gap is the one that opens between one participant (A) and another (B) wherein the first participant knows something that gives her an advantage over the second participant in pursuing her objective. Such a gap creates a simple two-step *hierarchy of awareness*: character B is one down; character A and the spectators are one up on character B. The dramatist can open multiple gaps, creating a hierarchy of three or more steps. Furthermore, the dramatist can open gaps that diverge, creating complex hierarchies that are more like networks of relative awareness, as happens in *The Taming of the Shrew*.

It is these gaps that are *exploitable gaps in awareness*. When he exploits such gaps, the dramatist creates a difference in awareness that confers an advantage on one character over another, and that advantage in awareness also shapes the consciousness of the spectators, creating effects that range from laughter at ignorance to moments when we hold our breath in suspense.

Finally, as we return to our exploration of *Richard III*, we need to recognize that one of the most pervasive ways of using discrepant awareness is to create dramatic irony, which is discussed more fully in the next section. Or to put this the other way around, dramatic irony is an especially effective and prominent product of relative awareness.

At this point, we enumerate the effects that follow from having Richard open with a direct address to the spectators. First, we gain access to Richard that no one else—not even Buckingham, as we later realize—shares. Second, this access makes us privy to the purposes he hides from the other dramatis personae. Third, we also gain some access to the plots he designs to achieve his objectives. Fourth, when he encounters other characters, we understand the tacit jokes he makes. Fifth, we become aware of the larger "joke" that is being perpetrated on the victims when their actions contribute not to their own objectives but rather to Richard's efforts to destroy them. This analysis also sets up the focus of the next segment, namely, that it is through Richard that Shakespeare creates the verbal and dramatic ironies that dominate the first half of the play.

Thus, in continuing our exploration of the different ways we can come to perceive a play's design, I have the students, individually or in groups, map the first two scenes by segments, asking themselves what pattern emerges, especially if they look at the flow of characters on and off the stage.

Richard solo / Richard + Clarence and Brackenbury

Richard solo / Richard + Hastings

Richard solo / [end of scene i]

Anne and Procession / + Richard / Richard and Procession / Richard solo

We thus begin to recognize a constitutive pattern to the play, which spectators will experience as a rhythm. It is a pattern of alternate segments of Richard alone with us, Richard with others, Richard alone with us. This pattern makes it seem that we are watching a play that Richard is presenting to us.

Concluding this introduction to discrepant awareness, I give an assignment. "Building on our work, and on the chart of the scenes just created, please write a short piece in which you chart the hierarchy of awareness in this play up through act III. Please also attempt to take into account the different point of view offered by Queen Margaret, who is the first character other than Richard to gain direct access to us, the spectators."

Richard as Dramatic Ironist

In this segment, students combine the questions that help them discern the form of a scene with new questions that help them delineate the shaping functions of discrepant awareness. These new questions focus on the complex manner in which discrepant awareness functions simultaneously as Richard's way of manipulating his reality and as Shakespeare's way of shaping our perception of that reality. As they answer these questions, students explore the design of the whole first half of the play by looking at Richard's designing activities. For it is primarily Richard's plotting that shapes these scenes, and it is Richard's consciousness that shapes how we respond to these scenes, even when, as in the murder of Clarence in act I, scene iv, Richard himself is not in the scene. In short, we focus on the way the dramatist uses the gap in awareness as a primary device to create action and shape consciousness. The effect Shakespeare achieves, I suggest, is that during the first three acts, spectators will become aware that they cannot easily discriminate Richard's design from the play's and thus cannot be sure what moral pattern, if any, governs the events unfolding in this universe. At the same time—and this would probably have mattered more to the original audience—the fact that they know Richard will be defeated makes this tension less threatening.

This is also the logical moment to introduce a distinction between *dramatic irony* and *verbal irony*. Dramatic irony emerges from the very structure of a play, from the discrepancies between what characters intend to do or intend to mean and what we know their actions and words are in fact doing or meaning; spectators can articulate such irony even if it is never directly articulated in the words of the script. Verbal irony, by contrast, inheres in the specific words spoken by a specific character at a given moment; one or more of the characters may be aware of such irony, as Richard clearly is at many moments in the first three acts.

As noted, one cue for beginning this activity is the short assignment to identify the pattern of the first two scenes in terms of the alternation between Richard alone and Richard with others. You can also use a fuller assignment of five interlocking questions, presented below, which can be given instead of or in addition to the first assignment. This second assignment asks students to produce an analysis of the playlets that Richard's histrionic action creates and to analyze the complex roles and functions that Richard performs in the course of carrying out his histrionic plots. When I introduce these assignments, I define a *playlet* as a moment, like the moments with Clarence, Hastings, and Anne, in which Richard produces a miniature drama as he manipulates his victims into performing a scene in which their apparently free choices are in fact shaped by his own script.

What we are doing here is extending our discussion of discrepant awareness to its most prominent effect, dramatic irony. To learn precisely how Shakespeare's design exploits dramatic irony, please answer, in writing, the following questions:

1. *Richard as onstage playwright: Scripted and improvised scenes.* If we think of Richard as an onstage playwright, we see that throughout the first three acts, Richard is busy creating his own scenes or *playlets.* Starting from act I, scene i, please list all the playlets you see Richard create through act III.

2. *Richard as star actor: Playing roles.* Richard is also the star of the play he is improvising as he makes history from his histrionic talent. Returning to act I, scene i, please list all the roles he plays in these scenes. How does his role playing work on stage? What does his skill in each role and his facility in shifting roles do to us?

3. *Richard as ironic comedian: Creating dramatic irony.* These playlets offer many instances of dramatic irony because Richard is creating situations in which what other characters do and say often has the opposite effect from what they intend: their words have the opposite meaning, their actions have the opposite outcome. Within each of the playlets you list, detail some of the dramatic ironies. What patterns do you begin to perceive?

4. *Richard as comedian: Playing tragedy for laughs.* These playlets also offer instances of verbal irony; many of these ironies are uttered by Richard himself, as in the aside where he mocks his mother's blessing (II.ii.109–111). Within each of the playlets, please note some of the verbal ironies in the scene. Again, jot down the immediate response you might have as a spectator. How would your responses begin to interact to produce an emerging pattern of response?

5. *Richard's ironies, Shakespeare's design(s).* Write a paragraph summarizing the dramatic ironies and verbal ironies you have discovered. Now please ask yourself, "What does this ensemble of ironies *do* first in the world of the play and then to me as a spectator?"

As a guide, I share the beginning of my own list of Richard's playlets:

I.i [162 lines] Rich: 3 sols; 2 playlets to deceive Clarence & Hastings

I.ii [263 lines] Rich & Anne, 3rd playlet: conversion of Anne; Rich's 4th sol

I.iii [354 lines] Rich: 4th playlet, with court; 5th sol

I.iv [283 lines] Murder of Clarence, 5th playlet: murderers playing Richard

In this or the next class, students work in small groups before we compare analyses to arrive at a consensus. Eventually we have a map that looks like this:

I.ii	Richard	Soliloquy	#1	
		Playlet	#1	with Clarence and Brackenbury
	Richard	Soliloquy	#2	
		Playlet	#2	with Hastings
	Richard	Soliloquy	#3	
I.ii	Anne	Monologue		
	Richard	Playlet	#3	Pseudo-conversion elicits conversion of Anne.
	Richard	Soliloquy	#4	
I.iii	Richard	Playlet	#4	with court
		Soliloquy	#5	
I.iv	(Richard)	Playlet	#5	Execution #1: of Clarence; murderers play Richard's part as humorists.
II.i	Richard	Playlet	#6	with king et al.: news of Clarence's death.
II.ii	Richard	Playlet	#7	with queen, duchess, children et al.
	Richard	Duet	#1	with Buckingham, planning next step.
II.iii	3 Citizens			Offer an alternate frame & alignment?
II.iv	Queen et al.			
III.i	Richard	Playlet	#8	with princes
	Rich & Buck	Duet	#2	Planning next step.
III.ii	Catesby	Playlet	#9	Testing Hastings.
	Buck	Playlet	#10	Testing Hastings.
III.iii	Vaughan et al.			Execution #2

III.iv	Rich/Buck	Duet	#3	Planning fate of Hastings.
	Richard	Playlet	#11	Trapping Hastings.
	Hastings	Soliloquy		Execution #3
III.v	Rich/Buck	Duet	#4	Planning next step.
	Rich/Buck	Playlet	#12	Fooling Lord Mayor.
III.vi	Scrivener			Points out discrepancy: alternate frame.
III.vii	Rich/Buck	Duet	#5	Planning the wooing of Richard.
	Rich/Buck	Playlet	#13	Conversion of Richard to accept throne.

This analysis also provides a foundation for answering the other questions.

For questions 2 to 5, the class can work in small groups. Depending on your objectives, you can have groups work on different questions, or you might have each group work on one scene, starting with act I, scene iii and going through act III, scene vi (leaving act III, scene vii for a separate whole-class activity). In the latter case, you might have each group put its answer to question 2 on the board; then answer question 3 by having each group list the three ironies they find most prominent; and for question 4, ask that they note all the explicit commentary by Richard that calls attention to the ironies, as well as the examples they responded to most strongly. By the time we have moved through the first four questions, we are usually well into a discussion of the fifth.

The list that emerges in answer to question 2 looks like this:

I.i	Playlet	#1	Loyal and grieving brother with Clarence.
			Haughty nobleman putting Brackenbury in his place.
	Playlet	#2	Fellow sufferer and statesman with Hastings.
I.ii	Playlet	#3	Masterful wooer and penitent murderer with Anne.
I.iii	Playlet	#4	A "plain" man, righteously indignant at being slandered.

With Margaret, the righteous rebuker of murderers.

"And seem a saint when most I play the devil."

Then with the murderers he plays the hearty killer.

| I.iv | Playlet | #5 | Clarence's unwittingly correct image of Richard as accidentally killing Clarence. |

Clarence captures Richard's doubleness.

The double image is also apparent in the conflict between Clarence's mistaken and murderers' accurate descriptions.

II.i	Playlet	#6	Again plain, honest man, bearer of sad news, righteously angry at being mocked, piously censoring others' guilt.
II.ii	Playlet	#7	Dutiful son, consoling brother-in-law, cautious advisor.
III.i	Playlet	#8	Protector: devoted uncle, deferential and protective, both subject and kinsman. His wicked asides make him "like the Vice" (82).
III.ii	Playlet	#9	Catesby tests Hastings.
	Playlet	#10	Buckingham seems just to mock, not even test Hastings.
III.iv	Playlet	#11	Injured victim of witchcraft treachery. (Not witty or believable.)
III.v	Playlet	#12	Buckingham and Richard play defenders of the kingdom, honest, plain men barely able to escape treason.
III.vi	Scrivener		Points out discrepancy—implies an alternate frame.
III.vii	Playlet	#13	Climactic role: Richard as pious, Henry VI–like prince, so holy and proper that swearing offends him, so reluctant he must be asked three times before he accepts the crown.

You have probably been imagining just how easily answering questions 3 and 4 could consume an entire class period. Each teacher will judge for herself or himself how much detail to go into in order to achieve specific objectives and to answer the question "What does Richard's irony do?"

Here I include a few of the most significant elements that either the students articulate or that I offer as a supplement to their analysis. In particular, my own remarks concentrate on the element that is usually, though not always, the most difficult for students to perceive, namely, the way in which Shakespeare's play uses Richard to instruct the spectators on how to respond to the events that constitute the play's action.

Richard's first soliloquy immediately opens a gap between us as spectators and the action that follows, but that gap is made ironic specifically by the last part of the soliloquy, which announces that Richard has already begun to weave plots to ensnare those who block his path. When he commands, "Dive thoughts, down to my soul, here Clarence comes," he not only instructs himself to assume his first (or, we may suspect later, his second) persona but also tacitly instructs us, as his confidants, to watch the performance that follows. As Janet Adelman has put it, "A play must teach us how to see it" (11) and what is crucial, therefore, is not just *what* we watch but *how* we watch. More precisely, during this playlet we are being taught how to watch, respond to, and appreciate the type of action that Richard will continue to script in subsequent playlets. What we see, as our earlier activity has shown, is Clarence caught in an ironic situation in which not only is his trust in Richard betrayed but the words he finds most reassuring—such as "We are not are safe" or "I shall deliver you or lie for you"—are the words we are prompted to hear as lethal comedy, since they announce Richard's murderous intentions. As first-time spectators, if we catch these verbal ironies they are the means by which Shakespeare begins to instruct us in how best to listen to Richard's speeches. What we discover is not only the general comedy of the ironic situation, in which many of Clarence's speeches are comic because he has things backwards, but also the verbal comedy actively created by Richard's ability to articulate pun-laced speeches that take advantage of the situation by having a public and safe meaning, which is what Clarence and Brackenbury hear, and a private and subversive meaning, which only we can share with him. The repetition of this set of maneuvers with Hastings confirms that we are being taught to watch the play in this manner. We are thus invited to align ourselves with Richard, and we are tempted to accept this invitation because it enables us to align ourselves with the manipulator rather than with the one being manipulated—and "the part of the dupe," as Anthony Trollope remarked in *Barchester Towers*, "is never dignified" (122).

Here are some answers to the question "What does Richard's irony do?" Richard's irony flatters us because we discover we have the wit to get the jokes that he has the wit to create. Thus, by the end of this scene, we have been introduced to the moves Richard's irony makes possible and the verbal rewards Richard will reap from the ironic situation. It is also crucial that the soliloquies in the first two scenes teach us that no matter how completely Richard seems immersed in his role, he is always secretly appreciating his own wit and the verbal ironies he creates through that wit. In effect, another complex function of his irony is that we are invited to imagine Richard's inner dialogue as he savors the verbal felicities.

I add one further point since it usually does not emerge in the students' analyses. Earlier I noted that if we look at what Richard does with Anne, we discover that underneath his satirical argument Richard has been wooing us, the spectators, just as he was wooing Anne. I noted also that you can see that he is wooing someone in almost every scene. But we can add that when he acquires Buckingham as his onstage confidant, the pattern of wooing changes because Richard changes his action: in the terms I am using here and that Buckingham makes explicit when he urges Richard "to play the maid's part," Richard goes from being the wooer to being wooed.

Contesting Frames

To extend this analysis, I return to two terms I have already used but not defined. They are part of the language of the stage and key elements in understanding what the dramatist can design his or her play to do. These two terms are *frame* and *alignment*, and what we need to explore, especially in order to understand the next scene we are going to look at, is precisely how a dramatist can frame not just the action but also the audience, and thereby induce the audience to align and realign itself. I use the interlocking definitions of *frame* and *alignment* that come from a bestselling book by Deborah Tannen, *You Just Don't Understand*, from the section titled "Framing":

> Another way to think about metamessages is that they *frame* a conversation, much as a picture frame provides a context for the images in the picture. Metamessages let you know how to interpret what someone is saying by identifying the activity that is going on: Is this an argument or a chat? Is it helping, advising, or scolding? At the same time, they let you know what position the speaker is assuming in the activity, and what position you are being assigned.
>
> Sociologist Erving Goffman uses the term *alignment* to express this aspect of framing. If you put me down, you are taking a superior alignment with respect to me. Furthermore, by showing the alignment that you take with regard to others, what you say frames you, just as you are framing what you say. For example, if you talk to others as if you were a teacher and they were your students, they may perceive that your way of talking frames you as condescending or pedantic. If you talk to others as if you were a student seeking help and explanations, they may perceive you as insecure, incompetent, or naive. Our reactions to what others say or do are often sparked by how we feel we are being framed. (33–34)

Even if you do not have time to stage the first scene with Queen Margaret, it is worth at least setting up the scene, placing the court in a possible blocking, and then asking questions about how Margaret functions, what her presence does. In answering these questions, the class will begin to delineate both the dramatic and the dramaturgic functions Margaret performs here: dramatically, she is the opponent of all the Yorkists, although Richard is her supreme enemy and target; dramaturgically, she is the first figure seriously to contest the frame and alignment proposed by Richard. Note, however, that the full significance of her challenge in offering an alternate frame reaches fruition only in act IV, scene iv, which we explore in a later activity.

It is worth asking, for example, where Margaret enters, where she places herself, and how she delivers her asides. Presumably, following the original staging, she enters from one of the two upstage doors, unseen because the court is so intently arguing, stirred up by Richard's ironic act of injured innocence. But she must startle us and catch our attention, the blindness of the onstage characters sharpening the intensity of our curiosity about and focus on this newest figure. We will be asking ourselves, "Who is this? What will she do? Will she be noticed?" She must also move downstage if her asides are to be delivered to us. By her second speech, as she speaks of "my husband Henry," we know she is Queen Margaret, the widow of the king whose corpse we have just seen (or not seen) in act I, scene ii. "What is she doing here? What does she want to accomplish? Is she in any danger? After all, the Yorkists, Richard in particular, have killed her husband and her son. Will she be noticed? What will she do?"

As they immerse themselves in the choreography of the scene, students begin to sense its compelling shape and energy. In Margaret's long exchanges, we focus on two elements: the pattern projected by her curse(s) and the challenge of her direct confrontation with Richard. At this point, we can begin to articulate most of the functions this apparently simple, even monotonous, and yet dramaturgically complex figure performs. The primary focus is clearly on Margaret's curses, for the pattern established by her curses is the pattern whose gradual fulfillment will produce essential elements of the frame that opposes and finally subsumes the frame proposed by Richard. (Whereas Anne specifically cursed Richard, Margaret moves to curse the entire Yorkist line, so she extends Anne's action.) Thus it is highly productive to have the students enumerate the curse: since Margaret's curse is fulfilled in every point, delineating the curse is a crucial step in grasping the larger design we might call super-scenic form. The assignment, then, is for students to list the elements of the curse and to analyze the effect of this sequence:

1. King Edward will die by surfeit.

2. Prince Edward will die a violent death: more specifically, of course, he will be indirectly murdered by Richard, as the

Lancastrian Prince Edward, Anne's husband, was directly murdered by Richard.

3. Queen Elizabeth will become a widow and lose her royal sons.

4. Rivers, Dorset, and Hastings: "unlook'd accident cut off!"

5. Richard: this is complex because on the one hand Margaret utters the most ferocious curse of all on Richard; on the other
   hand, he apparently wards it off with his quick-witted insertion
   of her name. But eventually he too succumbs, fulfilling the pattern.

6. Buckingham she spares—but then predicts his demise.

Interestingly, when Margaret tries to spare Buckingham and then,
although not cursing him, predicts his fate, a new key word rings
out: "And say poor Margaret was a prophetess" (I.iii.300). The
word *prophetess*, when we come to look back on the play as a
completed design, subtly transforms the pattern, for it lets us
recognize that a curse that comes true does indeed function as a
form of prophecy.

What Margaret projects here, then, is an alternate vision of
the pattern of the play's universe, and an alternative specifically
to the pattern projected by Richard. Immediately, then, Margaret's
curse raises a question of how we are to frame the action and
how we are to respond to the way Richard aligns himself and
asks us to align ourselves with the action as framed. That is, we
must ask ourselves, "Does Margaret offer us an alternative to
Richard's vision of the universe, or the same vision of the universe?" Margaret's vision offers an alternative in designating good
and evil, yet, as A. P. Rossiter notes, her vision is also identical to
Richard's in being a vision of retribution (21–22). If we ask, "What
is missing from the alternate vision that Margaret offers us?,"
the answer must be mercy. Margaret's god seems to be the god
Richard appeals to also. The difference is that Richard has no
serious concern for where people spend eternity: they can all go
to heaven so long as he rules on earth.

Thus Margaret's most encompassing dramatic and dramaturgic function is to offer an alternate frame, although in these
early acts, I think that for many, perhaps most, spectators this
frame remains unpersuasive compared to Richard's, and the fram-

ing potential of Margaret's vision, as I suggest later, is realized only when Margaret herself reappears in act IV, scene iv. The point can be made another way: until we see whether Richard does become a victim, there is no way to distinguish Margaret's and Richard's visions insofar as both project an identical path of destruction for the rest of the Yorkist line. And at the end, whatever vision we synthesize cannot simply be Margaret's unless we are willing to identify the Christian god with Nemesis, and see that god as ruling a universe of justice without mercy.

In completing this activity, we turn to the pattern of the play as a whole with the following assignment: "It seems clear that the structure of this play is in two parts: Richard's rise, completed in act III, scene vii, and his fall, which begins in act IV. Look back at the playtext to see how you might define the two parts in more detail. In particular, what patterns can you discover that unite the two parts so that they are similar even though opposite in the rise-and-fall action?" This is also a moment to return to Emrys Jones because his analysis of the play coincides with the analysis developed here. In that analysis, Jones shows that the play's design has two halves (although his inference that this design coincided with a break in performances is not supported by evidence):

> There is, however, a further structural feature, well exemplified in *Richard III*, which is clarified by being seen in the setting of a two-part structure. This is the placing of an elaborately developed climactic sequence in the third act. Bradley had noticed that such scenes or sequences tended to occur at this position: . . . But he had not related this feature with the possible occurrence of an interval shortly after it. In Shakespeare's two-part arrangement the exciting material of his third acts was no doubt a highly satisfactory way of leading up to a break in the performance. We have reached a point of partial fulfillment and rest (a provisional ending), but the situation is rich in unrealized potentialities (a provisional beginning). . . . The play now makes a fresh start; the dramatist has to re-engage his audience's interest, in some cases win their sympathy for an unfamiliar group of characters or a new kind of dramatic material. (73–74)

The nature of this larger dramatic or trans-scenic design will become clearer as we move through the next three activities.

The Turning Point

In this next activity, we start from a narrow focus on a single scene as the key to the larger design of the second half of the play. Phrased in the terms introduced earlier, we examine how the playwright moves us through a process of reframing and re-aligning. Specifically, an anatomy of act IV, scene ii reveals the combination of dramatic and dramaturgic maneuvers through which the play transforms our relation to Richard. By studying this transformation, students gain a sharper sense of how a dramatist, through control of what Thomas Van Laan (*Idiom*) calls the *idiom of drama*, invites us to adopt a new frame and a new alignment. This activity also continues our exploration of drama's temporal dimension, for it demonstrates how reframing the action impels us to retrospectively reinterpret the events we thought we had comprehended. Studying this process helps students reflect on their tacit knowledge, and since they use this tacit knowledge in reading nondramatic literature as well, this work helps them recognize analogous devices in fiction and poetry. Here is a more detailed version of the assignment.

> *Assignment: How is Richard reframed? How are we realigned?*
> Having established your initial sense of the two-part structure of this play, please concentrate on what happens in act IV, scene ii, the scene after or of Richard's coronation. How does this scene not only initiate the second half of the play but also prompt a new relation between Richard and us, the spectators? That is, how does Shakespeare *reframe* Richard and the action as a whole and enact this reframing in such a way that he also induces us to assume a new alignment? Be as precise as you can in delineating not only the dramatic but also the dramaturgic means by which Shakespeare produces this transformation in how we frame and align ourselves in relation to that action.

In conducting this discussion, one of my aims is to integrate key elements of drama, discrepant awareness and the process of framing actions, which have been introduced as tools for exploring a play. Looking at the larger pattern of the course, we can see that in exploring *The Taming of the Shrew* you introduce a concept of action; in exploring *Richard III*, you show how the action is framed, and how that frame itself can be transformed by the unfolding action even as the action is first given meaning by the process of being framed. Furthermore, although this next point about what Bernard Beckerman (*Dynamics*) called the *dynamics of drama* is one that students almost never articulate themselves, you can show that this integration is embodied in the play's complex irony: it is the pivotal shift in the ironic relation that reverses the hierarchy of awareness, and it is this reversed hierarchy of awareness that is designed to induce spectators to reframe the protagonist.

You can also initiate this discussion by asking "How does the gap opened in act I, scene i close? And how does a new gap, between Richard and us, open?" If the students have begun to incorporate the concept of discrepant awareness into their critical practice, they will recognize, at least intuitively, that the gap starts to dissolve in this scene, and something else happens as well. As one student noted, "When you're king, you're watched more closely!" "Excellent!" I responded. "In a few minutes we can return to this point and ask it from a different angle: how does the power of the Crown, what the Elizabethans called the *office of king*, differ from the power Richard had before?"

As we discuss the scene, the students gradually enumerate the different elements that transform our relation to the play, causing us to reframe the action and realign ourselves in a way that situates us in the one-up position in relation to Richard. What they come to recognize is that we detach ourselves from Richard because Shakespeare contrives to have Richard become detached from us. Like the onstage subjects who revolt, there is a sense in which we also refuse to accept Richard's rule and thus refuse to be the subjects of this disabling but now disabled king. One can even argue that in this way we too join in the revolt that, with Richmond as its leader, eventually brings Richard down.

To put it another way: When Richard becomes king, he automatically reframes his world, but he is also realigned quite differently in his new office as king. Yet he does not realize that within the dramatic world of the play the office of king automatically entails a radical transformation, reframing the identity of anyone who holds that office. Nor does he realize that this is an identity that it is not in the power of anyone, no matter how brilliant a plotter or how stupendous an actor, to refuse. And of course as a character within the fiction, he cannot realize that assuming the office of king entails a radical shift in his dramaturgic identity as well.

The change in Richard's behavior begins immediately, for no sooner does Richard ascend the throne than he is possessed by anxiety, an emotion previously foreign to his risk-seeking nature— although eventually a student will remember that Anne's comment on Richard's nightmare-riddled sleep in the previous scene (IV.i.82–84) prepares us to note this change. He is nervous about the continued existence of the rightful heirs, his brother's sons, and he turns to Buckingham for advice. And this produces a second change, for Buckingham has become suddenly uncomprehending, and his obtuse replies drive Richard to ask:

> Shall I be plain? I wish the bastards dead,
> And I would have it suddenly perform'd.
> What say'st thou now? Speak suddenly, be brief. (IV.ii.18–20)

What we hear and see is a very different Richard, one whose anxiety is so intense that his only concern now is for the speed and certainty with which the deed can be accomplished, and not at all for the style in which it is performed. The maintenance of his crown, not the production of comedy, is now his paramount concern, and Richard displays no interest in contriving the sort of performance he staged in duping Clarence, nor in contriving the complex scene of the murder itself. When Buckingham "grows circumspect" (31), Richard simply looks for another accomplice he can hire with "corrupting gold" (34); and when he converses with Tyrrel, he simply reiterates that he wants "those bastards in the Tower" (74) eliminated. The emphasis is entirely on what he hopes to gain and not at all on the entertainment his show might provide—indeed, there is no show since the murder takes place offstage, since it is narrated by Tyrrel in act IV, scene iii, and since Tyrrel stresses the gravity of the deed:

> The tyrannous and bloody act is done,
> The most arch deed of piteous massacre
> That ever yet this land was guilty of. (1–3)

In the murder of Clarence, Richard's motives are subordinated to the macabre levity of the performance, but in the murder of the princes Richard's fearful motives and their criminal results are emphasized. The contrast is made unmistakable by the *lack* of irony when Richard asks, "Kind Tyrrel, am I happy in thy news?" (24); the earlier Richard would have heard the brutal joke—it interestingly anticipates Hamlet's first words to Claudius (*Hamlet* I.ii.65)—in calling "kind" the man who has just supervised the execution of Richard's kindred.

This lack of verbal irony on Richard's part is a symptom of a larger shift, for in the course of these two scenes the gap Richard opened between the spectators and the other characters disappears and is replaced by a new gap between the spectators and Richard. As discussion continues, students discover that four main elements contribute to the process by which we gradually reverse our alignment and find ourselves looking at Richard as being in a one-down position.

First, a gap is opened by Buckingham, whose refusal to take a hint about the princes when Richard implores him to "think now what I would speak" (IV.ii.10) compels Richard's blunt "I wish the bastards dead" (18). Like Richard earlier, so now Buckingham plays the *eiron*, and his choice to play dumb compels Richard to state what he wants in morally self-condemning language. In short, Richard shifts from wooing to command and thereby demonstrates that being in command renders him more, not less, vulnerable to public moral judgment.

Second, Buckingham's deliberate obtuseness produces another step that separates the spectators from Richard; as the duke departs, Catesby whispers to a courtier, "The King is angry, see, he gnaws his lip" (27). Until this moment, Richard has been a perfect actor, never betraying any discrepancy between his various personae and his true feelings, but now Catesby succeeds in doing what Hastings so miserably failed to do in act III, scene iv, namely, infer Richard's mood from his manner.

Third, the gap widens further as Richard, having decided that Buckingham "No more shall be the neighbor to my counsels" (43), makes no effort to dissemble his anger and ensures the duke's hostility by refusing to grant him the promised rewards. Buckingham realizes Richard's enmity, and his words invite us to make the comparison implicit in Catesby's remark when he concludes his soliloquy, "O, let me think on Hastings, and be gone / To Brecknock while my fearful head is on" (121–122). Buckingham is immediately followed by Tyrrel, who appears "To bear this tidings [the murder of the princes] to the bloody King" (IV.iii.22).

Fourth, dramaturgically there is a crucial shift in the type of speeches offered by Buckingham and Tyrrel, as well as in their sequence. They speak in soliloquy, the instrument Richard previously used to direct spectators' perceptions, and their soliloquies come in sequence. On the open stage, the lack of scene break will emphasize the point so that two commentators who offer negative perspectives on Richard speak directly to us and without pause, the second speech giving weight to the first as a new pattern unfolds.

This discussion often prompts someone to see that this shift is initiated by a fifth element—the very first words in the scene—which is actually the first element contributing to the closing of one gap and the opening of another. "Stand all apart," which at first sight might seem to emphasize our special relation with Richard, as Richard himself uses it to emphasize his special relation with Buckingham, actually serves as the prelude to the dissolution of that relation and the reversal of the pattern of discrepant awareness.

These five elements contribute to a single effect, for in all of them Richard is treated as an observed participant, while his erstwhile confederates take on his role as participant observer. They interpose themselves between Richard and us, thereby suggesting that Richard himself is now the legitimate object of the type of detached observation and ironic scorn with which he has taught us to regard his victims.

We can take a further step in this analysis since Richard himself makes the most explicit contribution to the opening of this new ironic gap. Even as he awaits Tyrrell, he is already thinking ahead to the wooing of young Elizabeth:

> I must be married to my brother's daughter,
> Or else my kingdom stands on brittle glass.
> Murther her brothers and then marry her—

Uncertain way of gain! But I am in
So far in blood that sin will pluck on sin. (IV.ii.60–64)

The question to ask here is "What is different in this speech from
the comparable speech at the end of act I, scene i, especially if we
see the two scenes as parallel in that in each of them Richard is
initiating his reign, first as the king of irony, then as the king of
England?" The answer is that the zest with which he looked forward to the wooing of Anne has disappeared, as have the aesthetic terms in which he anticipated that challenge. Instead, he
uses unambiguously the moral terms that have always previously
elicited one of his bursts of parody. His very lack of irony is ironic,
for in speaking this way Richard testifies to the reality of the
moral order he has always mocked, and thus validates his enemies' point of view. In this way, Richard tacitly acknowledges
the moral considerations he has, up to this moment, sought to
persuade the spectators to suspend.

Richard, however, is not yet conscious of his transformation
from comedian to criminal and, with the princes disposed of, he
speaks a soliloquy in which he seems to renew his intimacy with
the audience. Reviewing the steps he has taken, he decides it is
time to approach young Elizabeth and concludes, "To her go I, a
jolly thriving wooer" (IV.iii.43). He seems to have regained his
confidence and to promise another of his spectacular performances
in which the spectators can once again enjoy not only the show
itself but also the honesty that renders Richard superior to his
foolish or hypocritical victims. Furthermore, this speech, coming
as the climax of the two-scene sequence, also contains the cue for
understanding the design of the second half of the play as a whole.
What Richard does in his first scenes as king of England is propose to repeat his earlier play making, as though his reign is to be
the sequel to his rise as the king of ironic comedians: he began by
plotting the death of Clarence, and now he plots the murder of
his nephews; he married Anne, the widow of one of his earlier
victims, and now he plans to marry his niece Elizabeth, the sister
of the soon-to-be-slain princes. Yet while Richard seems determined to reproduce his previous successes, his histrionic skill disappears, his irony disintegrates, and his special relation with the
spectators, the basis for his honesty, vanishes.

With this aspect of the larger design laid out, you may want to spend a few minutes examining Richard's next wooing. (In an ideal teaching situation, we would explore this scene as we explored act I, scene ii, starting with a sound-and-movement exercise before grappling with the language.) The question to ask is "Are we meant to think that Richard fools Elizabeth, or to think that she fools him?" It is worth noting that many literary critics, perhaps even the majority, speak of this scene as a straight repetition in which Richard fools Elizabeth as he has fooled Anne. But they surely ignore not only the performance potentials of the scene but even some key features of the words of the text. The point here is not that there is a right answer but rather that from a performance view the scene is open, and that any argument about how to play the scene should attend to both the specific words of the scene and the design of the play as a whole.

Whether or not you explore the replay of a part one scene in part two, at this point the discussion reaches a crucial formulation that is also a perfect cue to initiate the next activity. This activity focuses again on the larger pattern of the play's two-part structure and also introduces another of the constitutive features of drama, formulated as a question students need to practice, namely, "What does repetition do?" Once they note that the wooing scene promised here is a repetition of Richard's wooing of Anne in the first act, we enumerate the complete set of parallels by which the second half echoes the first:

1. Wooing Anne	1. Wooing Elizabeth
Triumphant soliloquy	Triumphant soliloquy cut short
2. The murder of Clarence	2. The murder of the princes
Gleeful dialogue with murders	Pure business dialogue with agent
Show: Staged as black comedy	Tell: Reported as tragedy
3. Execution of Hastings	3. Execution of Buckingham
4. Executing Queen's relatives	4. Holding young Stanley hostage
5. Clarence's dream	5. Ghosts come back to haunt Richard
Clarence's monologue	Richard's own desperate soliloquy

6. Climactic playlet wins crown   6. Climactic battle, loses crown
and life

Having compiled this list, we pause for written reflections on what students have learned about the dramatic form of the play and the dramaturgic means Shakespeare discovered for enacting this transforming moment.

What Does Repetition Do?

Repetition is an element in all human communication, of course, but when we remember that two of the constitutive elements of drama are that its medium is the actor and that it unfolds through time, we can see that repetition will have unique realizations and dimensions as an aspect of performance. First, the fact that the medium is the actor means that we must analyze both verbal and nonverbal repetition since spectators at a performance are responding to a much wider array of signals than the purely verbal signals encountered by a reader, and a much more complex interplay between these signals. Second, the fact that this is a temporal medium means that the spectators are called on to use their memory in a more urgent and focused fashion than readers of prose fiction, for example, need to do. Therefore the topic of repetition leads us to consider the way in which drama employs the capacities of human memory to achieve effects ranging from creating the largest elements of a design, such as the two-part structure of *Richard III*, to the smallest elements, such as the recall of a single word or image up to two or three hours after it was first sounded. These concerns lead me to lecture more than in most segments of the course. I present the material in this extended form because, as I noted in the prologue, the students I teach need some analysis of the differences between drama, narrative, and poetry that, in an ideal curriculum, would be provided at an earlier phase of their education in the performing arts.

Assignment: As you reread *Richard III*, please note all the repetitions, of any sort and on any level, and any type, literary and theatrical, verbal and visual, that you hear or see. These can range from the largest structural repetitions, at the level of major actions like those we have listed, to the most specific repetitions of words or sound patterns. Then ask yourself: "If I noticed this repetition during a performance, or if I notice it now in reading and let it guide the imaginary performance in my mind, then what do I make of the connection? What has the dramatist or the performance invited me to discover? What meaning emerges from the experience of this repetition?" Come to class with a written list of some of the repetitions you have noted and begin to develop your answer as to how you would interpret those repetitions.

An indirect aim of this assignment is to initiate the sort of intense discussion that occurs among engaged spectators after a performance. This is the sort of discussion you have with friends as each of you starts to voice your understanding of the play through sharing the connections you have made. In the interplay of perception and interpretation, each person can sharpen a sense of the patterns that emerge as we turn sight into vision.

As we open the class discussion, I suggest that to answer the question "What does repetition do?" we can start with the question "What is repetition?" The question is so apparently simple-minded that it elicits giggles from some students, but they offer the obvious answer: "The same thing over again." And then the question becomes "How does repetition work?" First of all, you have to perceive the repetition. And when you do perceive a present moment as repeating an earlier moment, the question becomes, as I have already suggested, "If I noticed this repetition during a performance, or if I notice it now in reading and let it guide the imaginary performance in my mind, then what do I make of the connection? What has the dramatist or the performance invited me to discover in making the connection?"

Obviously, the primary action such a repetition triggers is that we compare the second moment with the first. At the simplest, we confront a connection that impels us to recognize stasis or change. Or we discover a spectrum of modulations between complete stasis and the sort of change we might call revolution or reversal. Or we discover apparent change but real stasis. Or apparent stasis but real change. Or change that leaves things the same. Other connections are not about change but rather a means of getting us to see something. And these are only some of the functions of repetition.

How the Dramatist Shapes and Focuses Our Attention

Before we continue, I want to spend a few minutes situating our discussion of repetition in terms of human memory as the dramatist confronts it, operating in a temporal medium in which the spectators have no means to stop the flow of the staged event nor any means to return to and examine earlier moments in that event. As we have noted before, this makes "seeing and hearing a play" an experience much more directly dependent on memory—a situation presented with great clarity by Gary Taylor in *To Analyze Delight*:

> In one very real sense a performed play is a "show": it is pure appearance: what is not "seen" (aurally or visually or intellectually) does not exist. In modern theatrical usage a "show" is something with little or no working relation between its parts, each of which asks to be appreciated simply in and for itself. . . . A play, so defined, differs from a show only in that the impact of its individual moments vitally depends upon our perception of their relationship with other moments, this perception of relation itself depending on whether we remember or recall an earlier moment or moments (or anticipate a future one). If we imagine a show as a sequence of discrete illuminations, which appear and disappear without ever coexisting, then a play is a sequence of illuminations which persist, accumulate and overlap; which gradually fade, rather than merely disappear; and—this is fundamental—which fade at different rates, and vary in their initial brightness or magnitude. Whether the dramatist succeeds in creating the impression of what we call "organic unity" thus depends upon his command of immediate perception and continued retention; consequently any description of the organizing principles of a dramatic work depends, finally, upon an understanding of the processes of human perception and memory. Moreover, such a description must concentrate on the individual illuminations themselves, the moments . . . —how they make their impression upon us, and how they bid for relative emphasis, for intellectual and emotional longevity. (16–17)

Furthermore, at the same time that a performed play is more dependent on memory than is a play read by an individual, it also places more extensive demands on memory since it offers the spectator a much greater sensory input, over a wider range of channels—including the crucial influence of the responses of other spectators. Reading gives you both fewer stimuli and more time in which to connect those stimuli, whereas a performance gives you more stimuli in a wider variety of channels, combined with less time in which to connect those stimuli. And it is out of this cascade of what Styan [*Elements* 68] calls "shifting impressions" that we create tentative gestalts, hypotheses about what the play is meaning up to that point, and then revise them as the play surprises us with new impressions.

The fundamental point, as Taylor develops it, is that our ability to profit from this greater richness depends on what we can remember:

> When, in a well-known experiment, a set of twelve numbers (in three rows of four) is flashed briefly on a screen, subjects can only recall an average of 4.3 numbers; but when, after seeing the entire set, they are asked to recall the numbers in one specific row, they can recall three of the four. This means that they have seen nine of the twelve, for they can recall three of any four: nine numbers are available for recall, but in the time it takes to write down four numbers the other five are forgotten. This experiment might serve as a model of the relation between the spectator and the play. Into any given moment, Shakespeare compacts (let us say) twelve elements, but so quickly does the moment pass that no spectator, on a first encounter, can perceive more than nine— although *which* nine will vary from spectator to spectator. These nine factors all contribute to the spectator's impression of that moment, but five will be almost immediately forgotten, as another moment crowded with detail demands his attention. As the play proceeds, our memory of the details of individual moments will progressively deteriorate. But by returning to the play we can perceive elements we missed at first, and we can retain more, so that, after many readings or viewings, we could theoretically perceive all twelve elements simultaneously, and retain them for the duration of the play. In fact, this model will have to be modified. We pay closer attention to some moments than others; the dramatist can sometimes strongly discourage us from seeing certain elements; the theoretical goal, of complete perception and recall, is not only impossible but undesirable. (10–11)

At the same time, it is important to realize that the dramatist also works to orchestrate our perceptions, in part by creating a hierarchy of attention. It seems evident, for example, that the basic hierarchy of attention is such that we usually focus first on the speaker, then on the person(s) being spoken to, and then on the person(s) spoken about, if present, or on other people in the scene. That is, our attention moves from first to second to third person. A clear example is

offered by the last scene of *Hamlet*, during which Shakespeare carefully controls where we are looking, in part by the action itself and in
part by the bids for attention explicitly made by various characters.

As Alan Dessen [*Elizabethan* 103] has pointed out, dramatists
and performers employ many nonverbal means to produce what he
terms *theatrical italics*: nonverbal moves that draw attention to or
throw a spotlight on a particular moment of action. Repetition in
blocking, for example, can italicize a later moment in a play, inviting us to connect that moment with an earlier moment we might
otherwise have been unlikely to connect with it. Theatrical italics,
then, are one way the dramatist establishes a hierarchy within the
wide range of connections we might make between different moments or elements in the play.

Exploring Repetition

In what follows, the primary objective is to gain greater skill in
realizing both the literary patterns of repetition and the potentials for theatrical or visual repetition, and to gain greater sensitivity to the interplay of visual and verbal repetition that is one
of the medium's most powerful resources. When you start to deal
with repetition in this fashion, one problem is how to categorize
the phenomena. I offer a three-part categorization I have found
useful.

First are the issues raised by those who, like Jones, attend to
the larger elements of design. These design elements include (1)
repeated actions within scenes; (2) repeated actions across separated scenes; (3) repeated actions of sequences of scenes; and (4)
repeated actions entailing the entire play, such as a division into
two or three or four segments or arcs.

Second is a set of categories articulated by, among many others, Dessen (*Elizabethan*), McGuire (*Speechless*), Slater, and
Urkowitz (*Shakespeare's*), whose work suggests what might be
called "A List of Visual Stylistic Devices or Theatrical Figures":
(1) entrances and exits, (2) interruptions, (3) repeated actions
and blocking, (4) silences, (5) kneelings, (6) kisses, (7) props, (8)
corpses.

Third is Van Laan's list of "verbal stylistic devices" in *The
Idiom of Drama*: (1) sound patterns, (2) words, (3) allusions, (4)
image patterns, (5) repetition of ideas, (6) symbols.

Once we get started, there is in fact a superabundance that makes it hard to keep up with, let alone categorize, all the items offered. Sometimes, therefore, I preorganize or precategorize what follows in a simple way by asking that we hear all the items that might in any way be thought of as verbal repetition before we hear the items we might call visual repetition.

VERBAL REPETITION

Words and Key Words. *Crown, curse, pray, love, conscience. . . .* A number of these words we have discussed already.

Repeated Phrases. There can, of course, be syntactic as well as semantic repetition. The most vivid example is the stichomythia we explored in act I, scene ii, which mixes both syntactic and semantic repetition. That is, within the syntactically parallel structure the same word may be used again, although reversed, or else part of that word may reappear in a word with a contrasting meaning, as when Richard says, "By such despair I should accuse myself," and Anne responds, "And by despairing shalt thou stand excused" (I.ii.85–86).

Rhyme. Rhyme is also a form of repetition, of course, and in these plays it may end a scene, signaling closure in a couplet, the form of iambic pentameter we have learned to hear as providing closed-sounding poetry.

Imagery. Many students will at least know the concept of imagery and of an image cluster. If you are using the *Riverside Shakespeare*, you can turn to the introduction on imagery by Harry Levin:

> The basic trope, or figure of speech, can be illustrated by an obvious example from the Old English. Literally, we say that a ship *sails* the sea. But figuratively, speaking the language of connotation rather than denotation, we may say that the ship *ploughs* the sea. This implies a correspondence which can be stated logically:

$$\frac{\text{Ship}}{\text{Sea}} = \frac{\text{Plough}}{\text{(Land)}}$$

The literal reality is the first term of the equation; the figurative expression is the second; and "land" is in parentheses because it is out of sight. . . .

The sphere of Shakespeare's images is so vast and rich in itself that it has been investigated and charted for clues to his personal temperament. But though we can follow up associations of thought through his image-clusters, these are subordinated to his controlling purposes as a playwright. The imagery fulfills a structural and a thematic function, linking together a train of ideas or projecting a scheme of values. . . . The sun, a traditional emblem of kingship from the time of the Pharaohs, sheds its light on Shakespeare's procession of English kings, detaching itself from Richard II after his downfall to shine on the erstwhile Bullingbrook, now King Henry IV. . . . But though we cannot overrate the importance of the poetry, its function is to orchestrate the drama, to integrate the words at every turn with the actions and the ideas. (13, 14)

There are a number of major images in *Richard III*, many of which we discuss in enumerating key words. The *sun*—Edward IV's badge, as the notes say—sets up much of the play on light and shadow and recurs at the end in the exchanges about whether the sun will appear. The *crown* is another primary image. A subtler cluster pointed out by Rossiter is the images from the classical afterlife:

> *Queen Margaret.* Witness my son, now in the shade of death,
> Whose bright out-shining beams thy cloudy wrath
> Hath in eternal darkness folded up. (I.iii.266–268)

> *Clarence.* O then began the tempest to my soul!
> I pass'd (methought) the melancholy flood,
> With that sour ferryman which poets write of,
> Unto the kingdom of perpetual night. (I.iv.44–47)

Clarence's imagery also foreshadows the ghosts who materialize in the last act.

Queen Elizabeth. If you will live, lament; if die, be brief,
That our swift-winged souls may catch the King's,
Or like obedient subjects follow him
To his new kingdom of ne'er changing night. (II.ii.43–46)

And, of course, there is the incredibly dense animal imagery applied to Richard, so plentiful that it can be instructive to let students try to compile a complete enumeration and thereby discover just how pervasive and extraordinarily vituperative this imagery is. Besides being a dog, "Richard III appears further as poisonous toad, as foul hunch-back'd toad, bottled spider, as hedgehog, elvish-mark'd, abortive, rooting hog," as Wolfgang Clemen notes in *The Development of Shakespeare's Imagery*. Clemen summarizes:

> We cannot exaggerate the imaginative value of these revolting animal-images. Without our becoming conscious of it, the repulsive figure of the hunch-backed Richard as we see it upon the stage is repeatedly transformed into animal bodies conforming to his nature, and thus his brutal, animal character is illuminated from this angle too. *Richard III* is Shakespeare's first play in which the chief character is delineated by symbolical images recurring as a *leitmotif*. In *Henry VI* the animal-images, which are occasionally employed for individual combatants, are not yet differentiated. . . . In *Richard III*, however, the imagery begins to serve individual characterization. (51–52)

Ideas. Perhaps the most important repeated idea is that people who take oaths will be destroyed if they break those oaths: it is, of course, a form of ironic reversal that connects this play with *Hamlet* (Van Laan [*Idiom*] offers a comprehensive reading of this motif in *Hamlet*). Here we begin to see how the verbal and visual patterns interlock in the execution speeches given by Richard's victims: this is a pattern in which the speaker recalls his oath, recalls Margaret's warning, admits his guilt, and accepts his fate, ending with a final prayer for England and perhaps a prophecy. These prophetic speeches serve to frame the eventual triumph of Richmond, who is made to appear as the answer to a series of prayers and prophecies. The example of execution scenes is also, of course, an example of visual repetition and thus offers a cue for turning to this topic.

VISUAL REPETITION

Entrances and Exits. The complex pattern of act I, scene ii has already been noted, where the entrance and exit of King Henry's coffin is an emblem of Anne's reversal and the rise of Richard's fortunes: having killed this king, he now gains control of his burial. The sequence of exits to the executions fits here as well.

Repeated Actions/Blocking. In this play, we have a sequence in which Anne kneels to lament for Henry VI and curse his murderer; Richard kneels when he offers Anne the chance to kill him, in effect seeking to have her reverse her curse; and Stanley kneels to secure a pardon for a murderous servant from King Edward. There will be other kneelings, as when the Duke of York must kneel to his brother as the new King Edward. The final kneelings that seem mandated will be those of Richmond, who may kneel in act V, scene iii when Stanley offers Richmond his mother's blessing, and who surely kneels when he prays to God before he sleeps. His kneeling will not only complete a pattern but also highlight differences: like Anne, Richmond kneels to pray, but he does not curse; and he kneels to pray as Richard, a few minutes before, does not. Furthermore, it is likely that Richmond will kneel when he is crowned, and again we have a moment when the verbal and the visual unite: the image of the crown, the literal crown, and the act of kneeling combine as Richmond at once gains power and announces his submission to power.

Corpses. We have examined the second most notable appearance of a corpse in the body of King Henry VI, the ironic outcome in which Richard climaxes his "counterfeit profession" of penitence by requesting Anne's permission to inter the corpse. Of course, the most notable corpse is that of Richard himself, and what happens to his corpse can resonate with the treatment of Henry VI.

Eventually I ask the class to reformulate the different types of repetition they have enumerated into a more coherent array. One class organized the material by returning to the categories of visual and verbal:

Visual	*Verbal*
Entrances/Exits	Exact word repeated (semantic)
Costumes	Stichomythia, other syntactic repeats
Properties	Rhyme, other repeated sounds
Gestures	Imagery
Expression	Allusions
Blocking	Ideas
Symbols	Symbols
Whole scenes/scenic forms	Larger verbal patterns,
Execution scenes	Execution speeches

This list returns us to asking, "How can I teach myself to read so that I am able to discern these elements more precisely, or invent ways of realizing these patterns more fully?"

As I have already stated, we are working to develop students' ability to imagine how visual repetition and verbal recollection can combine to create meaning through their interaction. This occurs, for example, when the dramatist has a character note a repetition or articulate its significance. The richest cases will be those in which the action literalizes the language, as happens frequently in Shakespeare when a key metaphor is enacted on stage, or, conversely, when a carefully developed series of actions is suddenly articulated in a climactic verbal pattern. In *King Lear*, for example, Edgar, seeking to understand the nature of "the worst," suddenly recognizes the inadequacy of his just-completed formulation when he confronts the worst he has never imagined in the appearance of his newly blinded father.

Given the work we have done on the two-part structure, this discussion of repetition can become a cue for further unpacking these patterns. One of the most elegant analyses occurs when a student focuses on the ghosts at the end of the play. When we ask, "What do the ghosts do?," the answer is, "The ghosts provide an onstage review of the action":

1. Prince Edward, son to Henry VI: referred to in I.ii

2. King Henry VI: coffin and perhaps corpse seen in I.ii

3. Clarence: murdered in I.iv

4–6. Rivers, Grey, Vaughan: executed after (in) III.iii

7–8. Two young princes: murdered between IV.ii and IV.ii

9. Lord Hastings: executed after III.iv, head appears III.v

10. Lady Anne: dies, poisoned, after IV.ii

11. Duke of Buckingham: executed after V.i—pattern carries over into act V, and would be continued if young George Stanley were executed

Thus we come to see how the eleven ghosts serve as an *external memory*, a means by which the dramatist compensates for any potential weakness of memory (Taylor), and in doing so prompts us to enumerate the interlocking complex of patterns:

1. The Curses and Prophesies: Where Are the Curses Laid Out?
   I.i   Richard's prophesy about "G" turns out to be about himself.
   I.ii   Anne's curse of Richard and, unwittingly, of herself.
   I.iii Margaret's curses/prophecies: King Edward, Prince Edward, Queen Elizabeth, Rivers, Dorset, Hastings, Richard, Buckingham.
   II.i   Nobles swear to king, set up their own downfalls: Rivers, Hastings, Queen Elizabeth, Dorset, Buckingham.
          Richard avoids an actual oath.
          King tries to ward off his own guilt falling on his wife and children.

2. The Curses Come True—and Lead to the Prayed-for Salvation of England
   I.iv   Clarence murdered/executed, tries to ward off curse on family.
   III.iii Woodvilles executed.

III.iv Hastings executed.
IV.i Anne foresees her own death.
V.i Buckingham executed.
V.v Richard killed in battle.

3. The Curses Come True: Lamentations
   I.ii Anne laments King Henry and Prince Edward.
   I.iii Margaret laments, hence enumerates, Lancastrian losses and predicts Yorkist losses—hence sets up future laments.
   II.ii Duchess of York and Clarence's children lament Clarence.
          Queen Elizabeth laments King Edward.
   IV.i Queen Elizabeth, Duchess of York, Anne pray for and proleptically lament the fate of the princes.
   IV.iv Queen Elizabeth and the Duchess of York lament the princes.
           Queen Margaret joins them, enumerates how her curse is fulfilled.
   V.iii The ghosts are also, of course, posthumous lamenters.

Within these unfolding, interlocking, and encompassing patterns is the pattern created by Richard himself, which occurs as a form of repetition in the two halves of the play, since Richard, as we noted earlier, seeks to replay the scenes that were his hits in the first half.

4. Richard Replays or Seeks to Replay His Previous Hits
   a. Murder of Clarence / Murder of princes

| I.iii Richard + Murderers | I.iv Clarence murdered onstage |
| IV.ii Richard + Tyrrell | IV.iii Princes murdered offstage |

   b. Richard woos a woman he has wronged

| I.ii Anne | IV.iv Young Eliz. through Queen Elizabeth |

5. Curse Completer or Liberator Foreshadowed and Arrives
  IV.i   Duchess sends people, mentions Richmond.
  IV.iv   Richard hears of Richmond.
  IV.v   Stanley and Urswick.
  V.ii   Richmond's first appearance.
  V.iii   Richard & Richmond: ghosts, orations.
  V.v   Richard versus Richmond: duel, and only one
          orator left.

6. Margaret's Two Appearances: I.iii, IV.iv
  What is the logic here? Especially *after* princes' death?
  Subtle connection: "A dire induction" as echo of Richard's
    induction—his opening soliloquy.
  Winter/summer, now become autumn.
  Bridge: completion of most but not all of her curses;
    she passes on the cursing torch to duchess and Queen
    Elizabeth.

7. Richard's Last Soliloquy
  Impels us to remember others and discover transformation(s)
  in Richard: "acquisition of conscience."
  Prompts us to ask: "What is the relation between the transformation in Richard (if there is one) and the transformation
  in our relation to Richard?"

This charting also enables students to see how pervasively patterned the play is: of its twenty-three scenes, one or more of these
patterns shape all but four, and there is another subpattern in
those four scenes. In the two scenes in the first half, the citizens
(II.iii) and the scrivener (III.vi) comment on the condition of England and, at least in the scrivener's scene, indicate they see the
plotting going on. In the two scenes in the second half, the plotting against Richard goes forward: in act IV, scene v, Stanley sends
Urswick to tell Richmond that Elizabeth has promised her daughter to Richmond, as well as warn of the plight of Stanley's own
son George; and in act V, scene ii, Richmond makes his first appearance. In a play of 3,800 lines, these four scenes comprise a
total of 106 lines. These elements make this one of the most
densely patterned efforts in Shakespeare's canon, and unlike some

of the later plays' subtler designs, this patterning is so explicit that it seems intended to be perceived by spectators. It is also available to readers, for whom pattern perception may serve as a cue to re-create what a performance does to and with a live audience.

Staging Richard's Death: What Does the Ending Do?

As part of the ongoing project of learning about the different potentials of the modern naturalistic stage and the Elizabethan symbolic stage, students imagine and orchestrate various ways to stage the duel between Richard and Richmond. As they perform this activity, they learn how their imagined performances embody alternate stage logics, and how these alternate endings complete what turn out to be alternate designs in the play's text. They thus will also be working toward answering the question "What does or can an ending do?"

> *Assignment*: Review our discussion of Alan Dessen's distinction between the two *stage logics*, symbolic and naturalistic (*Elizabethan* 1–3). Then turn to act V, scene v and ask yourself, "How do I want to stage the final battle, especially the duel between Richard and Richmond?" Think first about how it might be staged in a modern, naturalistic version, with the emphasis on the fight itself; and then begin to imagine how you might stage it in terms of the symbolic dimension that Dessen describes. For this second version, ask yourself how the staging might indicate some meaning or meanings in a symbolic dimension. How might the fight be staged to connect with and complete some of the patterns created by the play up to this moment? Use your imagination to think about alternative possibilities and about how symbols can be enacted. As Dessen says, "a climactic Shakespearean fight, like a climactic Shakespearean speech, may weave together various threads into a highly theatrical yet intensely meaningful moment and may leave an audience with an epitome of what has gone before, a realization in action of central motifs or images or oppositions" (*Elizabethan* 129).

In developing the model for teaching offered here, I have found that just as Dessen's essay is useful for students, so his *Elizabethan Stage Conventions and Modern Interpreters* is useful for teachers. In particular, his presentation of alternate stagings for the Richard-Richmond battle is a compact model, combining his knowledge of actual performances with his own inventive abilities as a creator of imaginary stagings. Here is the core of his presentation:

> To see both the potential and the difficulties in reconstructing Elizabethan stage violence, consider one last Shakespearean example, the rather unhelpful Folio stage direction for the final fight in *Richard III*: "*Alarum, Enter Richard and Richmond, they fight, Richard is slain.*" Clearly, this combat serves as an exciting climax to a long play, but "*they fight*" leaves open many possibilities. Thus, if the critic or director prizes the logic of patterning, the blow that kills Richard can echo unmistakably the thrust he asks for but does not receive from Lady Anne in I.ii. . . . If the emphasis is placed upon Richmond as God's captain (see especially V.iii.109–18, 240–71), his blows could fall with more than human force upon Richard. . . . If Richard eventually is killed with his own weapon . . . his fate could confirm Buckingham's assertion of the power of "that high All-seer" who forces "the swords of wicked men / To turn their own points in their masters' bosoms" (V.i.20–4). If Richard dies when forsaken by Ratcliff or others in the final moments, his demise could be linked to Margaret's curse: "Thy friends suspect for traitors while thou liv'st, / And take deep traitors for thy dearest friends" (I.iii.222–3). If the staging suggests not Richmond's strength but Richard's weakness or surprising ineptness, the fight could be the final moment in a series started by the "myself myself confound" oath (IV.iv.397–405), where Richard pawns his future success, and continued in the "coward conscience" soliloquy, with its emphasis upon guilt and revenging "myself upon myself" (V.iii.178–207).
>
> Note that not all of these choices are incompatible with stage "realism" nor are they mutually exclusive, but each draws its potential meaning or force from a somewhat different logic, whether that logic is based upon patterning or surprise or symbolism or iterative imagery. From the limited evidence we cannot determine how this moment would have been staged in the original production, yet the director or critic who fails to consider such options may unwittingly be diminishing an important moment in a rich play by considering only those possibilities consonant with our prevailing tastes or assumptions. (128–29)

When they present the naturalistic stagings, students often concentrate on the fight itself and—influenced, surely, by the elaborate stagings of fights in movies and, more recently, I expect, by the complex choreography of video games—on the sustained possibilities of physical combat itself. But as we move into Elizabethan stagings and into considering the symbolic possibilities such action may produce, they offer an intriguing array of imagined duels.

One striking possibility was offered by Jackie, who proposed that the ghosts return and surround Richard and Richmond as they fight. Her staging suggested that Richard brings about his own death by his success: in her staging, we would see that those he has had murdered or executed come back to join the army that defeats him. This continues the pattern of the dreams and shows us the dead as well as the living enlisting with Richmond. Just as a number of the ghosts end by encouraging Richmond with an echo of Buckingham's "God and good angels fight on Richmond's side" (V.iii.175), so also the souls of the dead would fight on Richmond's side and thereby obtain revenge. This powerful production idea suggested another, which was to have the women who are left alive watch the scene, perhaps from the upper stage: thus the women who have chorally spent their time lamenting the dead, uttering curses, and praying for revenge now witness the fulfillment of their prayers. The student who suggested this had not seen the BBC production in which the final image shows Margaret seated on top of a pile of corpses and, in Robert Potter's words, "cradling the body of the dead King Richard like some demonic anti-Pieta, her golden curls shaking exultantly, gorgon-like" (118).

In this same class, Mary asked, "But who actually kills Richard?" This question surprised some people because the Folio stage direction presented in the text seems clearly to mandate that Richmond kills Richard:

Alarum. Enter [King] Richard *and* Richmond; *they fight; Richard is slain. Then, retreat being sounded, [flourish and] enter* Richmond, [Stanley, *Earl of*] Derby, *bearing the crown, with other* Lords, *etc.* [The Folio has "diuers other Lords" and no "etc."] (793)

But of course it does not have to be Richmond or Richmond alone: as in Laurence Olivier's film, where Richard is surrounded by soldiers, hemmed in, and impaled on their spears, such an ending can complete a literalization of Richard as the boar. So one answer to the questions "How is the duel staged?" and "What does the ending do?" can be: "The duel is staged so that Richard is killed as if he were the wild boar, and the ending shows us how he has progressed from being a villain to being an animal hunted and killed as if he were not human at all."

In this class, I quoted Dessen's (*Elizabethan* 128–29) record of two productions in which Richmond drove Richard to his knees, and then killed him, with a blocking that made it evident that Richmond was completing the stroke that Anne started but could not finish. This is an excellent example of how different endings can realize different patterns latent in the play's text. This blocking completes a pattern by urging us to recall act I, scene ii so as to make a series of interlocking connections. It will unite Richmond with Anne and suggest that he is completing the revenge she prayed for. And since Anne herself has been murdered by Richard, Richmond is now also taking vengeance for Anne. Furthermore, since Anne wanted vengeance for the murder of the Lancastrian King Henry VI and his son Prince Edward, Richmond can seem to be an agent avenging the House of Lancaster, and thus an agent for Margaret as well. Even if no production actually brings the women on stage, we are invited to make this connection with the final prayer-curse Margaret utters:

> Richard yet lives, hell's black intelligencer,
> Only reserv'd their factor to buy souls
> And send them thither; but at hand, at hand,
> Ensues his piteous and unpitied end.
> Earth gapes, hell burns, fiends roar, saints pray,
> To have him suddenly convey'd from hence.
> Cancel his bond of life, dear God, I pray,
> That I may live and say, "The dog is dead." (IV.iv 71–78)

Thus, as Richmond completes the vengeance called for by Richard's victims, he does indeed seem to be acting for England insofar as "England" is in part embodied by all those nobles who, while themselves guilty of sins or moral violations such as murder and treason, nonetheless at the moment of death recognize the need for a ruler who will end the seemingly endless cycle of what Rossiter memorably called retributive reaction (1–22, 40–64) and restore England by restoring a just king to the throne—a man whose acquisition of the crown is stained only with the blood of the man who had least right to wear it and who hideously abused it.

With the completion of this discussion, we move into the last activity, which focuses on a specific moment and also attempts to step back in order to gain perspective on the play as a whole.

Richard's End versus the Ending of *Richard III*

As several critics have suggested, the ending reflects a tension in the emerging genres that Shakespeare was in part re-creating but in part inventing in this play. On the one hand, coming after the Henry VI plays, *Richard III* embodies a clearer conception of what a history play could be and do; on the other hand, coming at some point in time not far from *Titus Andronicus*, his first essay at tragedy, *Richard III*, as its Senecan elements suggest, embodies Shakespeare's interest in creating a tragic dimension to history. Yet it seems clear that while the play was and is an enormous theatrical success, the elements of history and tragedy are not quite integrated into a harmonious design. Richard's final soliloquy, for example, so different from any of his earlier soliloquies and so much closer to Clarence's account of and response to *his* dream, represents an experiment in creating tragedy, but there is general critical agreement that this speech by itself cannot and does not transform Richard into a tragic hero.[2] Furthermore, the design of the play obviously requires that at the end Richard be seen as pure villain. Yet perhaps Shakespeare did see this ending as fitting the older sense of tragedy defined as "the fall of princes." As the opening for our closing discussion of this play, I offer a two-part assignment. You may assign each part separately, or divide them among groups in class; and if you want a simpler focus, you can assign only the first part.

Assignment: The play is titled *The Tragedy of King Richard III*, but in the Folio it is placed in the section called Histories. Thus the printing history of the play suggests a question: Is the play a history or a tragedy? or somehow both? Perhaps this is not a good way to ask the question. Perhaps we should try this: For the next class meeting, please offer us a preliminary definition of a *tragedy* as you understand that term. And then present all the reasons that make you believe this play is best seen as a tragedy. Then repeat the procedure for a *history*: define the term as you understand it, or cite a definition, and then present the reasons this play is best seen as a history. Does one case seem more plausible to you than the other? Why? Present your third set of reasons for choosing one over the other—or for choosing neither. Can you argue for some other term?

To help you think about this issue more concretely, ask yourself, "How does Richard's final soliloquy, which he speaks after waking from the 'nightmare' of the ghosts, support a case for calling this a history? for calling this a tragedy?" In short, consider the question "What does Richard's final soliloquy do?" and also "What does Shakespeare manage to do by having Richard speak this soliloquy?" Other questions and other connections will no doubt occur to you as you immerse yourself in this work.

Exploring the Relation of the Play's Genre and Design

In one class, the discussion of genre first emerged in response to an earlier assignment, but I include that discussion here because it shows how the questions that are the core of this course can interlock in richly varied ways; how the set of questions as a whole is flexible; and how one aspect of the approach is an invitation for the teacher to improvise, yet improvise within the suite of concepts that frame the course.

In this class, the students had just completed the assignment of examining Richard's opening scene looking for the potential for comedy. I asked, "So how did you discover potential for comedy in Richard?"

> LISA: The play is called a tragedy, so I don't think Shakespeare would create comedy; it would confuse spectators because it would not be tragic. They thought tragedy was serious, had an unhappy ending. So it can't be comedy!

> INSTRUCTOR: Good! You raise an essential issue here, the issue of

genre—and what genre *does*. You are exemplifying one use of genre, namely, labeling. And in English classes, this is often how the concept of genre is or seems to be used: you are assigned a paper or exam question and you write an essay saying "X is a comedy because it has a happy ending and . . ." But that type of labeling tends to be done as a static, detached vision. I would like us to think about genre as a dynamic phenomenon and to ask another version of my basic question "What does a genre do?" So write for a few minutes, please.

NANCY: Genre lets you know what to expect. It gives you a sense of control and safety: you won't be surprised.

JAK: I think the opposite. Genre often closes down people's thinking because it involves categories and stereotypes. I've seen productions where the audience wants to laugh at something funny but they stop themselves because they think it is a tragedy, they shouldn't laugh.

INSTRUCTOR: And you can also see directors who cut out the funny parts of a tragedy because they think that must be irrelevant. So it can go both ways.

JAK: But then that's bad directing!

INSTRUCTOR: Ah! But what else can genre do? Or what else can a dramatist do with genre? Play against it. Why might Shakespeare do that? For example: the original audience for this play, even without knowing the title, would expect what?

TERRI: Richard the king killer!

Two Steps in Exploring the Ending

Exploring the relation of genre and design can be sharpened by a two step-move, first imagining an alternative ending and then using this imagined alternative to probe and sharpen what we see in the words of the actual ending. The first step is to ask, "Suppose Richard won?"

Suppose, that is, that Richard defeated Richmond and then turned to the audience in a final soliloquy, saying, "Ah ha! So you thought I would be defeated? You believed in Margaret's curses and Richmond's god? But I have triumphed, and my explanatory system turns out to be the accurate description of the universe!" What would happen?

In some classes, this question produces ripples of laughter and contrasting responses. "That would be shocking!" say some students. "That would be great!" is the response from others. And indeed this would be a great play, but in a different way.

The question is: "What would happen to the pattern of the play? How would Richard's triumph complete the action? And what *genre* would the play belong to?"

For Richard the play would be or become pure comedy. For those he defeats, the play would become a tragedy of a specific sort, namely, a tragedy in which people are not merely defeated and destroyed, but in which they must face the destruction of their explanatory system. And for audiences? Or for us in this classroom? For audiences or readers, a triumphant Richard would prove not merely his brilliance as a Machiavellian politician-actor but also the apparent validity of his vision. Thus the play would be deeply unnerving, too unnerving to be pure comedy, because Richard both attacks and satirizes normative values, and as the successful satirist he would have stunningly proved his vision triumphant. The play would be comic history for him but satiric history for spectators and readers. Or perhaps worse, it would be a tragedy in reverse: not so much that good people die—Richmond is probably not someone we care enough about, the princes are too innocent to be tragic—as that the most unnerving exponent of amorality triumphs. So satirical history would have the tones of nihilism for us, ending with empty laughter.

With this contrast established, we can look again more clearly at the ending we actually have, which is Richmond's final speech, and ask, "What does this ending do?" We read the speech again and ask, "What relation to us does Richard's successor establish? Compared to Richard's opening soliloquy in particular, what does Richmond's speech *do*?"

> *Richmond.* Inter their bodies as becomes their births.
> Proclaim a pardon to the soldiers fled
> That in submission will return to us,
> And then as we have ta'en the sacrament,
> We will unite the White Rose and the Red.
> Smile heaven upon this fair conjunction,
> That long have frown'd upon their enmity!
> What traitor hears me, and says not amen? (V.v.15–22)

After detailing the virtuous actions he will perform, which indicate that Richmond will carry out the office of king as truly as Richard was performing it falsely, he speaks a powerful line: "What traitor hears me, and says not amen?" I suggest that once again the play cues us to explore a question about address, namely, "Who does the actor playing Richmond address?" Onstage he can direct his words to captives from Richard's army, if there are any. But Richmond can also include us, the spectators, and then the question becomes "How does he include us and what type of response can we make?"

From Richmond's point of view, he may be indicating what we hope is his genial presumption that only those on his side will be there alive; or he may be assuming that we will be happy to enlist on his side, whether because it is victorious or because right and victorious cannot be distinguished. But we can also imagine, as Wilbur Sanders invites us to imagine (72), the full force of the word *traitor* in the 1590s, when we would have walked through a city where the heads of traitors were regularly stuck up on poles. So we can also imagine or hear Richmond as not merely addressing the spectators but as uttering a threat, saying, "Only traitors will not join in, so not to join in is to arouse suspicion that one is a traitor." And suddenly we discover another pattern that can be italicized in completing the action. Strikingly, Richmond like Richard asks for our complicity, but in a way that is at once much more reassuring and potentially much more threatening than Richard's tacit request for our silent complicity in act I, scene i or act I, scene ii. At the same time, there is a striking parallel, because Richard begins with an action that looks comic for a minute but that soon leads to Clarence's death as a traitor.

What are our choices? We may by this point indeed give the wholehearted assent that Richmond's speech assumes. But if we have any impulse to respond to the question as more than rhetorical, his words make us aware of the price to be paid for withheld response or resistance, at least by those who were onstage in this virtual world. If Antony Hammond is right, as it seems he is when he suggests (in his note on this line in the Arden edition), "Presumably the onlookers pronounce the word in response" (330), then if all those onstage do indeed say "Amen," their act informs us that we too would have to participate. Again, we can imagine ourselves in the original audience of the play, looking at this actor who represents the grandfather of the present ruler—in whose presence we would indeed be well advised to say "Amen" if urged to do so. After all, it might be the case that for some of us our grandfathers or great-grandfathers had in fact confronted and made this choice.

I do not expect this analysis to convince even a majority of teachers of Shakespeare's plays, any more than it convinces all students. But it does illustrate why devoting time to learning to read a play differently is so powerful. As I have said before, doing so means that we must learn to imagine and analyze the complex interplay of verbal and visual elements, and that we must learn to recognize both what is mandated and what is open in a play's design. And as I hope the discussion of Richmond's apparently simple line demonstrates, even when we have grasped the design in great detail, the way in which that design is projected and emphasized still remains open to interesting, creative (and yes, of course, potentially distorting) acts of invention by the players, who mediate between the playwright and the playgoers, and whose work, at its best, can cause us to resee the pattern we thought we knew so well.

Hamlet:

Opening Playtexts, Closing Performances

Prologue: When Is a Soliloquy Not a Soliloquy?

> What would one not give to go backward through the centuries
> to see the first performance of *Hamlet*, played as Shakespeare
> had it played! . . . Though, in a sense, there was no first perfor-
> mance of *Hamlet*. And doubtless many of the audience for
> Shakespeare's new version of the old play only thought he had
> spoiled a good story of murder and revenge by adding too much
> talk to it. (Granville-Barker 8)

William Empson titled a provocative essay about the play "*Hamlet*
When New," and Harley Granville-Barker noted that we sometimes need a "reminder that here is a play, not a collection of
ritualized quotations" (18). Their remarks emphasize the fact that
one challenge we face when we begin *Hamlet* is that many students think they "know" the play or know what the play is
"about," and these preconceptions often prevent them from seeing the play as "new."

Certainly, when I ask them to do so, students will list what
they already know about *Hamlet*, even if they have neither read
nor seen the play. They know that *Hamlet* is the play in which
there is a skull, a skull that provokes the words "Alas, poor
Yorick"; that there is a ghost; that Hamlet says, "There are more
things in heaven and earth, Horatio, / Than are dreamt of in
your philosophy"; that we hear that "There's something rotten
in the state of Denmark"; that Shakespeare advises us "to thine
own self be true, / And it must follow, as the night the day, / Thou
canst not then be false to any man." Some of them have seen the
Olivier film and thus know that *Hamlet* is "the tragedy of a man
who could not make up his mind." And students know that *Ham-*

let is "the play with all those soliloquies," and that the most famous soliloquy commences "To be, or not to be."

Yet in thinking they know that "To be, or not to be" is a soliloquy, students exemplify the distorting effects of familiarity. When we look at the speech in context, one of the most striking facts about "To be, or not to be" is that it is and is not a soliloquy. In fact, the phrasing I have just used is itself an enactment of the problem the playtext provokes. Using this phrasing, I once said to a class: "It *is* a soliloquy insofar as Hamlet speaks *as if* he were alone—and speaking *as if* alone has traditionally been how critics have articulated what they believe to be the convention constituting soliloquies. But it is *not* what has sometimes been called a 'full-blown' soliloquy because Hamlet is not alone. Claudius and Polonius are in hiding somewhere onstage, waiting to observe Ophelia's encounter with Hamlet; and Ophelia herself is, as far as the texts of the play mandate, onstage and, in some productions, visible throughout the speech. The most famous soliloquy in all of Shakespeare's plays is an overseen (and perhaps overheard) speech, not a full-blown soliloquy." But in terms of our focus on performance, this analysis itself is askew, and considering the multiple potentials of the text, it seems more accurate to say this: The speech has the potential to be performed as a full-blown soliloquy, by a Hamlet who voices his thoughts while alone on stage, neither overheard nor overseen. But it can also be performed by a Hamlet who speaks thinking he is alone while Ophelia or Ophelia, Polonius, and the King are visible to us. Or it can be performed by a Hamlet who knows that one or more of these people are present and only pretends to voice his private thoughts—in which case, the speech is Hamlet's *performance* of a soliloquy, intended to function as indirect address to his onstage audience. Or it can be performed, and has been performed, by a Hamlet who not only sees but also chooses to address Ophelia directly. In what seems an apposite irony, then, it turns out to be very hard indeed to use forms of the verb *to be* in describing the most famous speech to begin with and focus on this verb. Furthermore, much of the dramatic function of the speech lies precisely in its both being and not being a soliloquy: for this peculiar situation indicates that, as Thomas Van Laan notes, "even in the midst of the others, then, Hamlet is profoundly alone" (*Idiom* 238); conversely, even in his efforts to be alone, Hamlet is surrounded by those who cause his alienation.[1]

This example captures what happens when we begin to attend to the play as if it were new and to follow its moment-by-moment unfolding. We might be tempted to say that we have simply made a mistake that we should correct by calling this speech a dramatic monologue. The problem, however, is intrinsic, for as designed the speech both is and is not a soliloquy—and indeed it is clear that we will go on speaking of it, as I sometimes do in class and in this chapter, as a soliloquy. Part of what is fundamental to how the play does what it does, as Stephen Booth has demonstrated, resides in the way it persistently maneuvers spectators and readers into misformulated perceptions and misdirected expectations. It is not so much that we make mistakes, but rather that the world of *Hamlet* often presents a complex reality while directing attention to only one part of that reality—until a later event impels us to notice the inadequacy of a formulation the play itself invited us to make. As Booth has said, *Hamlet* often seems to be "the tragedy of an audience that cannot make up its mind" (152).

The combination of the play's misdirecting energies and the students' culturally shared knowledge of the play provides the starting point for our activities. Thus, as indicated above, I start by collecting the students' answers to the question "What do you know about *Hamlet*, even if you have never read the play or seen it performed?" and looking at the patterns of what they know. If we cannot recapture what watching Shakespeare's *Hamlet* was like for its first audiences, we can begin studying *Hamlet* by using activities that seek to "defamiliarize" the play, and I offer two such activities here. One is a brilliant assignment designed by Barbara Hodgdon titled "Defamiliarizing *Hamlet*," which impels students to ask, "What do the soliloquies do?" The second is a complementary activity called "Reexploring the Play's Design: Rethinking the Act-Scene Divisions," which compels students to examine the play's design as a whole as a complement to their first Hamlet-centered double reading.

Completing these opening investigations, the class has a much clearer grasp of the intricacies of the play's design, with its interlocking yet distinct arcs, as well as of the complex functions of the soliloquies that are a major element not only in constituting Hamlet but also in shaping his relation(s) with spectators. We reimmerse ourselves in the play by asking, "What does the beginning do?" We answer this question by comparing alternate ways of segmenting the opening scene, which also enables students to delineate how the playwright initiates the action, establishes the play–audience relation, and encourages spectators to ask questions and formulate expectations. Similarly, we explore how characters introduce themselves in act I, scene ii, learning who Claudius is through the way he speaks and who Hamlet is through the way he acts. We complete our exploration of act I by using the actor's questions to rehearse and perform Hamlet's first soliloquy.

Investigating the middle of the play, we work with a pair of duets. The first duet centers on Ophelia's role, examining the dramatist's choice between showing and telling in act II, scene i. Specifically, we look at how the dramatist chooses to show one scene yet also makes us imagine a simultaneous scene occurring offstage, with Ophelia the central figure in both scenes. We examine how her responses to her would-be lover and her father serve as choices by which a particular performer transforms the role into the character. The second segment looks at the staging of the prayer scene (III.iii). Here, students explore in detail how near (in both senses) Hamlet does or does not come to killing Claudius, as well as the range of possible performances of Claudius.

We turn to the ending, exploring the duel by examining the choice-points and choices by which a production closes a performance. In this activity, students individually mark key choice-points in the final segment of the play and then, as a class, debate how different choices can combine to create divergent yet equally producible endings. Mirroring what we did earlier, we step back to reexamine the design of the play as a whole in two further activities. Students answer the question "What is the action of *Hamlet*?" by examining and reflecting on their suites of choices in staging the duel in order to understand which of (at least) three potential designs latent in the text—a providential universe, a malign universe, and an amoral universe—they have (re)created, and why that vision makes sense to them. They conclude by answering the question "What if the Ghost came back?"

Finally, at the end of this chapter I offer three paper assignments. The first assignment prompts students to explore act III, scene iii, the moment when Hamlet does not kill Claudius, by writing speeches for three "angels" who articulate the three codes operating in the play, and then using their own added speeches to help them delineate both the arguments and the dramaturgic choices Shakespeare did make. The second assignment was made in conjunction with an on-campus production of *Hamlet*, in which we read act I of the director's text before students attended the performance; in the essay, students examine three major choices by the director and three major choices or inventions by the actors, using these observations as a starting point for capturing the interpretation projected by this production. The third assignment is a multipart exploration of elements of the text, followed by their own imaginary staging of the end of the play, with further reflections.

Defamiliarizing *Hamlet*: "What do the soliloquies do?"

Here is the assignment designed by Barbara Hodgdon ("Making Changes") that initiates our (re)engagement with *Hamlet*, bringing us a bit nearer to seeing it as new.

Defamiliarizing *Hamlet*

What we'll be doing for the next several meetings might be described as cracking *Hamlet* open. This assignment has four parts; it requires reading, rereading, and a bit of writing.

1. Read *Hamlet*, omitting the following sections. Cover them up, forget they're there, ignore them. If you have any preconceived notions about the content and the "meaning" of these sections, try to erase them from your response. Act, scene, and line references are to *The Riverside Shakespeare*, ed. G. Blakemore Evans (Boston: Houghton Mifflin, 1997).

   I.ii.129–159: "O that this too too sallied flesh would melt . . . But break my heart, for I must hold my tongue."

   I.v.92–112: "O all you host of heaven! . . . I have sworn't."

II.ii.549–605: "Ay so, God buy to you . . . Wherein I'll catch the conscience of the King."

III.i.55–87: "To be, or not to be . . . And lose the name of action."

III.iii.73–96: "Now might I do it [pat] . . . This physic but prolongs thy sickly days."

IV.iv.32–66: "How all occasions do inform against me . . . My thoughts be bloody, or be nothing worth!"

2. Now, in a paragraph or so, address these questions: Do you understand what's happening in the play and to (or with) the character called Hamlet? If so, explain as precisely as you can that understanding. But if you also sense that you're missing some clues or information, what do you need to know (or want to know) in order to have a fuller understanding? Please do this writing *before* you go on to part 3.

3. Reread the play, including the omitted sections.

4. Now, in another paragraph or so, address these questions: How do the omitted sections work? That is, what sorts of information do they supply? Do they affect the narrative? Do they provide the understanding you felt you wanted in section 2? What can you say about the functions of these bits of text? Rank the sections of text according to their necessity—for Hamlet's understanding and for ours. That is, produce two different rankings. (Are these two understandings similar or different, by the way?) Which section seems most necessary? Which is least necessary? Briefly, justify your ordering.

5. Finally, why, in your opinion, are there no soliloquies in act V? Can you identify moments when a soliloquy might be useful or appropriate, given their placement elsewhere? In those moments, does anything substitute for soliloquy? If so, what does substitute? And to what effect?

[My thanks to Professor Barbara Hodgdon, who published this assignment in "Making Changes/Making Sense," in *FOCUS: Teaching Shakespeare, II*, ed. Ronald E. Salomone, 12:1 (Fall 1985): 2–11; and whose words I am quoting nearly verbatim. ELR]

One reason that "Defamiliarizing *Hamlet*" works so well is that it shifts the focus of inquiry to the question "What does each soliloquy do?" and, as we shall see, "What does the suite of soliloquies do?" This activity encourages students to concentrate on the dramatic functions of the soliloquies before immersing themselves in the subtler challenges of interpreting the complex poetry. And because this activity also focuses on the text as the product of choices Shakespeare made, it invites them to discover what even brilliant critics have often ignored, namely, the peculiar qualities of the soliloquies as they occur in time. That is, when you read the play without the soliloquies, you gain a sense of how the play suggests that each soliloquy will meet certain expectations; when you reread the play with the soliloquies, you discover how often what Hamlet says leaves you just as off balance as Barnardo, Marcellus, and Horatio are left by the appearances of the Ghost.

Step 1: Discussing Students' Two Readings and Discoveries

We begin the next class by discussing students' experience and their responses to the questions. A strong but not untypical response to part 2 of the assignment looks like this:

> I understand what is happening in the play and *to* the character called Hamlet. Hamlet's father has recently died, whereupon his uncle and his mother are married. The ghost of Hamlet's father appears to Hamlet and tells him that he was murdered by Claudius, Hamlet's uncle. The ghost demands that Hamlet avenge his father's murder; however, the ghost also commands that Hamlet not physically harm his mother. Hamlet is eventually murdered by Claudius but not before Hamlet is able to kill his uncle.
>
> In spite of my ability to follow what is happening in each scene, I do sense that I am missing clues or information regarding Hamlet's inner thoughts and emotions. I understand what is happening to Hamlet, but I do not understand what is happening *with* Hamlet. Hamlet appears to kill Claudius as an instinctual response to his own impending death. Throughout the play, Hamlet acts and reacts based on the acts and reactions of other characters. He does not appear to make any personal choices, does not suffer from internal conflict, and his involvement in events seems to be prescribed by fate. The supposedly distraught Hamlet who appears in Act I, Scene ii, does not expose himself to the reader. The human side of Hamlet is known only to the other characters in the play. —Kathy

Students also make interesting connections because they are coming from an unusual angle that foregrounds their own preconceptions:

> Reading the play *Hamlet* without his famous soliloquies creates for me a play much different than I expected. This reading gave me the sense of a kingdom plagued by a pestilence, similar to the play *Oedipus Tyrannus*. Claudius, by fouling the seat of power through murder and the marriage of his brother's wife (with its implications of incest and adultery), has tainted the entire kingdom and must be purged. The ghost seems less like an avenging angel and more like the Oracle at Delphi, speaking of what must be done. —Erik

A number of students comment on how the absence of the soliloquies makes the problem of Hamlet's madness more perplexing, and how the second soliloquy clarifies our knowledge of what Hamlet is doing when he reappears displaying the "antic disposition" he had suggested he might "put on" at the end of act I. Kathy answered part 4 thus:

> The omitted sections present and expound upon the inner conflicts that Hamlet experiences. These sections provided me with an opportunity to understand the inner conflicts and emotions of Hamlet's character. These omitted sections affect the narrative by humanizing the character of Hamlet. In addition, because Hamlet experiences inner conflicts, he must eventually decide what course of action he will follow. Fate does not control Hamlet; therefore, Hamlet's death is a human tragedy of his own making. The omitted sections do provide me with the understanding I wanted in part 2. These sections function as the catalysts for the play's tragic conclusion.

And at the end of her notes, Kathy discovers that the soliloquies "answer some questions about Hamlet's emotions but they also present more questions."

Particularly intense discussion comes when we look at the different ways students ranked the soliloquies (part 4). Below are Kathy's rankings:

For us	For Hamlet
1. II.ii	1. IV.iv
2. I.ii	2. I.v

3. III.i	3. III.iii
4. III.iii	4. III.i
5. I.v	5. I.ii
6. IV.iv	6. II.ii

Kathy offers a striking reversal. What is most important for us is to hear Hamlet describe his plan to trap the King—but this is least important to Hamlet because he would know his plan whether voiced or not. What is most important for Hamlet, as Kathy sees it, is his last soliloquy because he recommits himself to vengeance, but this soliloquy may seem least important to us because we have heard him make this commitment before. For contrast, here is Erik's arrangement:

For us	For Hamlet
1. III.iii	1. III.iii
2. III.i	2. II.ii
3. II.ii	3. IV.iv
4. IV.iv	4. I.v
5. I.ii	5. III.i
6. I.v	6. I.ii

For us, Erik suggests, the crucial variable is how fully a soliloquy reveals Hamlet's thoughts, whereas for Hamlet himself Erik ranks them in terms of making decisions. The soliloquy in act III, scene iii is a unique combination of action and thought, the one soliloquy in which Hamlet directly acts through the words he utters.

A number of students are surprised to realize that they have ranked "To be, or not to be" last, sometimes in both lists. Tina, who ranked the speech second, was troubled by this fact: "I've always thought that lines that are familiar to everybody are the most valuable passages in Shakespeare, so I feel almost blasphemous when I say this section was very abstract and difficult to grasp." How can the most famous speech appear to be the least "necessary" of the soliloquies? I point out that this is a question the play itself poses because of the remarkable contrast between Hamlet in this soliloquy and his immediately preceding "O what a rogue":

Further, not five minutes should elapse . . . between that passion-
ate soliloquy with its ringing and resolute end (the sound of it
will be still in our ears) and the pessimism of "To be or not to be
. . ." This is one of a series of such contrasts, a capital feature in
the presenting of the character. (Granville-Barker 35)

In performance especially the play puzzles us with the extreme
change in mood from the enormous excitement of Hamlet planning his trap to the apparent despair of Hamlet contemplating
suicide. Once again we are off balance, facing a challenge to our
understanding of the odyssey Hamlet is experiencing.

The fourth and fifth parts of the assignment also provoke
questions about Hamlet's relations to women in the play. Their
double reading has caused some students to perceive a powerful
tension between Hamlet's explicit commitment to revenge and
the way this commitment seems to be in conflict with Hamlet's
feelings about his mother, Ophelia, and women in general:

> Apparently he does not believe the king's sin to be the greatest. He
> sees depravity in everyone, even himself, and especially in women.
> His anger toward women is more apparent than his anger at his
> father's murder. This troubles him [so much] that he keeps forgetting
> his purpose of revenge. He continually has to remind himself and to
> re-excite himself into a frenzy of emotion which always ends in a
> vow to devote himself from then on to his sole purpose. But he is
> always being distracted and troubled by other matters, i.e., incest,
> women's frailties, doubts. His strongest emotions are aimed at his
> mother's marriage and Ophelia's change towards him. —Terri

This issue is prominent in Hamlet's first soliloquy, in which many
students see anger at his mother as stronger than his hatred of
the King, and the activity highlights how this misogyny seems to
subvert Hamlet's commitment to revenge.

In commenting on the lack of soliloquies in act V, many students say this is a time for action and a time when Hamlet talks
to Horatio. As one student noted, the absence of soliloquies also
signals a change in Hamlet:

> Hamlet is at peace with himself; he no longer suffers from internal
> conflict and self-doubt. Therefore I do not believe that a soliloquy
> would be useful or appropriate here in Act V. In moments where
> Hamlet previously would have soliloquized about suicide, he now

reacts with humor. For example, in Acts I through IV, the discovery of Yorick's skull would have prompted Hamlet to contemplate death as a means of escape from a cruel world. However, since Hamlet has come to terms with himself and what he believes he must accomplish, he jests about death. —Kathy

Interestingly, many students indicate that if there were to be a soliloquy, they would like to hear Hamlet say whether or how he had loved Ophelia; another student noted that a soliloquy from Gertrude would be especially effective "to let us know how much she knows and what her thoughts are."

Step 2: What Does the Sequence of Soliloquies Do?

The momentum created by "Defamiliarizing *Hamlet*" often propels students to explore another question, namely, "What does the sequence or suite of soliloquies do?" That is, another answer to the question "What do the soliloquies do?" is that they prompt spectators and readers to identify patterns that, emerging from soliloquy sequences, underline larger patterns and issues of the play. I focus attention on this aspect of the design: "As each new soliloquy begins, the repetition of Hamlet's speaking alone, which may be theatrically reinforced by blocking, invites us to connect to one or more of the previous soliloquies and to extend an emerging pattern, reformulate an emerging pattern, or articulate a new pattern. Please take a few minutes to connect two or more soliloquies and articulate the pattern that emerges when you make these connections."

Some students find the most obvious connection between "To be" (III.i) and "O that this too too sallied flesh" (I.ii). Both speeches are about suicide, but the first is specific, and Hamlet counters the impulse to suicide by citing God's injunction against it, while in "To be" Hamlet speaks in general terms and does not mention God nor cite God's prohibition in explaining what deters him from the act this time.

It is equally rewarding to connect the first two soliloquies—"O that this too too sallied flesh" (I.ii) and "O all you host of heaven" (I.v)—because this pair establishes a pattern of oscillation, moving from near-suicidal despair at his vision of a corrupted world to a vow to murder the apparent cause of this

corruption. Similarly, the last soliloquy (IV.iv) embodies a vari-
ant on this pattern, for Hamlet moves from his inability to explain why he has not yet killed Claudius to his vow, made in act
I, scene v and renewed yet postponed in act III, scene iii, to have
"bloody thoughts"—a moment some students comment on because they again register an incongruity: "I expect him to kill the
king immediately—and instead he goes off to England!"

As the discussion unfolds, it becomes clear that each soliloquy can prompt multiple connections. During "To be, or not to
be" (III.i), for example, Hamlet argues about whether to commit
suicide, whereas in "Now might I do it pat" (III.iii) he debates
whether to kill Claudius—and also imagines the fate of the King's
soul in a way that presupposes the existence of an afterlife that
seemed in question in the earlier speech. Even more striking, just
as "To be" is a soliloquy that may not be performed as a soliloquy, in part because Claudius is spying on Hamlet, so Hamlet's
"Now might I do it [pat]" is spoken as he spies on Claudius. This
observation leads to a connection between "To be, or not to be"
and "O, what a rogue and peasant slave": as in the latter speech
Hamlet moves from lashing himself to planning to trap the King,
so in these two speeches he moves from contemplating suicide to
almost killing the King. In this way, act II, scene ii, act III, scene
i, and act III, scene iii can be perceived as a unit in which the
cycle first embodied in act I, scene ii and act I, scene v is repeated
but with greater intensity.

As we work through these dense connections, we come to
perceive one of the most fundamental patterns formed by the set
of soliloquies: *the soliloquies erupt at moments when Hamlet
contemplates either suicide or homicide.* To see these patterns
opens a door to further reflection. As Nancy wrote: "I think he
does not want to kill anyone, but he has made a vow to kill the
King, his uncle, and feels so trapped by the vow that he often
thinks of killing himself to get out of that vow."

If you decide not to use "Defamiliarizing *Hamlet,*" you can
deploy an alternate activity in which you divide the class into six
groups, assign one soliloquy to each group, and ask each group
to answer five questions about their soliloquy:

1. What is the immediate event leading into or precipitating the soliloquy?

2. What is the focus and action of the soliloquy? Or what does Hamlet *do* during and through speaking this speech?

3. What is the action coming out of the soliloquy?

4. Which soliloquies are in fact not soliloquies?

5. What do you discover about the patterns of the play?

This activity produced one of the more remarkable moments of response to this play that I have experienced in class. As we finished looking at "To be, or not to be," the students noted that this was the second time Hamlet was considering suicide, and their observation enabled me to ask, "So if that makes these two soliloquies the same, what makes them different?" They noted that Hamlet does not mention God in "To be," and this observation triggered a powerful connection for Maureen (a psychology major who confessed she kept thinking about majoring in English), who burst out with her insight and provoked the following dialogue:

"I think he has lost faith not just in god but in the universe!"

"Because?"

"Because his father is dead, murdered by his brother, who has either seduced or committed adultery with Hamlet's mother. Because the universe—the universe no longer makes sense to him!"

"And?"

"And therefore he thinks about killing himself because it makes no sense! He wants it to make sense again, decides that *he* must make it make sense again. Either by killing the King or getting justice—or killing himself because he can't get it to make sense again!"

"What does Hamlet say that prompts you to make these connections?" After a few minutes while she and her classmates searched the text, Maureen found the speech that she realized had triggered her insight: "The time is out of joint—O cursed spite / That ever I was born to set it right!" (I.v.188–189).

"Did the Ghost ask him to do this, 'to set it right'?"

"No, the Ghost only said to take vengeance on Claudius—and leave Gertrude to heaven!"

"So why does Hamlet reinterpret his task as setting the time back in joint, setting the world right?"

"Because he couldn't accept a disjointed universe, one that didn't make sense to him. And that's one reason why Hamlet seems like an adolescent early in the play! Because he can't accept a world that doesn't follow the patterns it's supposed to follow. He sounds like an adolescent because adolescents want the world to make sense, to live up to how things *should* be, and they have a very hard time accepting it when the world does not follow the rules."[2]

This was a satisfying moment indeed. I also know, from her comments once the course was over, that the moment remained a touchstone for Maureen as well: a moment when she felt herself stretching her interpretive skills, the very skills she will need whether she becomes a psychologist-therapist, as she plans to do, or turns to teaching literature.

Reexploring the Design through Act Divisions

Provocative and exciting as it is, our work defamiliarizing *Hamlet* focuses so intensely on Hamlet that it naturally tends (as does the play itself, of course) to privilege Hamlet's point of view at the expense of the competing points of view of the other dramatis personae and of the design of the play as a whole. Furthermore, as noted earlier, using a performance approach makes it even less possible than do traditional literary approaches to achieve the aim of "covering" the play. But the following activity does offer us a chance to talk about the larger temporal patterns as they will be experienced by spectators; it also helps set up a later activity in which we examine the play as a completed event with its patterns visible. Moreover, it (re)opens discussion of the ways in which editors have worked with the text and, indeed, must be seen not only as editing the performance text but also as tacitly performing the text in the very act of editing it.

We want to turn our attention now from looking at Hamlet to looking at *Hamlet* as a complete design—that is, from the point of view of the dramatist's conception as embodied in the playtext as a whole. One way to think about this encompassing design is to examine how the play is and might be divided into acts, and how those act divisions, especially the accepted act division imposed by later editors, does and does not help us perceive the different arcs within the action or the overall trajectory of that action. So your assignment is to redivide the play into acts, which can also be thought of as arcs of action.

An alternate prompt for this activity is as follows:

As the *Riverside Shakespeare*'s note on the text and textual notes for *Hamlet* inform us, the First and Second Quartos have no act-scene divisions, and the Folio marks only act I, scene i through act I, scene iii and act II, scene i through act II, scene ii. All other act-scene divisions are the work of later editors, with the *Riverside* text following the divisions suggested by Edward Capell in his 1767–68 text (1235). But Capell's work, as fine as it may be, is hardly sacrosanct, and in terms of perceiving the design of *Hamlet* it may even seem to create problems. Would you please reexamine the text in order to suggest other possible act divisions. Think about what might be called the *arcs of the action*, asking yourself which scene sequences an audience will experience as forming larger coherent units—or, conversely, how your act division would itself serve as a tool to prompt readers to see the design as you see it at this moment.

To help students start on this assignment, I offer the following example, which not only illustrates the challenge but also focuses our attention on Gertrude, who is so often seen merely as a "weak woman." The example is the decision to separate the scenes editors mark as act III, scene iv and act IV, scene i. Here is what the notes in the *Riverside Shakespeare* tell us about the end of act III, scene iv and beginning of act IV, scene i:

217 s.d. **Exeunt . . . Polonius.**] *F1 (Capell adding* severally*);* Exit. *Q2–4;* Exit Hamlet with the dead body. *Q1.*

IV.i] *Q (1676); Q2-4, F1, Q1 indicate no scene or act break here, the Queen remaining on stage to meet Claudius (see III.iv.217 s.d.); Q2–4, however also re-enter the Queen as for a new scene.* (1241)

While it may be true that Gertrude exits as or after Hamlet drags off the body of Polonius, it is equally plausible that Claudius has been waiting outside the room and that Gertrude simply remains, staring after her son even as she prepares to confront her husband. Among its virtues, this staging affords the actor playing Gertrude an opportunity to show the Queen sorting out her conflicting loyalties to the son she has just seen murder the King's chief counselor and to the second husband that son has told her murdered her first husband. This is a profound dilemma the traditional division downplays, thereby eliminating an opportunity for performances that foreground Gertrude as an agent making the most profound moral choices amongst her incompatible commitments.

This activity invites students to grasp the logic of the five-act paradigm used by editors, helps them recognize that this paradigm may not accurately underline the play's latent design, and seeks to assist them become readers whose interpretations are not inadvertently limited by these editorial choices.

As with other segmenting activities, the point is not for students to discover some correct division. Rather, in redividing the play, they will discover new aspects of its interlocking patterns that are one source of its theatrical power. Thus when they share mappings, the contrasts become the stimulus for the group to achieve further insight into the play's design. As one example of such a contrast, Kelly told us that she saw the scenes from act II, scene i to act IV, scene iv as a single unit "because all these scenes are concerned with Hamlet's madness." No one else had perceived this pattern, but once Kelly offered it we could see how it phrased the play in an intriguing manner. Kelly's map also provided a natural cue to discuss what students made of Hamlet's madness and for tracing its course through the action, from its first hint in act I, scene v, when he announces the antic disposition, to the last mention in act V, scene i, when he speaks of "Hamlet's madness" as he apologizes to Laertes.

If you use this activity, you will discover that it prompts students to discover other aspects of its design. One of the most important aspects it illuminates is rhythm. Rhythm is one of the dramatist's more powerful means for creating what Andrew Gurr calls "the emotional sweep of the story" (*Studying* 13), which produces "the cumulative development of the play's emotional power" (3). But, as with the alternations of emptying and filling the stage that, as shown earlier, can be demonstrated by looking at a scene such as *Romeo and Juliet* act I, scene i, this fundamental aspect of performance is difficult even for trained readers to imagine and cannot easily be re-created in the study.

Here I use my own analysis, which I share with the class after we have discussed some of theirs, as a starting point for talking about not only the design but also the rhythm of *Hamlet*. I certainly do not expect you to agree with this analysis completely, and indeed I urge you to analyze the play yourself. (Robert Hapgood offers a similar analysis in *Shakespeare the Theatre-Poet* [96–105], dividing the play into four phases. It is testimony to the clarity of the play's design that my own analysis, arrived at before reading his book, parallels the analysis offered by Hapgood.)

ARC 1   I.i–I.v. 30 hours. Discovering what's "rotten" in Denmark. Hamlet learns of the murder and accepts the mission of revenge.

          2 soliloquies mark the beginning and the end of this movement.

ARC 2   II.i–III.ii. Several days. Hamlet puts on "an antic disposition."

          Antic Hamlet convinces observers he is mad and looks for an opening: he plans the play in order to trap the King and test the Ghost.

          3 soliloquies: despair + plan. Suicide? Resolution: hot blood.

ARC 3   III.iii–IV.iv. One night stretching into day. Hamlet plays the god.

          The trap/test succeeds and liberates Hamlet into frenzied action: he spares the King, kills Polonius, shrives the Queen, sees the Ghost, and promises to "answer" for murdering Polonius.

          2 soliloquies: deciding not to murder the King. Vowing bloody action.

ARC 4   IV.v–IV.vii. Several days. The recoil from Hamlet's burst of action.

In Hamlet's absence, Ophelia and Laertes respond to the murder of Polonius. They act out the impulses that have governed Hamlet: Ophelia goes mad and commits suicide, Laertes seeks revenge. Claudius plots his trap.

No *soliloquies*: antic Ophelia replaces antic Hamlet—songs instead of soliloquies.

ARC 5   V.i–V.ii. One or two days. The acting of revenge.

Hamlet returns transformed, yet his new calm and old fury collide.

Duel: Hamlet kills Laertes and King in self-defense, forbids suicide for Horatio, votes for Fortinbras.

No *soliloquies*: speech on Yorick's skull, dialogues with Horatio.

When I present this map in class, it is not to close discussion but to initiate further analysis. I welcome questions because they compel me to clarify other aspects of the design I am trying to illuminate, and they encourage students themselves to discover aspects of the design this analysis downplays or even obscures.

What Does a Beginning Do? Segmenting a Scene

The extensive work we do in "Defamiliarizing *Hamlet*" and examining the play's design leads to the moment when we initiate a much more detailed exploration of how the play does what it does. If, however, you decide not to use "Defamiliarizing *Hamlet*," the activity presented here can be the move through which you stage the opening scene in slow motion, either before or after the students first read the play. If *Hamlet* is the concluding play of the term, it also becomes the play in which your students last practice the new patterns of reading you have spent a term rehearsing. On the other hand, if *Hamlet* is the opening play of the term, this activity is also the moment when the class begins to enact one of the fundamental practices of reading differently.

In the traditional study of drama, the opening of a play is often described as the exposition: the part where the dramatist lays out the elements of the story. As I have suggested, framing an inquiry in "What is X?" form helps perpetuate a static sense of the play and a passive sense of the audience since the term *exposition* emphasizes that the play must "transmit information" to the audience. Of course, weak exposition does operate in this manner. The butler answers the phone and for five minutes proceeds to answer questions from a never-to-be-heard-from-again caller: these questions allow him to describe the family genealogy and detail the secrets, sins, and dilemmas of all the members of the family he so indiscreetly serves. When we witness such a minimally dramatized beginning, we do indeed murmur, "Ah, the exposition!" as we take in as much of the torrent as we can manage—and sit further back in our seats, fairly certain that nothing will happen until the exposition is completed.

Many playwrights, however, find ways to make the opening arresting, so that we lean forward in our seats, involved in a scene whose own dramatic logic motivates us to take in the required information even as we are becoming engaged with the play's world. When dealing with such fully dramatized openings, it seems a poor choice to ask, "What is the exposition of the play?" since the very shape of that question directs us to see the play as static object rather than dynamic event. Thus I suggest that we ask "What does the beginning do?" or "How does the dramatist frame the action and the audience?" More specifically, the class analyzes the beginning of *Hamlet* by asking three fundamental questions:

1. How does the beginning set the action in motion?

2. How does the beginning establish the play–audience relation or set up the conditions under which we participate in the play?

3. How does the beginning provoke questions and arouse expectations in the spectator's mind?

This is also the moment to reiterate the fact that we need to see the play in performance as a double communication: we are asking, "What are the characters doing to one another?," which in this instance means "What are Barnardo and Marcellus doing to Horatio?," and we are asking "What is the dramatist using the performed play to do to us?," which in this instance means "What does staging this encounter with the Ghost do to us?"

Segmenting a Scene

I ask students to segment the scene, noting that typically people find anywhere from four to twelve segments in the opening 175 lines. I call these *audience segments* as an indication that this type of segmenting is concerned with how an audience might divide the scene, and that this type of segment is distinct from the unit or beat used to analyze the scene as an actor. After ten minutes, I ask, "Who has three segments?" and so on up to whatever the largest number turns out to be, so that we get a range between more inclusive and more precisely focused divisions. In one class, the range went from ten down to four segments. The ten-segment division offered by Kathy went like this:

1. Up to "bid them make haste" (1–13)
2. Up to Francisco's exit (14–18)
3. Up to "Well sit we down . . ." (18–34)
4. Up to "Enter Ghost" (35–39)
5. Up to "Exit Ghost" (40–51)
6. Up to "Some strange eruption" (52–69)
7. From "Good now, sit down" up to "climatures and countrymen" (70–125)
8. From "Enter Ghost" to "stay and speak!" (126–139)
9. From "Stop it, Marcellus" to "Exit Ghost" (139–141)
10. The rest of scene (142–175)

The four-segment analysis offered by Margaret looked like this:

1. From opening line up to "Strange eruption" (1–69)
2. "Good now, sit down," offering history (70–125)
3. Ghost, up to "about to speak"(126–146)
4. The rest: conclusion, leads to what comes next (147–175).

It is useful to get several intermediate segmentings, which make it clear that there is a good deal of overlap, so that, as is the case here, segments 1–6 of one analysis form segment 1 of the other.

The middle range is five or six segments, and students realize that much of their segmenting is based on entrances and exits; you can mention that segmenting in this fashion leads to the model sometimes called "French scenes" commonly used in the classic French theater. If we use this provisional criterion—and there are clearly cases where an entrance or exit occurs within a segment—we will analyze the scene as having six segments: (1) The initial encounter of Barnardo and Francisco. (2) Marcellus and Horatio join Barnardo and discuss the Ghost. (3) The Ghost's first appearance and exit. (4) The ensuing discussion, in which the three men speculate about what the Ghost might signify. (5) The Ghost's second appearance, with Horatio's unsuccessful attempt to elicit answers to his questions. (6) The discussion of the Ghost's significance and the trio's decision to inform "young Hamlet" of the Ghost's appearance. Following is a more detailed exploration of each segment—which draws on analyses of act I, scene i by Van Laan (*Idiom* 150–55) and Booth (139–47)—to show some of the issues and insights that emerge from this activity.

Segment 1: "Who's there?" (1–19)
This segment establishes the outdoor setting, the time as late at night, the cold weather, and the tense atmosphere. "'Tis now strook twelf" (6) suggests the option of having the play open with a bell tolling twelve. I point out that on the nonscenic stage, if we simply see the figure of Francisco and hear the bell, we must ask, "Twelve noon or twelve midnight?" This is an appropriate note of uncertainty on which to begin our engagement with what Harry Levin has called the interrogative world of this play, a world he elegantly summarizes when he writes that "[t]he play has kept us guessing; it leaves us wondering" (42). And a bell, of course, would also prepare us for the later description of the Ghost appearing at "The bell then beating one" (39), which can happen in this scene also.

Interestingly, students can miss the reversal by which Barnardo challenges rather than waits to be challenged, although they may sense that something is wrong. "Why this mistake?" I ask, and they see that, especially when coupled with the question "Have you had quiet guard?," the mistake makes us wonder why Barnardo is so anxious. This question is soon answered when we learn that he is tensely wondering whether the Ghost is there or whether Francisco has seen the ghost. In discussing this mistake, we can discuss how the password "Long live the King!" soon takes on disturbing overtones since in a few minutes we meet the Ghost of the recently deceased king.

Segment 2: "Tush, tush, 'twill not appear" (19–39)
In examining the second movement, we (re)turn to the concept of action or Action $_2$ as I ask, "How can we best describe the action of this segment? What is the best verb for describing the primary act performed in this segment? What is it that Barnardo and Marcellus are trying to do?" The answer is that they have invited Horatio along in order to convince him of the Ghost's reality, and then to have him, a scholar, deal with the Ghost and advise them what to do.

As we prepare to explore the third segment, students often ask, "What is the Ghost like?" and sometimes, "Does it appear at all?" Wrestling with how the Ghost is staged—which means not only what it looks like but also where it enters—provides another moment to explore the resources of the Globe and to invite students to use their own creativity to imagine as many different possible ways of staging the Ghost as they are capable of inventing, asking of each, "What meaning will the spectators create from this staging?"

Segment 3: "How now, Horatio? you tremble and look pale"
(40–69)
Within the world of the play, the initial test of Horatio's skepticism is immediately enacted, and the segment functions to show us the conversion of Horatio from confident skepticism to awed belief. In fact, even before Horatio says a word, his nonverbal response indicates his stunned condition, a condition Barnardo highlights by asking, "How now, Horatio? you tremble and look pale. / Is not this something more than fantasy?" (53–54). His words are also another example of internal stage directions and evidence that some proportion of a play's reality is created by

unspoken reactions in one character and descriptions of those reactions by other characters. Barnardo's words create a pallor the actor of Horatio may not be able to command at will. This answer from within the world of the play also provides a cue to turn our attention to the dimension of the play–audience relation and ask, "What does Shakespeare seek to accomplish through staging the conversion?" Given the original open stage and the daylight performance, Shakespeare uses Horatio to deal with two challenges: first, the challenge of making a Ghost convincing in a daylight performance; and second, the challenge of dealing with the skepticism of at least some of his spectators, since the existence and nature of ghosts was a highly controversial topic in Elizabethan England.

Thus in exploring the third segment, you can offer a concrete instance of the general point that at every moment a Shakespearean play is performing an action within the world of the play and through that action performing its complex dance with the spectators. At times, as is true in this segment, these two actions are nearly identical, so that in many ways Horatio functions as our onstage double. This is certainly true here since the Ghost's silence provokes speculation about its motives and meanings in the minds of both the characters and the spectators. At other times, as is true when there is discrepant awareness, there can be a sharp divergence between a scene's onstage and offstage functions.

Segment 4: "Who is't that can inform me?" (70–125)
The fourth segment is one that some students say is boring "because it just gives us a lot of history," and of course the bulk of the fourth segment does perform an expository function. But the real point here is to show how expository functions are embedded in dramatic ones. Horatio's exposition is the means by which he offers speculations about what motivates the Ghost's appearance. Again, we are in a position nearly identical to the position of those onstage, who recognize that the Ghost "bodes some strange eruption to our state" (69) and thus naturally begin to form hypotheses about what might erupt. Like the trio onstage, furthermore, we will want to test these guesses when the Ghost next appears. Thus, to regard the speech purely as exposition is

to ignore its vital function in establishing a wider dynastic frame that, while kept subordinate, is nonetheless crucial for raising larger political and metaphysical issues. At the same time, its expository dimension is what has often prompted directors to cut some of the speech—and, if they omit the whole Fortinbras plot, to cut all of it. This is also the segment for which you can ask students to focus on the key images offered in Horatio's description of Denmark's war preparations: as Van Laan (*Idiom*) points out, they echo the opening reversal of the sentries insofar as the boundaries between day and night and between profane workdays and the sacred Sabbath are being disrupted, and insofar as the state seems to face the threat of invasion from young Fortinbras, who is bent on altering the boundaries between the kingdoms. Shakespeare also achieves misdirection by leading us to expect that a war between Denmark and Norway will be at the center of the tragedy.

Segment 5: "Speak of it, stay and speak!" (126–146)
A question to ask here is "Why does Shakespeare have the Ghost appear a second time?" One answer is that the converted Horatio is now the primary figure who confronts the apparition. The three men are united, whereas at the Ghost's first appearance they had divergent objectives. This segment is also useful for renewing exploration of Shakespeare's verse since Horatio's speech offers a particularly clear instance of how that verse functions as implicit instructions to the actors about how the words are to be spoken and what thought lies behind them. So I ask students what they make of the fact that the repeated plea to speak always occupies a short line:

> *Horatio.* I'll cross it though it blast me. Stay, illusion!
> If thou hast any sound or use of voice,
> Speak to me.
> If there be any good thing to be done
> That may to thee do ease, and grace to me,
> Speak to me.
> If thou art privy to thy country's fate,
> Which happily foreknowing may avoid,
> O speak!
> Or if thou hast uphoarded in thy life

Extorted treasure in the womb of earth,
For which, they say, your spirits oft walk in death,
Speak of it, stay and speak! (I.i.127–139)

That is, as readers students may simply read through the white space, failing to imagine what must happen when you implore another creature, whether natural or supernatural, to speak—namely, you pause to allow time for a response. Students with theatrical experience will help here since they are more likely to have learned that the short line can indicate a pause, and that the length of the pause can be equivalent to the missing syllables—to the three or four feet necessary to complete an iambic pentameter line. As we follow these cues, we begin to see how Shakespeare sought to control the way the actor playing Horatio speaks at this critical moment. Likewise, the way Horatio goes from one to two to three lines in successive pleadings indicates that he speaks with greater force and urgency the longer the silence endures. It is their increasing frustration that leads the three men to the desperate and, as it turns out, futile decision to attack the Ghost physically.

I also ask the class to explore the sequence of Horatio's ideas. Simply describing this sequence, they will see that he asks (1) if the Ghost needs some action taken to allow it peace; (2) if it has come to warn about the fate of Denmark; and (3) if it comes to reveal hidden treasure. Horatio justifies the sentries' faith in him as a scholar by moving through a series of guesses based on the most common reasons a Ghost was presumed to walk.[3]

Segment 6: "Do you consent we shall acquaint him with it?" *(147–175)*
The central feature of this segment is the first mention of "young Hamlet" (170), which introduces the play's hero in a way that immediately raises questions. If the previous king, whose ghost we have just seen, was named Hamlet, then why is "young Hamlet," who must be his son, not the new king? Students also usually provoke an interesting discussion of the cockcrow and of how this offstage noise highlights the silence of the Ghost. The discussion of the cockcrow between the three witnesses also introduces the doubts about the Ghost's origin that are precursors

to Hamlet's own doubts and help motivate the play-within-the-play. This is a suitable moment to introduce and assign readings on the controversy about ghosts that haunted thinking in this period.

Another small but telling example of the difference between reading and performing the play is useful here, that concerning how the sentries respond to Horatio's question "Do you consent we shall acquaint him with it?" While this is usually played so that Marcellus replies unhesitatingly, it can be played as a genuine question. All it takes is a look exchanged between Marcellus and Barnardo to make us realize that they *should* have reported what they had seen to the present king or to someone who would report it to the king. Something, we realize, must be inhibiting them from carrying out their duty. A first-time spectator should experience a little flicker of surprise here, a flicker that many of us have become too familiar with to notice, or to remember if we do notice. It also may provoke comment that Marcellus knows where Hamlet is, suggesting that despite his status as royalty, Hamlet is open to relatively low-ranking people. Certainly they, like Horatio, imply that they trust Hamlet—although, as one student suggested, they may also want to use Hamlet to protect themselves by having him pass on news that will not be welcome to the king.

QUESTIONS AND EXPECTATIONS AROUSED BY THE BEGINNING

At this point, we formulate the expectations and questions the scene is so obviously designed to arouse:

How did King Hamlet die?

Why has the Ghost of King Hamlet returned?

Why does the Ghost refuse to speak to these three?

What is its secret? Is the secret connected with war? or with his death?

Where does the Ghost come from? Heaven? Hell? Purgatory?

Does it have a genuine secret, or is it a devil sent to destroy someone?

Will it speak to young Hamlet; will it reveal its secret?

Does its secret have to do with the possible Norwegian invasion? And if young Fortinbras seeks revenge, will he succeed?

Will there be a war? And will young Hamlet and young Fortinbras re-create the single combat of their fathers? Who will win?

Who is king? How did he get to be king? What sort of king/person is he?

What is young Hamlet like?

Some of these questions, of course, articulate long-range expectations, but if we narrow our focus, our short-term expectations now include the following:

That we will meet young Hamlet in the next scene.

That this scene will take place with almost no time break.

That we will meet the King soon, if not in the next scene.

That Hamlet will confront the Ghost, who will/will not reveal his secret.

That whatever the Ghost's secret is, it will plunge young Hamlet into some conflict-filled situation.

At the end of this discussion, I often amplify the point that one thing the beginning does is to establish the play–audience relation. As noted, the beginning creates curiosity, arouses suspense, sets up surprise. I would suggest it does one other thing, namely, that in inviting us to form expectations of what we will see, it creates, as Kenneth Burke has insisted ("Psychology" 20–33, especially 21–22), a desire to have those expectations fulfilled and even commitments to outcomes we would prefer. The beginning often functions by causing us to change our attitude or, in a sense, our posture, so that instead of leaning back in our seats we are leaning forward. In this sense, we move from being spectators to being participants, not because we join the action but because we enter into the creation of the play as collaborators whom Shakespeare asks implicitly to do what the Chorus of *Henry V* asks us to do explicitly when he requests, "let us . . . /

On your imaginary forces work" (Prologue, 17–18), and when he exhorts us to "Piece out our imperfections with your thoughts" (23). The beginning makes us participate in creating the play even though we cannot, in terms of the implicit contract, become participants in its world.[4]

Defining What a Segment Is and Does

As one means of helping students integrate segmenting into their reading practices, you can ask them to segment the rest of the play, assigning one scene to each student, although I do not assign the last scene, because it is reserved for another activity. You can also have them segment the play in small groups. I ask that as they segment a scene, they focus on discovering the key action taking place in that scene. "Look for the verb that best defines what is going on in the scene, just as in examining act I, scene i we learned that the action is Marcellus and Barnardo converting Horatio to belief in the Ghost."

Based on their work, students come up with good definitions of the segment. Dawn wrote that "a segment is unified in thought, action, focus, often signified by entrances and exits." Joyce suggested that "a segment can be marked when the focus of conversation changes, when action changes, when an event or shift in conversation occurs." I like the way these two definitions complement each other, for where Dawn focuses on the center of the segment, Joyce calls attention to the border that separates and unites them. One of the fullest definitions a student has produced is this by David:

> Audience segmenting is the separation of a scene into individual segments [units] that perform distinct yet interrelated functions, such as directing the physical attention of the audience to a particular point in the stage or developing important aspects of the plot or characters. In performing such [analysis], we can relate the literary aspect of each segment to the dramatic, and gain a better insight into the author's purpose in writing that segment as it relates to the play as a whole.

Even if you do not work with the concept of scenic form introduced earlier, an ability to segment a scene and to find the core action/verb is a vital skill for learning to read the text of a play as a script.

Speech as Action and Action as Speech

> By enveloping the Prince from head to toe in a mourning cloak, Shakespeare insured that Hamlet would be the principal focus of the audience's attention from the first moment the court enters, even though the Prince does not speak until sixty-seven lines later. Hamlet is outweighed in power by Claudius, but it is equally true that Claudius is upstaged by Hamlet—which provides finely calibrated introduction to the contest between these two mighty opposites. (Frye 100)

I move into the next activity, focusing on the interplay of speech as action and action as speech in the first court scene, by returning to the nature of the open stage. I do so because some of the fundamental effects of Shakespeare's design arise from the way the performance exploits that stage's potentials. These effects are easily ignored because, while as spectators we will usually take them in without conscious effort, as readers we will not stop to imagine them. I introduce our work as follows.

> As we discussed earlier, scenes on a proscenium stage are contained within the box set, so they are separated from one another as the curtain opens and closes. But on the open stage that Shakespeare wrote for, scenes flow into one another: one group exits, another enters, and the dramatist creates powerful effects precisely by asking us to connect rather than separate adjacent scenes. So in the first two scenes of *Hamlet*, what seems obvious are the differences: we move from the outer guard of the castle, in cold weather, at night, watching a few dark-clad figures, to the inner world of the court, which is warm, well lit at midday, and filled with bright-clad figures. It is in the context created by these contrasts that the scene staged by Claudius emerges, and in his opening speech he seems to seek to dispel the darkness and menace that swirls around the castle and kingdom, and to assure us that the contrast between the dark outer guard and the well-lit inner court is as sharp, clear-cut, and complete as can be.
>
> In this next activity, we focus on what happens when we see the opening scenes of a play that is new to us, and on the way that we learn who someone is and what he means by what he does. More

specifically, we examine a character's speech as action and a character's action as speech. Looking at Claudius, we concentrate on speech as action, whereas looking at Hamlet, we concentrate on action as speech. As we begin this activity, recall the questions and expectations the class formulated at the end of the first scene; as spectators, we are not looking at act I, scene ii as passive receivers but rather as people actively searching for answers to our newly formulated questions. Our desire for answers and our need to learn how expectations are or are not fulfilled increase our engagement and our focus as we watch this scene.

Speech as Action: Meeting the King

In performance, then, we watch as Horatio, Marcellus, and Barnardo "Exeunt" to seek out Hamlet. Then we listen and watch as a trumpet flourish is played and the stage floods with people, and we realize that we are witnessing a formal gathering of a court. What I want to do now is look at Claudius's first speech and the way that, as they listen, the spectators will form those crucial first impressions of who the King is by what he does here.

At this point, I ask a student to read the opening sixteen lines, up to "For all, our thanks" (I.ii.1–16), with no attempt to do an oral interpretation, let alone a performance. We thus get to hear the words and, in particular, the blend of high diction and complex syntax that create the King. Then, borrowing a move that I, like many others, have learned from Miriam Gilbert ("Teaching Shakespeare" 605–6), I ask the students to write the speech as a telegram: "If you needed to get the gist into a telegram, where every word counts, what would you write?" A student may ask, "Who is the telegram addressed to?," and we will see that a crucial issue is how many audiences the King has. But for now, I simply say, "Do the best you can!" Here are the telegrams from one class:

1. Thanks for coming to the wedding funeral. (Cynthia)

2. My brother is dead; I am king, and Gertrude is now my wife—whether you like it or not. (Kathy)

3. We are sorry that Hamlet has died, but my marriage to his wife has lessened the sorrow. Thanks for your support. (Dawn)

4. Myself as well as others grieve for Hamlet's death, but I'm marrying his wife anyway. (Leslie)

5. The death of Young Hamlet's father is new. The kingdom is in grief. Let us think of the late king. Our sister lost her husband, remarried, and now is my wife—our Queen. (Meg)

6. Claudius to Hamlet: Sorry for your loss. Have married your mother and taken over kingdom in case of war. Still mourning, but thanks for understanding. (Margaret)

7. Dear King Brother is dead. Have married Queen in our warlike time as per your advice. (Susan)

8. We grieve at the death of the former King, Hamlet. We announce the marriage of the Queen to the new King, Hamlet's brother. Thanks for your support. (Mary)

9. Our hearts grieve for the death of King Hamlet. I have taken the queen as wife. Thanks! (Victoria)

10. Brother Hamlet dead. / Fond memories—grief. / Kingdom mourns. / His wife mine. / Still Queen. (Chris)

11. King is dead. Queen wed. Stop mourning. (Erik)

12. Hamlet dead. Too bad. He was nice guy, so is his wife. Country needs King, that's why we married. Thanks for understanding. (Irma)

13. To Council: Brother recently died. / Kingdom grieving. / I married my sister/queen. / Thanks for acquiescence to our marriage. (Terri)

14. Dear brother has died. / Remember and grieve him. / Taken queen as wife. / Thanks for wisdom and understanding. (Joyce)

Once students have stripped away the language, I ask, "Why does Shakespeare give the King this long complex speech? Why doesn't the King just say what we have in our telegrams? What's missing from the telegram?" And, conversely, "What does this speech—these specific words in this specific order—do that the telegram does not do?" I remind the class that they have said the dialogue invites a reader to reinvent the speaker and enables the actor to reinvent the character who would say just these words in just this order in just this situation (see Chapter 1).

I set them to work in pairs.

Ask yourselves, "What does the King's language *do*?" That is, how does the richness and complexity of this language guide you to create a particular king or range of possible kings? What *resources*—of syntax, diction, image, pauses, and rhythm—has Shakespeare built into the speech to enable the actor to re-create the King as the dramatist has imagined him? So we are exploring both "What does the King want to do through speaking in just this way?" and "What does Shakespeare want us to discover as we listen to a man who speaks in this way?"

As students work with the speech, and as I circulate, a problem often surfaces. Having read the play, students know the King is a villain, and some of them think his villainy should be evident in his first appearance. They claim that the speech is "too eloquent," so that we mistrust the King immediately. I ask them to imagine first-time spectators who hear the eloquence before they have learned about the villainy.

The first resource Shakespeare provides is the syntactic clarity of the speech: Though yet, Yet, Therefore, nor. Students quickly discover that many of their telegrams reflect the syntax very precisely. I ask, "What does the first word of his speech, *Though*, do?" "It signals that another clause is coming: Though this, Yet that." We move through the speech looking at syntax as action as we work out how each of these markers functions. Students often find it intriguing to learn that what they study as grammar can be seen as another type of action by which we shape how other people listen and respond. They move between noting how obvious the functions of the syntax are and realizing that they— or most of them—have never thought about these obvious functions from just this angle.

The most prominent syntactic feature is the way the King creates his speech as a sequence of carefully balanced phrases and clauses. So my next question is "What does this pattern of balanced elements signal?" "It signals, 'I am a rational man, balancing one consideration against another to reach judicious conclusions that you agree with.'" Then we begin to move into the interplay of syntax and semantics, looking at oxymoronic phrases such as "With mirth in funeral and with dirge in marriage." The balanced syntax plays against the phrases: even as the syntax signals "I am a reasonable man," the content signals, "who has broken the line of succession and committed incest—with your support." The speech thus introduces a man who can speak so as to make deeply disturbing actions appear the result of rational deliberation.

Those students who believe in a rhetoric of sincerity will argue that this formal, ornate style makes us mistrust a man whose artistry makes him seem insincere. On the other hand, some students will hear the balance as a form of control that seeks to convey the message "I really did not want to be King, but if you insist!" But of course the situation is more complex than this, as the earlier question, "Who should we address the telegram to?," hinted. Look, for example, at a phrase such as "with wisest sorrow." Specifically, I ask, if the King speaks of wisest sorrow, what would the opposite be? Unwise sorrow. And what would unwise sorrow be? Immoderate? Why might the King want to refer indirectly in this fashion to immoderate sorrow? The question points toward the second half of this activity, for it is clearly a rebuke to Hamlet. Claudius's speech is complex, then, because he is balancing contending pressures and because he is at once announcing the new reign, proving his own authority, securing assent, and seeking to forestall any potential dissent.

With this preliminary understanding of the scene and of the King's rhetoric and purposes, we move through the next segments. From the King's point of view, he must deal with three young men, two of them princes and heirs to their respective thrones, whose actions will directly shape the welfare of his kingdom. What does the King want to do? The King wants to show he has an agenda, show he is in control, unite the kingdom, and deal with the threat posed by "young Fortinbras." In addition to exploring the specifics of how Claudius deals with Fortinbras and Laertes, we look at the pattern established by the contrast in how he deals with the two men. This contrast can be highlighted by noting another example of reading differently, since the King may well be holding some of the messages that Fortinbras has "pestered" him with; and if this is the case, "So much for him" (25) may be a cue to do something with those messages. Perhaps the king rips them up and thereby establishes an attitude of contempt that will contrast with his solicitous treatment of Laertes.

When he turns to Hamlet, then, we have seen him move between extremes and will be more alert in noting the modulations in his treatment of this third young man.

Action as Speech: Meeting the Prince

As the scene reaches the moment when Claudius turns to Hamlet, we move into the second half of this activity.

In focusing on the King as the scene's first speaker, we have bypassed other elements that become prominent when the scene is performed and, in particular, ignored the way the nonverbal dimension precedes the verbal. Even before a word is spoken, what will catch our eye?

["The image of Hamlet dressed in black" is a frequent student response.]

Ah! that is a reader's response, but it is not quite how a first-time spectator will experience this moment: for the spectator, the striking thing will be the entrance of *someone* whose black clothes stand out from the brighter colors worn by the King, the Queen, and the rest of the court. We will ask ourselves, "Why is that man dressed in black?," a question that translates into the question "What is this figure *doing* by appearing dressed in black?"

So how do we make sense of that figure? Certainly by the time the King completes the first four lines, we realize what is going on: while the rest of the court has followed the King and Queen in shedding their mourning garments, this man has remained in black. And while the clothes worn by everyone else seem to testify to a harmonious transition, the black figure makes plain his belief that the entire court should still be in mourning. Thus we discover that by maintaining his mourning, this figure is publicly rebuking the King, the Queen, and the court, accusing them of an inappropriate celerity in ceasing to mourn the dead King. Here, then, is a paradigmatic instance of how nonverbal choices are not simply a means of self-expression but also a form of action. Simply by his dress, Hamlet has posed a challenge at the very moment the King most wants and needs harmony to prevail. The entire court will witness how Claudius chooses to handle that challenge—and thus Shakespeare stages the scene so that we too are challenged, challenged to learn about Claudius from how he handles this problem.

We must recognize, then, that the King's opening speech was meant to reach a double audience, as he speaks one way to the court in general and another way to the black figure in particular.

Claudius's "Yet," for example, is in part an indirect response to the discordant figure, and the manner in which he emphasizes his words, the direction of his address—perhaps ignoring, perhaps glancing at, perhaps looking directly at that black figure—may color the entire sixteen lines in which he begins his reign. And as the King finally turns to address "my cousin Hamlet," a very interesting choice must be made with the first words that Hamlet speaks.

Here we (re)turn to the example presented in the prologue of this book, the question raised by the brackets around "Aside": namely, "Is the line an aside or not?" The simplest way to answer is to ask, "What happens if it is or is not delivered as an aside? If it is not delivered as an aside but is audible to the court, what does the line do?" It becomes a direct insult to the King, a challenge that presents a fiery or sardonic Hamlet, who is ready to test the patience of the new King.[5] Delivered as an aside, the speech emphasizes the private nature of Hamlet's grief, his inwardness and isolation. And because he shares with us the grief and anger he chooses not to share with the court, this act draws us to him, so that even as he confides in us we lean toward him in the bond of a shared secret.

What we focus on now is the manner in which domestic and public politics mesh here. From Claudius's point of view, his nephew, whom he wants to treat as a son, is treating the uncle who has become his stepfather as his enemy. Given this context, we work through what the speeches of the King, Queen, and Prince are doing as Claudius struggles to keep control, as the Queen seeks to mediate between them, and as Hamlet seeks to maintain his integrity. In this ensuing discussion, the key points to explore are (1) how Hamlet's long speech about "seeming" provokes Claudius's even longer rebuke veiled as praise; (2) how the implicit reward of naming Hamlet heir to the throne is coupled with the implicit threat against leaving court; (3) how Hamlet both submits and refuses to submit, addressing his submission to his mother, the Queen, not to his uncle, the King, in a sentence that demands we experiment with alternate stresses; (4) how Claudius reframes this response as a "loving and a fair reply" (121) and a "gentle and unforc'd accord" (123); and (5) how the exit is performed.

BLOCKING: ENTRANCES AND EXITS

The end of this segment can, if you choose, lead to another brief activity, one I use when I want the class to continue concentrating on the physical issues of staging centered on the blocking of entrances and exits. I ask students to explore one particular blocking issue connected with the entrance, namely, where is Hamlet placed? Who controls his placement, Hamlet, the King, or the Queen? Does Hamlet attempt to isolate and distance himself from them? Does Claudius keep him from his mother? Or does Claudius try to surround Hamlet with courtiers, hiding his discordant dress? Is Hamlet passive and isolated by the court? Is Hamlet active and isolating himself physically as he distinguishes himself visually? And I ask students to consider the question "How is the exit played?" After all, it is not immediately evident from the text whether Claudius excludes Hamlet or Hamlet refuses an invitation to join in the feast. Many readers, I suspect, assume that a rebellious Hamlet excludes himself from the exit, continuing the resistance initiated by wearing mourning. But it is possible that Claudius foresees such a snub and prevents further embarrassment by leading the exit so as to exclude Hamlet. Introducing this focus is another step in learning to read the play's text as a script, for entrances and exits are mandatory events and, because of the simple pragmatic truth that you cannot not communicate, they always contain the potential to project meaning to the spectators.

An Acting Approach to Shakespeare's Language

Working with the King's speech and Hamlet's action brings us back to the first of the soliloquies already examined from the point of view of the playwright looking at the playtext's design. Now we work from the point of view of actors, who are trained to create a performance by having the words emerge through their nervous system. If studying *Hamlet* comes late in the term, you are continuing to work with the process of transforming the role in the text into the character on stage. If *Hamlet* is the first or only play you do, this is the moment you can introduce the process. For those who might want to introduce the practice of transforming role into character but do not want to use the explicit introduction of action, unit, and subtext presented in the handout "Playing an Action," this activity offers another mode of initiating this way of reading differently.

In turning the King's first lines into a telegram, we were in effect stripping away *how* Claudius creates meaning, and therefore stripping away much of what his speech *does*. When we turned back to the speech itself, we began to see how Shakespeare's language scripts a complex performance by the actor playing the role of the King, and how the patterns of the speech function as implicit directions about the way the King uses language to accomplish his complex mixture of public and private purposes.

Now we move into an even more detailed investigation of Shakespeare's language in Hamlet's first soliloquy. We will be (re)introducing concepts and practices to employ as you learn to work with Shakespeare's language as a remarkable resource that instructs us how to re-create a character's world through his words. In what follows, the goal, as Ellen O'Brien says, is to develop "an understanding of the role of poetry in Shakespeare's dramaturgy" (622). In following the model that O'Brien has developed, we will explore the different types of resources that speech offers us.

It seems obvious that in the plays we are studying the basic unit is the scene. Certainly the scene is the unit that is most obvious when we are in the role of spectators at a play. But while thinking about a scene as a whole yields rich insights, it can also prevent us from getting a more detailed perception of the internal movement of that scene, and we want to capture that movement to deepen our mental engagement with a play, to improve the performances we imagine, and to sharpen our perception of any productions we may see.

Another way into a play is to study the scene as an actor might be trained to explore it. Put most simply, the actor's task is to ask, "What are the words I have to say?" and "What are the actions I have to perform?" But that is still too general to be much help. The real challenge is to make sense of the role so that when the actor speaks the lines and performs the actions, we perceive them not as memorized speeches and rehearsed gestures but as springing from a unified life that is virtually present as it is re-presented before us. Thus actors are taught, as part of their discipline, to ask certain organizing questions as they begin to learn and rehearse a part: Who am I? Where am I? Who else is here? Why are we here? or Why am I here? What are we doing? or What am I doing? and, most important, *What do I want?*

Step 1: Dividing a Speech into Units

Actors have developed a number of techniques for moving from outside to inside so that, as Ellen O'Brien puts it, the actor can inhabit "the mental universe of his character" (625). To discover the answers to the questions listed above, it is often useful to break a speech into smaller units. In this case, please mark what you think are the smaller units within the speech. Once you have marked the units, please try to articulate what you see as the structure of thought and emotion embodied in the speech.

Here is an analysis typical of those that suggest there are three or four units in Hamlet's opening soliloquy:

O that this too too sallied flesh would melt,
Thaw, and resolve itself into a dew!   130
Or that the Everlasting had not fix'd
His canon 'gainst [self-]slaughter! O God, God,
How [weary] stale, flat, and unprofitable
Seem to me all the uses of this world!
Fie on't, ah fie! 'tis an unweeded garden   135
That grows to seed, things rank and gross in nature
Possess it merely.

                                 That it should come [to this]!
But two months dead, nay, not so much, not two.
So excellent a king, that was to this
Hyperion to a satyr, so loving to my mother   140
That he might not beteem the winds of heaven
Visit her face too roughly. Heaven and earth,
Must I remember? Why, she would hang on him
As if increase of appetite had grown
By what it fed on, and yet, within a month—   145
Let me not think on't! Frailty, thy name is woman!—

A little month, or ere those shoes were old
With which she followed my poor father's body,
Like Niobe, all tears—why she, [even she]—
O God, a beast that wants discourse of reason   150
Would have mourn'd longer—married with my uncle,
My father's brother, but no more like my father
Than I to Hercules. Within a month,
Ere yet the salt of most unrighteous tears
Had left the flushing in her galled eyes,   155

She married—O most wicked speed: to post
With such dexterity to incestuous sheets,

It is not, nor it cannot come to good,
But break my heart, for I must hold my tongue.

Dawn broke the speech into four units, with a question about
the exact break for the third unit: (1) In 129 to 137, she argued,
Hamlet expresses his despair. (2) In 138 to 143/146, Hamlet reflects on the relation between his parents before his father's abrupt
death. (3) In 147 to 157, Hamlet reviews his mother's actions as
a widow who remarried with such celerity. And in the last two
lines, she imagined a Hamlet who cried out in anguish.

In contrast, here is an analysis of the speech as eight units:

O that this too too sallied flesh would melt,
Thaw, and resolve itself into a dew!   130
Or that the Everlasting had not fix'd
His canon 'gainst [self-]slaughter!

                                  O God, God,
How [weary], stale, flat, and unprofitable
Seem to me all the uses of this world!
Fie on't, ah fie! 'tis an unweeded garden   135
That grows to seed, things rank and gross in nature
Possess it merely.

                    That it should come [to this]!
But two months dead, nay, not so much, not two.
So excellent a king, that was to this
Hyperion to a satyr, so loving to my mother   140
That he might not beteem the winds of heaven
Visit her face too roughly. Heaven and earth,
Must I remember?

                Why, she would hang on him
As if increase of appetite had grown
By what it fed on, and yet, within a month—   145
Let me not think on't! Frailty, thy name is woman!—

A little month, or ere those shoes were old
With which she followed my poor father's body,
Like Niobe, all tears—why she, [even she]—

O God, a beast that wants discourse of reason   150
Would have mourn'd longer—married with my uncle,
My father's brother, but no more like my father
Than I to Hercules.

                         Within a month,
Ere yet the salt of most unrighteous tears
Had left the flushing in her galled eyes,   155
She married—O most wicked speed: to post
With such dexterity to incestuous sheets,

It is not, nor it cannot come to good,
But break my heart, for I must hold my tongue.

In discussing students' analyses, as in discussing act I, scene i, the point is to use different segmentings as a stimulus for exploration. As they argue about units, students are arguing about whether some shift is a change in direction or simply a step in a continuing direction. The arguments about the first two segments are typical. Some students will argue that the talk of this world as a chaotic nightmare of contaminated growth begins a new thought, while others will argue that this is a single unit because the second half explains Hamlet's suicidal impulse. The discussion itself will help us all recognize that the unweeded garden image may function in both directions, reaching backward to connect the impulse toward suicide with that betrayal and reaching forward to his mother's incest.

Disagreement is especially sharp about the units in the middle of the speech, where Hamlet oscillates between a number of responses. But this disagreement reveals that it is the relative importance of Hamlet's feelings about his father, his mother, his uncle, and himself that is so difficult to define. Terri, for example, summarized her analysis by observing, "He is *not* suspicious of the circumstances of his father's death. He is *not* complaining that Claudius is king. He *is* upset about his mother's marriage." It is precisely in balancing the tensions between these competing impulses that each actor creates his or her unique incarnation of Hamlet.

In the course of this discussion, the basic trajectory of the speech comes into focus, and it is often seen as a climactic sequence:

Father's death; Mother's disloyalty, especially the sexuality manifested, as Hamlet believes, between the royal couple; intuition that this evil marriage must produce ill consequences; and resolve to remain silent, which presumably means to cease the provocative behavior he has just indulged in. Students also need to discover that this trajectory is in part created by the way in which Hamlet keeps trying to suppress the sense of personal and sexual betrayal: his resistance measures Hamlet's attempt to move beyond his nausea, while the repeated collapse of his resistance indicates how overwhelming that nausea is. Hamlet moves from general anguish to focused pain.

Step 2: Beginning to Explore the Resources of the Poetry

I ask students to identify the poetic resources that Shakespeare provides the actor to help project the character, a task they can begin by enumerating some of the patterns and striking features in the text. Soon a list emerges that includes items such as:

1. The repeated "O"s, which offer the actor the chance for expressive attack, indicating contained or released violent emotion.

2. The repetitions, "too too" and "O God, God," which can be played as rising or falling energies.

3. The dashes, which indicate that Hamlet repeatedly interrupts himself. These can represent the eruption of new thoughts, as in "Like Niobe, all tears—why she, even she— / O God, a beast that wants discourse of reason / Would have mourned longer— married with my uncle." Or the interruptions can represent moments when he tries to stop or suppress his thoughts, most notably "within a month—Let me not think on't!" which is rendered more telling by the fact that within a few lines it erupts again. Hamlet's inability to suppress the thought is a measure of its power, and also clear evidence that it is his mother's behavior, more than the death of his father or the unworthiness of his uncle, that is driving Hamlet to despair.

4. The progressive shortening of the time since his father's death, from "But two months dead, nay, not so much, not two" to "within a month" and "A little month" and "Within a month." This is a magnification of his mother's betrayal combined with Hamlet's vivid sense of still being near his father's death.

5. The suite of classical allusions, although at first students may see this resource as an obstacle. You will often need to work through these allusions for students to grasp the precise way in which they indicate the contours of Hamlet's thought.

6. The resources offered by the patterns of sound, especially in "to post / With such dexterity to incestuous sheets," with its extraordinary sequence of sibilants, practically compelling the actor to an expression either of explosive contempt or hissing disgust.

Our discussion frequently produces a debate about the last two lines, for students will disagree about whether Hamlet is saying, "I must *continue* to hold my tongue" or "I was overtly hostile to the King just now; I had better watch it—I am resolved to hold my tongue *from now on*." That is, we can ask how Hamlet understands his own behavior. Does he see his action as having betrayed his true feelings in the sense of revealing them or in the sense of concealing them? Does he feel as if he has maintained or betrayed his integrity?

Step 3: From Analysis to Synthesis

The descriptions of performances that follow demonstrate how the analysis has opened up the speech's potentials. In these performances, it is evident that students are no longer simply reading the words but rather infusing them with the thoughts and emotions and the nuances we have begun to discern. What also emerges is the diverse characters that actors can create from the role of Hamlet. Most of all, the dynamics of this challenging verbal solo begin to come into sharper focus. Let me illustrate with an account of three performances from one class.

The first performance in this class was by Erin, who offered a quiet Hamlet. There were tears in her voice, and her tense lips indicated a disgust forcefully held back. She paused before spitting out "Fie!," conveying a sense of disgust and the desire to expel the bad taste left by this scene. "Within a month" rose to a cry. The class heard this Hamlet as more sad than angry. One student suggested that in real adult anger the voice goes down, whereas Erin's voice had gotten louder but higher in pitch: her

Hamlet seemed anguished and moving toward self-paralyzing rage rather than the sort of anger that leads to action.

The second performance was by Mary Ann. Her jaw clenched and she trembled while contempt and pain writhed through her words. From beginning to end, her slow delivery indicated how much of her energy was being used to prevent tears, as her lips trembled and her chin quivered in repressed emotion, which made the tears that finally welled up even more disturbing. "Let me not" was spit out. "Frailty, thy name is woman" was a cry of deep fury at his mother. A lyrical note sounded as he recalled his father's love. This Hamlet was polarized between adoration of a dead father and contempt for a living mother.

The class was deeply affected. David said, "I felt like I should leave the room because I was overhearing something so private— the emotions were so raw. At the same time, I wanted to stay; I was fascinated." As the passage from Bert States (*Great Reckonings*) quoted in Chapter 2 implies, reading a speech of suffering is substantially different from hearing a suffering character speak because the performed version brings into play a complex array of biologically and culturally shaped responses we have when we witness another human being enact what would ordinarily be shared only with intimate others, or with no one. Other key points emerged as students articulated what Mary Ann had done. The intense privacy projected made it evident that Hamlet could not share his feelings with others, hence made suicide seem possible as a logical outcome to an impasse: "It seems as if his life can't go on." Even "Heaven and earth" was a revelation for one student, who commented, "I'd never really heard the words, it was just a phrase: here Heaven is where Hamlet assumes his father is, and earth is the place of betrayal!" And Mary Ann's delivery raised another issue about the last two lines. Do we hear the *certainty* of "Something evil will come inevitably from a just god" or the *desperation* of "Please, please don't let this happen or go on!" or yet again the *resolve* of "I will make sure it does not come to good"?

The third performance was by Dawnette, who offered a faster, angrier, and younger Hamlet. This Hamlet paced, flinging his arms about, exploding in disbelief, shouting, "That it should come to THIS!," uttering "Within a month" with contempt, only dropping his voice at the end. This time Hamlet did not evoke an impulse to leave the room, because students felt Hamlet himself to be less detached and more caught up in the play's world rather than standing outside in his own private world. "This Hamlet," said David, "is like a drowning rat in a bucket whirling round; I want to stay and watch!" Teresa added, "What surprised me was that I have thought of this only as an angry speech. But Erin and Mary Ann show me it can also be a sad speech, and they both seemed to be a more mature Hamlet, which makes it easier to see why Hamlet would *not* kill Claudius later on." Whereas if we ask the question "Would Dawnette's Hamlet kill Claudius?" the answer is "Immediately!" Another student added that this Hamlet might not have minded if Gertrude had only waited six months, because it seemed to be the timing, not incest, that was upsetting him. The other two Hamlets would be upset no matter how long Gertrude waited to remarry.

A discussion such as this will trigger a number of unexpected responses and often provoke students to share ideas they otherwise would have felt were too odd or private—and making it safe for students to share such responses is one of the aims of the performance approach. So in this class, Debbie noted that in reading the play she became deeply angry at Hamlet because he says nothing about wanting to be king; he seemed to be more interested in self-indulgent emotion. But Erin's and Mary Ann's performances showed her that grief might make any thought of being king irrelevant and aroused a response that left her more sympathetic than she had been to the Hamlet of her reading.

I asked the class to write a note here, and I wrote to myself: "What struck me today were the surprising engagements, which showed so clearly how your body or being can drop into the role's reality just by letting yourself speak the lines out loud. And I was delighted by the risk taking of these three performers—the risk taking that I hope for but know that only students can choose to do. And I am delighted also with the sharp, subtle response in this group." As we shared insights, the discussion enabled me to restate what seemed a key point in the session: "I suggest again that you read your speeches out loud to find out the range of things Shakespeare's words can do to you, or release in you. As

Mary Ann said, she could do the scene that way in front of us because 'You're not even yourself anymore, you lose yourself; the words read me, make me do things that Erin and I never planned in our rehearsal.'"

Showing and Telling

Act II, scene i is fascinating in part because of the way it begins to weave together the two plots revolving around the two main families of the Danish court. Thus, in examining this scene, we return to exploring the nature of multiplot drama even as we begin to consider the dramatist's choice between showing and telling different parts of the story. The two concepts intersect because Shakespeare stages one action within which he virtually shows another action: he thereby invites us to connect the simultaneous actions we encounter sequentially, demonstrating another, less obvious type of multiplot juxtaposition. I start by reintroducing the topic of multiplot drama.

In our work together, as I point out to the class, we transformed the question "What is the plot of X?" into the question "What does a plot do?" And we have asked this question of previous plays such as *The Taming of the Shrew* and *Richard III*. Similarly, we have recognized that the plot in these plays is multiple rather than single, and we have learned to ask the question "What does the interaction of the plots do?" In our work on the first act of *Hamlet*, we have already begun to delineate its three-part plot: act I, scene i establishes the Danish-Norwegian conflict, originating in the combat through which King Hamlet wins some Norwegian land by killing King Fortinbras of Norway; and act I, scene ii shows us Claudius dealing with the three young men, Fortinbras, Laertes, and Hamlet, each of whom will be at the center of one of the play's three plots.

But we can continue our exploration of multiplot drama by introducing another distinction. If we go back to our work of transforming dialogue into narrative, we can see that a fundamental choice the dramatist always faces is choosing which actions to *show* and which actions to *tell*. Act II, scene i provides an opportunity to see how Shakespeare handles the choice between showing and telling in an innovative fashion. Specifically, in this scene Shakespeare contrives to show one scene and tell another in order to escape one of the limits imposed by the linear nature of his medium. In fact, this is one of a number of scenes in which Shakespeare adroitly sets up a situation in which we not only see an action onstage but also imagine an action proceeding offstage. In all these scenes, when we grasp their simultaneity, we can begin to make powerful connections between the two actions, as if Shakespeare foresaw the split screen.

This second act can be said to begin with two scenes playing at once: even as Polonius is giving Reynaldo directions on how to spy on Laertes, Hamlet, as we soon learn, is visiting Ophelia in her "closet." When we make this connection, we also make an ironic discovery: at the very moment Polonius is giving Reynaldo instructions on how to spy on the far-off Laertes, whom he cheerfully assumes is busy frequenting brothels, his eye is not on his nearby daughter, who is being visited by the man he has ordered her to shun, in part because he fears Hamlet may compromise her virginity. This is an extraordinary effect to achieve, and it stimulates some interesting further reflections on the complex, double world of Elsinore. Most directly, it will at once connect yet distinguish Hamlet from Laertes.

Shakespeare clearly wants us to visualize the scene Ophelia describes, for her twenty-two-line speech is so full of detail that it virtually forces us to imagine the scene. Furthermore, because only a few minutes before we have heard Hamlet suggest that he might "put an antic disposition on," we must wonder whether the scene she reports is the moment when he has begun to put this plan in action. Thus, even though he grants us prior knowledge of the "antic disposition," Shakespeare places us in a situation in which, like the court, we must begin to use our most acute perceptions to figure out whether Hamlet is playing a part.

For this activity, I ask one student to read Ophelia's part while two others mime the action described. We do this straight through once and then begin to experiment with possible stagings in order to explore the different possible meanings the scene might have for Ophelia, for Hamlet, and for us. In the course of shaping these alternate performances, students will reinvent theories critics have offered about what Hamlet is doing. He may be beginning to feign madness, testing his ability to play this part first on the relatively innocent Ophelia, especially if he suspects she will tell her father, who will tell the King. He may visit her out of genuine love, hoping to find someone he can trust or rely on for support. He may, on the other hand, be visiting her to put an end to their love, perhaps because he feels he can rely only on Horatio, perhaps because he wishes to spare her the danger he fears his actions will provoke. He may visit her intending to ask why she has cut herself off from him. He may visit her planning to confide in her and then, for reasons having to do with his needs and with what he recognizes about her, change his mind. In developing these interpretations, we will also begin to discuss the tensions between his decision to act mad and the sense that he may be or at some point become mad.

Conversely, performing this scene enables us to concentrate on Ophelia and the unspoken choices we imagine Ophelia making. Overtly, Ophelia obeys her father's orders. But as feminist critics have insisted, she may not be the "chaste, silent, and obedient" woman Elizabethan conduct books extolled. Certainly in performance Ophelia has other options, and in thinking about what happens in the scene she describes we can consider her situation and choices and begin to imagine how her choices might manifest themselves in the way the actor playing Ophelia does or does not obey her father. What Ophelia does here helps prepare us for choices she makes later when her father uses her as bait to trap Hamlet, and for what she does in response when Hamlet murders her father.

At the end of this activity, I ask the class to write, exploring the interplay of showing and telling. I may ask specific questions: (1) What have you learned about what can happen when the dramatist chooses to show a scene versus what happens when he chooses to tell a scene? (2) What have you learned about what can happen when he has one character describe an unstaged scene in detail? (3) How does Shakespeare make Ophelia's narrative particularly effective? (4) What does Shakespeare achieve by having Ophelia narrate her scene with Hamlet rather than, for example, showing it, or having either Ophelia herself or Polonius narrate it to the King and Queen?

Performing Act III, Scene iii

> [We] can take Hamlet to that frozen moment when he stands,
> like Pyrrhus, sword drawn over the kneeling King, and stop right
> there, turning to challenge those who look on as mutes or audi-
> ences to this act: "What should Hamlet do now?" That question
> ... forces spectators of the outer action to become participants
> in the true and inner action, to share the dilemma of one whose
> task is *rightly* to be great but who finds no easy solution to the
> problem of how this is to be accomplished. Hamlet's heroism is
> not that he finds answers to his great question, but that in asking
> it, he speaks for all of us: "What should such fellows as I *do*,
> crawling between heaven and earth?" (Hawkins 518)

As Sherman Hawkins reminds us, the moment when Hamlet
stands debating whether to execute the praying King is one of
the supreme moments in drama because the very circumstances
that provide this opportunity for undetectable revenge are the
circumstances that make revenge seem unacceptable. Returning
to what I said earlier about the play's design, act III, scene iii is a
point at which the play moves from one arc to the next: the pivot
is the apparent success of *The Murder of Gonzago* in making
Claudius inadvertently reveal his guilty conscience, which propels Hamlet into ferocious action. (Although it is also the case
that how unequivocally the King's behavior seems to provide
evidence of his guilt is very much up to the actor or director, and
varies widely in the performances of which we have a record.) At
this moment, Hamlet shifts from indirect to direct action, a mode
he does not fully relinquish even on his way to England; when he
returns, we learn that it was his initiative that led him to discover
the nature of Claudius's letter to England, as it was his eagerness
for battle that led him to board the pirate vessel. At the end of
this third movement, Hamlet's offensive has failed, both because
Claudius is now aware that Hamlet knows the truth and because
killing Polonius gives Claudius the pretext to eradicate the threat
by dispatching Hamlet to an adroitly planned death in England.
At the same time, it is worth noting that the two arcs are also
unified by the way Hamlet's experience embodies a sense of the
contingency of human life. John Gielgud put this with beautiful
clarity when he directed Richard Burton's attention to the rhythm
of Hamlet's experience:

What I find so fascinating about the part is that Hamlet always begins a scene one way and has to end it in another because something has happened in the course of the scene. Rosencrantz and Guildenstern's spying doesn't occur to him until he catches them. The arrival of the Players causes another enormous change. He meets Ophelia in the nunnery scene and he doesn't know how she'll react to him. Then he realizes they are spying on him and there's another change. He goes to his mother, hears a voice, and kills Polonius, and this changes the whole course of his life. You never know in real life the actual time or moment when your whole life may be changed—when you meet someone who is going to be important to you, or somebody dies, or somebody forgets something vitally important. (Sterne 59)

Act III, scene iii is one of the most vivid examples of how Hamlet's life swerves in response to an encounter he does not and indeed could not anticipate.

Over the years I have been teaching *Hamlet*, I have developed a suite of three activities for exploring this scene over two class periods: (1) A direct exploration of performance options that starts by asking, "Does Hamlet actually come close enough to kill the king?" in order to ask, "How *close* does Hamlet come to killing the king?" (2) A second performance, which includes the soliloquy and final couplet by the King as well as Hamlet's "Now might I do it," adding a crown and a Bible to the mandated sword in order to unpack the invisible codes (ideologies) constituting Hamlet's field of choice. (3) A reflective writing assignment in which students rehearse the intersecting codes, wrestling with the forces that make Hamlet's choice so agonizing. Together these activities enable the class to experience the intricate design that ties King and Prince into a single Gordian knot that at once invites yet repels the temptation to replay Alexander's solution.

How Close Does Hamlet Come to Killing the King?

I begin our immersion in act III, scene iii halfway through the scene, starting with the monologue Hamlet speaks after he spies Claudius. Here is an account of one class's work. In this class, Jim volunteered to be Claudius and, reading the implicit stage direction, knelt as he started to pray. This simple move immediately forced the students to ask, "Which way is Claudius facing? Downstage, so that at least some of the spectators can see him? Or directly upstage, so that he is a mystery to us as he is to Hamlet?" They chose to have the King facing downstage since they wanted to see Hamlet, who, they argued, would enter behind Claudius and would therefore also be facing downstage. I asked each participant to imagine and be prepared either to perform or direct a staging, and we moved into the first performance.

Janet volunteered to go first. I took her through the actor's questions, followed by "Where are you going? Is Claudius in front of you, on your way? Do you walk straight at Claudius? Or is he peripheral?" Janet decided Claudius was glimpsed in passing, bringing Hamlet to a sudden halt. She took her position and began the speech:

> *Hamlet.* Now might I do it [pat], now 'a is a-praying;
> And now I'll do it—and so 'a goes to heaven,
> And so am I [reveng'd]. That would be scann'd:
> A villain kills my father, and for that
> I, his sole son, do this same villain send
> To heaven. (III.iii.73–78)

Stopping Janet here, I asked for observations. What struck the students was that Janet's Hamlet was too far away for it to be possible to kill Claudius. What happens, I asked, if Hamlet is played like this? "His speech shows Hamlet only imagining killing the King, and that he does not really mean to do it." So I walked directly behind the King, and on "And now I'll do it!" I began a downward stroke, which stopped with the imaginary blade inches short of the king. This stirred things up as people threw out suggestions, objecting to how close I was standing to the king, while Janet murmured, "None of this is how I imagined it!" This response was the cue to explain the conventions that might operate to let Hamlet speak when he was so close to Claudius that contemporary audiences, shaped by a paradigm of "realism," would find it *un*realistic of Claudius not to hear Hamlet.

At this point, I broke the class into groups to secure maximum participation and invention. As they worked in their groups and collected their work, students discovered complex choreographies of word and action, including a Hamlet who repeatedly raised and lowered the sword, so that we saw a man oscillating between enacting and suppressing his murderous impulse. As they argued about the logic of the different stagings, I connected this work with the larger issues of the play's design, asking. "What has Shakespeare designed this scene to do? To do to Hamlet? To do to us?" As they responded, students discovered that the scene is designed to do at least three things.

First, the scene is obviously designed to create enormous tension: Hamlet finally has proof, but at the moment he seems prepared to act he is diverted by the command to visit his mother. This becomes especially clear when we look back at the short soliloquy that ends act III, scene ii and recognize the full import of Hamlet's injunction "O heart, lose not thy nature! let not ever / The soul of Nero enter this firm bosom" (393–394). This speech indicates that his fury has reached such a pitch that he must tell himself not to yield to an impulse to murder his mother—an extraordinary revelation, and one that helps explain what happens when he comes upon the King at prayer and, later, finally releases his twice-repressed impulse to kill on the man hiding behind the arras.

Second, the scene is designed to force us to decide whether we want Hamlet to kill the King at this moment. In this class, as in many, an initial vote showed that a majority of students wanted Hamlet to kill Claudius. I am always struck by how bloodthirsty students seem to be, but I take this response as an indication of how Shakespeare's design works to arouse the desire for revenge in spectators. As often happens, a number of students said they were tired of what they saw as Hamlet's inability to act. "What's his problem?" they asked. Debate grew quite fierce, especially as students recalled the ways in which Hamlet's own speeches had raised issues about justice, religion, and nobility, and about his obligations as son, heir, prince, subject, and Christian soul. I asked, "If you think Hamlet has been delaying, when is the first time we see him alone with Claudius?" The answer to that question— namely, that this was the first such moment—did produce an interesting pause in their complaints.

Third, whether we do or do not want Hamlet to kill the King, the scene is designed to force us to evaluate the reasons Hamlet gives for his decision. Students found themselves torn between the decision Hamlet makes and the reasons Hamlet gives for that decision. As they discovered, there were four obvious possibilities: (1) spectators may agree with Hamlet's decision not to kill the King and agree with his reasons; (2) they may agree with Hamlet's decision not to kill and disagree with his reasons; (3) they may disagree with Hamlet's decision not to kill but agree with the reasons since they also hope Hamlet will find a way to send Claudius to hell; and (4) they may disagree with Hamlet's decision and disagree with his reasons, wanting him to achieve revenge but not stain his own soul with the blasphemous attempt to control the destiny of another human being's soul. Arguing about these divergent responses provides a powerful impetus to return to the earlier part of the scene.

Three Codes in Action: Sword, Crown, and Bible

Part of what has always appealed to me about employing a performance approach is the richness of the results in the classroom. A second appealing aspect has been the pedagogic richness that emerges when one teacher adapts a performance activity composed by another teacher, revealing untapped potentials in the original pedagogic design and setting up the possibility of further transformations. The activity that follows is a direct result of this recursive process. When *Teaching Shakespeare through Performance* (Riggio) was first published, I read David Kennedy Sauer and Evelyn Tribble's "Shakespeare in Performance: Theory in Practice and Practice in Theory," in which they present the following activity:

> Evelyn Tribble has developed an exercise that challenges students to produce different Ophelias. The exercise makes the character essentially an empty stage on which ideology, revealing the contradictions of our society, is enacted. She divides the class into three groups, giving one a sword (or two), one a bouquet of flowers, and one a Bible. The groups are then separated and told to rehearse act 1, scene 3, of *Hamlet*, integrating their props into the performance. After the three groups perform, they discuss their results. Every time this has been tried, the groups find that the interaction among text, actors, and props produces a different Ophelia (as well as a different Laertes and Polonius). (43)

Even before finishing this essay, I realized I could adapt Tribble's design to *Hamlet* act III, scene iii, adding a crown and a Bible to the mandated weapon, and I worked out the activity offered below. Then I read the footnote for this passage:

> [Garry] Walton inspired Tribble's experiment with his explanation of his work in the 1992–93 Folger Institute on Shakespeare and the Language of Performance conducted by Lois Potter, which we attended together. . . . Walton's work was based on Edward Rocklin's article ("Incarnational Art"), whose work in turn derives from Philip McGuire's *Speechless Dialect*. (Sauer and Tribble 47)

In the essay referred to, I presented an activity for performing *A Midsummer Night's Dream* act I, scene i by dividing the class into three groups, offering one group a rose, one group a book titled *The Laws of Athens*, and one group no prop at all. In responding to Tribble's adaptation of my own earlier design, I found myself embodying one way in which a performance approach invites ongoing pedagogic innovation.

The activity provides an opportunity to articulate the invisible but constitutive codes in which the dramatis personae of *Hamlet* operate, show how these codes are both different from and similar to codes at play in our own society, and formulate a definition of *tragedy* as being produced, in part, precisely by the conflict of codes.

You may not have access to a sword or dagger or a crown, and you may not want to use an actual copy of the Bible. The sword or dagger can be something as simple as a pen; if you are going to use a stage property sword, you will need to instruct students about the proper use of that weapon. Since I habitually wear hats, my hat can serve as a crown, but of course you can make a crown in any of a number of ways; I currently have a crown made and donated by a student who knew he was going to play Claudius in this scene and came to class prepared for his part. As for the Bible, you can simply print or use a computer to print a paper cover labeled "BIBLE," which you attach to a large book. If you can offer multiple copies of each property, so much the better. In any case, I divide the class into pairs: one-third of the groups have only the weapon; one-third add a crown; and one-third add a Bible. What follows is a description of how these properties contributed to the performances of one class.

SWORD and CROWN. Claudius = Aaron, Hamlet = Caroline
Throughout the first part of his speech, Aaron's king was a man who desperately wanted to repent but was barely able to force himself to kneel, even to God. He took slow steps forward (downstage toward us) and finally knelt. He took off his crown even as he said "my crown," looking at it and then putting it aside on the ground. He finally bowed down very slowly, making us see that his "stubborn knees" were the visible embodiment of an invisible civil war. Caroline's Hamlet projected anger, doubt, pain. He began to bring his weapon down but then had a three-second pause after beginning to strike. Later, he started and stopped again on "That would be scanned . . . ," looking at his own sword as he meditated on how the deed would be "scanned." Then, as his anger regathered a third time, he shifted his weapon to a more daggerlike position and almost brought it up again. At "Up sword," this Hamlet put the weapon away. His words projected strong appeals to heaven, and his anger was projected out at the universe, not turned inward. Finally, he left, his closing words accompanied by a harsh glare at the king. The king stood up, put on the crown, resumed his office. What we witnessed, then, seemed to be a performance in which Claudius prayed as a man, not as a king; but when his human prayer failed, he resumed the office of king. As we discussed this performance, what came into focus was the way in which this Claudius's choices demonstrated his recognition that remaining king and achieving salvation were incompatible objectives. Although he could put aside the crown, even to save his soul he could not put aside the ambition that compelled him to commit murder to secure the crown. Students found this performance elicited a respect for the king that they had not felt when reading the play and, some said, that they were reluctant to feel: it was respect not for his evil actions but for his clearsighted acknowledgment of his priorities and his explicit admission of his spiritual failure.

SWORD and BIBLE. Claudius = Carlos, Hamlet = Sonja
When this Claudius knelt, he was much more distressed by his crime, his condition, and the prospect of damnation. He clutched the Bible with fingers curling in desperate tension. His voice stressed "crown," "ambition," and "queen" as equal motives. At the self-command, he squatted, then knelt, then bent over so that he approached a fetal curl, with the Bible in front of him facing the ground. Hamlet entered, offering a quiet but forceful delivery that led him close enough that at "Now I'll do it!" he began to strike. At this moment, showing no awareness of Hamlet's presence, the king suddenly raised the Bible over his head, a gesture that made it look as though he were hoping the book would serve as a shield to ward off the wrath of heaven. So Hamlet, who had started his stroke, was stopped, at least in part, by the sudden appearance of the Bible. As Hamlet proceeded, the King lowered the Bible, again with no apparent awareness of Hamlet's presence, as Hamlet said, "When he is drunk, asleep . . ." What we witnessed was a moment in which religion stops Hamlet from revenge, even though some version of religion was compelling him to revenge. Our discussion raised the point that differently situated spectators at the Globe would have had somewhat different points of view of the actions. Aaron, for example, who was sitting on what would be the upstage left side, noted how striking it was when the Bible suddenly, almost magically, appeared over the head of the King, stopping Hamlet in the middle of his stroke. We agreed that this Claudius seemed not so much to be praying as begging to be spared, perhaps hoping that his complete abjection would win pardon through pity. I also pointed out that Carlos and Sonja had in effect re-created one aspect of the performance in the Olivier film; catching sight of Jesus on the cross, placed on the alcove in front of and above the praying but oblivious king, stops Olivier's Hamlet as he is about to kill. The difference is that Olivier's Hamlet stops or seems to stop himself, whereas in our performance the King accidentally manages to save his life at the very moment he is failing to save his soul. Even as the Bible in Claudius's hand seemed to counter yet mirror the sword in Hamlet's, so too did the king's failed attempt at prayer

counter yet mirror Hamlet's attempt to offer a Christian justification for seeking eternal revenge through assassination.

SWORD. Claudius = Elisabeth, Hamlet = Danielle
This was a Claudius who paced and thrust down his left hand to emphasize specific words. He looked up at each mention of heaven and touched his chest when admitting guilt and voicing hope. Hamlet used a two-handed stroke as he started to kill the King; he stopped himself, looked up to heaven as he said, "Why this is hire and salary, not revenge," and, with his arm still raised, continued his indignant meditation until he cried out "No!" Then he raised the sword as if to strike but suddenly stopped himself as an idea sprang to mind; he lowered his sword and worked out his new plan. This Hamlet relished the thought of killing the King: his eyes brightened as he imagined killing and damning Claudius, his head moved to follow the body as he imagined it rising and then plunging toward hell, and an evil grin appeared on his face. This Hamlet was animated and often looked directly at us, making eye contact as he spoke. He backed off very slowly, looking at Claudius while slipping stealthily away. He said, "My mother stays," took a few more steps, looked around, completed the couplet, and exited. In discussion, a number of students were struck by how Hamlet's imagination of damning the king had become a delight in picturing the King's eternal agony. They were startled by the hint that the praying, fratricidal brother-uncle and the murderous, pious son-nephew might have switched places, and that in attempting to fulfill his oath Hamlet may have become possessed of a devil-like taste for inflicting suffering—a result that raised further doubts about the origins and the intentions of the Ghost. Their focus on a suddenly evil Hamlet provided a cue to share Richard Burton's chillingly gleeful delivery of this line.

WHAT DOES A PROP DO?

After I asked students to write their responses to the question "What did each prop do for the performance and the spectators?," they shared answers. "The props emphasized one element over another. They emphasized different elements in different performances, so they helped create different performances. They focused our attention on specific words and actions together, making those words or actions stand out. They helped create the meaning of the scene."

I asked students how the prop had influenced their work together. In the most basic sense, the prop contributed to making performing the scene vividly different from reading the scene. It focused attention on the body of the actor experimenting with or wielding that prop. The sword in particular—and this will be especially true if you use a long object or have a property sword—also forced them to think much more explicitly about the distance between and relation of the two actors. They realized that the prop tended to become the focus of the rehearsal, that paying attention to the prop might also focus attention on a specific word or phrase, and that overall the props clearly shaped or focused their explorations. We could see that in the performances the prop often provoked key acting choices. Building on this perception, I noted that actors may use a prop in rehearsal and then discard it: it can be a tool for invention to focus attention more precisely on what you are saying, what you are doing, and, in particular, on *connections* between word and act—that is, on how what you are doing may incarnate the imagery of what you are saying.

WHAT CODE DID EACH PROP EMBODY?

We turned to the point made by Sauer and Tribble, namely, that "props are not ideologically neutral," and proceeded to articulate the codes embodied in each prop. The sword was at once the emblem and the instrument of honor—the weapon of a gentleman since only a gentleman, a member of the gentry or nobility, could have honor, as distinct from the honesty a man of lower rank could possess. This code of aristocratic honor regulates, or is supposed to regulate, the behavior of a gentleman, just as honesty—that is, chastity—regulates or is supposed to regulate the behavior of a gentlewoman. The code is embodied in the gentleman's word, which entails that gentlemen speak truth and fulfill their promises. This masculine honor entails a formal process for negotiating, rectifying, or punishing violations of that code, such as lying, violating the chastity of a woman, or murdering another gentleman. The mechanism for enforcing the code is the duel, in which one gentleman challenges another, alleging a violation of the code considered to have dishonored the challenging party. The party challenged must be ready to offer an apology; to negotiate with the challenger until they can perform an action other than a duel that satisfies the honor of both parties; or, if these maneuvers break down, to answer the accusation in combat. The duel is a highly codified event whose rules are designed to make it a fair fight between men of equal rank. Violating the rules of the duel itself (using swords of unequal length or a poisoned sword, as Laertes does) is also a code violation. The imperative for revenge could produce a vendetta, the type of feud that, as in *Romeo and Juliet*, not only provokes lethal duels over generations but, when followed to a logical conclusion, also destroys both families.

The crown was a symbol of the emerging system of state justice (which could also, of course, be seen as a system of state oppression), embodied in the monarch who was the head of state and the officer from whom justice flowed and to whom subjects looked as the ultimate judge. This system was designed, in part, to be impersonal and to eliminate the need for individuals to take justice into their own hands; it was also embodied in the institution of trial by jury. In this system, violations of the code were to be answered by having the state conduct a trial. More specifically, in a criminal (as distinct from civil) case, the state secured an indictment by a grand jury; conducted a trial, with a prosecution and a defense, before a jury of the accused's peers; proceeded to a verdict of guilty or not guilty; and, in the event of a guilty verdict, imposed a sentence, whether incarceration or execution.

The code of aristocratic honor was at the core of the older medieval form of organization, and however much it was becoming subordinated by the time Shakespeare wrote, it was still a pervasive element of English culture. It was also a code that was recognized as inherently subversive of the attempt to establish systems of impersonal, state-sponsored justice, and the monarchs of Europe, though aristocrats themselves, largely sought to prevent and indeed eliminate the effects of this corrosive code by forbidding their subjects from engaging in duels. Like the Prince of Verona in *Romeo and Juliet*, Queen Elizabeth I and King James I sought to prevent their subjects from engaging in duels. James I, for example, issued several proclamations outlawing dueling, although the fact that he issued several of them indicates that they did not succeed in ending this practice. In outlawing dueling, these edicts created a situation in which a man who killed his opponent in a duel was subject to prosecution for murder. For instructors who want to situate *Hamlet* explicitly in a historical context, sword and crown can be read as embodying what Raymond Williams (*Drama from Ibsen to Brecht*) and subsequent cultural materialist critics would present as the shift from one ideology to another.

The third code explicitly at work in the action and in Hamlet's choices is Christianity, symbolized by the Bible—and made more complex by differences between Catholic and Protestant theological understandings of ghosts. We can distinguish three crucial points within this code that shape Hamlet's action and the action of *Hamlet*. First is the shared Jewish and Christian commandment that forbids murder, coupled with God's proclamation that "Vengeance is mine" and not to be executed by human beings (Deuteronomy 32:35 and Romans 12:19). Second, this twofold command is intensified by Jesus imperative of mercy: he offers a new commandment which insists that victims must not only endure being wronged but also actively forgive their enemies, and, going still further, they must "turn the other cheek" to injuries. Third is the question of the Ghost's origin, since where the Ghost came from would clearly affect the validity of the Ghost's command. Catholic theology had added purgatory to heaven and hell, defining it as the place where the souls of those who have lived imperfect but not evil lives must suffer in order to purge their sins. But Catholic theology also held that however long they suffered, *all* the souls in purgatory would eventually reach heaven. Protestant theology, beginning with Luther's critique of indulgences, attacked purgatory as a fiction: it forbade prayers for the dead and eliminated the concept of purgatory and the license purgatory gave for the idea that some souls might return to plead for human assistance (or suffrage) in shortening their time of suffering. For Protestants, souls were in either heaven or hell—and the question of a ghost's origin became simpler yet more problematic. A ghost who admitted it was suffering pains and punishments would seem to be admitting it came from hell. A ghost who not only admitted to such suffering but also sought to persuade a human being to take revenge was a ghost whose actions would seem to indicate that it came from hell and, in all probability, that it was a devil seeking to damn a human soul gullible enough to violate the commandments of Jesus and God.[6]

Three Codes in Action: Rehearsing Hamlet's Choices

At this point, you reach a logical moment for taking a third step in immersing students fully in Hamlet's dilemma in act III, scene iii, which can be done with the following prompt: "Work out and write down the most immediate and most direct action Hamlet can take that will resolve his problem while fulfilling all three codes at once." Sooner or later, you will hear some quietly rueful or sardonic laughter as many students come to the conclusion that it is not possible to craft such a (re)solution. Depending on how you want the discussion to develop, you can ask for anyone who has a solution that fulfills all three codes to offer it, or you can start by asking students who think a solution is impossible to initiate discussion. If you start with those who claim there is no solution to the dilemma because there is no action Hamlet can take that will simultaneously fulfill all three codes, the discussion will offer an anatomy of the knot created by the three codes that looks something like the following analysis.

The aristocratic code comes into play through the Ghost of King Hamlet, whose plea for Hamlet to commit himself to revenge is a direct invocation of that code. The Ghost's claim is that since he was killed dishonorably by his brother, his son must restore their honor by killing the king, his uncle. Furthermore, although the Ghost does not say so, Hamlet and most if not all of the original spectators would instantly have been aware of the reasons why Hamlet has no recourse to the code of justice. First, he has no evidence to support the process of securing an indictment. (Hamlet secures evidence later when he seizes the commission from the King requesting or ordering that the English monarch execute Hamlet, but at that point he shares this evidence only with Horatio and, of course, the spectators.) Second, even if he had evidence, since the person to be indicted is the king, there is no possibility that Claudius would allow such a process to commence. Third, even if Hamlet could get Claudius indicted, as king Claudius would assert that no trial is possible because it is impossible to empanel a jury of his peers. Thus Hamlet confronts the question of whether he is justified in killing, which means assassinating, the king. Few students speak of the act Hamlet is contemplating as assassination (itself an interesting fact), but as Frye, among others, has demonstrated, a substantial number of the original spectators would have been aware that Hamlet was confronting one of the most fiercely contested issues of the day, namely, the question of the proper response to an evil or tyrannical monarch. While the Anglican church commanded subjects to obey the ruler, apparently licensing only passive resistance, writers ranging from the most fervent Protestants to the most ardent Catholics were working out theories that justified both organized armed resistance (the course of action finally chosen by the French Huguenot nobles who eventually ensured the triumph of Henri IV) and assassination by an individual (the course of action chosen by the individual Catholics who assassinated Henri III and Henri IV of France). Thus Shakespeare could have expected some members of the audience to consider Hamlet justified in assassinating Claudius because they would have situated Hamlet's act in the context created by the arguments justifying the murder of a usurper and tyrant.[7]

But what of the Christian code? Although neither Hamlet nor *Hamlet* ever overtly alludes to the doctrinal problem, many of the original spectators would have been well aware of the divergent theological understandings of the afterlife. In both Catholic and Protestant dispensations, it is clear that, given the too-horrifying-for-human-ears pains the Ghost claims to be suffering, he is not in heaven. The problem Hamlet confronts is deciding whether the Ghost is from hell or purgatory. In a Catholic universe, the Ghost might be the soul of a dead man, and that Ghost might be making a legitimate plea for action from the one to whom he appeared. Even in a Catholic universe, however, a true ghost would ask its human interlocutor to perform acts that would shorten its suffering, not solicit acts that would either damn the human agent or ensure that such an agent would himself spend time in purgatory. In a Protestant universe, such a ghost—presuming it was not a devil appearing as the soul of a specific human being—would come from hell, and its sufferings would be eternal, because its sins were not merely not-forgiven on earth, as the Ghost acknowledges King Hamlet's sins were not, but not forgiven by God. Yet during their first encounter, Hamlet becomes convinced that the apparition is indeed the Ghost of his father, and he swears an oath to seek revenge. Only later does Hamlet voice the horrifying suspicion (raised by Horatio [I.iv.69–78]) that the Ghost might be a devil tempting him to commit an action (homicide or, at moments, suicide) that would damn Hamlet's soul. But even during this skeptical period when he sets out to test the Ghost's veracity, Hamlet never overtly questions the legitimacy of its call for revenge. Despite his explicit fear (II.ii.598–603) that the Ghost might be a devil seeking to tempt him to perform a damnable act, Hamlet seems to reject this possibility, as he does when the apparent success of the play-within-a-play makes him exclaim, "I'll take the Ghost's word for a thousand pound" (III.ii.286–287). Moreover, once his test satisfies him that the Ghost's account of the crime is true, he seems to commit himself wholeheartedly to the task of achieving revenge. As Greenblatt puts it, "Hamlet understands that it is premeditated murder, not due process, that is demanded of him" (237). Yet Hamlet still invokes the religious beliefs that in his first anguished soliloquy, for example, prevented him from committing suicide.

Furthermore, even if Hamlet is trying to fulfill the honor code's demand for revenge, it is dishonorable to stab a man in the back, let alone kill him while he is at prayer. And it is un-Christian, of course, to kill at all. (You can ask the class to compare Hamlet's action here with the claim of Laertes that if he could he would "cut his [Hamlet's] throat i' th' church," and Claudius's agreement that "No place indeed should murder sanctuarize" [IV.vii.126–127].) Thus in wrestling with the Christian code, students will come to recognize that the play's design is deeply equivocal about whether its universe is governed by Catholic or Protestant theology. The Ghost's description of his sufferings clearly indicates he is not in heaven. On the one hand, if he is in hell, which must be true in a Protestant universe, then no matter how accurate the account of his own murder, and therefore no matter how guilty and damnable Claudius may appear, it would seem to be true that this is a devil using the truth to secure the damnation of Hamlet's own soul. On the other hand, if this is a Catholic universe and King Hamlet's soul is in purgatory, that soul will eventually complete its sufferings and be translated to heaven. In this case, it would seem more probable that the Ghost is not a devil but the soul of Hamlet's father—but this still does not alter the fact that what the Ghost is asking Hamlet to do runs counter to the commandments of God. Indeed, after looking at how thoroughly the evidence seems to support both sides of this long-running debate, Greenblatt concludes that Shakespeare de-signed his play so that "a young man from Wittenberg, with a distinctly Protestant temperament, is haunted by a distinctly Catholic ghost" (240).

At this point, it can be quite effective to play Richard Burton's performance of Hamlet's monologue in the version issued on the long-playing record.[8] What is most striking about this perfor-mance is how Burton delivers the climactic lines, which are printed in the "Prompt-script" in Richard Sterne's *John Gielgud Directs Richard Burton in* Hamlet (227) as follows:

> Then TRIP him that his heels may KICK at heaven,
> And that his soul may be as damned and black
> As hell, whereto it goes.

In some classes, I do not even have to ask "What strikes you about this Hamlet?" before a student will exclaim, "But Hamlet has become evil!" What is barely hinted at by the typography is the deeply gleeful way in which Burton utters the phrase "kick at heaven": his rising intonation, with a startling leap to a high and extremely intense note on "kick," the very slight pause that fol-lows, and the relish in his voice combine to produce a stunning effect. I ask what image Burton's delivery invites us to imagine is playing through Hamlet's mind or, perhaps more to the point, through his mind and body. Over the years, students have of-fered images such as this from Steve, who told us, "The image I have is of someone dangling from a noose, heels kicking in the air." For me, the kinetic power of Burton's voice suggests his Hamlet is imagining tripping Claudius at the very moment the latter seems to be reaching for heaven (as his praying position suggests he is) and trying desperately to grab onto the edge of heaven above him, before falling just short, beginning to somersault, tumbling down headfirst, and plunging into the abyss of hell. The sheer relish of Burton's performance suggests Hamlet's almost gustatory delight: here is a Hamlet who can almost taste the moment in which his uncle loses heaven and begins to suffer the torments the Ghost has hinted at. If part of Hamlet's assignment is to leave Gertrude to heaven, then at this moment, making this choice, Hamlet acts as though the other part of his assignment is to send Claudius to hell. This example demonstrates what a difference the actor's performance can make in what the text *does*, and hence what it *means*—and what it reveals about the speaker.

Burton's performance provides the perfect cue to introduce Samuel Johnson's comment on this speech:

> III.iii.93 HAMLET. Then trip him, that his heels may kick at
> heav'n;
> And that his soul may be as damn'd and black
> As hell, whereto it goes.

> The speech, in which Hamlet, represented as a virtuous character, is not content with taking blood for blood, but contrives damnation for the man that he would punish, is too horrible to be read or to be uttered.[9]

In effect, Burton's Hamlet *realizes* the Hamlet imagined by Johnson almost exactly two hundred years before Burton's performance. And it functions to elicit from at least some classroom auditors precisely the reaction Johnson registered. As Felice realized, the horrifying element of Burton's performance is that Hamlet seeks to play God in an attempt to control not merely the earthly fate of his uncle but also the eternal fate of his soul. Although he thought the speech "too horrible to be read or uttered," Johnson might have recognized that Burton's performance had the virtue of demonstrating the corrupting effect of revenge on the character of Hamlet. For what Hamlet seems to be trying to fashion is an action that might be called Christian revenge, although to formulate this phrase makes one immediately aware of what is almost certainly one motive for his not acknowledging this fact.[10]

At this point, we listen to the solutions put forward by students. Aaron, for example, proposed that if Hamlet walked away he could fulfill *all* the codes, including keeping his honor as an aristocrat, because he would not commit a dishonorable murder of a defenseless man. One problem with this solution is that Hamlet does not really achieve justice at that moment. Moreover, we recalled that Hamlet has sworn an oath to avenge the Ghost, and this imperative derives from the code of aristocratic honor, even if the oath is presumably made in the name of the Christian God. The fact that it is the Ghost who demands revenge adds an extra twist, since even as it evokes a merciless imperative to avenge murder, the Ghost seems to seek the sanction of the religious code.

In another class, Pam offered this solution: "Hamlet can fulfill all three codes *if* he can get Claudius to confess. If the king confesses, then Hamlet can get royal justice, he can avenge his father's death with honor, and he can also fulfill Christian precepts, first not to commit murder and second to leave vengeance to God, to only seek justice." Pam's solution elicited appreciation for its elegance, as well as comments from her classmates indicating that Pam had formulated what for the moment seemed to be the only possible solution. Although it is hard to imagine how a royal system of justice would actually deal with a king who confessed to murder—in particular, to imagine how a court could secure an indictment, trial, guilty verdict, sentence, and execution—Pam had indeed worked out an *action* that attempted to confront all the elements of Hamlet's dilemma.

As Hawkins suggests, asking students to invent a course of action for Hamlet at this moment is a move that "forces spectators of the outer action to become participants in the true and inner action, to share the dilemma" (518) that confronts Hamlet. Once they have become so engaged, students will be less likely to simply endorse their impatience with Hamlet because he does not fit our present culture's model of an "action hero." They will be less likely to echo the voice heard in many late-twentieth-century revenge movies—which is also the voice of Laertes when he returns to Denmark—saying, as a student once said, "He killed my father? He's going down!" They will be less likely, that is, to assume a position of superiority and to make the judgments that flow from such a position. Thus this suite of activities compels students to step away from an exclusive focus on Hamlet's psychology and to move toward an understanding of the constitutive conditions within which or against which he must make his choice. What the play insists on, and what the props italicize, is that the dilemma caused by the collision of codes is an impersonal dilemma that would confront anyone in Hamlet's position, no matter what his or her personal constitution might be. That dilemma also, of course, embodies one of the fundamental definitions of tragedy.

I often close this set of activities with a passage from the actor Michael Pennington, reflecting on his own performance of Hamlet:

> A man with a sword comes upon his enemy, whom he has sworn to destroy, at prayer. The promised act of revenge can at this point be performed with relatively little difficulty—indeed with no greater fear of discovery than that of the praying man on an earlier occasion when he destroyed *his* enemy in an orchard. With exultation the armed man approaches his victim and raises his sword.
>
> At this point we stop and see where we are. There is no question in the mind of the spectator but that the sword will certainly come down on the neck of the praying man with all the fury with which it was raised. There is also no question in the mind of the armed man but that he will now do the deed—no question at all. Most oddly of all, in the mind of the actor personifying the man with the sword there is a momentary certainty that tonight will be different, and that his colleague on the floor is about to suffer a severe and unexpected injury.
>
> The alarming question arises: who is actually in charge? If the actor himself is in doubt, then who is masterminding the event and guiding us towards the next action? Everyone waits, the spectators, the two men, the actors playing the two men, all held for a moment on the same edge, holding the same breath. (*"Hamlet"* 128)

This passage often elicits a murmured appreciation of the image of "all . . . holding the same breath."

Part of what I value about the performance approach is precisely that it offers us not only the chance for fierce debate but also the opportunity to achieve moments of powerful connection through art and our collaborative transaction with that art in the classroom. Indeed, one purpose of this book is to call attention to these pedagogic potentials, frequently ignored in our classrooms, for building engagement through collaborative exploration. So in the midst of a discussion about how the play asks us to contemplate what it might be like to murder another human being, we also sometimes reach a moment when the class comes into focus as we seek to balance our sharply conflicting points of view on Hamlet's decision not to murder Claudius.

Staging the Duel

For the next class, I ask students to analyze act V, scene ii, lines 224–403, from the moment when the court assembles for the last time to the death of Hamlet and final exit. In particular, they are to locate the major choice-points for performance, to suggest what they believe to be the primary production options for each such choice-point, and to make their own suite of choices. I also ask them to look at the design of the play, concentrating on patterns formed by the three court scenes from the beginning (I.ii), middle (III.ii), and end (V.ii). The point is to recognize that at the beginning, we have the King seeking to control three young men; that in the middle, one young man seeks to control the King; and that at the end, two of those young men kill each other and one of those young men kills the King and then votes for the third young man to become king.

Throughout our work together, I argue that one reason we need to consider questions of performance is that the choices the team of actors, director, and designers makes as they work out the script's potentials create the experience from which the spectators (re)create an imaginative vision. The crucial fact about the last scene of a play is that these choices complete the patterns embodied in the performance, and it is these choices that enable the spectators to create a whole from what has been an emerging gestalt.

When I introduced the map of the performance ensemble (see Figure 2.1), I pointed out that, given our predominantly literary training, when we read a play most of us collapse the triangle in a direct relation of playtext and play reader. But we can modify that point by also acknowledging that when reading a play many of us do imagine small elements of performance, although we are usually unaware of doing so, and are thus unaware that we are in fact making choices about possible performances. Literary critics and even those who focus on the theater, theater companies, and performance spaces provide frequent examples of this process. In Andrew Gurr's *Studying Shakespeare*, for instance, we read: "'You, Prince of Wales!' says Falstaff bitterly, thinking not of riot but of dishonour in this inverted setting for military valour" (30). That "bitterly" tells us how Gurr imagines Falstaff delivering the line, and this is certainly a suggestion to be taken seriously since it is offered by one of the most significant contributors to theater history in the last thirty years; nonetheless, Gurr's suggestion is clearly not the only possible performance for the actor playing Falstaff. Indeed, any time a critic writes a sentence such as "Hamlet's sullen reply to Polonius shows that—" he writes as if this is how the line must be performed. These critics make choices suggested by the script, but their choices may also function to banish other equally plausible options. So Hamlet can say his line in a way that is buoyant rather than sullen, and Falstaff can say his line with sunny contempt or playful mockery or—but you can imagine other possibilities. The point is not that we should stop making and publishing such choices, but rather that as readers of criticism we should be aware that, no matter how authoritative they sound, in many cases critics are not reading off a staging mandated by the text: they are reading a text they have already interpreted insofar as they have performed it in imagination. What Daniel Seltzer said about performance applies to much criticism as well: "performance, while by nature unlike an act of literary criticism, always has one of the same results: *it cannot avoid implying a point of view*" ("Shakespeare's Texts" 89).

So the activity being introduced here is designed to make us aware of the interpretive choices we make as readers, to discover the alternative choices made by other readers in this class, and to help us discover or invent the range of possibilities for the end of *Hamlet*. Or, to put it another way, this activity is designed to make us aware of ways in which even when we do read plays theatrically we may unwittingly limit the range of choices. The duel scene in particular, as is true of any scene dominated by action and especially by sustained violent action, is always open to widely varied staging choices, choices that can create divergent or even contradictory completions of the play's design.

1st Choice: The Setting. The essential questions seem to be these: "Are there thrones for the King and Queen? Where are the thrones placed? Where is the table placed? Between the thrones? To one side? Is the table in reach of the King's throne? Does an attendant bring the cup to the King? Does the King move to it? Who carries the weapons? Who carries the cup? How are the courtiers arranged?"

2nd Choice: The Apology and Handshake. It may be useful to have three students perform the exchange beginning at act V, scene ii, line 225, so that the class can explore the question "In what manner and for how long do they hold hands?" What does Laertes do? Does he take Hamlet's hand? How long does he hold it? Does he pull away? Does Laertes have trouble meeting Hamlet's gaze or does Hamlet have trouble meeting that of Laertes? If, for example, Laertes immediately pulls back, what does that indicate? Or if Hamlet insists on holding Laertes' hand through the entire speech, what does this do? Or what if Laertes pulls away as he starts his speech? If Laertes cannot meet Hamlet's gaze, if his conscience seems to be bothering him, does this give first-time spectators hope for Hamlet's survival? Or if Hamlet seems uneasy, does his tension suggest that he is uncomfortable in offering a version of an insanity defense?

3rd Choice: Choosing the Foils. Answering the question "How does Laertes know which foil to select?" leads to an explanation of what "unbated and envenom'd" means. Discussing how Laertes knows which weapon to select will also prompt students to wonder if Osric is part of the plot. And if Osric is in on the plot, what is emphasized? This point has been made explicit in a striking performance reported by Marvin Rosenberg (*Masks of* Hamlet 882), who writes:

> Hodek's [the translator's] compunctious Laertes, suddenly unwilling to go ahead with the plot, tried to give back the lethal foil—
>
>> loading his words with sharp irony, "This is too heavy. Let me see another." His fate is sealed as he is prevented in doing so by Osric and Claudius himself. (Stribrny [*sic*])

Hamlet's "These foils have all a length?" raises the question "Does Osric commit a direct lie?" It also creates a moment of possible suspense, noted by T. J. B. Spencer in his edition of *Hamlet*: Claudius assumes Hamlet is unsuspecting, but if Hamlet starts to inspect the foils, we hold our breath, watching how steady Claudius remains even as we begin to hope that Hamlet might avoid the trap (353).

4th Choice: What Are the Conditions for the Duel? To understand the trajectory of the duel, we need to turn back to the early part of the scene to clarify Osric's description of the wager and the structure of the bout:

> *Osric.* The King, sir, hath laid, sir, that in a dozen passes between yourself and him, he shall not exceed you three hits; he hath laid on twelve for nine; and it would come to immediate trial, if your lordship would vouchsafe the answer. (V.ii.165–169)

The *Riverside* editor's notes on the two halves of this speech are as follows:

> 166–67. **he ... hits.** Laertes must win by at least eight to four (if none of the "passes" or bouts are draws), since at seven to five he would be only two up.
> 167. **he ... nine.** Not satisfactorily explained despite much discussion. One suggestion is that Laertes has raised the odds against himself by wagering that out of twelve bouts he will win nine. (1231)

The critical point is that Laertes must win eight passes, and this helps explain why, after two passes and one apparent draw, Laertes becomes desperate: since Hamlet has scored two hits, he need win only three more passes for the duel to be over, thereby evading the poisoned weapon Laertes holds in his hand. And though Hamlet might well be assassinated by the poisoned cup, we might infer that the "fiery" Laertes will not be satisfied if he cannot personally exact revenge.

5th Choice: How Ferocious Is the Duel? "Is the duel playful at the beginning or in earnest from the start? Is there a contrast between Laertes, primed to kill, and Hamlet, liberated from attempts to control the world? Or does his foreboding weigh on Hamlet? Does Hamlet win the early bouts because he is a better fencer? Or because Laertes, though better, is made overeager by the conflict between his purposed revenge and his sense of honor?" Discussion elicits the wide variety of ways in which students imagine the flow of the duel, and compels them to attend to the ways each version would invite spectators to make meaning.

6th Choice: The King Lets Gertrude Die. As Gertrude reaches for the cup, the scene reaches its first climax: once someone drinks from the cup, the King passes a point of no return. In particular, anyone staging the scene must decide if the King is near enough to stop Gertrude simply by reaching out to grab the cup or stay her arm, or so far away that he would have to take more overt and hence self-incriminating action. If they are separated, the stress is on Claudius's loss of control, whereas if they are close, the stress is on his choice not to act. We also need to ask whether he lets his anguish show. The basic fact is incontestable: Claudius is willing to sacrifice Gertrude to save his throne and his skin— this in spite of the fact that in his attempt to pray his words seemed to imply that he was ready to risk damnation to keep his queen. But how much effort, if any, does he make to save her? And when she has drunk, does he quickly move away, abandoning her to the death he has unwittingly contrived for her?

Gertrude also has some choices, and in some performances they will function to indicate whether she has shifted her allegiance from Claudius to Hamlet. She may, for example, look at the cup, look at the King, intuit what he has done, and deliberately drink. In such a performance, it may be up to the spectators to infer whether she drinks to protect Hamlet or to punish herself for being deceived by Claudius, or, perhaps most simply, to escape an intolerable situation. If she commits suicide, Gertrude becomes an even more exact analogue to Ophelia, caught between loving her husband and her son as Ophelia is caught between loving her father and her suitor. A Gertrude who commits suicide completes the design in a substantially different way than one who dies by accident, particularly in how we see the fate of women in this play's world. At the same time, in a production in which Gertrude commits suicide, the performance probably needs to omit any gesture by which she seems to offer Hamlet the cup and certainly omit Hamlet's response, "I dare not drink yet, madam; by and by" (V.ii.293).

7th Choice: Laertes and the King. Next we focus on the crucial exchange between Laertes and the King, and on the question of how Laertes performs what can be a response to the King or an aside:

> *Laer.* My Lord, I'll hit him now.
> *King.*   I do not think't.
> *Laer.* [*Aside.*] And yet it is almost against my conscience. (295–296)

Obviously the King and Laertes are placed so that we can hear them while the court cannot. How does the King say his line? He has, in effect, just murdered his Queen, and he can see that Laertes may lose: is he filled with despair, anguish, or rage? Most of all, we want to know if he is still scheming or has begun to give up. Laertes' aside here—if it is an aside and not spoken to the King— is a key to what type of revenger he is. The more anguished he is, the more we see him as a man manipulated into a plot in which he is trying to restore the honor of his family through an act that destroys his own personal honor. This means that the more he seems to be a pawn, the more Claudius becomes the primary source of evil. Conversely, the less his conscience troubles Laertes, the more his action contrasts with Hamlet's extensive probing of the dilemmas of revenge. Moreover, an anguished Laertes suggests he may not be able to carry out his plot, again prompting a rush of hope for first-time spectators that Hamlet, with the poisoned cup now apparently disarmed, will somehow survive Laertes' doubly lethal weapon. Indeed, some students reading the play for the first time keep thinking that Hamlet might escape the duel. As Kathryn remarked, "I was so surprised that Hamlet got killed here in this way: I knew it was *The Tragedy of Hamlet*, so I knew he must die, but I thought he would get out of this, achieve revenge, and die in some other way!" Finally, Laertes has the choice of saying his second speech to the King or to himself, and this choice will create significantly different alignments.

8th Choice: How Are the Rapiers Exchanged? The two most important questions are "How and where does Laertes wound Hamlet?" and "How do they exchange rapiers?" The first question forces students to think in detail about the weapon Laertes is using, and about the fact that the weapon needs to be "unbated" as well as "envenom'd." The question "*How* does Laertes wound Hamlet?" leads us to ask, "*Where* does he wound him?" and then "*When* does Hamlet realize that he has been wounded?"[11] Discussion may, however, also begin with the second question, "How is it that the weapons come to be exchanged?" The bracketed stage directions in the *Riverside* text read "Laertes wounds Hamlet; then, in scuffling, they change rapiers," followed by "Hamlet wounds Laertes" and "The Queen falls," but we do not have to let the editors preempt our choices. The direction from the First Quarto (1603) presents what some editors and critics propose *may* be original stage practices:

> They catch one anothers Rapiers, and both are wounded,
> Leartes [sic] falles downe, the Queene falles downe and dies.

The most obvious answer is that this exchange results from confusion: Laertes hits Hamlet when he is unprepared, Hamlet becomes incensed by Laertes' cheating, he attacks ferociously, they both drop their weapons, and, in reaching for them, each grabs the other man's sword. The switch can be done so that even the spectators do not realize the exchange has taken place.

"When Laertes hits Hamlet, what happens? *Why does Hamlet die?*" The answer must be, "Because Laertes' weapon has broken Hamlet's skin and the poison enters his blood." Does any blood well up? Does Hamlet notice he has been hit? He may only feel the hit and become so enraged that he does not notice the wound, in which case the exchange can indeed be done as an accident. Or an accident on Hamlet's part, since if Laertes knows what has happened he must frantically try to regain his weapon when the "scuffle" ends and they resume their duel.

"But what else is possible?" It is possible that Hamlet does notice he has been hit, or that Horatio draws his attention to a tear in his clothing or to a wound. Hamlet does not know, as we know, that he has been mortally wounded, but he will realize, and we will see him realize, that Laertes is using an unbated sword and thus that, despite Laertes' protestations, he is in fact trying to kill Hamlet. The difference will be that this Hamlet deliberately tries to disarm Laertes. Whether they drop their weapons in a scuffle or he compels Laertes to lose his weapon, Hamlet may force Laertes to take the other weapon (as happens in the BBC-Shakespeare version, in which Hamlet puts his foot on Laertes' sword to force the exchange). This Hamlet knows what he is doing, and once he has the live weapon he goes after Laertes with the specific aim of wounding if not killing him. Meanwhile, Laertes is aware, as Hamlet is not, that the sword is not only unbated but also envenomed, so if he wants to survive, his task is not merely to avoid being seriously wounded but to avoid being hit at all. At the same time, he knows that if he can avoid being hit for only a few minutes, the poison will take effect. Thus the fight will quickly escalate to a level of desperation that gives Hamlet the opportunity to hit Laertes, knowing he has no risk from the sword Laertes now wields. (If the fight is staged with daggers as well as rapiers, Hamlet must also guard against Laertes' dagger, since he must now assume that the dagger is also a live weapon.) Although no student of mine has ever (re)invented it, there is an even more complicated version described by Rosenberg:

> Claudius has tried to save Laertes. . . . But he has also betrayed Laertes: when McKellen's Claudius came down to separate the two, before they had exchanged weapons, both on stage and

television, he gave Laertes Hamlet's sword and gave Hamlet the poisoned foil—as if deliberately arranging for his co-conspirator to be killed. Laertes knew he was betrayed. (*Masks of* Hamlet 893)

You will undoubtedly have realized that the staging questions form so complex a web of interrelated choices that there is not a single best order in which they should be asked. So, for example, you may have been impatiently thinking, "But they also have to answer the question of *where* is Hamlet hit." Indeed, we soon reach the point at which the question "Where does Laertes wound Hamlet?" becomes the focus of discussion, which means that students have to think about the sequence in which people die. If Hamlet outlives Laertes although Hamlet is wounded first, the implication must be that Hamlet wounds Laertes much more seriously than Laertes wounds Hamlet; it may not even be the poison that kills Laertes, and Laertes makes no mention that he feels the poison as he is dying. When he answers Osric's "How is't, Laertes?" by saying, "Why, as a woodcock to mine own springe, Osric: / I am justly kill'd with mine own treachery" (V.ii.306–307), it may be the wound inflicted by his own sword, not the poison, that he knows is mortal. Thus we conclude that Hamlet is probably wounded in an extremity, most likely his arm, whereas Laertes is probably wounded in his torso and bleeds to death before the poison can take full effect.

9th Choice: How, Where, and When Does the Queen Die? Even if we accept the most common staging, in which Gertrude drinks with no idea that the cup is poisoned and so has no idea why her husband tries to stop her, questions arise as to when and where Gertrude dies. So I suggest that we look at the death of Gertrude in more detail because just as she often seems to be the most ignored character in the play, so hers seems to be the least noticed death. Anne Pasternak Slater provides a wonderfully illuminating report by a performer of this role:

An actress once described to me how the audience reaction [to the death of Queen Gertrude] appeared from the stage. For a long while her playing of the poisoned Queen went unobserved; at Osric's words the faces of the audience swung round to her (a sudden swamp of pink in her direction), and then, as swiftly, back again, in obedience to Horatio's equally irresistible demand for attention. (32–33)

The *Riverside* text says, in brackets, "Hamlet wounds Laertes. The Queen falls." Then, after her last words, "The drink, the drink! I am pois'ned," this text says "Dies," which is editorially chosen and placed. But the First Quarto of 1603 says, as noted earlier, "They catch one anothers Rapiers, and both are wounded, Leartes falles downe, the Queene falles downe and dies." It says this several lines before the Queen's last words. The Second Quarto of 1604 has no stage direction for the duel and does not say when anyone dies, and the Folio of 1623 does not say when the Queen dies. So I ask, "When is the *latest* moment that the Queen can be alive? Or to put it the other way around, by what moment in the play does the text *mandate* that Gertrude has died?"

The obvious answer is that she dies before Hamlet, and it may seem obvious that she must die before the King as well. Students point to Hamlet's "Wretched Queen adieu!" (333), where, they argue, his use of the third person indicates that she is dead. This does not, however, preclude the possibility that she dies just a moment before, at roughly the same time as Laertes, who speaks just after the King's death. Other students notice Hamlet's words to the King, "Follow my mother" (327), which, they argue, almost certainly means she is already dead. Nonetheless, this still leaves the actual moment of death open between Gertrude's last words and some point up to Hamlet's speech to the King—and brings us to a crucial further question, namely, "If Gertrude lives past her words, how much does she see and hear *before* she dies?" Does she live long enough to learn that her son is dying? To learn that her second husband has arranged the murder of her son by her first husband? To see her son mortally wound her second husband? To see her second husband dying? If, for example, she lives until Hamlet wounds the King, she lives long enough to know that her second husband has caused the death of the entire family. Here is what T. J. B. Spencer wrote in his edition of *Hamlet*:

poisoned. The terrible word arouses Hamlet's fury.
  (stage direction) *She dies.* There is no indication in Q2 or F; perhaps the Queen, speechless, hears and sees some of the later words and actions before dying. Hamlet's *follow my mother* (line 321) implies that he knows she is dying, if not dead; his *Wretched Queen, adieu!* (line 327) may be an immediate response, accompanied by some gesture, to her death. (356)

As we work through these possibilities—you can share Spencer's note or offer a handout with notes from other editors—another question arises: "Where is Gertrude?" Is she downstage so that we can witness her registering these events? What does her face reveal about her dying moments? If, for example, she suspected the cup was poisoned and tried to save Hamlet by drinking from it, does her face register her realization that she has failed to save her son's life?

Exploring Gertrude's death leads us to speculate about Hamlet's relation to his dying mother and to wonder how her death helps shape the action around her. How do Claudius and Hamlet respond to this death? Where is she in relation to Hamlet and to Claudius? How close does Hamlet come to her? Does he hold her? Or is she abandoned by both men? Is this a moment when Gertrude is ignored or a moment when mother and son achieve some sort of reconciliation?

10th Choice: The Death of Claudius. While this climactic scene is designed to be experienced by a first-time spectator not only from Hamlet's point of view but also from a commitment to having Hamlet achieve revenge, it is important to see the scene through the eyes of the other main players in order to understand how the action emerges as the product of their conflicting intentions. I ask the students to return to the actor's basic questions. Startling as the thought may be, from the King's point of view his own survival may still seem possible up until the last moment. When Hamlet stabs Laertes, Claudius may calculate that if Laertes dies quickly and without revealing their conspiracy, and if Hamlet dies soon thereafter, he will have eliminated the only people who can expose him. How does Hamlet attack the King? And how, if at all, does the King defend himself? Does he flee? Stand his ground, as he did against Laertes? Does he try to wrest a weapon from one of his guards? Is he still a fighter, or has he given up? Has the death of his wife changed his will to survive? How does Hamlet stab him? Why does the court not stop it? When "All" cry "Treason! treason!" (323), who and what are they are responding to? And when the King cries out, "O, yet defend me, friends, I am but hurt!" (324), how badly hurt is he? Could he survive? Does anyone make a move to help the King? What stops them from completing such a move? What does the King die of? The wound or wounds Hamlet inflicts? The poison Hamlet forces on him? Or a combination of these? Where does he die? Near to or far from Gertrude? On or off the throne? Furthermore, in this discussion it is important to note, as Spencer does, that the King's death contrasts with that of Laertes: Claudius dies unrepentant, unforgiven, and unshriven, like the man he murdered.

As I have said before, part of what delights me in using a performance approach to teaching drama is that I cannot predict all the questions students will ask, nor what stagings they will invent. In a one class, for example, Margaret asked, "Why does the King drink the poisoned wine?" The obvious answer is that Hamlet forces him to, but then the question becomes "Does he actually swallow any of the liquor?" Margaret's own contribution was to ask, "What would happen if Claudius drank voluntarily, indicating that he was guilty and that he did repent?" This suggestion stunned the class, but it also galvanized them to formulate reasons why this seemed an unlikely possibility. Most directly, they noted Laertes' line "He is justly served, / It is a poison temper'd by himself" (327–328), which indicates that Hamlet succeeds in forcing at least some liquor into the King's throat. Unlikely as it seems, however, you can point out that Margaret's idea has been staged, as Robert Hapgood notes in the *Shakespeare in Production* edition of the play: "Anton Lesser/Jonathan Miller: John Shrapnel as Claudius, accepting his guilt, 'voluntarily swigs the dregs of the poisoned cup' (*New Statesman*, 27 August 1982)" (273).

Responding to Margaret's suggestion forced us to examine a question previously ignored, namely, "What happens to the cup when Gertrude drinks?" Does she set it down and then start to feel the poison? Does she feel the effects instantly so that the cup falls from her hands? If she drops it, how much is spilled? Or does she hand it to a courtier? Does someone pick it up or set it upright again? The amount of liquor that remains becomes important because Horatio will try to commit suicide by finishing what is left, and this point is one of the main reasons students may decide that Claudius could not voluntarily finish off the poison. But then what happens when Hamlet forces the wine on him? Does Claudius, for example, push or even fling the cup away? Does he drop the cup? The traditional staging is that Hamlet (too) drops the cup as he finishes poisoning the King and begins to feel the poison working in his own system. Horatio then seizes the cup, only to have Hamlet snatch it away. But this staging does not, of course, exhaust the possibilities.

Following Margaret's prompt, students wondered if a staging would work in which Hamlet drinks from the cup. When they suggested this move, they were reinventing actual stagings in which the actor playing Hamlet does indeed choose to drain the cup. In such a version, we discover that one possible completion to the play's design entails a Hamlet who fulfills *both* of his early wishes, for he has fulfilled the Ghost's command to revenge his murder and, if he does not exactly commit suicide, he has at least hastened his own death through a suicidelike act.

This particular discussion illustrates the cyclic nature of the process involved in many of these performance-oriented activities. In talking of Claudius as dying unrepentant, we tried to imagine how the King might die a penitent death, which forced us to return to the text to see if this would work, and then to ask if playing this choice could be made to fit with other possible choices. This discussion also illustrates a premise I want students to learn from *how* I teach this class: that we are well served by adopting the stance of an experimenter. What our exploration of this segment does is to enact a cycle in which we experiment by moving between invented stagings and the text in a process analogous to certain aspects of theatrical rehearsal. We thereby engage in a recursive process that attempts to assess the producibility of a choice as a means of assessing the validity of that choice.

There is another question you can ask here, or that you can ask instead of using the staging assignment, and that is the question asked by David Ball (16–18), namely, "What finally impels Hamlet to kill the King?" You can assign this as a short writing assignment so that students imagine their way into Hamlet's mind at the moment he discovers he is mortally wounded. Students will suggest reasons that include the following:

1. Knowing that he is dying, Hamlet vividly rediscovers the truth of his own remark "And a man's life no more than to say 'one'" (V.ii.74).

2. Knowing that the King has been caught at a moment "that has no relish of salvation in it," Hamlet now feels sure that the King will be damned.

3. Seeing his mother die goads him into action: it is his mother's murder, not his father's, which enables or impels him to take revenge.

4. Laertes' speech convicts the King and gives Hamlet the public testimony he needs to act.

5. Realizing his impending death, Hamlet acts out of a sense of being wronged himself, so that in killing the King the revenge he originally vowed is not the foremost motive.

6. Hearing Gertrude and Laertes speak of poison, as Spencer suggests, "the terrible word arouses Hamlet's fury" (356), and makes him delight in hoisting the engineer with his own petard.

This discussion is, of course, a complement to our discussion of why Hamlet does not kill the King in act III, scene iii.

I leave the remaining major choice-points open for your own exploration, noting that these include at least six items. *11th Choice*: How do Hamlet and Laertes exchange forgiveness? *12th Choice*: How strenuously does Horatio try to commit suicide, and how does Hamlet prevent him? *13th Choice*: In what spirit does Hamlet cast his vote for Fortinbras? *14th Choice*: Where and how does Hamlet die? In particular, does he die near or on throne, in which case he tacitly fulfills his earlier provocative self-definition when he announced "This is I, / Hamlet the Dane!" (V.i.257–258). Or does he die far away from the throne? Near his mother, perhaps? And in what relation to Horatio? *15th*

Choice: How do Fortinbras and the English ambassadors enter? What do they do? *16th Choice*: How is the final exit performed? What is the last sight and sound? You can remind students that the play may well have begun in sound even before sight, with the tolling of a bell at midnight. As the play ends with Fortinbras commanding "Go bid the soldiers shoot" (V.ii.403), the opening bell may thus be played off against the closing sound of the soldiers firing their weapons (presumably musket or cannon fire in the original productions). If the play has opened with the bell "beating" twelve, it now closes with the warlike sound of weapons fired in unison—and for spectators with sharp auditory memory, the bell may begin to sound like the bell that tolls for death. The two sounds, then, may be heard as two expressions of mourning.

With the conclusion of this detailed exploration of the play's potential realizations, you reach a point where you (re)turn to the question of what makes *Hamlet* a tragedy by asking, "Which code or codes does Hamlet fulfill in (finally) killing the King? Which code or codes does he fail to fulfill?" Returning to the issue of the three codes that shape Hamlet's choices works to connect the concluding tragedy with the play's central moment of choice in act III, scene iii, and therefore to reap a pedagogic reward for the intense focus on the earlier scene. Students can fruitfully propose that Hamlet fulfills one, two, or three of the codes in the complex way he murders the King, while other students will argue that he seems to be killing the King more out of self-defense than as revenge for his father's death, especially since Hamlet makes no mention of King Hamlet here. One of the more intriguing responses I have ever prompted by asking this question came from Sigita who, on her own initiative, submitted a three-page response on the problem of how Hamlet might solve the dilemma in act III, scene iii. She realized that if you allow Hamlet to be God's agent—and she recognized how the "scourge and minister" passage might indicate that Hamlet sometimes sees himself in precisely this role—then, although she could still not offer the solution of a single decisive action for Hamlet in act III, scene iii, she could propose that the actions Hamlet takes in the *final* scene do fulfill all three codes:

The other theory is that Hamlet found a way to avenge his father and live within the given codes. The first code is in order to maintain his gentlemanly honor he must be the one to end Claudius's life. This code is actually fulfilled in V.ii.321–327, when Hamlet personally stabs the king and forces him to drink the poisoned wine. The second code says that revenge belongs to God and he will handle it in his own way. It is also said that the Lord works in mysterious ways and that He uses man to carry out his will. If this is true, then Hamlet's killing of Claudius was an act of God working through Hamlet allowing him to live within that code. The third code is one of earthly justice or that of the royal court. This code was fulfilled by way of having compelling evidence of the king's treachery presented in a room filled with court members by Laertes and the Queen with their own last words, which of course is always taken as truth even today, for no one about to die would dare to tell a lie. Therefore Claudius must be sentenced to death and Hamlet is thus justified in this third and final code.

When shared with her classmates, Sigita's solution provoked praise and useful discussion, for while not all students agreed with her, the step-by-step manner in which she worked out the logic of Hamlet's spontaneous yet complex manner of killing the King elicited general admiration. For me, her entry was also evidence of how the performance approach can elicit deep immersion from a student whose previous engagements with Shakespeare, she told me, had left her skeptical about the appeal and power of these plays.

This discussion also logically provokes a parallel question, namely, "Which code or codes does Laertes fulfill when he mortally wounds Hamlet in their duel?" This prompt has the virtue of turning attention to a question students may ignore: "Why does Hamlet die?" or "Why does Hamlet have to die?" As they respond, students come to recognize that Hamlet's death also fulfills one of the codes, for he dies for having murdered Polonius. That is, in murdering a father, Hamlet becomes the legitimate target of a son's revenge. Laertes, it turns out, "needs no ghost ... come from the grave" (I.v.125) to command revenge in order to be prompted "to cut his throat i' th' church" (IV.vii.126). (This is a speech that will prompt alert spectators to remember Hamlet's decision not to murder the King when the latter was at prayer.) Even more crucial to grasping the play's design is understanding that Hamlet himself has promised that he "will answer well /

The death I gave him" (III.iv.176–177). That is, Hamlet admits that he has committed a criminal act for which he must answer, and thereby admits that he too is not exempt from the codes constituting his world. But his cryptic promise to "answer" for killing Polonius does not specify whether he believes he is subject to this accounting in terms of the code of aristocratic honor, state justice, or religious sin.

At the end of this detailed engagement with the scene, you have reached another moment to return to considering the question of reading differently. Here I ask the members of the class to write a response to what they have learned, beginning "One thing that is becoming clear to me about the duel scene is—." We follow this with an entry on "One thing I can see about *how* we explored this scene is—."

Opening a Playtext, Closing Performances

Having immersed ourselves so deeply in the act of making choices that, taken together, produce the final scene, we reach a point where students can reflect on their suite of choices in order to reexamine and clarify their own interpretations. In framing the following discussion, I often cite a point made by Janet Adelman:

> A play is an enormously complex entity in which many details are necessarily lost to us; and just as the eye must be trained to impose a pattern on the welter of visual stimuli in order to see, so the mind must be trained to impose pattern in order to construct meaning. As we experience a play, we make, I think, a multitude of small and usually unconscious adjustments toward it: decisions about what we will choose to find meaningful. But our decisions, if they are to be useful, must to a large extent be directed by the play itself. . . .
> A play must teach us how to see it; and a complex play will insist that we see it several ways at once. (1–2, 11)

One way to make this shift, which is a shift from riding in the car as the play unfolds to riding in the helicopter from which we can view the play as a completed event, is to start with the following handout:

What Is the ACTION of *Hamlet?*

As another way of beginning to answer the question "What is the Action of Hamlet?" I offer this passage from Thomas F. Van Laan's *The Idiom of Drama* (Ithaca, NY: Cornell UP, 1970). The passage comes from the concluding chapter, "Modes of Combination," and from The Multiple View—*Hamlet* section (pp. 340–55). I have added breaks to what is a single paragraph in order to make it easier to follow Van Laan's analysis.

"The universe within which the events of *Hamlet* occur and from which they derive their fullest significance lacks the lucid schematization that Aeschylus has given the universe of the *Oresteia*. Unlike Aeschylus, who employs such clear allegorical representations of cosmic forces as Apollo and the Furies, Shakespeare embodies the universe of *Hamlet* only in the Ghost and, more obliquely, in Fortinbras, and these figures evoke conflicting or equivocal responses; both suggest a universe that is essentially ambiguous. Other elements of the play particularize this ambiguity by asserting three separate and incompatible possibilities.

One of these, the one most frequently accepted in current criticism of the play, is that which Hamlet expresses in the final act. This view distinguishes a universal order, divine and perfect, governed by a benevolent providence, which manifests its influence even in such a seemingly trivial incident as the fall of a sparrow and which ensures that all human actions, however intended, will contribute to an ultimate good.

This view occurs late in the play, however. It is preceded by another that sees the universe as orderless and irrational but permeated with evil. This universe is one in which nothing thrives except corruption. Here brother kills brother, wife betrays husband, the lover tortures his beloved, and friends blithely lead each other to their deaths. In this universe contentment betokens superficiality, innocence is naïveté, and moral sensitivity produces only paralysis, despair, and further evil. Ultimately, all ordinary distinctions tend to become irrelevant as everyone in this universe helps exemplify the workings of the ubiquitous evil. Those who do not foster it experience its effects; some exemplify it in both ways. Hamlet suffers, but so does Claudius, the putative cause of Hamlet's suffering. Claudius, performing a willful murder for the basest motives, brings disorder to his kingdom. Hamlet, seeking an honorable revenge, increases it. In this universe death is the chief sign of evil, and it shows no discrimination in choosing its victims; the ideally good, the innocent, the guilty, the morally ambiguous, the ignorant—all meet the same fate.

These deaths also serve to illustrate the third view, one that seems to combine the other two. This view, which I developed extensively in Chapter 5, also pictures a universal order, but according to this view the order is malevolent. Like Hamlet's providence, it shapes the ends that man rough-hews, but it does so in order to punish him. It regards every human action, however intended, as an unwarranted self-assertion, and consequently it transforms every action into an instrument of self-destruction.

All three of these views are thoroughly established in the play. Each is perceived, with varying degrees of preciseness, by Hamlet, and each is also given objective verification through action, imagery, or the repetition of ideas." (350–51)

Whether I use this handout or simply summarize the three versions of the universe of *Hamlet* so elegantly delineated by Van Laan, I ask students to focus on answering this question: "Looking over the entire suite of choices you have made in directing your imaginary rehearsal, please ask yourself, 'What universe have I created from the potential universes latent in the design(s) of the playtext?' If you have not done so already, write your choices in the margin of your text. Now look at them and ask yourself, 'What pattern(s) do my choices form? And how might this pattern or these patterns prompt the spectators to make meaning from this performance?' Does the pattern project the interpretation that you currently would offer to us? If you change any of your choices, does the new pattern better project your interpretation?" You may want to break the class into pairs so that each person can share his or her pattern with one other person and hear another pattern laid out. You can then move into a whole-class discussion. In one class, several people offered their patterns as follows.

Marcella was the first to share her suite of choices and her interpretation-through-action. All the choices in her imagined production were deliberate, made by the dramatis personae as fully conscious agents. That is, Gertrude drank knowingly. She was within arm's reach, so Claudius was actively refusing to save her, making him a more deliberate villain. Hamlet knew the foil was a live weapon and he deliberately forced the exchange. When I asked Marcella, "Why does this set of choices not only seem right about the play but also appeal to you?" she replied, "Because I want Hamlet to be the hero!" And by hero she meant someone who succeeded in destroying evil or evil people even if the cost was his own destruction, and did so through a series of conscious decisions; an accidental success, she thought, would undermine the logic of a heroic enterprise. So Marcella was offering the positive universe that, as Van Laan (*Idiom*) noted, is commonly chosen by critics because it is the vision projected by Hamlet *and* apparently endorsed by the play given that Hamlet finally succeeds in carrying out the Ghost's command.

Next, Danny shared his pattern. In the previous class, Danny had begun articulating an interpretation based on a universe composed of accidents, the phrasing offered by Horatio immediately after all the deaths. Danny argued that Gertrude should drink unwittingly and the weapons should be exchanged unwittingly, and he worked out the other choices so that, wherever possible, the choice was unwitting or accidental. Again I asked, "Why does this set of choices, this interpretation, not only seem right about the play but also appeal to you?" He answered, "Because the world is like that—because that is how I see things now!" I asked, "If we see the world as largely controlled by accident, not conscious choice by logical agents, then what else follows?" He answered, "If we are not making conscious choices, then we are not responsible for consequences." In contrast to Marcella, then, Danny was offering a vision of the amoral universe, the universe of original accident. He put it this way: "They have ideals, they try to live up to those ideals, but then they become obsessed with those ideals—they become willing to go to extremes for those ideals; the ideals take over their lives and the very obsessive attempt to achieve those ideals creates havoc." Finally, Danny noted that he was surprised the Ghost did not come back—and I asked him to hold that thought since he had just provided a perfect cue for our last activity.

Just as I had students vote on their preferred outcome in act III, scene iii, so I now asked them to take a vote on the ending: "At this moment, are you leaning toward Marcella's vision of the universe or Danny's vision of the universe?" Four students were in favor of Marcella's reading of the play's universe, while nine were in favor of Danny's reading; Sigita voted for both readings because she saw the play as supporting both patterns.

These responses also gave me an opportunity to return to a point about shifting between engagement and detachment that I introduce in the outline for my courses. "Having made your choices, enacted your interpretation, you can now ask yourself, 'Why did I make, why did I want to make these choices? Why is it that I see the play in this way—at least at first?' To answer this question, you need to go beyond saying, as some of you have, 'That's just the way it is!'"

Again, Marcella offered her answer first. Her choices, she indicated, were made to compose this specific pattern because she wants a universe in which people have some control: they are free to make choices and to rely on the fact that they can achieve some predictable outcomes from these choices. She wants a universe in which there really are black-and-white choices, despite all the uncertainty that Hamlet experiences for so much of the action. Most of all, she added, she wants to ensure that we see Hamlet as the hero, and as a hero successful in fulfilling his mission. What she sees, and what she would want a production she directed to enable her audiences to see, is Hamlet as a hero who is unequivocally on the side of good, against the unmitigated evil of Claudius.

This was a crisp, clear projection of what has been a historically dominant reading, in part because it is the interpretation finally adopted by Hamlet when he accepts the governance of a "Special providence," which indicates that he has reconverted to believing in a Christian universe. The appeal of this vision from within the play is reinforced by the fact that now Hamlet does not talk of an unweeded garden but of a properly ordered world, temporarily infected by rampant evil but able to be healed. In short, Marcella wants a Hamlet who can "set it right." Danny, by contrast, offered his pattern because he believed the world is made up of choices that proceed from and help produce accidents, a vision of the universe that seems to be proposed in Horatio's focus on "accidental judgments, casual slaughters . . . purposes mistook / Fall'n on the inventor's heads" (V.ii.382, 384–385) in his speech after Hamlet's death.

Although it does not happen in every class, sometimes a student will also turn our attention to the very first and last example(s) of ironic reversal, that of King Fortinbras and young

Fortinbras. To analyze this aspect of the play, I ask students to respond, in class or as an assignment, to the question "What if the Ghost came back?"

What If the Ghost Came Back?

As we begin our last look at *Hamlet*, we visualize the scene. "Imagine that as the body of Hamlet is borne off, followed by Fortinbras and the others, the Ghost appears: he simply turns upstage and stands motionless, watching the procession. What would his final appearance do?"

In the discussion that follows, I am in part seeking to refocus on the idea of Shakespeare as someone who composed plays: the point is that however qualitatively superior we may (or may not) think Shakespeare to be as a writer, he engaged in a process of composition that is related to what other English Renaissance dramatists were doing. Specifically, we can imagine Shakespeare, in the process of composing this script, asking himself what he wanted the ending to do. Did he want his audience to feel that Hamlet had succeeded? Or did he want them to have a sense that Hamlet had failed? Or to recognize that Hamlet succeeded but at a price? Did he want them not only to exult at the successful revenge but also to assess the cost of that revenge? "What if the Ghost came back?" works by asking students to see how Shakespeare—who clearly wrote *Hamlet* in part as a rethinking of the most famous revenge play of his time, *The Spanish Tragedy* (composed between 1582 and 1592), in which the Ghost to be revenged is always onstage and has the final word—might have composed a different ending that would have elicited different responses.[12]

Students often start by offering a clear, positive response. The Ghost would seem to return in triumph to look at the fulfillment of his request, and of course he could make some gesture, perhaps a salute to the procession, which would indicate his sense that his request has been honored. Or he might exit upward or appear on the second level, indicating an ascent to heaven, so we would know that Hamlet's action had finally freed his father's spirit. (The fact that this staging might have been interpreted as implying that the universe of the play was Catholic, and that the Ghost had been freed from purgatory, is one strong reason for Shakespeare not to have composed this ending, since it could have invited the censor to demand revision of the scene.)

In contrast, other students suggest that the Ghost would witness the failure of his original command. Surely, they argue, he did not want his son or his wife to die, and he would want his son to be king. If we saw the Ghost again, we would be moved to think more about the cost of his plan and less about its success. As one student asked, "If the Ghost came back, wouldn't it emphasize that Hamlet has *failed* to carry out the revenge in the way the ghost wanted it carried out? If the Ghost came back, wouldn't we be forced to see another ironic reversal?" Thus it becomes clear that if the Ghost came back he would serve as what Alan Dessen calls a form of stage italics (*Elizabethan* 103); in this case, he would underline a riddle or mystery about the universe of the play.

Sometimes students start the discussion with a different response. "We would immediately ask, '*Why* should the Ghost return?' And we would wonder if the Ghost is still not resting peacefully and ask, 'Why not?' Is it because his plan has backfired? Claudius is dead, but so are Gertrude and Hamlet, his wife-widow and son. Or is he distressed that Hamlet did not kill the King for revenge of his father's death, but instead for his own murder or the murder of Gertrude? After all, when he kills Claudius, Hamlet says, 'Follow my mother'!"

Thus some students argue that an unresting Ghost could be disturbing in several ways. First, he would suggest that although Hamlet has avenged his murder this vengeance has cost too much. This would lead us to ask ourselves what in particular made the cost too high; it might be the cost in other lives, or the failure to heed his injunction to leave Gertrude to heaven, or because when Hamlet does kill Claudius it does not seem to be revenge for his father but for his own imminent death. Second, his return would emphasize the fact that the entire Danish royal family and the Danish court, insofar as the latter is embodied in the family of Polonius, was wiped out in the course of this revenge.

And third, the Ghost's reappearance would invite us to ask, "Is the Ghost *also* a victim of ironic reversal?" because we would also have to think about King Fortinbras. After all, it was King Fortinbras who initiated the challenge and who in defeat was in effect hoist with his own petard. Why should the Ghost be the "enginer" (III.iv.206) of his own destruction when he was trying to restore the kingdom by purging it of luxury and incest? Why should King Fortinbras be "revenged" when he was the initiator of the combat that touched off this whole sequence of events and therefore should have been hoist with his own challenge—and was? Why should the son and heir of this Norwegian engineer be rewarded?

In one spirited discussion, the emerging ideas stimulated Margaret to imagine another staging. Having earlier asked, "Why does Claudius let Hamlet force him to drink poison?," she now wondered what would happen if the Ghost came back *while the duel was in progress*? "Who would be able to see the Ghost? Would Claudius see the Ghost? And if he saw the Ghost of his brother, might this make Claudius accept his own defeat? If the Ghost came back while Claudius was alive, then Claudius might drink the poison himself out of remorse!"

What interested me when Margaret made her suggestion, and what interests me generally when students make such "wild" leaps, is precisely the way in which thinking about performance opens up a play for them. They may indeed imagine stagings that we would finally, or even immediately, think of as wrong, but at the same time a student who can think in this way has gained a different type of engagement with a Shakespeare play. This is a type of engagement that makes Margaret more fully immersed in the art and in the act of thinking about drama creatively. And as I have said before, one of my objectives in using this approach is to balance the emphasis on teaching students to be critical that seems to be the primary, even the only, objective of much current literary training, with an emphasis on teaching students to accept the invitation to disciplined creativity that a script offers all its readers.

As an example of how a director and actors can seize a scripted opportunity for disciplined creativity—and an example that may make some of the students' suggested stagings seem less wild—I describe here the staging of the Ghost in the Royal Shakespeare Company production of *Hamlet* directed by Michael Boyd in

2004. This was, by critical consensus, one of the most striking stagings of the Ghost in the past half-century. This production was mounted on the main stage of the RSC, a traditional proscenium stage that makes it difficult to create the close relation between performance and audience inherent in the arena theaters that Shakespeare wrote for. The director sought to compensate for this problem by using a ramp (also used in other RSC productions), made of an open mesh metal grid, that stretched from the edge of the stage to the right of center all the way to row L. In act I, scene ii, the Ghost entered on this ramp and moved through the audience. This Ghost, played by Greg Hicks, strikingly appeared not in full armor, but rather clothed only in a ragged garment wrapped around his waist and falling part way down his legs. His face and upper body were coated in white; trails of dried blood traced the path left by the poison in each ear; his eyes were surrounded by dark red bruises; and his mouth, when he opened it to gasp for air, appeared a dark red circle. He moved slowly, bent nearly horizontal at the waist, his chest heaving as he gasped and panted in pain. He dragged behind him a massive two-handed broadsword, as tall as himself, which, as he moved and paused, moved and paused, provided staccato sound— "clink-clink-clink-clink-clink-clink"—against the open mesh of the metal ramp. In his two appearances in act I, scene i, he reached the stage, horrifying Horatio, Barnardo, and Marcellus, continuing to pant in apparent agony, and did indeed seem about to speak when the crow of the cock caused him to hesitate and, as had happened at the end of his first appearance, run lightly and silently down the ramp, the sword now not clanking, and disappear. In act I, scene v, he made the same entry, dragging his sword against the metal grid and producing the same patter of clinking sounds, disappeared upstage and reappeared with Hamlet following him. When he spoke, he slowly became upright, and his "List, list, list!" was a rasping crescendo that moved into an even louder, more violent, and elongated call for "Revenge!" Just before he called for revenge, he swung the sword completely over his head, so that this demand came from a figure that towered twelve feet above the stage and dwarfed his robust son. He then lowered the sword and finished his speech, crying "Remember me!" He released the sword and plunged like a flying figure into the trap, which had silently opened in the course of the scene, producing a spectacular and heart-stopping exit. It was an exit that, it is worth noting, may well be a variation or echo of the original staging. In this production, then, what we saw was a figure who, unlike the Ghost mandated by the words of both the Second Quarto and the Folio, did not have the seeming invulnerability of the completely armored figure described by Horatio, but rather combined the intense vulnerability of a nearly naked body wracked by pain with the devouring hunger for revenge incarnated in the sword and in the towering figure that the naked body and the sword combined to make. But the final payoff of this remarkable staging came at the end of the play. This production did not have "four captains / Bear Hamlet like a soldier to the stage" (V.ii.395–396), but rather had the lights go down on Hamlet cradled in the arms of Horatio in a pietàlike image. And as the lights went down, we heard quiet music in a minor key—and a subdued "clink-clink-clink-clink-clink-clink." Since the Ghost did not actually appear, the spectators were invited to exit the theater speculating and debating about what this ghostly echo might signify.

Back in the classroom, when the exploration of these endings, hypothetical and actual, has brought out some of the key issues, we return our attention to the choice Shakespeare did make, for instead of the Ghost coming back, Fortinbras finally enters the scene. Thus our next question is "What does the entrance of Fortinbras do?"

One obvious answer emerges from what Fortinbras says: he praises Hamlet as a potentially great king and a hero in death. He validates the response of all those spectators and readers whose inclination is to see Hamlet as having succeeded, indeed triumphed, even at the cost of his own life. He thus articulates a vision of Hamlet as tragic hero. Another answer lies in what Fortinbras does: honoring Hamlet's dying vote, he claims the throne. On the one hand, he brings hope of a new order, free of the poison set loose by Claudius. On the other hand, he displaces the Danish royal line with the Norwegian, and thereby completes a breathtaking ironic reversal that now frames the entire action.

Another answer emerges in the way Fortinbras completes the pattern of the generational conflict. For, as many critics have noted, Fortinbras is the third young man who is seeking revenge. But he is at the opposite extreme from Laertes, who would commit murder in church to achieve revenge, because Fortinbras achieves revenge by not seeking it. Like Hamlet, he is a nephew (and one displaced from a direct line of succession) of a king. Unlike Hamlet, and like Laertes, he obeys his elders. Yet unlike Laertes, he does not seek revenge directly. And yet unlike both Laertes and Hamlet, he achieves his (unsought or, rather, apparently abandoned) revenge without dying. As he completes the pattern of generational conflict, Fortinbras may also suggest the regeneration of the poisoned and sterile kingdom—even as he raises intriguing issues about the place and price of revenge.

"How does the appearance, speech, and action of Fortinbras also help shape each of the three basic interpretations we have already articulated in our converging exploration of the duel and ironic reversal?" The discussion of this question becomes a cue for another written response, which asks students to define, as best they can, their sense of how this play is a tragedy. This writing can also be a starting point for discussion of how Shakespeare seems to have implicitly defined tragedy.

Finally, we are ready once again to reflect on the very processes of reading we have performed in our immersion in *Hamlet*, composing further writing to explore the act of reading differently and the students' ability to seize on the openings for co-creative action offered by this remarkable playtext.

Appendix

Three Essay Assignments for Exploring Hamlet

In this appendix, I offer three essay assignments for teaching *Hamlet*. These three prompts are:

1. *Hamlet*, III.iii.73–98: The Intersection of Honor, Justice, and Mercy—or, Imagining What Shakespeare Left Out

2. Observing in a Different Language: Text and Performance Choices in the Cal Poly Pomona *Hamlet*

3. Reading and Writing in a Different Language: Staging the Ending of *Hamlet*

The first assignment grows directly out of the work performed in the suite of activities that enables students to immerse themselves in act III, scene iii. The second assignment offers a model for students to observe an on-campus production of *Hamlet*; it can be adapted for productions of other Shakespeare plays. This assignment can be especially effective if you and the students have access to a portion of the script as adapted by the director. The third assignment asks students to direct the last scene of the play, and it offers a model I have used with *The Taming of the Shrew*, *Measure for Measure*, and *King Lear*.

ASSIGNMENT 1: *HAMLET* III.iii.73–98: THE INTERSECTION OF HONOR, JUSTICE, AND MERCY—OR, IMAGINING WHAT SHAKESPEARE LEFT OUT

Enter Hamlet

Hamlet. Now might I do it [pat], now 'a is a-praying;
And now I'll do't—

As E. A. J. Honigmann reminds us in the conclusion to *Shakespeare: Seven Tragedies Revisited; The Dramatist's Manipulation of Response*, "Shakespeare gave his unremitting attention to audience response in each of his plays. The question 'What should Hamlet do or say next?' must have been inseparable for the dramatist from the question 'How will it affect the audience?'" (247). And being an enormously inventive dramatist, he must always have been looking for solutions that would allow him to transform the tensions of Hamlet's situation into visible choices that, in turn, became legible actions for the spectators. Certainly, at the moment when Hamlet raises his weapon, proclaiming (perhaps with whispering, hissing, fury, perhaps with icy calm, perhaps with terrible agitation, perhaps with . . .), "And now I'll do it!," Shakespeare's design achieves one of the great moments of literal suspense and excruciating moral choice. The longer Hamlet pauses, the longer we have to consider all the reasons he should or should not complete the stroke that will kill his enemy the King.

Shakespeare does not have Hamlet articulate the entire range of issues that the play has already shown facing his protagonist. Yet if he had written his play following the model of Marlowe's *Doctor Faustus*, this might be a logical moment for those figures from an earlier dramaturgy, the good and bad angels, to appear, since it is precisely at moments of fundamental moral choice that they appear in Marlowe's play.

For this assignment, I want you to write the speeches Shakespeare neglected to write—only in your case you will be employing *three* angels because, as we have seen, throughout the play Hamlet is struggling to reconcile the imperatives of three codes. One angel will speak for the Christian code, which forbids murder, commands mercy to one's enemies, and proclaims that vengeance must be left to God. One angel will speak for the code of justice, in which crimes must be punished by the state through a formal process of indictment, trial, and, if the defendant is found guilty, sentence. And one angel will speak for the aristocratic code of honor, in which a crime such as murder must be avenged by one of the surviving members of the family, in a duel if possible, by other means if not. (You are free to find other designations for these figures, and you might want to think about their costumes.) These angels will present the arguments for each code, but do so in the terms established in the speeches and actions of the dramatis personae up to this point.

In writing these speeches, you will face a number of choices, which are the same choices that confront any dramatist as he or she writes a play. I can mention some of the most obvious choices, and leave to you the pleasure of discovering the less obvious ones. One major choice will be whether to have each angel give one long speech, or have them give short speeches that represent the thrust-and-parry of a verbal duel. Another choice will be whether to keep the speeches evenly balanced or give one angel the advantage—and again, which angel? If you do compose speeches that seem to favor one angel over the others, you will also need to decide if you want this apparent imbalance to foreshadow Hamlet's choice or surprise the audience by prompting them to formulate expectations that are not fulfilled. Finally, you can also think about questions such as "Do the three angels speak to one another? Or only to Hamlet? Or to the audience? Does Hamlet show any awareness of their presence?" Many more questions and choices are likely to occur to you as you immerse yourselves in the creative opportunities this project offers.

As a start, you may simply want to do some freewriting in which you capture all the arguments you can invent for each position. Or you may want to do three freewritings, one for each position. Once these are completed, you can begin to think about the choices of structure, sequence, language, image, and so on that you face. You are to write the speeches so that they can fit precisely into the existing text at this point. You can write the speeches in prose, but you are free to write them in blank verse.

As Honigmann notes, the question "'What should Hamlet do or say next?' must have been inseparable . . . from the question 'How will it affect the audience?'" Now that you have been given the opportunity to become a dramatic poet, working with both the conception and the enactment of this scene, the second half of this assignment asks you to shift into the receptive position, thinking about your scene as a spectator who becomes a dramatic critic writing a prose analysis. Use your recomposing of this scene to explore what the scene as written by Shakespeare does, can be made to do, or can "make the actor make the audience do" (Styan, *Elements* 2). Maybe there is a reason Shakespeare did not write the play with three angels after all. . . . What are the primary effects of this moment of choice? For example, does the moment seem designed to prompt spectators to support or dissent from Hamlet's decision? What meanings can we construct from our encounter with this designed experience? (You are free to draw on considerations about staging as they are relevant.) As part of this essay, please record whatever insights into Hamlet's mind and behavior you have gained through writing your own segment of the scene. The objective of your essay is, once again, to wrestle with our basic question "What does this moment *do* to us as we watch the play?" What types of responses are we compelled to make as we experience this moment of action? What patterns in the action so far does this moment extend, modify, twist, or reverse? And what sense do we or can we make of these aspects of the unfolding pattern? In short, you are also exploring the question "How does this moment compel us to re-create meaning from the designed action?"

Criteria for Evaluation. As I read your scene and essay, I will be asking:

1. How do the speeches of your three angels articulate the central concerns the play itself has raised up to this point? Do these speeches also function dramatically to intensify the moment of choice Shakespeare has so carefully shaped? Do your inferences about what issues might be in Hamlet's mind at this point have a firm basis in the text?

2. Does your essay present your analysis of what the scene *does* in a coherent and unified way, so that I can understand your vision of how meaning emerges from experience in this moment?

3. How well do you use your own invented text as a tool that, through contrast, helps you learn more about the script you are reading?

I know this is a challenging assignment, but I think these are challenges that your creativity, insight, and critical intelligence will find rewarding. I am looking forward to reading lively, thought-provoking essays. ELR 10/03

ASSIGNMENT 2: OBSERVING IN A DIFFERENT LANGUAGE: TEXT AND PERFORMANCE CHOICES IN THE CAL POLY POMONA *HAMLET*

Your assignment has four parts. (1) Attend a performance of the Cal Poly Pomona production of *Hamlet* directed by Bob Gilbert. (2) Describe what you perceive to be the three most important or most interesting textual decisions (cuts, splices, and so on), and the three most important or most interesting choices made by the actors in performing the play's mandates. (3) Analyze how these choices function as an interpretation of the play—which is to say, how they seem designed to prompt spectators to make meaning from their experience of the action. (4) Reflect on what you have discovered about the relation of the text of *Hamlet* to a performance of the play, using these reflections to articulate any new principles or practices for reading a playtext you can identify from your experience.

Thus, when you attend the performance (or performances: if you have time, you might attend one performance, start drafting your essay, and then attend a second performance to increase the precision of your observations and analysis), you will be looking for the text choices the director made in cutting and shaping the playtext (which range from single words, to sentences, to speeches, to large segments of scenes, to threads running throughout the play), and for the inventions of the actor—those moments where they accepted Shakespeare's invitation (even demand) to become co-creators of the performance. When you sit down to write, you will be seeking not only to capture these observations but also to use them to sharpen your reading of the production.

Remember that in all six cases, you want to describe what the choice does, what specific shaped experience it creates for us, and how we make meaning from or of that experience. You are *not* evaluating whether the choices are good or bad, but rather asking, "What does this choice do?" As I said, using a concept formulated by Peter Elbow (in the appendix to *Writing without Teachers*), your stance is that you are playing the believing game: more specifically, you are doing all you can to become the alert spectator who re-creates the interpretation that the team of director, designers, and actors has embodied in their production.

In a sense, this assignment is the mirror image of the first project: in the first project, you sought to direct your own production on the page, and to direct it in such clear detail that your reader could re-create your vision from the words on the page. This time, others have directed and enacted the performance, and your task is to perceive some of their choices as a key to re-creating their interpretation.

Criteria for Evaluation. As I read your essay, I will be asking:

1. Do you clearly describe what you perceive to be the three most important or most interesting textual decisions?

2. Do you clearly describe what you perceive to be the three most important or most interesting choices made by the actors in performing the play's mandates?

3. Does your analysis of these choices demonstrate how they function to project and prompt a specific interpretation of the play? Do you capture how these choices operate to prompt us to make meaning from our experience of the action?

4. Do your concluding reflections demonstrate what you have discovered about the relation of the text of *Hamlet* to a performance of the play? Do you succeed in articulating principles or practices for reading a playtext that you might apply to reading and seeing other Shakespeare plays?

Again, I know this is a challenging assignment, but as your first essays demonstrated you are up to meeting these challenges. I look forward to reading sharply observant and thought-provoking readings of this production of *Hamlet*.
ELR 2/01

ASSIGNMENT 3: READING AND WRITING IN A DIFFERENT LANGUAGE: STAGING THE ENDING OF *HAMLET*

A Shakespearean playtext is not a series of statements that specify in all respects—or even in all important respects—what must happen during performance. Its statements do specify what *cannot* happen, and in doing so they permit whatever possibilities are not prohibited.
—PHILIP McGUIRE, *Speechless Dialect:*
Shakespeare's Open Silences (1985): 139

Endings of plays are like the codas of music, and play directors take great pains orchestrating their movement and rhythm, for the simple reason that all characters in plays, even those of comedy, die before us in the end in the sense of completing their three-hour lives. Such time-deaths simply remind us that music is art's greatest regulator of the body's response systems: with enough violins you can make the death of a pet snake unbearable.
—BERT O. STATES, *The Pleasure of the Play* (1994): 85

For this essay, I am asking you to write a staging paper that will consist of three parts. (1) An introduction, in which you analyze a segment of a scene in order to enumerate what you believe are the major interpretive problems the scene presents: in terms of staging, these interpretive problems also define major performance choices that confront anyone staging this scene. (2) The main portion of the essay, in which you direct the scene: you will use a two-column format, with the words of the text (keep the verse form of the lines!) in the left-hand column and your stage directions and explanation of motives and relations embodied in those directions (the logic behind those choices) in the right-hand column. (3) A conclusion, in which you reflect on the ways in which, having developed your own imaginary staging, you understand the design of the play differently than you did earlier—say, at the moment you finished writing your expectation log.

The scene you will work with is *Hamlet* act V, scene ii, lines 225–403, including the stage direction immediately preceding the king's "Come, Hamlet." Again, you are staging the scene on a Shakespearean stage but for a twenty-first-century audience.

Let me say a bit more about the logic of the assignment and about each of the three segments you must perform.

Just as it is always illuminating to ask, "What does the beginning of a play do?," so it is always illuminating to ask, "What does the ending do?" and then "What can the ending be made to do?" This is especially true for *Hamlet* because while the text mandates the duel and deaths, how that duel is carried out, how the dramatis personae make their life-and-death decisions, and precisely when, for example, each of the dramatis personae dies, all involve choices. Certainly, in each production the choices made shape how the spectators make meaning from the action. Most obviously, how Hamlet completes his revenge shapes how we understand the nature of tragedy in this particular world: does Hamlet, for example, seem to have succeeded or failed in whatever task he has undertaken? Overall, you are seeking to orchestrate your ensemble of choices in a way that you believe is producible *and* that offers a coherent closure to the play's design.

The introduction is vital because you need to develop, and share with your reader, a clear grasp of the problems and opportunities the script of this segment offers to anyone who wants to do more than simply read the words on the page. You need to think carefully about the issues any production must consider before staging the scene. The choices include questions about the relationships between characters; the nature of the occasion; the atmosphere of the occasion, given what has happened earlier in the scene; and so on. You also need to indicate lines that you feel offer particularly important choices for interpretation. And then there are the mandated actions: for example, does Claudius take any action in addition to asking Gertrude not to drink from the poisoned cup? How does he say his aside? How does the exchange of weapons happen? Is it by accident or by design? And if by design, whose design? You want to be clear about what you believe to be the most important interpretive problems.

As for the second part, let me quote from Miriam Gilbert:

As you work with the lines of the scene, show why people are saying what they say—or why they say nothing. Avoid words

such as "dramatically," "forcefully," "emotionally," which tell
the reader little about the actual feelings involved. Precise adverbs will help greatly. [Furthermore,] moving people around on
an imaginary stage ("Kent moves stage left") without explaining
why or how they're moving isn't good enough. In fact, internal
movement and response are the most important considerations
for the paper. The double-column approach, with the words of
the text on the left and your comments on the right, should help
you look closely at the pattern of feeling and response. ("Writing
about Performance, Writing as Performance," *Teaching Shakespeare through Performance*, ed. Milla Cozart Riggio [New York:
MLA, 1999]: 308–9).

The conclusion is important because here you have the opportunity to
learn from your own action. What you can discover for yourself and
share with readers is not only knowledge about how you understand
this particular play but also knowledge about reading differently—that
is to say, knowledge about how to read any Shakespeare play with greater
engagement, precision, and richness.
    Criteria for Evaluation. As I read your essay, I will be asking:

1. Does your introduction clearly frame your project by demonstrating your perception of the key interpretive issues in this
   scene?

2. Does your double-column staging not only orchestrate the final
   scene with a suite of plausible choices, but also project those
   choices in sufficient detail for your readers to grasp your interpretation?

3. Do your reflections demonstrate how your interpretation of this
   scene and *Hamlet* have unfolded from your earlier reading of
   the play?

I know this is a challenging assignment, but I think these are challenges
that your creativity, insight, and critical intelligence will find rewarding. Again, I encourage you to come to my office hours with a draft in
hand. I look forward to reading lively, thought-provoking essays!
ELR 5/00

Epilogue:

Shakespeare's Script as a Cue
for Pedagogic Invention

*Curiously most of us, lay people and educators alike,
tend to underrate teaching. We rarely underestimate the
difficulties of learning. Having had to learn, we know
that it is a complicated and unpredictable business. Likewise, the craft of provoking us to learn—the act of teaching—is itself complicated.*

THEODORE SIZER, *Horace's Compromise:
The Dilemma of the American High School*

*When a practitioner sets a problem, he [or she] chooses
and names the things he [or she] will notice. . . . So problem setting is an ontological process—in Nelson
Goodman's memorable word, a form of worldmaking.*

DONALD SCHÖN, *Educating the Reflective Practitioner*

*We can allow Shakespeare's dramatic technique to cue
our teaching technique.*

ROBERT ORNSTEIN, *Shakespeare in the Classroom*

Prologue: Articulating a Tacit Premise of the Performance Approach

In developing, employing, and discussing the variety of pedagogical methods collectively called "the performance approach
to drama," we often focus on aspects such as the performance of
students in action together, the knowledge those students produce through their transactions with the text, and the knowledge
they produce about themselves as well as about the plays in their

interactions with one another. I want to examine another aspect of the performance approach, however, namely, its effect on our work as teachers. In particular, I want to focus on the dramatic nature of the pedagogic production and teachers as pedagogic designers who participate in their own designed occasions. This less-noticed and less-discussed aspect of the performance approach emerges when we recognize a parallel between what we ask students to learn to do in a performance-centered class and what we ask ourselves to learn to do in designing and conducting such classes. Stated in the simplest terms, what the performance approach seeks to do *directly* for students is what employing the approach can and is likely to do *indirectly* for teachers.

What does the approach seek to do for students? First, as I hope this book explicitly demonstrates, the model offers students the opportunity to learn how the script of a Shakespeare play is a cue for invention and how they can accept the invitation it offers them to collaborate in reinventing the play. Second, as they rehearse this model of reading, students are invited to widen their imaginative powers so that they re-create the play from something more nearly approaching its total range of possibilities.

What does the approach seek to do for teachers? First, as I hope this book tacitly demonstrates, the model offers teachers the opportunity to learn how the text of a Shakespeare play functions as a cue for pedagogic invention, and how we can accept the indirect invitation the script offers us to teach people how to read and imaginatively perform the play. Second, as we rehearse both the act of creating a scenario and the action through which students learn to read the plays differently, we encounter varied opportunities to develop our creativity as teachers and learners. In this way, teaching Shakespeare's plays offers us an opportunity to extend our creative energies as designers of what Patricia Bizzell calls "inventive environments" in which other people can learn (485–86).

The parallel is implied but not worked out by Robert Ornstein when he suggests that "[w]e can allow Shakespeare's dramatic technique to cue our teaching technique" (15). The Shakespeare play becomes the core element in the classes we design: in learning to recognize and respond to the dramatic text as offering cues for invention by actors, we also learn how to create pedagogic scenes that offer cues for invention, discovery, the rehearsal of new practices, and reflection by students.

Just as we invite students to learn to read differently *through* the languages of the stage, which are centrally the languages of the body and voice in action, so also we can widen our pedagogic inventiveness precisely by employing approaches that restore the body-and-mind in action to a more prominent role in the classroom. Employing a grander vocabulary than Ornstein's, we can say that in learning something about the poetics of Shakespeare's drama, we can also learn about the poetics of our own pedagogy.

As you will have noted, I am assuming that most instructors teach in ways that employ only a narrow part of the full spectrum of classroom activities that make learning possible—and I include myself in this statement. This is a point that university teachers who have begun to make connections with elementary and secondary school teachers are coming to recognize as a critical issue. Testimony of this recognition comes from Stanley Katz, president of the American Council of Learned Societies (ACLS), in the speech that inaugurated the first major ACLS program for revising the humanities curriculum in K–12 education:

> The underlying premise of the program in which we are engaged is that there is an unnecessary and counterproductive fracture within the teaching profession, between those who teach youngsters in the K through12 years and those who teach grades 13–16. . . .
> What happens educationally in the schools is important to post-secondary educators not only because precollegiate teachers prepare some of their students for us, but also because they have both experiential and theoretical knowledge about pedagogy (both teaching and learning) to impart to us, though we have seldom taken their expertise with sufficient seriousness (2, 3).[1]

Further testimony comes from Edward Berenson, professor of history at UCLA, in an essay describing his tenure as the first director of the California State History-Social Science Project, one of the California Subject Matter Projects devoted to improving teaching:

Most professors operate within an extremely narrow pedagogical range, limiting themselves almost exclusively to lecture and
discussion. After observing the work of K–12 teachers over the
past few years, I now realize that there is so much more I can do.
. . . Not all of these techniques are appropriate for university
students, but the principle of making the classroom more interactive could not be more relevant to undergraduates bored by
"discussion" sections in which little discussion takes place. (24)

I think that readers can supply abundant examples from their
own years as students to support Berenson's claim that many
professors do limit their methods to lecture and some form of
discussion.

The most obvious symptoms of how we narrow our options
are in front of us in many classrooms: students sit in rows looking at the back of the head of the person in front of them, and
they take notes while the teacher lectures. These symptoms point
toward what is being limited, which is student participation and,
in particular, the use of the body as a source of learning. But this
exclusion of the body is itself symptomatic of what is really excluded—*action* in which the focus is on people doing things, experimenting, and trying new moves. What is missing in our
classrooms is what is sometimes spoken of as "learning through
doing."

A more interactive classroom is not an incidental pedagogical choice but a choice that shapes how students learn and what
students learn—and, crucially, how they learn to learn. An interactive classroom is a necessary condition for enabling students to
return to being the active learners most of them were when they
entered kindergarten or first grade. The "fracture" that Katz and
Berenson have come to recognize is much more fundamental and
disabling than either of these educational leaders or many other
university professors realize. In contrast, the model offered in
this book assumes that teachers who use a wider range of the
modes in which human beings learn can improve student learning, that employing such a wider pedagogy will enable more students to learn, and that a widened spectrum of approaches will
enable teachers themselves to learn more about both the plays
and how students learn.

Just as we can invite students to learn to read differently in part by reading in the language(s) of the body, so also we can invite ourselves to learn to write our pedagogic scripts differently, widening our pedagogic range by restoring the body to the classroom—an action that will also bring more of each student's mind into play as well.

Teaching as Art and Action

If we choose to see teaching as a form of action, it is an easy step to recognize a profitable analogy with the dramatic medium itself. Such an analogy suggests a twofold relation between the dramatist and the teacher: like the dramatist, what the teacher composes is a script, although a pedagogic rather than a dramatic script; and what the teacher orchestrates is a drama, although a pedagogic drama. In exploring teaching as an art, an understanding of drama becomes an instrument for thinking about how to function as pedagogic composers and what choices we make as our students play out our "scripts." In the still useful terms first articulated by Aristotle, the analogy enables us to delineate more precisely aspects of our identity as both makers and doers, engaged as we are in both productive and practical arts.

Teachers are engaged in a *productive art* when they are composing the script for an entire course or the scenario for a single class. In this phase of the work, teachers operate with some of the attributes, skills, and constraints of the poet, the maker of a designed object. Teachers are engaged in a *practical art* when they move into the performance of the script in a course and in a class. While teachers can be seen in part as directors or stage managers, coaches, facilitators, and observers, we must also recognize their ethical role as people who, in the perceptive phrasing of Louise Wetherbee Phelps, "inhabit a world of choice calling for judgments based on inadequate knowledge and conflicting values" ("Practical Wisdom" 877). Furthermore, it becomes evident that, in this phase, teachers' aesthetic concerns with the elegance of the script must be subordinated to the pedagogic and ethical concerns of offering students an opportunity to learn while respecting their purposes, needs, and limits.

Teachers in the role of composer of scripts are like poets, and especially like the poets we call dramatists, since what teachers create is more directly a form of making than of doing. As people who initiate the enactment of a script, teachers are engaged in practice: what they create is the unfolding, collaborative action of a group of people who have some resemblance to a cast of actors, though more to actors in a rehearsal than to actors in a performance. And what they are engaged in is a form of doing. Thus, in knowing how to study a play so as to own the text, teachers are makers, practicing a productive art; in knowing how to teach others to achieve ownership of a text and produce criticism, teachers are doers, participating in a practical art.

Teachers as Makers: Pedagogic Designers

In the first of the two phases, then, teachers are analogous to dramatists insofar as they are engaged in a productive art or poetics—the composition of a course of study. Phelps's formulation of this moment as *speculative theorizing* offers a concise account of what teachers do in "making" a course:

> In planning a curriculum . . . there is a starting point that occurs without the student. At this point the teacher . . . must, like any composer, imagine the student audience for which they are "scripting" a learning experience. . . . This teaching moment is speculative thinking. ("Developmental Challenges" 410)

To view this designed event through the lens of the dramatic event, we might employ an analysis of the specific elements that constitute the dramatic medium.

I present, therefore, a rearticulated list of eight of the constitutive elements of drama delineated in the first chapter. I often use this list as a heuristic to design my own pedagogic script. First are the tacit conventions that form the contract between the performers and the audience and that are in effect the enabling conditions for the re-creative actions that follow. Second is what Peter Brook has called the empty space, in which performers and audience come together to enact the script. Third is the presence of actors, the medium of the performance, in whose actions the words of the script become incarnated, and who ensure that no two performances are identical. Fourth is the presence of the spectators, present to one another so that one person's response can influence the response of others, and present to the actors as the actors are present to them. Fifth is the objective form of presentation in which speech follows speech and action follows action without a narrator to instruct the spectators to adopt a specific point of view. Sixth is the temporal dimension, the movement of the play in time so that, unlike a reader, a spectator cannot stop the experience; this unstoppability of time mimics our human subjection to choice and contingency. Seventh is the verbal medium, the specific multiple forms of language deployed in the classroom and in the course assignments, in which the language is seen not only as the dialogue between characters but also as instructions to the actors to transform the words into character. Eighth is the script that functions as the performance's blueprint, shaping the experience the spectators will undergo; while scripts vary in specificity, many scripts mandate some actions, delimit other options, and leave some areas open to the performers' decisions.

Each of these elements can provide a starting point for inquiry into a corresponding element in the act of teaching and the drama of the classroom event. Teachers can, for example, explore different uses of the empty space. The most common arrangement of a teacher up front and students in rows corresponds to the proscenium stage, with the teacher as performer and the students as audience. But other arrangements allow us to initiate other kinds of performance. One obvious alternative is the circle, which enables the teacher to dissolve the stage/auditorium division and transform the entire room into the stage, thus foregrounding the complex ways in which students can be asked to shift between roles as actors and spectators. In this arrangement, the students can be much more fully present to one another, verbally and nonverbally, and hence be much more likely to create complex connections among themselves.

Another alternative, better known to elementary and junior high school teachers than to those teaching in universities, is the arrangement called the fishbowl, in which a small group of actors sits inside a larger group of observers. The inner group performs an action or activity. The outer group then discusses both content and process, analyzing not only what was said but also how things were said. Here we begin to initiate the sort of complex interplay between being an actor and being a spectator that makes a student a successful performer in any discipline. I have used the fishbowl arrangement in composition classes by having an inner group of five students, four of whom offer feedback to the author of a paper. Such an arrangement dramatizes the entire act of responding to the draft of an essay and enables the group to discuss the process of giving feedback in useful ways. When successful, this dramatized scene enables the class to talk about tacit knowledge of several kinds and focus on the elusive but crucial skills needed to improve as critical readers, writers, speakers, and listeners. Similarly, I have used the fishbowl arrangement in my Shakespeare class by having an inner group rehearse a scene and the larger outer group of spectators subsequently discuss the process of the rehearsal and the categories of reading and invention employed by the group conducting the rehearsal. In this maneuver, it is easier for the students not only to discuss a specific rehearsal or performance but also to talk about where the inner group was successful in reading as co-creators and where they may have limited themselves unnecessarily in the categories and process of invention.

In discussing the use of the fishbowl, we automatically begin to examine the tacit conventions that bring together students, teachers, and the texts that students read and write. As is true in the theater, the tacit conventions of teaching and learning are givens that go largely unexamined until those conventions are modified or violated. Thus, when asked to adopt innovations such as a performance approach, students are likely to feel they are being asked to learn in a new way and to step outside conventions they have spent years in mastering. These conventions include the roles they expect teachers and students to play; the sources of knowledge and power in the classroom; the relative authority of the participants; the nature of the actions they are asked to perform; and what counts as a legitimate performance of the various roles in reading, discussing, and writing. A colleague of mine once outraged his students in the first class meeting by asking them to write the speech they "knew" he was going to give on the importance of the subject of the course. Group activities often elicit challenges from students who believe the teacher is the sole source of authority and there is nothing to be learned from other students. If teachers not only use group performances of scenes but also decide to assign a single grade for group performance, they may be perceived as violating the conventional assignment of grades. By reflecting on the tacit contract, teachers may become aware of other elements, rules, roles, and patterns of action they might want to experiment with and think about—including conventions they might find it difficult to challenge. And, as is true with some forms of metatheatrical drama, the conventions themselves can be a focus of inquiry.

Turning to the third and fourth elements, it is apparent that in the classroom the presence of actors and spectators takes many forms. Some instructors use such a pure form of lecturing as their sole medium that they become teacher-actors delivering monologues to their student-spectators—and they may produce brilliant performances that educate and entertain their student auditors and, in the best cases, implicitly model a disciplined process of inquiry that is as important as the content of the presentation. But when we alter this theatrical model, we can, for example, ask students to shift between the roles of actor and spectator, first performing an action and then becoming spectators who reflect on those performances. A teacher with some theater experience and with both literature and theater majors in class could also have the theater majors realize performances suggested by the other students. We can also shift our roles. Many teachers, for example, reserve the role of actor for themselves, while others serve mainly as stage managers so that students can take center stage. Teachers can reverse the roles in interesting ways, making students dramatists or directors and even, on occasion, having the students direct the teacher. One teacher I know demonstrates the writing process by having his students assign him a topic and then writing an essay on the board, talking through his choices as he writes. Certainly a teacher with enough skill as an actor could invite students to direct him or her in alternative performances of a scene or character. As a teacher, you can also ask yourself how much you perform the activities you ask students to perform. Do you act? When you ask them to do writing for discovery in class or in journals, do you share writing with them? Do you present yourself as an expert? a learner? a practitioner? Do you share drafts of your work? Do you ask for critical or editorial responses? Such questions can sharpen your awareness of the way you present opportunities for students to move through cycles of action, reflection, and reaction during the term.

In looking at the temporal dimension of our pedagogic medium, we can ask, "What does the beginning do?" The beginning of a play, as we have seen, sets the event in motion, establishes the relation between the event and the spectators, and establishes expectations and questions that become the premises from which spectators begin to construct meaning. In the first class meeting, then, you are performing a scene that can be likened to a prologue to the course, and you can ask yourself what the beginning of your course is doing. Can you, for example, define what you want the action of your course to be and what you are doing to set that action in motion? What relations do you want to establish between yourself, your students, and the texts they will be writing and reading? What roles do you want students to take? If these are difficult roles, how does your opening class or classes work to make it safe for them to take the necessary risks? What expectations do you establish and what questions do you invite students to formulate? Exploring the wide array of options lets you imagine and test out moves you have not attempted. If you break some familiar rituals of many opening classes—in which the teacher comes in, takes roll, adds or drops students if necessary, reads the syllabus, and dismisses the class—you can pose a challenge for the students: can they assimilate what you are doing to an alternative schema? Or are they discovering the limits of their existing categories? Changing the arrangement of the space, for example, is one way to challenge students to predict what will follow; the very act of making a prediction begins to alter the nature of their participation in the action, just as beginning to predict what will happen to Fortinbras, Laertes, and Hamlet changes the nature of our participation and investment in a performance of *Hamlet*.

When we examine a Shakespeare play, the verbal medium is the verse and prose in which the dialogue is cast. In our classes, the texts are Shakespeare's plays and whatever critical writings we assign, but we may ask students to share other types of writing, ranging from in-class entries to more considered journals to formal papers or their own experiments in composing blank verse or sonnets. We can even go beyond the verbal medium. One well-known example proposed by Miriam Gilbert ("Teaching Shakespeare" 604–5) is the sound-and-movement exercise in which students are asked to take a scene, as I ask students to do with *Richard III* act I, scene ii, and perform it without any words, using only nonverbal sound and motion. As Gilbert notes, the point is twofold: on the one hand, it forces students to concentrate on the action of the scene; on the other, the act of suspending Shakespeare's language sharpens students' perception of what that language accomplishes that sound and motion cannot capture. Working with drama in performance is also likely to sharpen our perceptions of the ways in which we and our students react to each other through reading body language and other nonverbal cues.

As I noted in Chapter 1, the script in drama is a peculiar constitutive element. First of all, the spectrum ranges from scriptless drama to the fully scripted performance. Second, even in forms of drama such as the plays of Shakespeare, which are based on mandated dialogue, the written document evaporates when the play is performed. So too we can explore not only the constituting function of the pedagogic scripts we employ but also the range of scripts from the most improvisatory to the most fully constructed. Teachers vary enormously in how completely they script the course as a whole, the individual class session, or smaller units of time. As teachers, if we become more conscious of our scripts and even more explicit in writing them out, we add another element of experiment to our own pedagogy in which we can use our students' performances to revise our script. This might at first seem simply to formalize what many teachers do when they improve their teaching through a trial-and-error process, but foregrounding that process will also change it and make us focus on the differences between our productive and practical phases. I also suspect that in the long term the widespread use of computers is going to sharpen our awareness of teaching as a design profession in the sense suggested by Sizer and Schön (*Educating*; *Reflective*), and thus compel us to pay more attention to our own pedagogic scripts.

As these examples suggest, this heuristic use of the dramatic medium can enable you to probe the alternative pedagogic choices available to you at any point in the unfolding action, to imagine the different scenes you might create, and to illuminate surprising moments during your own classroom experiences—and, in a recursive spiral, use such illuminated moments to add new cues and scripts to your pedagogic repertory. Using such a heuristic may lead you to invent moves and combinations of moves you and your students have never tried before. I once, for example, combined the fishbowl with an exploration of the four categories of voice, stage business, stage movement, and address offered by Daniel Seltzer ("Actors") to comprehensively explore what actors do when they translate the text into performance. I combined these two elements with Miriam Gilbert's principle of taking away an element so that you can use it with greater control and precision. In this case, I realized I could remove one of these four categories from a fishbowl performance and have the observers discuss what becomes clearer about the design of the text and the options for performance. So when I thought students were not paying adequate attention to their stage movement, I had pairs of students hold the ends of a four-foot rod to immobilize themselves as they rehearsed and performed a scene; observers then commented on what they discovered not only about the scene but also about how movement could best be used to convey or create meaning in that scene. Indeed, I would suggest one reason to internalize the heuristic I am developing here is that it offers a precise, detailed map of the pedagogic scene, and can thereby sharpen your own sense of the specific dimensions you may wish to play with.

Furthermore, since one of the plots in teaching based on any performance model is to have students cross the gap between knowing that something is true and knowing how to do an activity, scripting our pedagogic scenes in terms of these specific dimensions can help us design classroom events more likely to prompt students to make the move from tacit to explicit knowledge, and from theory to practice.

Teachers as Doers

The second part of the analogy between the dramatist and the teacher suggests that when we move into the classroom we see ourselves as performers, analogous to the director's role as performer-coach. In this phase, we are, in Aristotle's terms, people engaged in a practical art. As is true when we move from text to performance in drama, when we move from planning to conducting a class we are also (again) shifting into Clurman's "different language," the language of action. When a class session begins, we start to speak in a language that is both verbal and nonverbal and that includes a much wider range of stimuli than the words on the page or in our minds as we first compose our script. In this language, speech is action and action speaks. And, whereas in the first phase we can textualize in imagining the play in the classroom, in the second phase, as that pedagogic script is realized, we find ourselves operating in a complex unfolding event that is difficult to describe or analyze in detail, and is certainly not fully under our control.

What goes on in the classroom is difficult to talk about just as a dramatic performance is difficult to talk about because, while much of it is explicit and visible, much of it is also subtextual, based on a network of considerations that are largely tacit and unarticulated. Insofar as we have a plot for a given session, one powerful imperative is to guide the action so that students move toward the learning that our plot aims to make possible—but we are also subject to a competing imperative to let unplanned and surprising actions lead us in alternative directions. Thus one aspect of our performance as teachers as we immerse ourselves in the scripts and scenarios we have created is maneuvering to balance an imperative to do the script as planned against the impulse to follow out unplanned cues in improvised actions. At the same time, our openness to and tolerance for improvisatory scenes will vary widely, not simply between one teacher and another, but within the work of one teacher in one term or in one class. The range of variation even within the work of a single teacher will be based on both conscious choices and tacit limits, including the limits of risk that each teacher is willing to take at any given moment.

Enumerating the elements shaping this dimension of teaching is a challenge for another effort outside the scope of this book, but the work of Donald Schön, especially in *Educating the Reflective Practitioner*, offers useful ways to begin unpacking some of the complexities of the classroom phase of the drama-teaching analogy. Examining the competing imperatives I have just sketched out, Schön describes the manner in which a reflective practitioner, having named and framed a situation in composing a script, enters into a dialogue with the unfolding event:

> From time to time, their efforts to give order to a situation provoke unexpected outcomes—"back talk" that gives the situation a new meaning. They listen and reframe the problem. It is this ensemble of problem framing, on-spot-experiment, detection of consequences and implications, back-talk and response to back-talk, that constitutes a reflective conversation with the materials of a situation—the designlike artistry of professional practice. Several features make this process learnable, coachable, but not teachable. (157–58)

In balancing our competing imperatives, we encounter back talk as we attend to our students; and as we monitor both what and how students are learning, we find ourselves revising the script for a particular class session. When such back talk is extensive enough, we learn things that force us to revise not just the scene but also major elements of the script. In transforming a pedagogic script into a classroom event, we play the director, shaping the event in order to move through a script or scenario; we play the experimenter who, while participating in that performance, is also trying to observe how students are learning in order to revise the script both during and after that performance; and we play the reflective practitioner who, like some dramatists, seeks to compose a better design by watching how the auditors respond—how the students learn from the design at hand.

I would add that if we employ another distinction from Aristotle, namely, the distinction between theoretical, productive, and practical knowledge, not only will we discard the theory/practice dichotomy, but we will also begin to articulate more complex relations between these three types of knowledge than the bipolar model suggests. Teaching has traditionally been seen as a sort of stepchild, not quite elevated enough to turn the dyad into a triad. Indeed, the accepted model still assumes that to choose the type of pedagogy we will employ is simply to choose the appropriate methods for "delivering" the content of the course, the theory and practice that students need to acquire. I hope it is evident from the material presented here, however, and from the logic of a performance approach itself, that teaching is not separable and subordinate in this way, because *how* we teach shapes *what* we teach, and it shapes both how, or even if, students learn what we teach. Teaching is not, or not just, the transmission of information. The relation of theory to production and practice is mutual, not hierarchic; cyclic, not linear; reciprocal, not unidirectional. Theory does indeed shape production and practice, but production and practice in turn demand that we revise theory. Teachers designing their classes can be thought of as revising their theories based on the results of production and practice. Again, this is a topic that demands another book if it is to be successfully anatomized and usefully developed for practicing teachers.

Conclusion

If we can begin to see our classes through the lens of drama and use drama-framed concepts to reflect more searchingly and more productively on our work as teachers, this analogy might enable us not only to analyze what we already do but also to redesign our pedagogic scripts to elicit better—meaning richer and more reflective—performances by our students and ourselves. At the core of this model, the parallel suggests that just as the dramatic script is the actor's cue for invention, so too when we teach Shakespeare's plays we can design our own pedagogic scripts to offer our students cues for invention in the classroom, some of them versions of the cues in Shakespeare's plays, some of them the cues in our own pedagogic scenes.

The dramatist can be seen as someone who engages in the craft of provoking us to respond to the performance of an action. The teacher, Theodore Sizer notes, can be seen as someone who engages in "the craft of provoking us to learn" (2). Shakespeare, Robert Hapgood suggests, "seems . . . much less interested in telling his audience *what* to think about a given play than in suggesting *how* best to go about understanding it" (38). The performance-oriented teacher is often much less interested in telling his or her students what to learn from a particular play-text than in suggesting how they might best go about exploring its potentials and learning from their own performance. What the dramatist and the teacher share, then, is a poetics, whether a poetics of drama or a poetics of pedagogy. Despite the differences in their mediums and goals, the dramatist and the teacher share the challenges that arise when we seek to compose designs that, when performed, will provoke both actors and spectators to learn more about their worlds and their ways of world making.

NOTES

Prologue

1. This first part of this prologue is adapted from my essay "How Does One '*Teach*' a Play, Anyway?" published in *California English* 5.1 (Fall 1999): 12–13.

2. Throughout this book, all quotations from Shakespeare's plays not attributed to another source are from *The Riverside Shakespeare* edited by G. Blakemore Evans.

Chapter 1

1. Berthoff presents her model of the double-entry journal in a number of books and essays, but I am referring specifically to "Dialectical Notebooks and the Audit of Meaning," which appears in *The Journal Book* edited by Toby Fulwiler (11–18). This volume is extremely useful for teachers who want to explore a wide range of options for using journals.

2. This pair of sentences comes from the conclusion of Fish's essay "Literature in the Reader" in *Is There a Text in This Class?* (66–67). The reader will recognize that my use of the formula "What does X do?" parallels Fish's formula "What does that _____ do?" although we develop the paradigm differently.

3. Wilder notes that "[t]he theatre is unfolding action and in the disposition of events the authors may exercise a governance so complete that the distortions effected by the physical appearance of actors, by the fancies of scene-painters and the misunderstandings of directors, fall into relative insignificance" (108). Originally published in *The Intent of the Artist* (1941), Wilder's essay is reprinted in *Playwrights on Playwrighting: The Meaning and Making of Modern Drama from Ibsen to Ionesco* (1960) edited by Toby Cole, and I am quoting from this reprinted version. Robert Hapgood's "The Playwright in the Play,"

Chapter 5 of *Shakespeare the Theatre-Poet*, is an illuminating development of Wilder's essay. See also the chapter "Orchestration and Theatrical Structure" in Jean Howard's *Shakespeare's Art of Orchestration*.

4. "A Brief Drama" is my own title for this excerpt from Stan Freberg's "Washington Crosses the Delaware," one of the scenes on his LP album *Stan Freberg Presents the United States of America, Volume 1: The Early Years*. Volumes 1 and 2 have been reissued on CD by Rhino Records Inc.

5. For a much fuller anatomy of the possible points of view in fiction, see James Moffett's presentation in *Points of View* (Moffett and McElheny 1966), where he notes that "[a] point of view, naturally, is both a physical vantage point and a personal way of perceiving events" (313). Moffett enumerates eleven points of view, as follows: (1) interior monologue; (2) dramatic monologue; (3) letter narration; (4) diary narration; (5) subjective narration; (6) detached autobiography; (7) memoir, or observer narration; (8) biography, or anonymous narration: single character point of view; (9) anonymous narration: dual character point of view; (10) anonymous narration: multiple character point of view; and (11) anonymous narration: no character point of view.

6. In her essay "Dialogue," Lynne Magnusson presents a model for reading Shakespeare's dialogue that makes explicit the concepts from pragmatics and politeness theory that are implicit in the moment being analyzed here. Although I developed this analysis long before Magnusson published her essay, I was certainly influenced by some of the same studies that shaped her work, and I recommend the models of systematic analysis she offers. See also Magnusson's own *Shakespeare and Social Dialogue: Dramatic Language and Elizabethan Letters*.

7. In "Making Changes/Making Sense," Hodgdon in turn acknowledges her debt to Miriam Gilbert, who has taught so many of us to introduce the challenges of reading Shakespeare's language by asking our students to explore the question "What's going on here?" As readers will discover, I use Hodgdon's richly productive "Defamiliarizing *Hamlet*" as the opening activity through which students become (re)engaged with that play.

8. See John Rawls's "Two Concepts of Rules" and John R. Searle's *Speech Acts: An Essay in the Philosophy of Language*. The distinction has been applied to teaching grammar by Richard McLain in "The Role of Explanation in Teaching Standard English: Constitutive and Regulative Rules in Language."

9. Alan Dessen has produced a number of important books in which he has sought to rearticulate some of the specific terms on which the audiences for English Renaissance drama "agreed to meet." See, for example, the first chapter of *Elizabethan Stage Conventions and Modern Interpreters*. Also worth consulting is the fascinating volume he has produced with Leslie Thomson, *A Dictionary of Stage Directions in English Drama, 1580–1642*. In addition to the introduction, you might start your exploration of this volume by looking at the entry on "aside" (15–16).

10. One passage from Brook that is particularly relevant to the way this course is framed, and that I sometimes use in class, is as follows:

> Shakespeare's words are records of the words that he wanted to be spoken, words issuing as sounds from people's mouths, with pitch, pause, rhythm and gesture as part of their meaning. A word does not start as a word—it is an end product which begins as an impulse, stimulated by attitude and behavior which dictates the need for expression. (15)

For anyone who chooses a performance approach to drama in the classroom, this passage usefully emphasizes the incarnational nature of the medium, hence the central place that using their own bodies occupies in having students explore a playtext. Brook's passage itself echoes a passage by T. S. Eliot:

> Behind the drama of words is the drama of action, the timbre of voice and voice, the uplifted hand or tense muscle, and the particular emotion. The spoken play, the words which we read, are symbols, a shorthand, and often, as in the best of Shakespeare, a very abbreviated shorthand indeed, for the actual and felt play, which is always the real thing. The phrase, beautiful as it may be, stands for a greater beauty still. (53–54)

This passage is from Eliot's essay "Seneca in Elizabethan Translation," originally published in 1927 and republished in *Selected Essays* (1950).

Chapter 2

1. My encounter with Patrick Stewart's presentation occurred at a workshop titled "Teaching Shakespeare" sponsored by the Globe Shakespeare Institute and held at the Huntington Library, San Marino, California,

on September 9, 1989. Stewart began by saying that he had given two-hour workshops on this segment of the play alone, but that we would get the shorter version, which in fact lasted about half an hour. James P. Lusardi and June Schlueter also begin their examination of "The Anonymous Captain: 5.3" using Stewart's workshop as their cue in their book *Reading Shakespeare in Performance: King Lear* (122–28).

2. This is from *The Riverside Shakespeare*. As many readers will know, there is an ongoing debate about the nature of and relationships between the three early texts of *King Lear*, and in particular over the claim that the Folio (1623) represents Shakespeare's systematic revision of the First Quarto (1608). Here, I need only note that the two important early texts of the play, the First Quarto (1608) and the Folio (1623), offer nearly identical readings: "the worst is not, / As long as we can say, this is the worst" (Quarto) and "the worst is not, / So long as we can say this is the worst" (Folio), and add that we can ignore the Second Quarto (1619) since editors who disagree about the sources for and the relations of Quarto (1608) and Folio (1623) nonetheless agree that this Quarto is a reprint of the first with no independent authority. I am citing the Quarto and Folio from the photographic facsimile by Michael Warren in *The Parallel King Lear, 1608–1623* (96–97). With Gary Taylor, Warren edited *The Division of the Kingdoms: Shakespeare's Two Versions of King Lear*, a volume in which a number of essays argue for the hypothesis that the Folio text represents Shakespeare's revision of the play's design. This hypothesis is also developed in detail in *Shakespeare's Revision of King Lear* by Steven Urkowitz. For a contrasting account, the reader might turn to Rene Weis's introduction to his modernized *King Lear: A Parallel Text Edition*, in which he demonstrates some problems with the hypothesis of systematic revision.

3. Among the books that have contributed powerfully to performance-centered criticism, and also been especially important for my own development, are those by Raymond Williams (1954/1972); J. L. Styan (*Elements*); John Russell Brown (*Discovering*); Alan C. Dessen (*Elizabethan*); Philip McGuire (*Speechless*); and Judith Milhous and Robert Hume. Valuable pioneering essays on using a performance-centered approach in the classroom include those by Miriam Gilbert ("Teaching Dramatic"; "Teaching Shakespeare"); Bernard Beckerman ("Some Problems"; "Shakespeare's"); Charles Frey ("Teaching"); Ellen O'Brien; and Homer Swander. *Shakespeare Quarterly* has also published issues devoted to teaching Shakespeare in volume 35 (1984), volume 41 (1990), and volume 46 (1995); these contain a wide array of developments in this approach. In addition, the Modern Language Association of America (MLA) has published a number of volumes in its Approaches to Teaching series, including volumes on *King Lear* (Ray), *The Tempest* (Hunt),

Romeo and Juliet (Hunt), and *Hamlet* (Kliman). MLA has also published *Teaching Shakespeare through Performance* edited by Milla Cozart Riggio, and a version of the present chapter appeared in this collection under the title "Performance Is More Than an 'Approach' to Teaching Shakespeare" (48–62).

4. Here I am drawing most directly on Burke's *A Rhetoric of Motives* (1–55), but my reading of many other books and essays by Burke lies behind this framing.

5. Stephen Booth can be said to have composed an entire body of criticism by asking this question and developing answers of great penetration and subtlety. For my purposes, the most relevant formulation still is that offered in his essay "On the Value of *Hamlet*" (137–76) in *Reinterpretations of Elizabethan Drama* edited by Norman Rabkin.

6. Hapgood focuses on a constitutive element of the pedagogy developed in this model. *Shakespeare the Theatre-Poet* provides a systematic framework and offers richly detailed examples that demonstrate how to discern the mandated and open elements of a playtext; how to delineate the range of options and experiment with those options in what he calls "imaginary rehearsals"; and how to compose suites of performance choices that produce alternate but equally valid realizations of the text or elements of the text.

7. One such paper, written by Leeann Cretser (as a graduate student in the master's program at Cal Poly Pomona) and analyzing *The Courtier* and *Utopia*, was awarded first prize as the best piece of critical writing at the 1999 national conference of Sigma Tau Delta, the English Honors Society. The paper on dialogue in D. H. Lawrence's *Women in Love* by Wendy Gullett was awarded an honorable mention at the 1996 Sigma Tau Delta conference.

Chapter 3

1. Frances E. Dolan has produced a useful edition that brings together the playtext and a wide array of contemporary documents in *The Taming of the Shrew: Texts and Contexts*. There are performance histories by Tori Haring-Smith and Graham Holderness (*Shakespeare in Performance*), as well as Elizabeth Schafer's edition of the play in the Shakespeare in Production series. In Carol Rutter's *Clamorous Voices*, Paola Dionisotti, Sinead Cusack, and Fiona Shaw discuss their experience of transforming the role of Katherina into the performed character and

offer perspectives on three productions. In addition, Michael Sibbery, in *Players of Shakespeare 4*, presents an account of his Petruchio in the production directed by Gale Edwards; and Gale Edwards is among the directors interviewed in Elizabeth Schafer's book on *Ms-Directing Shakespeare*. There are illuminating chapters on the play in the books by Gay, Hodgdon ("Katherina"), Newman, and Werner; Lynda Boose has written two powerful and often-cited essays, and other essays such as that by Shirley Nelson Garner offer stimulating perspectives. The reader can also consult Nancy Lenz Harvey's annotated bibliography, which has entries on materials up to 1992. For an interesting model of a cultural studies approach that might be adapted to this play, see Paul Skrebels's "Transhistoricizing *Much Ado about Nothing*." In her updated edition of the play, Ann Thompson notes that in an anthology she coedited with Sasha Roberts, *Women Reading Shakespeare, 1660–1900*, "we were able to include a range of views which tend to support my assumption that this has always been a 'problem play'" (49).

2. In composing this handout, I read the core trilogy of books in which Stanislavski articulated his ideas, *An Actor Prepares, Building a Character*, and *Creating a Role*, as well as *Stanislavski's Legacy* and *An Actor's Handbook*, all in the Elizabeth Reynolds Hapgood translations; *Stanislavski on the Art of the Stage*, translated by David Magarshack; and the books on Stanislavski by Sonia Moore and Jean Benedetti cited in the bibliography. I should note that in suggesting that when transforming role into character the actor take account of what is said about that character by the other dramatis personae, I follow modern practice, but that this practice is an anachronism. It assumes the modern situation in which every actor has easy access to the whole text of the play. But this was not true in Shakespeare's theater, where the company had one complete copy—the "book of the play" approved by the censor—and then distributed handwritten parts to each actor. The "part" consisted of the speeches constituting a role, with each speech preceded by a cue, namely, the last few words of the previous speaker. It is startling to realize that the English theater continued to use this part system well into the twentieth century, long after it was possible for each actor to own a text of the complete play. For an introduction to the nature of this part system and the consequences for our understanding both of the nature of Shakespeare's text and of how actors rehearsed their parts, see Tiffany Stern's *Making Shakespeare: From Stage to Page*, especially pp. 123–36. Stern's work in this chapter offers material that might well prompt teachers in advanced classes to develop assignments for *Hamlet* about the verse/prose shifts in that play, and for *Macbeth* about the patterns of address between Macbeth and Lady Macbeth.

Chapter 4

1. In an interesting essay titled "Active Reading: Shakespeare's Stage-craft," Peter Reynolds offers a model for enabling students to become active readers of Shakespeare's plays that is very close to the model presented in this book. Furthermore, to exemplify his argument, he looks at issues of casting, silent characters, and props in *Richard III* act I, scene ii. His imagined rehearsal of the scene is rich and provocative, he emphasizes aspects of the scene I have downplayed, and anyone interested in examining the variety of options within the performance approach should read this essay, which appears in *Teaching Shakespeare: Essays on Approaches to Shakespeare in Schools and Colleges* edited by Richard Adams.

2. In the section "Identity and Choice" in the introduction to her edition of *Richard III*, Janis Lull presents a strong argument for the claim that in his final soliloquy and subsequent choices Richard does achieve tragic stature:

> Richard does not really love Richard, in the sense that he harbours no tender feelings for himself, but neither will he hate himself. His remarkable self-overhearing on the day of battle results in the same outcome as if he had despaired, fallen into self-hatred, and so taken revenge on himself, as Anne once predicted (1.2.86–7). He will die and be damned. Yet psychologically, there is a difference. By electing to remain himself, Richard insists on free will in the face of determinism. As Coriolanus banishes Rome rather than passively suffer banishment, so Richard assumes his predestined identity as his own choice. This interior moment is the play's final gloss on the paradoxical pun of the opening soliloquy. Richard is—he always has been—"determined to prove a villain," and he refuses to surrender his own part of the pun, his human determination, to cosmic determinism. He has no choice, but he chooses anyway, and in this gesture against fate he partakes of tragic heroism. (14)

I find this analysis cogent and worth sharing with the class. Pedagogically, Lull's argument also suggests how effectively this play could be taught in conjunction with *Doctor Faustus*.

Chapter 5

1. For an illuminating exploration of how the potentials of this complex scene have been realized, see the chapter titled "Act III, Scene i (*Part 2*)" in Marvin Rosenberg's *The Masks of Hamlet* (465–74). I take the term *full-blown soliloquy* from Daniel Seltzer's compact survey of the soliloquy in "The Actors and the Staging," especially pp. 45–52. Seltzer's effort to distinguish types of soliloquy nicely illustrates the problem of retroactively articulating a convention that clearly was not rigid and that evolved as the dramaturgy changed over the course of Shakespeare's career.

2. Although she did not know this, Maureen was rearticulating a point worked out by Philip Edwards who, commenting on Hamlet's last speech in act I, scene v in the introduction to his edition of *Hamlet* (first published in 1985), writes: "This is a terrible moment as, all exhilaration gone, he faces the burden of his responsibilities. But who has told him that it is his responsibility to put the world to rights? to restore the disjointed frame of things to its true shape? No one but himself. It is the entirely self-imposed burden of cleansing the world that he now groans under" (45).

3. On the need for a scholar versed in the proper way to interrogate a ghost, see J. Dover Wilson's *What Happens in* Hamlet (75–76). See also Stephen Greenblatt's illuminating discussion in Hamlet *in Purgatory* of the motives for ghosts to return (41) and on the questions to ask a ghost (103, 209–10).

4. The relevance of the Chorus's request has been emphasized by Alan Dessen in *Elizabethan Stage Conventions and Modern Interpreters* (11–12). In an interesting and provocative analysis, Robert Hapgood suggests that these requests by the Chorus might be seen as inviting the spectators to other self-transforming experiences (15–23).

5. In an essay on Shakespeare's stage directions, E. A. J. Honigmann forcefully challenges the editorial consensus that Hamlet's first line is an aside: "When an editor adds '*Aside*' he often implies that the speaker would not have dared to utter the same words openly; in short, he passes judgement on the relationship of two or more dramatic characters. Clearly, if the situation includes an impudent speaker or an inattentive listener the case for an aside is weakened" (*Myriad* 177). Turning to the case of Hamlet's first speech, Honigmann argues, "Traditionally printed as an aside (since Theobald), Hamlet's first speech expresses the riddling impudence that is characteristic of all his exchanges with Claudius before Act V. Are we to assume that he would not have dared to speak

out loud, and that the only alternative is an aside? There is surely evidence enough in the play that Hamlet's angry contemptuousness could not be muzzled. Nevertheless, a third possibility should be considered: that Hamlet, the arch-soliloquiser, not infrequently mutters to himself and cares not a rap whether or not others catch his words. Shakespeare had earlier broken the convention of 'inaudible soliloquy' when it suited him (as in the balcony-scene in *Romeo and Juliet*); now he modifies the aside, which becomes audible or semi-audible as he chooses, so that many of Hamlet's speeches resemble an aside being partly addressed to himself" (*Myriad* 177). Honigmann's point can be supported by Alan Dessen and Leslie Thomson's entry on *aside* in their *A Dictionary of Stage Directions in English Drama, 1580–1642*. They note that "the majority of *asides* signaled in today's editions are not marked as such in the original manuscripts and printed editions, particularly in the Shakespeare canon where the only designated spoken *asides* are Quarto *Merry Wives*, E1r, 3.3.139 and *Pericles*, D4v, 2.5.74,78" (16). The material from Honigmann and from Dessen and Thomson can be used to compose another handout for the class.

6. On the controversies provoked by the Ghost, see *The Renaissance Hamlet: Issues and Responses in 1600* by Roland Mushat Frye, especially pp. 14–28, and Stephen Greenblatt's book-length exploration of the issues raised by the ghost.

7. On the arguments for and against tyrannicide, see Frye, especially pp. 29–38. You can illuminate these issues by bringing in a copy of the warrant for the execution of Charles I.

8. The reissue of a videotape and, more recently, a DVD of the Gielgud-Burton production, along with a CD and cassettes offering the sound track, combined with the earlier release of a studio-recorded LP, has revealed a striking yet apt exemplification of the point that performances vary even within a single production. Burton's diabolically gleeful delivery of the line occurs in the original long-playing record issued in 1964 shortly after the brief theatrical release of the film, and he is not nearly as emphatic in the performance recorded during the original Broadway production. I would speculate that the increased glee of the LP version was Burton's compensation—whether conscious or instinctive—for the absence of the visual dimension, the full performance on stage that was registered on the film. But having said that, I must also acknowledge that Burton was notorious for varying his delivery from performance to performance.

9. Samuel Johnson's note in his edition of Shakespeare (1765) is cited from *The Yale Edition of the Works of Samuel Johnson* (990).

10. An argument for Christian revenge has been made by Father I. J. Semper in Hamlet *without Tears*. Greenblatt offers this note on the subject: "The issue has been the subject of extensive scholarly discussion. Arguing for the Catholic position, I. J. Semper has suggested that, under certain circumstances, vengeance could be called for, but there is no evidence that Hamlet's circumstances in any way match those that might possibly justify the assassination of Claudius. . . . For the dominant counterview, see Prosser, *Hamlet and Revenge*" (308). It might be argued that the action of Portia, sanctioned by the Duke of Venice, presents an interesting case when she uses the law to seize the wealth and force the conversion of Shylock in act IV of *The Merchant of Venice*: while the Christians within the play present themselves as merely carrying out the dictates of the impersonal code of state justice, spectators have the option of seeing this as the Christians not only piously following both law and the dictates of faith but also using the law to take revenge—in an act that might come to seem, as it indeed seems in many modern productions, to be Christian revenge. Certainly, with Portia's eloquent plea for mercy ringing in their ears, the spectators may see the action of the court, when coupled with the gleefully malicious comments of the bystanders, as constituting a form of merciless mercy that is hard to distinguish from revenge.

11. For an interesting analysis of the duel, see James Jackson's "'They Catch One Another's Rapiers': The Exchange of Weapons in *Hamlet*." Jackson argues that the duel is indeed fought with rapier (and dagger), not the modern foil, and that the significantly different style of combat necessitated by the fearsomely lethal rapier provides the most plausible explanation of how the exchange happens.

12. In *Staging in Shakespeare's Theatres*, Andrew Gurr and Mariko Ichikawa also make this point: "Shakespeare's text introduced changes to the revenge archetype [embodied in *The Spanish Tragedy* by Thomas Kyd], and the original audiences would have recognized those changes more easily than we can. Chief among them is the number of appearances of the ghost as an advocate of revenge. In Kyd's play the ghost of Don Andrea is personified as the initiator of and observer of all the actions of the play. He returns as the play ends to gloat over the success of the policy of revenge. Hamlet's dead father, on the other hand, does not return at the end of the play. Instead he appears in the form of a surrogate presence [namely, Fortinbras, wearing the same full armor the Ghost wore in his initial appearance] which would have been recognized in its visual features in the original staging, but of which we are deprived by our blind reading of the words. He returned in a distinctive shape which has some striking implications for our reading of the play" (49). In their last chapter, "The Early Staging of *Hamlet*," Gurr and

Ichikawa offer a hypothetical staging of the play, which you might use either to stimulate your own pedagogic designs or to share with students. This chapter includes their schematic renderings of the "chief moves" in Ophelia's burial (V.i) and the duel (V.ii). In *Enter the Whole Army*, C. Walter Hodges offers sixty illustrations, including his conjectural versions of Hamlet act I, scene iv and act I, v (the Ghost), Hamlet act III, scene ii (the Mousetrap); and act V, scene i (Ophelia's grave), as well as an illustration of the induction from *The Taming of the Shrew*. Michael W. Shurgot, in *Stages of Play: Shakespeare's Theatrical Energies in Elizabethan Performance*, devotes his last chapter to the staging of the Mousetrap (199–213), with a useful schematic illustration.

Epilogue

1. The ACLS Elementary and Secondary Schools Teacher Curriculum Development Project ran from 1992 to 1995; my own participation in the project, serving as a faculty member working with high school teachers from the Los Angeles Unified School District's Humanitas Program, was an enormously enriching experience. The released time provided by the ACLS grant, furthermore, enabled me to compose an earlier version of this chapter, and I thank then-ACLS President Stanley Katz and Michael Holzman, at that time project director, for their support. My essay appeared in *Shakespeare Quarterly* 46 (1995): 135–44.

BIBLIOGRAPHY

Abbs, Peter. *A Is for Aesthetic: Essays on Creative and Aesthetic Education*. London: Falmer Press, 1989.

———. "The Meaning of English within the Arts." *Critical Quarterly* 26 (1984): 168–74.

Adams, Richard, ed. *Teaching Shakespeare: Essays on Approaches to Shakespeare in Schools and Colleges*. London: Robert Royce, 1985.

Adamson, Sylvia, Lynette Hunter, Lynne Magnusson, Ann Thompson, and Katie Wells, eds. *Reading Shakespeare's Dramatic Language: A Guide*. London: Thomson Learning, 2001.

Adelman, Janet. *The Common Liar: An Essay on* Antony & Cleopatra. New Haven: Yale UP, 1973.

Aers, Lesley, and Nigel Wheale, eds. *Shakespeare in the Changing Curriculum*. London: Routledge, 1991.

Allen, Michael. "From Dialogue to Rhetoric: Berthoff's Double Entry Notebook with a Lanham Twist." *The Writing Instructor* 5 (1986): 122–31.

Allen, Michael J. B., and Kenneth Muir, eds. *Shakespeare's Plays in Quarto: A Facsimile Edition of Copies Primarily from the Henry E. Huntington Library*. Berkeley: U of California P, 1981.

Andrews, John F. "Cedric Messina Discusses *The Shakespeare Plays*." *Shakespeare Quarterly* 30 (1979): 134–37.

———, ed. *Teaching Shakespeare*. Spec. issue of *Shakespeare Quarterly* 35.5 (1984): 515–656.

Austin, J. L. *How to Do Things with Words*. Cambridge: Harvard UP, 1962.

Ball, David. *Backwards and Forwards: A Technical Manual for Reading Plays*. Carbondale: Southern Illinois UP, 1983.

Barton, John. *Playing Shakespeare*. London: Methuen, 1984. Also on videotape.

Beckerman, Bernard. *Dynamics of Drama: Theory and Method of Analysis*. 1970. New York: Drama Book Specialists, 1979.

———. *Shakespeare at the Globe, 1599–1609*. New York: Macmillan, 1962.

———. "Shakespeare's Industrious Scenes." *Shakespeare Quarterly* 30 (1979): 138–50.

———. "Some Problems in Teaching Shakespeare's Plays as Works of Drama." *Teaching Shakespeare*. Ed. Walter Edens, Christopher Durer, Walter Eggers, Duncan Harris, and Keith Hull. Princeton: Princeton UP, 1977. 306–16.

———. *Theatrical Presentation: Performer, Audience and Act*. Ed. Gloria Brim Beckerman and William Coco. New York: Routledge, 1990.

Beehler, Sharon A. "Censorship and the Teaching of Shakespeare." *Ideological Approaches to Teaching Shakespeare: The Practice of Theory*. Ed. Robert P. Merrix and Nicholas Ranson. Lewiston, NY: Mellen, 1992. 215–28.

———. Introduction. *Shakespeare and Higher Education: A Global Perspective*. *Shakespeare Yearbook* 12 (2001): 1–4.

———. "Making Media Matter in the Shakespeare Classroom." *Teaching Shakespeare into the Twenty-First Century*. Ed. Ronald E. Salomone and James E. Davis. Athens: Ohio UP, 1997. 247–54.

———. "'Such Impossible Passages of Grossness': Education and the Censoring of Shakespeare." *Nebraska English Journal* 35.3/4 (1990): 16–31.

———. "Teaching Shakespeare's Dramatic Dialogue." *Teaching Shakespeare Today: Practical Approaches and Productive Strategies*. Ed. James E. Davis and Ronald E. Salomone. Urbana, IL: National Council of Teachers of English, 1993. 14–23.

———. "'That's a Certain Text': Problematizing Shakespeare Instruction in American High Schools and Colleges." *Shakespeare Quarterly* 41 (1990): 195–205.

Beehler, Sharon A., and Holger Klein, eds. *Shakespeare and Higher Education: A Global Perspective*. *Shakespeare Yearbook* 12 (2001).

Bibliography

Benedetti, Jean. *Stanislavski and the Actor.* New York: Routledge/Theatre Arts Books, 1998.

Berenson, Edward. "The California History-Social Science Project: Developing History Education in the Schools." *Perspectives: The Newsletter of the American Historical Association* (December 1993): 21–24.

Berger, Harry. *Imaginary Audition: Shakespeare on Stage and Page.* Berkeley: U of California P, 1989.

Berkeley, David S. "'Determined' in *Richard III*, I.i.30." *Shakespeare Quarterly* 14 (163): 483–84.

Berry, Ralph. Rev. of *The Taming of the Shrew,* by William Shakespeare. CBC, 1982. *Shakespeare Quarterly* 33 (1982): 199–201. Rpt. in *Shakespeare on Television: An Anthology of Essays and Reviews.* Ed. James C. Bulman and H. R. Coursen. Hanover, NH: UP of New England, 1998. 285–86.

———. *Shakespeare in Performance: Castings and Metamorphoses.* New York: St. Martin's Press, 1993.

Berthoff, Ann. "Dialectical Notebooks and the Audit of Meaning." *The Journal Book.* Ed. Toby Fulwiler. Portsmouth, NH: Boynton/Cook, 1987. 11–18.

Bertram, Paul, and Bernice Kliman. *The Three-Text Hamlet: Parallel Texts of the First and Second Quartos and the First Folio.* New York: AMS Press, 1991.

Billington, Michael. *One Night Stands: A Critic's View of Modern British Theatre.* 1993. London: Nick Hern, 2001. xii–xiii and 123–24.

Bizzell, Patricia. Rev. of *Invention as a Social Act,* by Karen LeFevre. *College Composition and Communication* 38 (1987): 485–86.

Blayney, Peter W. M. *The First Folio of Shakespeare.* Washington, D.C.: Folger Shakespeare Library, 1991.

Boose, Lynda E. "Scolding Brides and Bridling Scolds: Taming the Woman's Unruly Member." *Shakespeare Quarterly* 42 (1991): 179–213.

———. "*The Taming of the Shrew*: Good Husbandry and Enclosure." *Shakespeare Reread: The Texts in New Contexts.* Ed. Russ McDonald. Ithaca, NY: Cornell UP, 1994. 193–225.

Booth, Stephen. "On the Value of *Hamlet.*" *Reinterpretations of Elizabethan Drama.* Ed. Norman Rabkin. New York: Columbia UP, 1969. 137–76.

Brook, Peter. *The Empty Space.* Harmondsworth, Eng.: Penguin, 1972.

Brown, John Russell. *Discovering Shakespeare: A New Guide to the Plays.* New York: Columbia UP, 1981.

———. *Shakespeare's Plays in Performance.* 1966. Harmondsworth, Eng.: Penguin, 1969.

———. *William Shakespeare: Writing for Performance.* New York: St. Martin's Press, 1996.

Brown, Roger. *Words and Things: An Introduction to Language.* New York: Free Press, 1958.

Brown, Stephen J. "The Use of Shakespeare in America: A Study in Class Domination." *Shakespeare: Pattern of Excelling Nature.* Ed. David Bevington and Jay L. Halio. Newark: U of Delaware P, 1978. 230–40.

Bullough, Geoffrey, ed. *Narrative and Dramatic Sources of Shakespeare.* Vol. I: *Early Comedies, Poems,* Romeo and Juliet. New York: Columbia UP, 1977.

Bulman, J. C., and H. R. Coursen, eds. *Shakespeare on Television: An Anthology of Essays and Reviews.* Hanover, NH: UP of New England, 1988.

Burke, Kenneth. *The Philosophy of Literary Form: Studies in Symbolic Action.* Baton Rouge: Louisiana State UP, 1941.

———. "Psychology of Form." 1924. *Perspectives by Incongruity.* Ed. S. E. Hyman. Bloomington: Indiana UP, 1964. 20–33.

———. *A Rhetoric of Motives.* Berkeley: U of California P, 1969.

———. "Terministic Screens." *Language as Symbolic Action: Essays on Life, Literature, and Method.* Berkeley: U of California P, 1966.

Calderwood, James. *To Be and Not To Be: Negation and Metadrama in* Hamlet. New York: Columbia UP, 1983.

Carnovsky, Morris, with Peter Sander. "The Eye of the Storm: On Playing King Lear." *Shakespeare Quarterly* 28 (1977): 144-50.

Cartwright, Kent. *Shakespearean Tragedy and Its Double: The Rhythms of Audience Response.* University Park: Pennsylvania State University, 1991.

Bibliography

Chapman, Gerald. *Teaching Young Playwrights*. Ed. Lisa A. Barnett. Portsmouth, NH: Heinemann, 1991.

Charney, Maurice. *How to Read Shakespeare*. New York: McGraw-Hill, 1971.

———. "Shakespearean Anglophilia: The BBC-TV Series and American Audiences." *Shakespeare Quarterly* 31 (1980): 287–92.

Clemen, Wolfgang. *The Development of Shakespeare's Imagery*. New York: Hill and Wang, 1951.

Clurman, Harold. "In a Different Language." *Theatre Arts* 34 (January 1950): 18–20. Rpt. in *Directors on Directing: A Source Book of the Modern Theater*. Ed. Toby Cole and Helen Krich Chinoy. Indianapolis: Bobbs-Merrill, 1976. 272–78.

Cohen, Ralph A. "Original Staging and the Shakespeare Classroom." *Teaching Shakespeare through Performance*. Ed. Milla Cozart Riggio. New York: MLA, 1999. 78–101.

———, ed. *Teaching Shakespeare*. Spec. issue of *Shakespeare Quarterly* 41.2 (1990): iii–v, 139–268.

———, ed. *Teaching Shakespeare*. Spec. issue of *Shakespeare Quarterly* 46.2 (1995): iii–v, 125–251.

Cohen, Robert. *Acting in Shakespeare*. Mountain View, CA: Mayfield, 1991.

Coursen, H. R. *Reading Shakespeare on Stage*. Newark: U of Delaware P, 1995.

———, ed. *Shakespeare and the Classroom* 1 (Spring 1993), and subsequent issues.

———. *Shakespeare in Production: Whose History?* Athens: Ohio UP, 1996.

Croall, Jonathan. Hamlet *Observed: The National Theatre at Work*. London: National Theatre Publications, 2001.

Cullum, Albert. *Shake Hands with Shakespeare*. New York: Citation Press, 1968.

David, Richard. *Shakespeare in the Theatre*. Cambridge: Cambridge UP, 1981.

Davis, James E., ed. *Teaching Shakespeare*. SOCTE Focus. Urbana, IL: National Council of Teachers of English, 1976.

Davis, James E., and Ronald E. Salomone, eds. *Teaching Shakespeare Today: Practical Approaches and Productive Strategies.* Urbana, IL: National Council of Teachers of English, 1993.

Davis, Ken. *Rehearsing the Audience: Ways to Develop Student Perceptions of Theatre.* Urbana, IL: ERIC/National Council of Teachers of English, 1988.

Dawson, Anthony B. *Watching Shakespeare: A Playgoer's Guide.* London: Macmillan, 1988.

Dessen, Alan C. Editorial Note to *Renaissance Drama* ns 12 (1981). N. pag.

———. *Elizabethan Stage Conventions and Modern Interpreters.* Cambridge: Cambridge UP, 1984.

———. *Rescripting Shakespeare: The Text, the Director, and Modern Productions.* Cambridge: Cambridge UP, 2002. See especially "The Editor as Rescriptor" 209–34.

———. *Shakespeare and the Late Moral Plays.* Lincoln and London: U of Nebraska P, 1986.

———. "Shakespeare and the Theatrical Conventions of His Time." *The Cambridge Companion to Shakespeare Studies.* Ed. Stanley Wells. Cambridge: Cambridge UP, 1986. 85–99.

Dessen, Alan, and Leslie Thomson. *A Dictionary of Stage Directions in English Drama, 1580–1642.* Cambridge: Cambridge UP, 1999.

Devine, Mary Elizabeth, and Constance M. Clark. "The Stanislavski System as a Tool for Teaching Dramatic Literature." *College English* 38 (1976): 15–24.

Dolan, Frances E. *The Taming of the Shrew: Texts and Contexts.* Boston: Bedford/St. Martin's, 1996.

Earthman, Elise Ann. "Enter the Madcap Prince of Wales: Students Directing *Henry IV, Part I.*" *English Journal* 82.4 (1993): 54–60.

Eaves, Morris. "The Real Thing: A Plan for Producing Shakespeare in the Classroom." *College English* 31 (1970): 463–72.

Edens, Walter, Christopher Durer, Walter Eggers, Duncan Harris, and Keith Hull, eds. *Teaching Shakespeare.* Princeton: Princeton UP, 1977.

Elbow, Peter. *Writing without Teachers.* New York: Oxford UP, 1973. 147–91.

Eliot, T. S. *Selected Essays*. New York: Harcourt, Brace, 1950.

Empson, William. "*Hamlet* When New" in the *Sewanee Review* 61 (Winter and Spring 1953). Rpt. as "*Hamlet*" in *Essays on Shakespeare*. Ed. David B. Pirie. Cambridge: Cambridge UP, 1986. 79–136.

Engell, James, and David Perkins, eds. *Teaching Literature: What Is Needed Now*. Cambridge: Harvard UP, 1988.

Esslin, Martin. *An Anatomy of Drama*. New York: Hill and Wang, 1977.

Evans, Bertrand. *Shakespeare's Comedies*. Oxford: Clarendon Press, 1960.

———. *Shakespeare's Tragic Practice*. Oxford: Clarendon Press, 1979.

Ferguson, Margaret. "Afterword." *Shakespeare Reproduced*. Ed. Jean R. Howard and Marion F. O'Connor. London: Methuen, 1987. 273–83.

Fish, Stanley. *Is There a Text in This Class? The Authority of Interpretive Communities*. Cambridge: Harvard UP, 1980.

Foakes, Reginald A. *Illustrations of the English Stage, 1580–1642*. London: Scolar Press, 1985.

Freberg, Stan. *Stan Freberg Presents The United States of America, Volume 1: The Early Years*. LP. Capitol, 1961; Capitol, 1989; EMI-Capitol, 1996. CD. Rhino, 1996.

Frey, Charles. *Experiencing Shakespeare: Essays on Text, Classroom, and Performance*. Columbia: U of Missouri P, 1988.

———. *Making Sense of Shakespeare*. Madison, NJ: Fairleigh Dickinson UP, 1999.

———. "Shakespeare in Seattle." *Shakespeare Quarterly* 31 (1980): 285–86.

———. "Teaching Shakespeare in America." *Teaching Shakespeare*. Spec. issue of *Shakespeare Quarterly* 35.5 (1984): 541–58.

Frye, Roland Mushat. *The Renaissance Hamlet: Issues and Responses in 1600*. Princeton: Princeton UP, 1984.

Garner, Shirley Nelson. "*The Taming of the Shrew*: Inside or Outside of the Joke?" "*Bad*" *Shakespeare: Revaluations of the Shakespeare Canon*. Ed. Maurice Charney. Rutherford, NJ: Fairleigh Dickinson UP; London: Associated University Presses, 1988. 105–19.

Gay, Penny. "*The Taming of the Shrew*: Avoiding the Feminist Challenge." *As She Likes It: Shakespeare's Unruly Women*. London: Routledge, 1994. 86–119.

George, David. Rev. of *Shakespeare's Second Globe: The Missing Monument*, by C. Walter Hodges. *Shakespeare Quarterly* 28 (1977): 268–71.

Gibson, Rex. *Teaching Shakespeare*. Cambridge: Cambridge UP, 1998.

Gibson, Rex, and Janet Field-Pickering. *Discovering Shakespeare's Language*. Cambridge: Cambridge UP, 1998.

Gilbert, Miriam. *Shakespeare in Performance*: Love's Labour's Lost. Manchester: Manchester UP, 1993.

———. "Teaching Dramatic Literature." *Educational Theatre Journal* 25 (1973): 86–94.

———. "Teaching Shakespeare through Performance." *Teaching Shakespeare*. Spec. issue of *Shakespeare Quarterly* 35.5 (1984): 601–8.

———. "Writing about Performance, Writing as Performance." In *Teaching Shakespeare through Performance*, ed. Milla Cozart Riggio. New York: MLA, 1999. 307–17.

Goldman, Michael. *Acting and Action in Shakespearean Tragedy*. Princeton: Princeton UP, 1985.

———. *The Actor's Freedom: Toward a Theory of Drama*. New York: Viking, 1975.

Granville-Barker, Harley. *Prefaces to Shakespeare: Hamlet*. 1946. Princeton: Princeton UP, 1965.

Greenblatt, Stephen. Hamlet *in Purgatory*. Princeton: Princeton UP, 2001.

Guare, John. Foreword. *From Ibsen's Workshop: Notes, Scenarios, and Drafts of the Modern Plays*. Trans. A. G. Chater. Ed. William Archer. 1913. New York: Da Capo Press, 1978. N. pag.

Gurr, Andrew. *Playgoing in Shakespeare's London*. 3rd ed. Cambridge: Cambridge UP, 2004.

———. *The Shakespearean Stage, 1574–1642*. 3rd ed. Cambridge: Cambridge UP, 1992.

———. *Studying Shakespeare: An Introduction*. London: Edward Arnold, 1988.

Gurr, Andrew, and Mariko Ichikawa. *Staging in Shakespeare's Theatres.* Oxford: Oxford UP, 2000.

Hageman, Elizabeth H., and Sara Jayne Steen, eds. *Teaching Judith Shakespeare.* Spec. issue of *Shakespeare Quarterly* 47.4 (1996): v–viii, 361–489.

Halio, Jay L. *Understanding Shakespeare's Plays in Performance.* 1988. Houston, TX: Scrivenery Press, 2000.

Hall, Peter. *Shakespeare's Advice to the Players.* London: Oberon Books, 2003.

Hallett, Charles A. "A Shakespeare Workshop." *College English* 32 (1971): 790–96.

Hallett, Charles A., and Elaine S. Hallett. *Analyzing Shakespeare's Action: Scene Versus Sequence.* Cambridge: Cambridge UP, 1991.

Hapgood, Robert. *Shakespeare the Theatre-Poet.* Oxford: Oxford UP, 1988.

Haring-Smith, Tori. *From Farce to Metadrama: A Stage History of* The Taming of the Shrew, *1594–1983.* Westport, CT: Greenwood Press, 1985.

Harvey, Nancy Lenz. The Taming of the Shrew: *An Annotated Bibliography.* Boston: Garland, 1994.

Hawkins, Sherman. "Teaching the Theatre of the Imagination." *Teaching Shakespeare.* Spec. issue of *Shakespeare Quarterly* 35:5 (1984): 517–27.

Hayman, Ronald. *How to Read a Play.* New York: Grove Press, 1977.

Heathcote, Dorothy. *Dorothy Heathcote: Collected Writings on Education and Drama.* Ed. Liz Johnson and Cecily O'Neill. London: Hutchinson, 1984.

Heathcote, Dorothy, and Gavin Bolton. *Drama for Learning: Dorothy Heathcote's Mantle of the Expert Approach to Education.* Portsmouth, NH: Heinemann, 1995.

Hinman, Charlton, ed. *The Norton Facsimile: The First Folio of Shakespeare.* New York: Norton, 1968. 2nd ed. Introduction by Peter W. M. Blayney. New York: Norton: 1996.

Hodgdon, Barbara. "Defamiliarizing *Hamlet*: Hamlet with and without His Soliloquies." *Approaches to Teaching Shakespeare's* Hamlet. Ed. Bernice W. Kliman. New York: MLA, 2001. 222.

———. "Katherina Bound, or Play(k)ating the Strictures of Everyday Life." *The Shakespeare Trade: Performances and Appropriations.* Philadelphia: U of Pennsylvania P, 1998. 1–38.

———. "Making Changes/Making Sense" in *FOCUS: Teaching Shakespeare II.* Ed. Ronald E. Salomone, 12.1 (Fall 1985): 2–11.

Hodges, C. Walter. *Enter the Whole Army: A Pictorial Study of Shakespearean Staging 1576–1616.* Cambridge: Cambridge UP, 1999.

———. *The Globe Restored.* London: Ernest Benn, 1953.

Holderness, Graham. *Shakespeare in Performance: The Taming of the Shrew.* Manchester: Manchester UP, 1989.

———, ed. *The Shakespeare Myth.* Manchester: Manchester UP, 1988.

Homan, Sidney, ed. *Shakespeare and the Triple Play: From Study to Stage to Classsroom.* Bucknell, PA: Bucknell UP, 1988.

Honigmann, E. A. J. *Myriad-Minded Shakespeare: Essays, Chiefly on the Tragedies and Problem Comedies.* New York: St. Martin's, 1989.

———. *Shakespeare: Seven Tragedies: The Dramatist's Manipulation of Response.* London: Macmillan, 1976.

———. *Shakespeare: Seven Tragedies Revisited: The Dramatist's Manipulation of Response.* Houndsmill, Eng.: Palgrave, 2002.

———. "Shakespeare as Reviser." *Textual Criticism and Literary Interpretation.* Ed. Jerome J. McGann. Chicago: U of Chicago P, 1985. 1–22.

Hornby, Richard. *The End of Acting: A Radical View.* New York: Applause Theatre Books, 1992.

———. *Script into Performance: A Structuralist View of Play Production.* Austin: U of Texas P, 1977.

Howard, Jean. *Shakespeare's Art of Orchestration.* Urbana: U of Illinois P, 1984.

Howard, Jean R., and Marion F. O'Connor. "Introduction." *Shakespeare Reproduced: The Text in History and Ideology.* Ed. Howard and O'Connor. London: Methuen, 1987. 1–17

Hunt, Maurice, ed. *Approaches to Teaching Shakespeare's* Romeo and Juliet. New York: MLA, 2000.

————. *Approaches to Teaching Shakespeare's* The Tempest *and Other Late Romances.* New York: MLA, 1992.

Jackson, James. "'They Catch One Another's Rapiers': The Exchange of Weapons in *Hamlet.*" *Shakespeare Quarterly* 41 (1990): 281–98.

Johnson, Samuel. *Johnson on Shakespeare.* Ed. Arthur Sherbo. *The Yale Edition of the Works of Samuel Johnson.* Vols. 7–8. New Haven: Yale UP, 1968.

Johnston, A. F., ed. *Editing Early English Drama: Special Problems and New Directions.* New York: AMS Press, 1987.

Johnstone, Keith. *IMPRO: Improvisation and the Theatre.* London: Methuen, 1979.

Jones, Emrys. *Scenic Form in Shakespeare.* Oxford: Clarendon Press, 1971.

Kahn, Coppélia. *Man's Estate: Masculine Identity in Shakespeare.* Berkeley: U of California P, 1981. 104–18.

Kamps, Ivo, ed. *Shakespeare Left and Right.* London: Routledge, 1991.

Katz, Stanley. "The Humanities and Public Education." *The Humanities in the Schools.* American Council of Learned Societies Occasional Paper No. 20. New York: ACLS, 1993. 2–3.

Kinney, Arthur F. *Shakespeare by Stages: An Historical Introduction.* Malden, MA: Blackwell, 2003.

Kliman, Bernice W., ed. *Approaches to Teaching Shakespeare's* Hamlet. New York: MLA, 2001.

Krieger, Elliot. "Shakespearean Crossroads: Teaching Shakespeare through Induction." *College English* 39 (1977): 286–89.

Langer, Susanne K. *Feeling and Form: A Theory of Art.* New York: Scribner's, 1953.

Lanham, Richard. *A Handlist of Rhetorical Terms.* 2nd ed. Berkeley: U of California P, 1991.

Levin, Harry. *The Question of* Hamlet. New York: Viking, 1964.

Lewis. C. S. *English Literature in the Sixteenth Century.* Oxford: Clarendon Press, 1954.

Lewis, Robert. *Madness—or Method.* New York: Samuel French, 1958.

Luckyj, Christina. "Historicizing Gender: Mapping Cultural Space in Webster's *The Duchess of Malfi* and Cary's *The Tragedy of Mariam*." *Approaches to Teaching English Renaissance Drama*. Ed. Karen Bamford and Alexander Leggatt. New York: MLA, 2002. 134–41.

Lusardi, James P., and June Schlueter. *Reading Shakespeare in Performance*: King Lear. Rutherford, NJ: Fairleigh Dickinson UP; London: Associated University Presses, 1991.

Magnusson, Lynne. "Dialogue." *Reading Shakespeare's Language: A Guide*. Ed. Sylvia Adamson, Lynette Hunter, Lynne Magnussion, Ann Thompson, and Katie Wells. London: Thomson Learning, 2001. 130–43.

———. *Shakespeare and Social Dialogue: Dramatic Language and Elizabethan Letters*. Cambridge: Cambridge UP, 1999.

Maguire, Laurie E. *Studying Shakespeare: A Guide to the Plays*. Malden, MA: Blackwell, 2004.

Mallick, David. *How Tall Is This Ghost, John?* Adelaide: Australian Association for the Teaching of English, 1984.

Mandel, Barrett John. *Literature and the English Department*. Urbana, IL: National Council of Teachers of English, 1970.

Mazer, Cary M. "Playing the Action: Building an Interpretation from the Scene Up." *Teaching Shakespeare through Performance*. Ed. Milla Cozart Riggio. New York: MLA, 1999. 155–68.

McCloskey, Susan. "Teaching Dramatic Literature." *College English* 46 (1984): 385–91.

McDonald, Joseph P. "Raising the Teacher's Voice and the Ironic Role of Theory." *Harvard Educational Review* 56 (1986): 355–78.

———. "A Reflective Conversation about Teacher Education." Rev. of *Educating the Reflective Practitioner*, by Donald Schön. *Harvard Educational Review* 59 (1989): 251–59.

McDonald, Russ. *Shakespeare and the Arts of Language*. Oxford: Oxford UP, 2001.

McGuire, Philip C. *Shakespeare: The Jacobean Plays*. Basingstroke, Eng.: Macmillan, 1994.

———. *Speechless Dialect: Shakespeare's Open Silences*. Berkeley: U of California P, 1985.

McGuire, Philip C., and David Samuelson, eds. *Shakespeare: The Theatrical Dimension.* New York: AMS Press, 1979.

McLain, Richard. "The Role of Explanation in Teaching Standard English: Constitutive and Regulative Rules in Language." *College English* 38 (1976): 242–49.

McLean, Andrew M. *Shakespeare: Annotated Bibliographies and Media Guides for Teachers.* Urbana, IL: National Council of Teachers of English, 1980.

Mellor, Bronwyn. *Reading* Hamlet. The NCTE Chalkface Series. 1989; Urbana, IL: National Council of Teachers of English, 1999.

Merrix, Robert P., and Nicholas Ranson, eds. *Ideological Approaches to Teaching Shakespeare: The Practice of Theory.* Lewiston, NY: Mellen, 1992.

Metz, G. Harold. "Stage History of *Titus Andronicus.*" *Shakespeare Quarterly* 28 (1977): 154–69.

Milhous, Judith, and Robert Hume. *Producible Interpretation: Eight English Plays, 1675–1707.* Carbondale: Southern Illinois UP, 1985.

Miller, Naomi J. ed. *Reimagining Shakespeare for Children and Young Adults.* London: Routledge, 2003.

Moffett, James, and Kenneth R. McElheny, eds. *Points of View: An Anthology of Short Stories.* New York: Mentor/New American Library, 1966. Rev. and updated ed. New York: Mentor/Penguin, 1995.

Moore, Sonia. *The Stanislavski System: The Professional Training of an Actor.* New York: Penguin, 1974.

———. *Training an Actor: The Stanislavski System in Class.* Rev. ed. New York: Penguin, 1979.

Mousley, Andy. *Renaissance Drama and Contemporary Theory.* Basingstroke, Eng.: Macmillan, 2000.

Nelsen, Paul. "Positing Pillars at the Globe." *Shakespeare Quarterly* 48 (1997): 324–35.

Newman, Karen. "Renaissance Family Politics and *The Taming of the Shrew.*" *Fashioning Femininity and English Renaissance Drama.* Chicago: U of Chicago P, 1991. 33–50.

O'Brien, Ellen. "Inside Shakespeare: Using Performance Techniques to Achieve Traditional Goals." *Teaching Shakespeare.* Spec. issue of *Shakespeare Quarterly* 35.5 (1984): 621–31.

O'Brien, Peggy, with Jeanne Addison Roberts, Michael Tolaydo, and Nancy Goodwin. *Shakespeare Set Free: Teaching* Hamlet *and* Henry IV, Part 1. New York: Washington Square Press, 1994.

———. *Shakespeare Set Free: Teaching* Romeo and Juliet, Macbeth, *and* A Midsummer Night's Dream. New York: Washington Square Press, 1993.

———. *Shakespeare Set Free: Teaching* Twelfth Night *and* Othello. New York: Washington Square Press, 1995.

Orgel, Stephen. "Shakespeare Observed." *Shakespeare Quarterly* 31 (1980): 133–41.

Ornstein, Robert. *Shakespeare in the Classroom.* Urbana, IL: Educational Illustrators, 1960.

Pavis, Patrice. *Languages of the Stage: Essays in the Semiology of the Theatre.* New York: Performing Arts Journal Publications, 1982.

Peat, Derek. "Teaching Shakespeare through Performance: An Interview with J. L. Styan." *Shakespeare Quarterly* 31 (1980): 142–52.

Peck, John, and Martin Coyle. *How to Study a Shakespeare Play.* London: Macmillan, 1985.

Pennington, Michael. "*Hamlet.*" *Players of Shakespeare: Essays in Shakespearean Performance.* Ed. Philip Brockbank. Cambridge: Cambridge UP, 1985. 115–28.

———. Hamlet: *A User's Guide.* New York: Limelight Editions, 1996.

Phelps, Louise Wetherbee. *Composition as a Human Science: Contributions to the Self-Understanding of a Discipline.* Oxford: Oxford UP, 1988.

———. "Developmental Challenges, Developmental Tensions: A Heuristic for Curricular Thinking." *Developing Discourse Practices in Adolescence and Adulthood.* Ed. Richard Beach and Susan Hynds. Norwood, NJ: Ablex, 1990. 386–414.

———. "Practical Wisdom and the Geography of Knowledge in Composition." *College English* 53 (1991): 863–85.

Potter, Robert. "The Rediscovery of Queen Margaret: *The Wars of the Roses,* 1963." *NTQ: New Theatre Quarterly* 4 (1988): 105–19.

Pratt, Mary Louise. *Toward a Speech Act Theory of Literary Discourse.* Bloomington: Indiana UP, 1977.

Proudfoot, Richard. *Shakespeare: Text, Stage and Canon.* Foreword by R. A. Foakes. London: Thomson Learning, 2001.

Qualley, Donna J. *Turns of Thought: Teaching Composition as Reflexive Inquiry.* Portsmouth, NH: Boynton/Cook, 1997.

Rawls, John. "Two Concepts of Rules." *Philosophical Review* 64 (1955): 3–32.

Ray, Robert H., ed. *Approaches to Teaching Shakespeare's* King Lear. New York: MLA, 1986.

Reviews of *The Taming of the Shrew,* by William Shakespeare (Royal Shakespeare Theatre, opened April 9, 2003) and *The Tamer Tamed,* by John Fletcher (Swan Theatre, opened April 9, 2003), directed by Gregory Doran. Compiled in *Theatre Record* 8 (9–22 April 2003): 495–501.

Reynolds, Peter. "Active Reading: Shakespeare's Stagecraft." *Teaching Shakespeare: Essays on Approaches to Shakespeare in Schools and Colleges.* Ed. Richard Adams. London: Robert Royce, 1985. 118–32.

———. *Practical Approaches to Teaching Shakespeare.* Oxford: Oxford UP, 1991.

Riggio, Milla Cozart, ed. *Teaching Shakespeare through Performance.* New York: MLA, 1999.

Roach, Joseph. *The Player's Passion: Studies in the Science of Acting.* 1985. Ann Arbor: U of Michigan P, 1993.

Robinson, Randal. "Improvisation and the Language of Shakespeare's Plays." *Nebraska English Journal* 35.3/4 (1990): 54–64.

———. *Unlocking Shakespeare's Language: Help for the Teacher and the Student.* Urbana, IL: National Council of Teachers of English, 1988.

Rocklin, Edward L. "Converging Transformations in Teaching Composition, Literature, and Drama." *College English* 53 (1991): 177–94.

———. "Exploring *Hamlet*: Opening Playtexts, Closing Performances." *Approaches to Teaching* Hamlet. Ed. Bernice W. Kliman. New York: MLA, 2001. 73–76.

———. "Framing *Macbeth*: How Three Films Create the Play's World." *California English* 5.3 (Spring 2000): 10–11.

———. "How Does One 'Teach' a Play, Anyway?" *California English* 5.1 (Fall 1999): 12–13.

———. "'An Incarnational Art': Teaching Shakespeare." *Shakespeare Quarterly* 41.2 (Summer 1990): 147–59.

———. "Mapping the Scene of Learning Through the Lens of Drama." *Feminine Principles and Women's Experience in American Composition and Rhetoric.* Ed. Louise Wetherbee Phelps and Janet Emig. Pittsburgh: U of Pittsburgh P, 1995. 361–73.

———. "Performance Is More Than an 'Approach' to Teaching Shakespeare." *Teaching Shakespeare through Performance.* Ed. Milla Cozart Riggio. New York: MLA, 1999. 48–62.

———. "Performing Pedagogy." *Reimagining Shakespeare for Children and Young Adults.* Ed. Naomi Miller. London: Routledge, 2003. 289–97.

———. "Shakespeare's Script as a Cue for Pedagogic Invention." *Shakespeare Quarterly* 46.2 (Summer 1995): 135–44.

Rocklin, Edward L., and Sarah Innerst-Peterson. "Examining *Measure for Measure* through Performance." *Shakespeare Yearbook* 12 (2001): 356–70.

Rosenbaum, Ron. "Shakespeare in Rewrite." Onward and Upward with the Arts. *The New Yorker* (13 May 2002): 68–77.

Rosenberg, Marvin. *The Masks of* Hamlet. Newark: U of Delaware P; London: Associated University Presses, 1992.

———. *The Masks of* King Lear. Berkeley: U of California P, 1972.

———. *The Masks of* Macbeth. Berkeley: U of California P, 1978.

———. *The Masks of* Othello: *The Search for the Identity of Othello, Iago, and Desdemona by Three Centuries of Actors and Critics.* 1961. Berkeley: U of California P, 1971.

Rossiter, A. P. *Angel with Horns and Other Shakespeare Lectures.* Ed. Graham Storey. New York: Theatre Arts Books, 1961.

Rozett, Martha Tuck. *Talking Back to Shakespeare.* Newark: U of Delaware P, 1994.

Rutter, Carol, with Sinead Cusack et al. "Kate: Interpreting the Silence." *Clamorous Voices: Shakespeare's Women Today.* Ed. Faith Evans. New York: Routledge/Theatre Arts, 1989. 1–25.

Rygiel, Mary Ann. *Shakespeare Among School Children: Approaches to the Secondary Classroom.* Urbana, IL: National Council of Teachers of English, 1992.

Salomone, Ronald E., ed. *Teaching Shakespeare II.* SOCTE Focus. Urbana, IL: National Council of Teachers of English, 1985.

Salomone, Ronald E., and James E. Davis, eds. *Teaching Shakespeare into the Twenty-First Century.* Athens: Ohio UP, 1997.

Sanders, Wilbur. *The Dramatist and the Received Idea: Studies in the Plays of Marlowe and Shakespeare.* Cambridge: Cambridge UP, 1968.

Sauer, David Kennedy, and Evelyn Tribble. "Shakespeare in Performance: Theory in Practice and Practice in Theory." *Teaching Shakespeare through Performance.* Ed. Milla Cozart Riggio. New York: MLA, 1999. 33–47.

Schafer, Elizabeth. *Ms-Directing Shakespeare: Women Direct Shakespeare.* New York: St. Martin's Press, 2000. 57–72.

Schanzer, Ernest. *The Problem Plays of Shakespeare.* London: Routledge and Kegan Paul, 1963.

Schoenbaum, S. *Shakespeare: His Life, His Language, His Theater.* New York: New American Library, 1990.

Schön, Donald A. *Educating the Reflective Practitioner: Toward a New Design for Teaching and Learning in the Professions.* San Francisco: Jossey-Bass, 1987.

———. *The Reflective Practitioner: How Professionals Think in Action.* New York: Basic Books, 1983.

Searle, John R. *Speech Acts: An Essay in the Philosophy of Language.* Cambridge: Cambridge UP, 1969.

Sedgwick, Fred. *Shakespeare and the Young Writer.* New York: Routledge, 1999.

Selbourne, David. *The Making of A Midsummer Night's Dream: An Eye-witness Account of Peter Brook's Production from First Rehearsal to First Night.* London: Methuen, 1983.

Seltzer, Daniel. "The Actors and the Staging." *A New Companion to Shakespeare Studies.* Ed. Kenneth Muir and S. Schoenbaum. Cambridge: Cambridge UP, 1971. 35–54.

———. "Shakespeare's Texts and Modern Productions." *Reinterpretations of Elizabethan Drama.* Ed. Norman Rabkin. New York: Columbia UP, 1969. 89–115.

Semper, I. J. Hamlet *without Tears.* Dubuque, Iowa: Loras College Press, 1946.

Shakespeare, William. *The Riverside Shakespeare.* Ed. G. Blakemore Evans, with J. J. Tobin. 2nd ed. Boston: Houghton Mifflin, 1997.

———. *The First Quarto of Hamlet.* Ed. Kathleen O. Irace. Cambridge: Cambridge UP, 1998.

———. *Hamlet.* Ed. G. R. Hibbard. Oxford: Oxford UP, 1987.

———. *Hamlet.* Ed. Harold Jenkins. London: Methuen, 1982.

———. *Hamlet.* Ed. T. J. B. Spencer; with an Introduction by Anne Barton. Harmondsworth, Eng.: Penguin, 1980.

———. *Hamlet, Prince of Denmark.* 1985. Ed. Philip Edwards. Updated ed. Cambridge: Cambridge UP, 2003.

———. *Hamlet Prince of Denmark: Shakespeare in Production.* Ed. Robert Hapgood. Text ed. Philip Edwards. Cambridge: Cambridge UP, 1999.

———. *Hamlet: The First Quarto of 1603.* Ed. Albert B. Weiner; with a Foreword by Hardin Craig. Great Neck, New York: Barron's, 1962.

———. *The Tragedy of Hamlet, Prince of Denmark.* Ed. Edward Hubler. 2nd ed. New York: Signet, 1987.

———. *King Lear: A Parallel Text Edition.* Ed. René Weis. New York: Longman, 1993.

———. *The Parallel King Lear, 1608–1623.* Prep. Michael Warren. Berkeley: U of California P, 1989.

———. *King Richard III.* Ed. Janis Lull. Cambridge: Cambridge UP, 2003.

———. *Richard III.* Ed. Antony Hammond. London: Methuen, 1981.

————. *Richard III*. Ed. Julie Hankey. London: Junction Books; Totowa, NJ: Barnes and Noble, 1981.

————. *Richard III*. Ed. E. A. J. Honigmann. Harmondsworth, Eng.: Penguin, 1968.

————. *The Tragedy of Richard the Third*. Ed. Mark Eccles. 2nd ed. New York: Signet, 1998.

————. *The Tragedy of Richard III*. Ed. John Jowett. Oxford: Oxford UP, 2000.

————. *The Taming of the Shrew*. Ed. Robert B. Heilman. 2nd ed. New York: Signet, 1987.

————. *The Taming of the Shrew*. Ed. G. R. Hibbard. Harmondsworth, Eng.: Penguin, 1968.

————. *The Taming of the Shrew*. Ed. Brian Morris. London: Methuen, 1981.

————. *The Taming of the Shrew*. Ed. H. J. Oliver. Oxford: Oxford UP, 1984.

————. *The Taming of the Shrew*. Ed. Ann Thompson. Updated ed. Cambridge: Cambridge UP, 2003.

————. *The Taming of the Shrew: Shakespeare in Production*. Ed. Elizabeth Schafer. Text ed. Ann Thomson. Cambridge: Cambridge UP, 2002.

————. *The Taming of the Shrew: Texts and Contexts*. Ed. Frances E. Dolan. Boston: Bedford/St. Martin's, 1996.

————. *The Tempest*. Ed. Stephen Orgel. Oxford Shakespeare. Oxford: Oxford UP, 1987.

Sher, Antony. *Year of the King: An Actor's Diary and Sketchbook*. London: Methuen, 1985.

Showalter, Elaine. *Teaching Literature*. Malden, MA: Blackwell, 2003.

Shurgot, Michael W. *Stages of Play: Theatrical Energies in Elizabethan Performance*. Newark: U of Delaware P, 1998.

Sibbery, Michael. "Petruccio in *The Taming of the Shrew*." *Players of Shakespeare 4*. Ed. Robert Smallwood. Cambridge: Cambridge UP, 1998. 45–59.

Sinfield, Alan. "Give an Account of Shakespeare and Education ..." *Political Shakespeare: New Essays in Cultural Materialism.* Ed. Jonathan Dollimore and Alan Sinfield. Ithaca, NY: Cornell UP, 1985. 134–57.

Sizer, Theodore. *Horace's Compromise: The Dilemma of the American High School.* Boston: Houghton Mifflin, 1992.

Sklar, Daniel Judah. *Playmaking: Children Writing and Performing Their Own Plays.* New York: Teachers and Writers Collaborative, 1991.

Skrebels, Paul. "Transhistoricizing *Much Ado about Nothing.*" *Teaching Shakespeare into the Twenty-First Century.* Ed. Ronald E. Salomone and James E. Davis. Athens: Ohio UP, 1997. 81–95.

Skura, Meredith Anne. *Shakespeare the Actor and the Purposes of Playing.* Chicago: U of Chicago P, 1993.

Slater, Ann Pasternak. *Shakespeare the Director.* Sussex, Eng.: Harvester, 1982.

Slover, George. "Video versus Voice: Teaching Students and Teachers Shakespeare." *Nebraska English Journal* 35.3/4 (1990): 32–53.

Snyder, Susan. *The Comic Matrix of Shakespeare's Tragedies.* Princeton: Princeton UP, 1979.

———. "*Romeo and Juliet*: Comedy into Tragedy." *Essays in Criticism* 20 (1970): 391–402. Rpt. in Romeo and Juliet: *Critical Essays.* Ed. John Andrews. New York: Garland, 1993. 73–83.

Spencer, T. J. B. "Shakespeare: The Elizabethan Theatre-Poet." *The Elizabethan Theatre I.* Ed. David Galloway. Toronto: Macmillan, 1969. 1–20.

Spolin, Viola. *Improvisation for the Theatre.* Evanston: Northwestern UP, 1983.

———. *Theatre Games for the Classroom: A Teacher's Handbook.* Evanston: Northwestern UP, 1986.

Sprigg, Douglas C. "Shakespeare's Visual Stagecraft: The Seduction of Cressida." *Shakespeare: The Theatrical Dimension.* Ed. Philip C. McGuire and David A. Samuelson. New York: AMS Press, 1979. 149–63.

Stafford-Clark, Max. "The Man Who Saved the Stage." Program for the double bill of *She Stoops to Conquer* by Oliver Goldsmith and *A Laughing Matter* by April De Angelis. Presented by the National

Theatre in a co-production with Out of Joint theater company, 2002–2003.

Stanislavski, Constantin. *An Actor Prepares.* Trans. Elizabeth Reynolds Hapgood. New York: Theatre Arts Books, 1936.

———. *An Actor's Handbook: An Alphabetical Arrangement of Concise Statements on Aspects of Acting.* Ed. and trans. Elizabeth Reynolds Hapgood. New York: Theatre Arts Books, 1963.

———. *Building a Character.* Trans. Elizabeth Reynolds Hapgood. New York: Theatre Arts Books, 1949.

———. *Creating a Role.* Trans. Elizabeth Reynolds Hapgood. New York: Theatre Arts Books, 1961.

———. *Stanislavski on the Art of the Stage.* Trans. David Magarshack. New York: Hill and Wang, 1961.

———. *Stanislavski's Legacy: A Collection of Comments on a Variety of Aspects of an Actor's Art and Life.* Ed. and trans. Elizabeth Reynolds Hapgood. New York: Theatre Arts Books, 1968.

States, Bert O. *Great Reckonings in Little Rooms: On the Phenomenology of Theater.* Berkeley: U of California P, 1985.

———. *The Pleasure of the Play.* Ithaca, NY: Cornell UP, 1994.

Stern, Tiffany. *Making Shakespeare: From Stage to Page.* London: Routledge, 2004.

Sterne, Richard L. *John Gielgud Directs Richard Burton in* Hamlet: *A Journal of Rehearsals.* New York: Random House, 1967.

Stewart, Patrick. Workshop on Teaching Shakespeare. Sponsored by the Globe Shakespeare Institute. Huntington Library, San Marino, California, 9 Sept. 1989.

Stodder, Joseph H. "Shakespeare in Southern California and Visalia." *Shakespeare Quarterly* 31 (1980): 254–74.

Stodder, Joseph H., and Lillian Wilds. "Shakespeare in Southern California." *Shakespeare Quarterly* 30 (1979): 232–45.

Stříbrný, Zdeněk. "Recent *Hamlets* in Prague." *Shakespeare Quarterly* 35 (1984): 208–14.

Styan, J. L. "Direct Method Shakespeare." *Shakespeare Quarterly* 25 (1974): 198–200.

————. *The Elements of Drama.* Cambridge: Cambridge UP, 1960.

————. "Quince's Questions and the Mystery of the Play Experience." *Journal of Dramatic Theory and Criticism* 1.1 (1986): 3–16.

————. Rev. of *Shakespeare's Playhous Practice,* by Warren D. Smith. *Shakespeare Quarterly* 28 (Spring 1977): 266–68.

————. *Shakespeare's Stagecraft.* Cambridge: Cambridge UP, 1975.

————. "Stage Space and the Shakespeare Experience." *Shakespeare and the Sense of Performance.* Ed. Marvin and Ruth Thompson. Newark: U of Delaware P; London: Associated University Presses, 1989. 195–209.

Swander, Homer. "Such Audiences as We Wish Him." *Teaching Shakespeare.* Spec. issue of *Shakespeare Quarterly* 35.5 (1984): 621–31.

Tannen, Deborah. *You Just Don't Understand: Women and Men in Conversation.* New York: William Morrow, 1990.

Taylor, Gary. *To Analyze Delight: A Hedonist Criticism of Shakespeare.* Newark: U of Delaware P, 1985.

Taylor, Gary, and Michael Warren, eds. *The Division of the Kingdoms: Shakespeare's Two Versions of* King Lear. Oxford: Clarendon Press, 1986.

Thompson, Ann, and Thomas L. Berger, A. R. Braunmiller, Philip Edwards, and Lois Potter, eds. *Which Shakespeare? A User's Guide to Editions.* London: Open UP, 1992.

Thompson, Ann, and Gordon McMullan, eds. *In Arden: Editing Shakespeare: Essays in Honor of Richard Proudfoot.* London: Thomson Learning, 2003.

Thompson, Ann, and Sasha Roberts, eds. *Women Reading Shakespeare, 1660–1900: An Anthology of Criticism.* Manchester: Manchester UP, 1997.

Thompson, Marvin, and Ruth Thompson, eds. *Shakespeare and the Sense of Performance: Essays in the Tradition of Performance Criticism in Honor of Bernard Beckerman.* Newark: U of Delaware P; London and Toronto: Associated University Presses, 1989.

Tillyard, E. M. W. *The Elizabethan World Picture.* 1943. New York: Vintage Books/Random House, 1959.

Bibliography

Trewin, J. C. *Five and Eighty Hamlets*. New York: New Amsterdam, 1987.

Trewin, J. C., and Robert Speaight, "Talking about Shakespeareans." *Shakespeare Quarterly* 28 (1977): 133–43.

Trollope, Anthony. *Barchester Towers*. 1906. London: Dent, 1978.

Twain, Mark. *The Adventures of Huckleberry Finn*. Introduction by Hamlin Hill. New York: Harper and Row, 1987.

———. *Big River: The Adventures of Huckleberry Finn*. A Musical Play. Book by William Hauptmann, adapted from the novel by Mark Twain. Music and Lyrics by Roger Miller. New York: Grove Press, 1986.

Umland, Sam, ed. *Shakespeare in Our High Schools*. Spec. issue of *Nebraska English Journal*, Spring/Summer 1990. Urbana, IL: National Council of Teachers of English.

Urkowitz, Steven. "'Good News about 'Bad' Quartos." *"Bad" Shakespeare: Revaluations of the Shakespeare Canon*. Ed. Maurice Charney. Rutherford, NJ: Fairleigh Dickinson UP; Toronto: Associated University Presses, 1988. 189–206.

———. *Shakespeare's Revision of* King Lear. Princeton: Princeton UP, 1980.

———. "'Well-sayd olde Mole': Burying Three *Hamlets* in Modern Editions." *Shakespeare Studies Today* (1986): 37–70.

Van Laan, Thomas. *The Idiom of Drama*. Ithaca, NY: Cornell UP, 1970.

———. *Roleplaying in Shakespeare*. Toronto: U of Toronto P, 1978.

Waller, Gary. "Decentering the Bard: The BBC-TV Shakespeare and Some Implications for Criticism and Teaching." *Shakespeare on Television: An Anthology of Essays and Reviews*. Ed. J. C. Bulman and H. R. Coursen. Hanover, NH: UP of New England, 1988. 18–30.

Warren, Michael J. *The Parallel King Lear, 1608–1623*. Berkeley: U of California P, 1989.

———. "Repunctuation as Interpretation in Editions of Shakespeare." *ELR* 7 (1977): 155–69.

———, ed. *Shakespeare: Life, Language, and Linguistics, Textual Studies, and the Canon: An Annotated Bibliography of Shakespeare Studies 1623–2000*. Fairview, NC: Pegasus Press, 2002.

Watson, Robert N. "Teaching 'Shakespeare': Theory versus Practice." *Teaching Literature: What Is Needed Now.* Ed. James Engell and David Perkins. Cambridge: Harvard UP, 1988. 121–50.

Weis, René, ed. *King Lear: A Parallel Text Edition.* New York: Longman, 1993.

Wells, Stanley. *Shakespeare: The Writer and His Work.* New York: Scribers, 1978.

Wells, Stanley, and Gary Taylor. *Modernizing Shakespeare's Spelling with Three Studies in the Text of* Henry V. Oxford: Clarendon Press, 1979.

Wells, Stanley, and Gary Taylor, with John Jowett and William Montgomery. *William Shakespeare: A Textual Companion.* 1987. New York: Norton, 1997.

Werner, Sarah. "*The Taming of the Shrew*: A Case Study in Performance Criticism." *Shakespeare and Feminist Performance: Ideology on Stage.* London: Routledge, 2001.

White, Martin. *Renaissance Drama in Action: An Introduction to Aspects of Theatre Practice and Performance.* London: Routledge, 1998.

Widdicombe, Toby. *Simply Shakespeare.* White Plains, NY: Longman, 2001.

Wilder, Thornton. "Some Thoughts on Playwrighting." *The Intent of the Artist.* Ed. A. Centeno. Princeton: Princeton UP, 1941. 83–98. Rpt. in *Playwrights on Playwrighting: The Meaning and Making of Modern Drama from Ibsen to Ionesco.* Ed. Toby Cole. New York: Hill and Wang, 1960. 106–15.

Wilhelm, Jeffrey D. "*You Gotta BE the Book*": Teaching Engaged and Reflective Reading with Adolescents.* New York: Teachers College Press; Urbana, IL: National Council of Teachers of English, 1997.

Williams, Raymond. *Drama from Ibsen to Brecht.* New York: Oxford UP, 1969

———. *Drama in Performance.* 1954. Harmondsworth, Eng.: Penguin, 1972.

Willinsky, John, and Jim Bedard. *The Fearful Passage*: Romeo and Juliet in the High School—A Feminist Perspective.* Urbana, IL: National Council of Teachers of English, 1989.

Wilson, J. Dover. *The Manuscript of Shakespeare's* Hamlet *and the Problems of Its Transmission.* 2 vols. Cambridge: Cambridge UP, 1934.

————. *What Happens in* Hamlet? 1935. 3rd ed. Cambridge: Cambridge UP, 1967.

Wilson, Thomas. *The Art of Rhetorique.* 1553. *English Literary Criticism: The Renaissance.* Ed. O. B. Hardison, Jr. New York: Appleton-Century Crofts, 1968.

Wittgenstein, Ludwig. *Philosophical Investigations.* Trans. G. E. M. Anscombe. 3rd ed. 1958. New York: Macmillan, 1989.

————. *Tractatus Logico-Philosophicus.* 1921. Trans. C. K. Ogden. London: Routledge, 1981.

————. *Tractatus Logico-Philosophicus.* Trans. D. F. Pears and B. F. McGuiness. New York: Humanities Press, 1972.

Worster, David. "Performance Options and Pedagogy: *Macbeth.*" *Shakespeare Quarterly* (53) 2002: 362–78.

Worthan, W. B. *Shakespeare and the Authority of Performance.* Cambridge: Cambridge UP, 1997.

————. *Shakespeare and the Force of Modern Performance.* Cambridge: Cambridge UP, 2003.

Wright, George T. *Shakespeare's Metrical Art.* Berkeley: U of California P, 1988.

Wright, Louis B., et al. *Shakespeare in School and College.* Champaign, IL: National Council of Teachers of English, 1964.

Zahorski, Kenneth J. "The Next Best Thing . . . Shakespeare in Stereo." *College English* 39 (1977): 290–93.

INDEX

AUTHOR

Photo by Sonja Stump.

Edward L. Rocklin received his BA magna cum laude from Harvard College (1970) and his MA (1974) and PhD (1981) from Rutgers University. He taught for five years at Clarion University in Pennsylvania and has been teaching at California State Polytechnic University, Pomona, since 1986. Rocklin has published essays in *Shakespeare Quarterly*, *Shakespeare Survey*, *Shakespeare Yearbook*, *Shakespeare Bulletin*, *The Journal of Dramatic Theory and Criticism*, *College English*, and *California English*. In addition, he has been a fellow of the American Council of Learned Societies (1992–1993) and a participant in a yearlong program, funded by the National Endowment for the Humanities, titled "Shakespeare Examined through Performance," which was conducted at the Folger Shakespeare Library (1995–1996). From 1996 to 2000, he served as a regional director of the California Reading and Literature Project. Rocklin is working on a performance history of *Measure for Measure* to be published in the Manchester University Press series *Shakespeare in Performance*.

This book was typeset in Sabon and Futura by Electronic Imaging.
Typefaces used on the cover include Poetica Chancery II and Giovanni.
The book was printed on 50-lb. Accent Opaque paper by Versa Press, Inc.